Lecture Notes in Computer Science 8708

Commenced Publication in 1973
Founding and Former Series Editors:
Gerhard Goos, Juris Hartmanis, and Jan van Leeuwen

T0213756

Stephanie Teufel   Tjoa A Min   Ilsun You
Edgar Weippl (Eds.)

Availability, Reliability, and Security in Information Systems

IFIP WG 8.4, 8.9, TC 5 International
Cross-Domain Conference, CD-ARES 2014 and
4th International Workshop on Security and Cognitive
Informatics for Homeland Defense, SeCIHD 2014
Fribourg, Switzerland, September 8-12, 2014
Proceedings

Springer

Volume Editors

Stephanie Teufel
University of Fribourg
iimt - international institute of management in technology
Fribourg, Switzerland
E-mail: stephanie.teufel@unifr.ch

Tjoa A Min
Vienna University of Technology
Institute of Software Technology and Interactive Systems
Vienna, Austria
E-mail: amin@ifs.tuwien.ac.at

Ilsun You
Korean Bible University
School of Informatic Science, Seoul, South Korea
E-mail: isyou@bible.ac.kr

Edgar Weippl
Vienna University of Technology and SBA Research
Institute of Software Technology in Interactive Systems
Vienna, Austria
E-mail: eweippl@sba-research.org

ISSN 0302-9743   e-ISSN 1611-3349
ISBN 978-3-319-10974-9   e-ISBN 978-3-319-10975-6
DOI 10.1007/978-3-319-10975-6
Springer Cham Heidelberg New York Dordrecht London

Library of Congress Control Number: 2014946921

LNCS Sublibrary: SL 3 – Information Systems and Application,
incl. Internet/Web and HCI

© IFIP International Federation for Information Processing 2014

Typesetting: Camera-ready by author, data conversion by Scientific Publishing Services, Chennai, India

Printed on acid-free paper

Springer is part of Springer Science+Business Media (www.springer.com)

Preface

The Cross-Domain Conference and Workshop CD-ARES is focused on the holistic and scientific view of applications in the domain of information systems.

The idea of organizing cross-domain scientific events originated from a concept presented by the IFIP president Leon Strous at the IFIP 2010 World Computer Congress in Brisbane, which was seconded by many IFIP delegates in further discussions. Therefore CD-ARES concentrates on the many aspects of information systems in bridging the gap between the research results in computer science and the many application fields.

This effort led us to consider the various important issues of massive information sharing and data integration that will (in our opinion) dominate scientific work and discussions in the area of information systems in the second decade of this century.

The organizers of this event who are engaged within IFIP in the area of Enterprise Information Systems (WG 8.9), Business Information Systems (WG 8.4), and Information Technology Applications (TC 5) very much welcomed the typical cross-domain aspect of this event.

Out of 27 submissions, we assembled a program for CD-ARES 2014 consisting of 10 papers. CD-ARES 2014 provided a good mix of topics ranging from knowledge management and software security to mobile and social computing.

The collocation with the SeCIHD 2014 Workshop was another possibility to discuss the most essential application factors. Due to its great success and echo in the scientific community, this special track was held this year for the fourth time.

The main goal of SeCIHD 2014 was to collect and discuss new ideas and solutions for homeland defense.

To handle the complex research challenges of homeland defense, it is necessary to adopt a "multi-disciplinary" approach, which is the core spirit of CD-ARES 2014. This year, SeCIHD 2014 comprised 14 papers, which introduce the latest technologies of homeland defense including security issues and protocols for Internet services, anomaly detection, cryptographic models, security and privacy in ambient intelligence and so forth.

The papers presented at this conference were selected after extensive reviews by the Program Committee with the essential help of associated reviewers.

We would like to thank all the Program Committee members and the reviewers who made great effort contributing their time, knowledge, and expertise and foremost the authors for their contributions.

September 2014

Stephanie Teufel
A. Min Tjoa
Ilsun You
Edgar Weippl

Organization

Cross-Domain Conference and Workshop on Multidisciplinary Research and Practice for Information Systems (CD-ARES 2014)

General Chair

Stephanie Teufel   University of Fribourg, Switzerland

Program Committee Chair

A. Min Tjoa   Vienna University of Technology, Austria

Program Committee

Cristina Alcaraz Tello	University of Malaga, Spain
Markus Aleksy	ABB AG, Germany
Amin Anjomshoaa	Vienna University of Technology, Austria
Kristian Beckers	University of Duisburg-Essen, Germany
Svetla Boytcheva	Bulgaria
Elzbieta Bukowska	Poznan University of Economics, Poland
Stephan Faßbender	University of Duisburg-Essen, Germany
Stefan Hofbauer	Amadeus Data Processing GmbH, Germany
Andreas Holzinger	Med University Graz, Austria
Stefan Jakoubi	SBA Research, Austria
Massimo Mecella	Sapienza Università di Roma, Italy
Bela Mutschler	University of Applied Sciences Ravensburg-Weingarten, Germany
Richard Overill	King's College London, UK
Andreas Peter	University of Twente, The Netherlands
Simon Tjoa	St. Poelten University of Applied Sciences, Austria
A. Min Tjoa	Vienna University of Technology, Austria
Edgar Weippl	Vienna University of Technology & SBA Research, Austria

4th International Workshop on Security and Cognitive Informatics for Homeland Defense (SeCIHD 2014)

General Chair

Ilsun You	Korean Bible University, Republic of Korea
Fang-Yie Leu	Tunghai University, Taiwan

General Vice-Chair

Marek Ogiela   AGH University of Science and Technology,
                                    Poland
Aniello Castiglione   University of Salerno, Italy

Program Committee Chairs

Francesco Palmieri   Second University of Naples, Italy
Ugo Fiore   University of Naples "Federico II", Italy

International Liaison Chair

Kangbin Yim   SCH University, Korea

Program Committee

Benjamin Aziz   University of Portsmouth, UK
Joonsang Baek   Khalifa University of Science, Technology
                                    & Research, UAE
Wolfgang Boehmer   Technische Universität Darmstadt, Germany
Clara Maria Colombini   University of Milan UNIMI, Italy
Massimo Ficco   Second University of Naples, Italy
Dominique Genoud   University of Applied Sciences Western
                                    Switzerland, Switzerland
Tomasz Hachaj   Pedagogical University in Krakow, Poland
Jean Hennebert   University of Applied Science - HES-SO,
                                    Switzerland
Antonio J. Jara   University of Applied Sciences
                                    Western Switzerland, Switzerland
Shinsaku Kiyomoto   KDDI R&D Laboratories Inc., Japan
Mauro Migliardi   University of Padova, Italy
Lidia Ogiela   AGH University of Science and Technology,
                                    Poland
Kyung-Hyune Rhee   Pukyong National University, Republic of
                                    Korea
Sergio Ricciardi   Universitat Politènica de Catalunya, Barcelona,
                                    Spain
Kangbin Yim   Soonchunhyang University, Republic of Korea
Shuichiro Yamamoto   Nagoya University, Japan
Akihiro Yamamura   Akita University, Japan
Toshihiro Yamauchi   Okayama University, Japan
Wei Yu   Towson University, USA

Table of Contents

Cross-Domain Conference and Workshop on Multidisciplinary Research and Practice for Information Systems (CD-ARES 2014)

Knowledge Management

Software Security

Mobile and Social Computing

4th International Workshop on Security and Cognitive Informatics for Homeland Defense (SeCIHD 2014)

Argumentation-Based Group Decision Support for Collectivist Communities

Marijke Coetzee

Academy for Computer Science and Software engineering,
University of Johannesburg, South Africa
marijkec@uj.ac.za

Abstract. In collectivist communities, decisions are taken by groups of people who prefer to consider the opinions of their in-group. For them it is important to reach group consensus by focusing on the group's preferences and goals. Such decision processes can be supported by multi-criteria decision analysis that identifies sets of objectives, representing subjective values used in decision making, to better generate recommendations. Recently, several attempts have been made to explain and suggest alternatives in decision-making problems by using arguments. Argumentation theory is the process of bringing together arguments so that conclusions can be justified and explained. Each potential decision usually has arguments for or against it, of various strengths. For collectivist communities, the non-monotonicity of argumentation theory is useful as it supports an adaptive decision-making style. The fact that the opinions of group members can be evaluated and replaced, if they are found lacking via a group opinion strategy, fits well with collectivist decision-making. This paper proposes a framework that allows a group of users, belonging to a collectivist and mostly rural community, to share their opinions when making decisions such as buying goods in bulk in order by incorporating their cultural beliefs in the system design.

Keywords: Collectivist culture, group decisions, multi-criteria decision-making, argumentation.

1 Introduction

In the developing economies of Africa, South America, India and Asia, very small enterprises (VSEs) find it challenging to conduct business supported by ecommerce [1]. VSEs are part of the informal economic sector and have an important role to play in the growth of developing economies. It is therefore vital that these, and other types of VSEs, are supported by technology to enable growth and expansion. To answer this need, recent research projects investigate how to support VSE owners by means of m-commerce applications backed by cloud-based technologies [5] [6] to allow them to conduct their business from a mobile phone. For such applications to be successful, VSE owners should be encouraged to collaborate, and together decided to buy products in bulk from large retail suppliers in order to become more profitable.

S. Teufel et al. (Eds.): CD-ARES 2014, LNCS 8708, pp. 1–16, 2014.

An analysis of data collected in the U.S. (highly individualistic) and Ghana (highly collectivist) points to the fact that culture affects decision making [2]. It is thus important for researchers who are designing decision-making tools to be aware of the fact that individualist are inclined to be more rational, and collectivist are inclined to be more dependent when making decisions. Individualistic consumers would rather evaluate the features of a product before they purchase it, in contrast to collectivists in Asia or Africa who consider factors such as status and symbolism [7]. Therefore the role of culture on group decision-making needs to be investigated as currently, no culturally adapted group decision-making tool exists that incorporates collectivist behavior and beliefs.

In order to address this, this research contributes a framework where humans interact with an application on their mobile phone that accumulates the preferences of all members of a collaborative group and addresses cultural factors when decisions are made. The reasoning model is based on an argumentative multi-criteria decision framework [8] to assist members to make decisions. The focus is to determine a collective choice that will satisfy at most of the goals of the group. Arguments provide the pros and cons to support decisions and are not of equal strengths, which makes it possible to compare pairs of arguments. When arguments are compared, it is done using different principles, it is done on the basis of their relevant strengths and whether they are for or against a choice. The process of argumentative decision-making is supported by decision-making strategies that meet the needs of collectivists such as a group opinion strategy and a group customisation strategy.

The paper is structured as follows: The next section gives a motivating example that highlights the environment of the collectivist consumer that is considered by this research. The influence of culture on decisions is described by identifying main cultural approaches and the effect of collectivism on decision-making and social position. Group decision methods are discussed and multi-criteria decision analysis is identified as a promising approach for this problem area. To assist a collectivist decision-maker in his decision processes, argumentation theory can be used with multi-criteria decision analysis to provide not only a decision, but also the explanation to the decision. A framework is presented that illustrates how different group decision strategies are implemented with examples. Finally, the paper is concluded.

2   Motivating Example

There is an acute need for culturally-adapted technology to assist VSEs to collaborate more. Today, rural collectivist business owners in Africa, Asia and South America interact in a face-to-face manner with each other in a culturally involved manner to ensure that their businesses will survive in the face of adversity. Figure 1 gives nodes representing VSEs, as well as a large retail supplier of goods. Each of these VSEs operate on their own and buy good from the supplier individually, at more expensive prices. The focus of such a collaboration tool would for example be to assist business owners to group together to buy goods in bulk at a cheaper price from this or any other supplier.

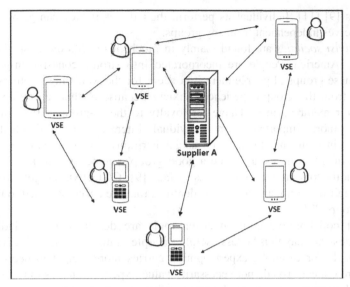

Fig. 1. Very small enterprises collaborating

Due to the size of VSEs and their informal nature, owners tend to run the business and make business decisions based on personal relationships and understandings, where social capital and social ties support and influence all decisions. Their behavior is strongly influenced by their cultural norms and beliefs [9]. This is even more relevant when collaborations occur since it involves committing to and trusting in a relationship with another business owner. In order to be able to implement such systems successfully, the collectivist approach to consumer decision-making needs to be understood for such systems to be useful. The aim is to ensure that participants are comfortable with the manner in which the system enables them to collaborate in a group.

3   Culture and Decisions

Culture is generally described as the shared symbols, norms, and values in a social group such as an organisation or country [9]. Hofstede [9] [11] has identified dimensions of national culture of which individualism vs. collectivism is the most prominent. Other dimensions include power distance, uncertainty avoidance, and masculinity vs. femininity. These dimensions are generally applied by other researchers even though Hofstede's model has been criticized as too simplistic and not refined. Yet Hofstede's model has been validated by as many as 140 studies [12], making it useful in many different situations.

Individualist societies are found mainly in North America and much of Western Europe. For them, ties between members of the community are loose where people make a life for themselves and their direct family members only. The interest of a specific person is more important than the interest of the group. Individualists are more goal-oriented and self-motivated, and use guilt and loss of self-respect as motivators [9] [11]. Individualists perform their duties if they can gain from it, and see themselves independent from any groups.

Collectivist societies are found mainly in much of the Middle East, Asia, Africa, and South America. People are incorporated into strong, cohesive in-groups from birth. In these groups of people there is concern for the wellbeing of others. A person separated from the group experiences anxiety because of this separation. In-groups protect their members in exchange for loyalty to the in-group. Group interests and goals are more important than individual interests, and individuals conduct themselves in a manner to maintain social harmony. Such individuals acquire the skills and qualities necessary to be a good group member and to keep to tradition. Typical motivators are shame and loss of face [9]. Collectivists enjoy doing what is right for their in-group, and have self-identities that are strongly linked to the features of their group [27].

Current collaborative group decision tools are designed to suit individualistic communities and may thus be less useful to people in many of the collectivist cultures in the world. For example, expert opinion carries more weight in decision-making [17], where collectivists do not necessarily value expert opinion as much as it may be to the detriment of group harmony. Based on a review of collectivists decision-making tendencies that now follows, this research aims to present strategies to be used in the design of decision-making tools for a collectivist audience.

3.1   Collectivism and Decisions

Studies have investigated the impact of culture on group decision making [13] [14] [15] and has highlighted that the importance of group opinion, maintenance of consensus, and decisions of people with high social positions in the group cannot be underestimated. Collectivists follow an adaptive and more dependent decision-making style to maintain group harmony where the needs of the group outweigh the needs of individuals' opinion of a group leader.

Group Opinion - Collectivists generally give more weight to the opinions of their in-group than individualists do, and thus these opinions strongly influence their decisions. When collectivists perform an activity in isolation, they feel isolated and are less effective [9]. A *group opinion strategy* to consider may be to provide the user with the opinions of the other in-group members when they make a decision. [14]. This lessens the user's feelings of isolation, and reduces the time taken to seek advice from members of the in-group regarding their opinions. [14].

Consensus Change - Collectivists values consensus highly. They have less change in consensus between themselves than individualists [13] and rather strive to maintain consensus.

Group Polarization - Polarization is the inclination of individuals in a group setting to hold very different opinions to the group [13]. Polarization is a largely individualistic trait where individuals want to showcase their ideas and influence others to promote self-interest. In contrast, collectivist opinions do not lead to polarization in the group's decision and persuasive arguments.

Persuasive Arguments - Collectivists experience lower levels of persuasive content from arguments presented, due to the collective and high power distance of the culture [13]. They may rather support the arguments of powerful people in the group than arguments with more merit.

Adaptive Decision-Making - Collectivists adapt their decisions as needed as they are part of a group and are more receptive to social consequences of their decisions. Individualists view themselves as independent and responsible for their decisions [15] and keep to the same decision strategies.

Group Surveillance - Individualists use guilt as a negative motivational force, whereas collectivists use shame of the in-group as a result of their actions [9]. This strategy sets to track the behaviour of an individual or a group of individuals, to either reward or punish them later [14]. Collectivists' identities are strongly tied to that of their in-group and they are want to contribute as team members. An entire group is thus rewarded or punished for the actions of the individual.

Disapproval Conditioning - Individualists make use of positive reinforcement as a motivational strategy, but collectivists are use negative reinforcement to be motivated [14].

Deviation Monitoring - As collectivists desire to fit in with their in-group, they change their behaviours to adapt to the group and situation to ensure they do not stand out [14]. Collectivist cultures agree on what expected behaviour is deemed to be and they are given severe criticism for small deviations from the norm.

Group Customisation - In collectivist cultures it is important to put in-group goals ahead of one's own goals [11]. This means that in-group preferences may out-weigh individual preferences in different circumstances, particularly where members of the same in-group are together. A *group customisation strategy* can permit one member of an in-group, or perhaps various members, to modify application settings on behalf of the in-group's needs, preferences, and goals [14].

Previous research indicates that the ignorance of such culture differences cause the failure of systems [25]. Currently, many group decision-making tools are designed by individualists in the Western world, who do not consciously set out to focus on the individualistic culture. They are not aware of the features they design in this manner, but when such tools are used by different cultural groups, these same features surface to become problematic.

3.2   Collectivism and Social Position

Decisions are not only influenced by culture, but also by the opinions of group leaders. Such leaders are members of a group whose exercises strong influence over the members of the group [16]. In collectivist cultures, members look up to other group members for guidance who have a higher social in the community. Such a leader is trusted by its group members where there is more trust as the social position of the leader increase. Well connected leaders can provide access to a wider range of resources [24] and are beneficial to the group. Such leaders form potential collaborations with others outside the group, leading to potential business opportunities.

When groups are formed, new members are generally only invited if they are personal friends or well-know to current members [24]. Since current members are held responsible, to a certain degree, for the new member's behaviour, it is crucial that new member should behave according to the norms of the group. Collectivist cultures encourage individuals to relate to those in their in-groups and rely less on others outside the in-group to instill strong loyalty towards the group.

4   Group Decisions

A Group Decision can be defined as "a decision problem that is shared by two or more parties who make a choice for which all parties will bear some responsibility" [18]. Group Decision Support System (GDSS) enables the definition of alternatives, the choice of criteria and their weights, performance and final recommendations [17]. In order to obtain a recommendation a complete decision process is supported by formulating and structuring the problem, defining an evaluation model, finding an answer to the problem, and finally constructing a recommendation [19]. Many GDSS tools have been proposed that support brainstorming to generate ideas, blackboards to share information, argumentation models for decision analysis, and multiple criteria decision models for alternative evaluations. Recent research on GDSS implement consensus models that take into account coincidence among preferences, similarity criteria among the solutions obtained from the experts' preferences, and the agreement between the experts' individual opinions and the group opinion using fuzzy measures [26] illustrating the trend in these systems to focus only on rational decision-making. Social parameters such as trust or culture are generally ignored by the research community, leaving a gap to be explored.

Of the available set of GDSS decision models, multi-criteria decision analysis shows promise to support collectivist decision-making. It provides a set of techniques and principles to compare and evaluate alternatives according to criteria [18] [19]. A recommendation is constructed, based on formal preference models defined by users in the decision process, making it possible to explain why a preference is preferred over another. This aspect is relevant to decision-making in collectivist communities, as group members can be given access to the opinions of other group members, to make them more comfortable and effective in their decision-making. A group member can be given a recommendation, and also the reasons that underlie this recommendation by making use of argumentation. Amgoud et al. [8] proposes an approach that explicitly links argumentation to multi-criteria decision making, discussed next.

5   Argumentation

When considering classical logical reasoning such as propositional or predicate logic it is inferred that a conclusion can be found to be true despite any new additions made to the set of proposition which supported the conclusion. This is defined as monotonicity, where additional information does not cause conclusions to be modified or withdrawn [19]. For human reasoning this is not natural as people can change their minds when new information is made available. Decisions are based on the available information at a specific moment in time, and can be modified at any time. Non-monotonic reasoning formalisms have emerged over time of which argumentation theory is considered by this research. Argumentation theory enables reasoning, by constructing and comparing arguments for and against conclusions [20].

Non-monotonicity arises as new facts enable the construction of new arguments to support new conclusions, or support stronger counter-arguments against existing conclusions. Those arguments are intended to support, explain, or attack statements that can be decision, opinions, preferences, and values. Argumentation thus fits more naturally with human decision-making as people use arguments to support the claims that contribute to these decisions [21] [28]. Each potential decision usually has a set of arguments for or against it, of various strengths. The adoption of argumentation to a decision support system has direct benefits as the user can be provided with a choice that is not only well-founded, but is also accompanied by the reasons underlying the decision. Furthermore, as argumentation-based decision making is similar to the manner in which humans mull over options to finally make a decision [8], it is more natural to use.

When one wants to solve a decision problem, a set of X possible choices or decisions needs to be ordered, based on the different consequences of each decision. Here, argumentation can be used to define such an ordering. In order to achieve this arguments are to be constructed in favour of, and against each decision. This enables a comparison of possible decisions on the basis of the arguments and their quality or strengths. An argumentation-based decision process can be decomposed into the following steps:

- Constructing arguments in favour of or against each decision in X.
- Evaluating the strength of each argument.
- Comparing decisions on the basis of their arguments.
- Defining a pre-ordering on X.

Formally, following [8] an argumentation-based decision framework is defined as follows:

An argumentation-based decision framework is a tuple $<X, A, \geq, \quad \Delta_{Princ}>$ where:

X is a set of all possible decisions.

A is a set of arguments.

$\geq$ is a (partial or complete) pre-ordering on A.

Δ_{Princ} a principle for comparing decisions defines a partial or complete pre-ordering on X, defined on the basis of arguments.

Each decision that can be made may have arguments in its favour, and arguments against it. If there are multiple criteria to be considered, an argument in favour of a decision (pro) will be criteria that are positively satisfied. On the other hand, an argument against a decision (con) gives the criteria which are insufficiently satisfied. Arguments may have forces of various strengths [22] that enable an agent to compare different arguments in order to select the *best* ones, and consequently to select the best decisions.

Arguments pro/con Let $x \in X$ [8]
- $\text{Arg}_{\text{Pro}}(x)$ = the set of arguments in A which are in favour of x.
- $\text{Arg}_{\text{Con}}(x)$ = the set of arguments in A which are against x.

In order to support an argument-based comparison of decisions, a principle is required. A simple principle can be defined by merely counting the arguments in favor of each decision. This principle prefers the decision which has more supporting arguments.

An argument supporting a decision takes the form of an explanation. An argument is a 4-tuple $A = <S, x, g, c>$ where:
 S is the support of the argument,
 x is the conclusion of the argument,
 c is the criterion which is evaluated for x
 g represents the manner in which c is satisfied by x.
 where K represents a knowledge base gathering the available information about the world; X is the set of all possible decision; C is a base containing the different criteria and G is the set of all goals.

To be able to further refine the comparison principle, the strengths of arguments and of the preference relations between arguments are considered. Criteria in C may not have equal importance. The base C is partitioned and stratified into $C = (C_1 \cup \ldots \cup Cn)$ such that all criteria in C_i have the same importance level and are more important than criteria in Cj where $j < i$. Each criterion can be translated into a set of consequences, which may not be equally satisfactory. For example, consider the criterion "price" for a product on sale. If the price is 10 or less the user may be fully satisfied, but if it is more than 20, the user may be unsatisfied. This leads to the fact that there are sets of goals that are either positive G^+ or negative G^-. A decision to purchase a product is either made or not.

Once it is decided what are considered as pro and con arguments for each possible decision, it is necessary to aggregate them to finally decide what alternative to select. Here, one needs to consider how to manage the potential interactions between arguments that refer to different criteria. Bonnefon and Fargier [23] provide an overview of possible approaches to aggregate sets of pro and cons. These approaches take into account the fact that the arguments are bipolar and qualitative. Amgoud et al. [8] shows that it is possible to make use of classical aggregation operators in their framework. They compare decisions in terms of positive and negative arguments and show that the presented framework can capture different multiple criteria decision rules to select the best decision. The rule for the choice is characterized by the fact that criteria have or do not have the same level of importance.

6   Framework for Collectivist Decision Support

To illustrate the framework, a mobile eProcurement application, the Virtual Store, is used as example. It solves the challenges of VSEs such as the replenishment of stock using bulk buying. Users are provided with a mobile application to register, login and navigate through a supplier product catalogue. The catalogue contains real-time pricing information and specials that enables VSEs and other retailers to purchase goods in a group. The system allows the formation of collaborative groups where an identified group leader invites group members to be part of the group via the application. Before this can happen, face-to-face agreements are made between group members. A group needs to agree on basic aspects such as the types of products that they will purchase together as well as the threshold amount that they are willing to spend. The goals of the system are to take into account the collectivist nature of the end-user when a decision is make to buy stock in bulk.

The framework is defined next by describing the system architecture, the Virtual Store Agent, and the how collectivist group decision strategies are applied.

6.1 System Architecture

The architecture of the system is depicted in Figure 2. At the back-end there is a Virtual Store Server agent and on the mobile device of the users there is a User agent. The Virtual Store Server agent can access the product catalogue of the Virtual Store containing all products that can be purchased.

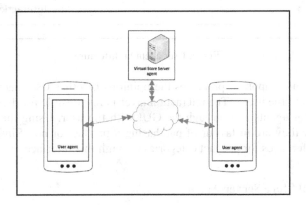

Fig. 2. Virtual store system architecture

These products are sent to the User agent that displays them to users simultaneously, when a session starts. In addition to the image of the products, the Virtual Store agent supports categories that represent particular aspects of products such as price, type or colour. The User agent is defined by subcomponents found in three layers shown in Figure 3 namely the interaction, reasoning and knowledge layers.

In the knowledge layer the User agent stores information about the environment of the user and profile information of other group members and the profile of the user consisting of preferences and goals. The social system component keeps track of the all group members and their relative social position to include this in the group decision computation Knowledge is accumulated over time, as the user interacts with the system. The reasoning layer forms a bridge between the knowledge and interaction layers and contains two components namely the argumentation component and decision component. The argumentation component is responsible for the generation of arguments when the human makes choices.

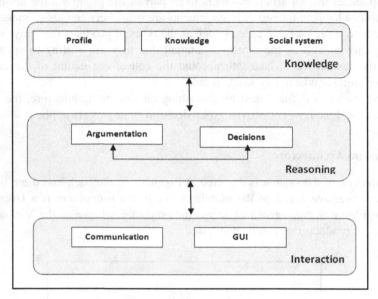

Fig. 3. User agent architecture

The decision component processes the opinions of other User agents to provide a group opinion to the user. The interaction layer is responsible for the communication with other User agents and through the GUI with the user. Using the GUI, users express whether they are in favour of purchasing a product or not. Similarly, they provide their preferences for product categories through this interface.

6.2   Virtual Store Server Agent

The Virtual Store Server agent stores product records of a large number of products P that can be purchased. For example, a group of VSE owners collaborate to buy products such as bread and milk in bulk. As a group, they need to create a shopping cart containing products that has been chosen by a group consensus process. They are provided with sets of products. The set of products is defined by $P = p_1, \ldots\ldots p_k$, where $k > 2$ is the set of available products.

Each product is described with a finite set of categories or features. The set $C = c_1, \ldots\ldots c_n$ contains all the possible categories where $n > 2$. A category may be associated with more than one product. For example, in Table 1, the following three bread products and their four categories are made available by the Virtual Store for bulk buying.

Table 1. Product categories

Price (c_1)	Quantity (c_2)	Supplier (c_3)	Type (c_4)
100	60	New bakeries	White
100	80	Smiths	Brown
80	50	ABC	White

The Virtual Store sends each product and its categories to the User agent, where it is displayed graphically to the user who evaluates it. The application supports strategies for collectivist decision-making, described next.

6.3   Collectivist Group Decision Making

The reasoning of the group is now described. A decision protocol is defined to allow the group to reason. To support the collectivist approach to decision-making the decision protocol has two main strategies namely the group customization strategy and group opinion strategy. Then follows a description of the process.

Group Customization Strategy. In-group preferences may be more important than individual preferences in scenarios such as the Virtual Store application. A group customisation strategy allows one member or leader, or various respected members, to customise the Virtual Store application configurations with the in-group's needs, preferences, and goals. Other in-group members can then accept and use the group-level customisation for themselves, thereby saving time and preventing possible uncomfortableness stemming from acting in isolation. It would be possible for group members to set a "personal level" customisation, and they should control which setting will be used in which sitautions. Data can be stored of all in-group preferences, to allow in-group members to stay up to date with group decisions and matters.

Group Opinion Strategy. The group opinion strategy provides the user with opinions of other in-group members while the user is making a decision. This ensures that the user's is not isolated from the group and reduces the time that he may take to consult each member of the in-group regarding their opinions. The group opinion can be presented in a visual manner by giving a graphical representation of categories that may be sized according to the strength of group preference.

The Group Decision Protocol. The group decision protocol is shown in Figure 4. The first step is the formation of a group when a group leader invites members to the group. The invited members accept requests. The group leader and respected members customises the goals and preferences of the group to best represent their requirements. The group leader starts a session to select products for bulk buying by the group. The Virtual Store agent send products to the User agent of each user. Members analyse categories and decide their preferences. Each user expresses his opinion about the product categories through the GUI of the User agent. User agents provide their users a report on the aggregated opinion of the group to determine if an agreement was reached. If so, the decision is made to buy the product. If no agreement is reached, the group opinion formation process starts. Users create new opinions as arguments that are exchanged between User agents following an adaptive decision-making style. The decision-module of the User agent determines the modified opinion of the group and whether an agreement was reached. This process continues until an agreement is reached to buy or reject the product. If no agreement can be reached, the group leader makes the final decision.

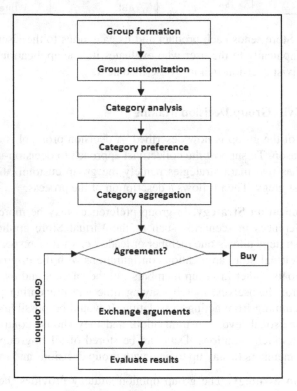

Fig. 4. Group decision protocol

Group decision-making is now described in more detail using the Virtual Store application.

Group Customisation

Using the group customisation strategy, the group leader of the group of retailers configures the Virtual Store with the products and their related categories the group will prefer to buy in bulk where the set of products for the group is defined by $PG = p_1, ...p_k$, where $k > 2$ is the set of available products and $PG \in P$.

Category Analysis

When making decisions, the user interacts with the system via the GUI, depicted in Figure 2. Each user expresses an opinion about each category of product sent by the Virtual Store Server agent. To ensure ease of use, the opinion is defined by the use of a slider on the GUI of the application.

Users provide their preferences and rejections for each category. This is done through a value, in the opinion range $Op = [0, 100]$ for each category associated with the product. In this context, the best preferred option is assigned a score of 100, and the least preferred a score of 0. This range can be customised according to the specific scenario. Assigning a value more than 50 to a product means that the product should be bought in bulk by the group.

Category Preference

The preferences of a user is defined as follows:

$U_i = \{s_{ij}\}$ is the score assigned by user i to category j. This preference represent the user's opinion of a product. For example $U_1 = \{70, 20, 90, 70\}$ gives the opinions of user 1 for each category c_1 to c_4 of a single product. The user gives a high preference to the baker (c3) Shown in Table 1 that provides the bread. The user may be able to change his opinion, based on what the group decides.

The overall score for each option, Si is given by summing the preference score for option i on criterion j.

$$Si = \sum_{j=1}^{n} sij /n$$

For user 1, $S_1 = 63$, indicating the user is in favour of buying the product.

After being provided a report on the ratings of other group members, a user can revise his opinion.

Category Aggregation

It is very important for each user to know the opinion of the group as the user may want to revise his opinion to accommodate the preferences of the group.

For example, given are the opinions of a set of 4 users for a product and their total scores:

$U_1 = \{70, 20, 90, 70\}$ $S_1 = 63$
$U_2 = \{50, 30, 20, 65\}$ $S_2 = 42$
$U_3 = \{70, 40, 20, 80\}$ $S_3 = 53$
$U_4 = \{50, 30, 30, 70\}$ $S_4 = 45$

The opinion of the group Op_i is calculated for each category as follows:

$$op_i = \sum_{j=1}^{n} oij /n$$

$op_i = \{60, 30, 40, 72\}$ $S_i = 50$

The opinion of user 1(63) is thus out of bounds with the group (42, 53, 45).

Group Opinion

As collectivist consumers prefer an adaptive decision-making style, they should be supported to change their mind when confronted with the opinion of the group. The focus of this research thus to support a group to reach consensus on a joint decision. Each member of the group can give their opinion, and change their mind when needed. This gives these consumers more confidence when making decisions, as they feel that they are complying to the preferences and goals of the group.

For this purpose, arguments pro and con to be used with multi-criteria decision analysis are now defined.

pro p_g is a pair $((c, o), p_g)$ where $c \in C$ and $o \in O$ and $o > 50$.
con p_g is a pair $((c, o), p_g)$ where $c \in C$ and $o \in O$ and $o \leq 50$.

The pair (c,o) represents the opinion of a user for a given category of a product. If the opinion is more than 50, the argument is in favour to buy the product, and if the opinion is less or equal to 50, the opinion is in favour to reject the product.

When a user changes his opinion about a given category, the initial argument is removed and replaced by another. For example, if the user decides to give a low preference to the baker, he can decrease the opinion to 30 from 90. The argument $((c_3, 90), p)$ is replaced by $((c_3, 30), p)$. The first argument is thus completely removed from the set of arguments of the user.

User 1 views the opinion of the group provided by his User agent and sees that the group is not in favour of the product. Similarly, user 3 sees that he is also out of the norms of the group. Both users modify their opinion by providing new arguments as follows: $U_1 = ((c_3, 30), p)$ and $U_3 = ((c_2, 30), p)$ resulting in the following set of opinions:

$U_1 = \{70, 20, \mathbf{30}, 70\}$ $S_1 = 48$
$U_2 = \{50, 30, 20, 65\}$ $S_2 = 42$
$U_3 = \{70, \mathbf{30}, 20, 80\}$ $S_3 = 50$
$U_4 = \{50, 30, 30, 70\}$ $S_4 = 45$

The opinion of the group changes to:
$op_i = \{60, 28, 25, 72\}$ $S_i = 46$
The group is now in agreement to reject this product.

7   Conclusion

This paper proposes a framework for the Virtual Store application to enable a group of users such as VSE owners to create a shared shopping cart containing products that have been agreed to as a group. In the framework, users are provided with products and related criteria over which to define their preferences, which are the strengths of their arguments that they present. A joint group opinion is formed which is reported to all users to assist them to feel part of the group and to ensure that they can comply to the group opinion if needed. The architecture consists of two parts namely the Virtual Store server agent and the User agent through which users interact with the system.

To the knowledge of the authors, the framework to address collectivist decision-making is the first of its kind. The framework is a step towards supporting collectivist beliefs and behaviours relating to decisions and group opinions by using argumentation-based decision for a multi- criteria decision problem. This approach naturally support the manner in which opinions can be changed as new facts come to light.

Next research is addressing the refinement of features to be addressed in the decision framework, the implementation of a prototype and the evaluation of the framework.

Acknowledgments. The support of the National Research Foundation (NRF) under grant number 81201 toward this research is hereby acknowledged. Opinions expressed and conclusions arrived at are those of the authors and not necessarily to be attributed to the NRF.

References

1. Economic Report on Africa, "Governing development in Africa – the role of the state in economic transactions", http://www.uneca.org/era2011/ (accessed February 8, 2012)
2. LeFebvre, R., Franke, V.: Culture Matters: Individualism vs. Collectivism in Conflict Decision-Making. Societies 3(1), 128–146 (2013)
3. e-spaza (2011), http://www.e-spaza.com/?p=251 (accessed February 9, 2012)
4. Radebe, K.: R7bn worth of untapped township potential (December 27, 2012), http://www.moneyweb.co.za/moneyweb-mybusiness/r7bn-worth-of-untapped-township-potential (date accessed: June 19, 2013)
5. Dörflinger, J., Friedland, C., Mengistu, M., Merz, C., Stadtrecher, S., Pabst, K., de Louw, R.: Mobile commerce in rural South Africa — Proof of concept of mobile solutions for the next billion mobile consumers. In: Proceedings of the 10th IEEE International Symposium on a World of Wireless, Mobile and Multimedia Networks – WOWMOM 2009, Kos Island, Greece, June 15-19 (2009)
6. Ntawanga, F., Eloff, J.H.P., Ngassam, E.K., Kandie, W.: User Experience Evaluation of a Lightweight Mobile EProcurement Application for Rural Small-Scale Retailers. In: Proceedings of the Fourth International IEEE EAI Conference on eInfrastructure and eServices for Developing Countries, Yaoundé, Cameroon, November 12-14 (2012)
7. Dhar, M.: Brand Management 101-101 Lessons from Real World Marketing. John Wiley & Sons (Asia) Pte Ltd., Singapore (2007)
8. Amgoud, L., Bonnefon, J.-F., Prade, H.: An argumentation-based approach to multiple criteria decision. In: Godo, L. (ed.) ECSQARU 2005. LNCS (LNAI), vol. 3571, pp. 269–280. Springer, Heidelberg (2005)
9. Hofstede, G., Hofstede, G.J., Minkov, M.: Cultures and organizations. McGraw-Hill, London (1991)
10. Martin, R., Hewstone, M.: Social-influence processes of control and change: Conformity, obedience to authority and innovation. In: Hogg, M.A., Cooper, J. (eds.) The SAGE Handbook of Social Psychology, pp. 347–366. Sage, London (2003)
11. Hofstede, G.: Culture's consequences: International differences in work-related values. Sage Publications, Incorporated (1980)
12. Usunier, J.C.: International and Cross-Cultural Management Research. Sage, London
13. Yetim, F.: Cultural Aspects of Group Support Systems. In: Zimmermann, H., Schramm, V. (eds.) Knowledge Management and Communication Systems, Proceedings of 6th International Symposium on Information Science, ISI 1998, Prague, November 4-7, Universitätsverlag, Konstanz (1998)
14. Khaled, R., Biddle, R., Noble, J., Barr, P., Fischer, R.: Persuasive interaction for collectivist cultures. In: Piekarski, W. (ed.) The Seventh Australasian User Interface Conference (AUIC 2006), pp. 73–80 (2006)
15. Güss, D.: Decision making in individualistic and collectivist cultures. In: Lonner, W.J., Dinnel, D.L., Hayes, S.A., Sattler, D.N. (eds.) OnLine Readings in Psychology and Culture, Western Washington University, Department of Psychology, Center for Cross-Cultural Research (2002)

16. Yeboah, A.: The Influence of Culture on Consumer Choice: A Case of the Fast Moving Consumer Goods In Ghana. International Journal of Business and Management Tomorrow 2(2) (February 2012)
17. Salo, A., Hämäläinen, R.P.: Multicriteria Decision Analysis in Group Decision Processes. In: Kilgour, D.M., Eden, C. (eds.) Handbook of Group Decision and Negotiation. Springer, Dordrecht (2010)
18. Kilgour, D., Chen, Y., Hipel, K.: Chapter 11 - Trends in Multiple Criteria Decision Analysis. In: Greco, S., Ehrgott, M., Figueira, J.R. (eds.). XVI. International Series in Operations Research & Management Science, vol. 142, p. 412 (2010)
19. Ouerdane, W., Maudet, N., Tsoukias, A.: Chapter 7 - Argumentation Theory and Decision Aiding. In: Greco, S., Ehrgott, M., Figueira, J.R. (eds.) XVI. International Series in Operations Research & Management Science, vol. 142, p. 412 (2010)
20. Ouerdane, W., Maudet, N., Tsoukiàs, A.: Argumentation theory and decision aiding. In: Figueira, J., Greco, S., Ehrgott, M. (eds.) International Series in Operations Research and Management Science, 1,Trends in Multiple Criteria Decision Analysis, vol. 142, pp. 177–208 (2010)
21. Chesnevar, C., Maguitman, A.G., Loui, R.P.: Logical Models of Argument. ACM Computing Surveys 32(4), 337–383 (2000)
22. Ouerdane, W., Dimopoulos, Y., Liapis, K., Moraitis, P.: Towards automating decision aiding through argumentation. Journal of Multi-Criteria Decision Analysis 18, 289–309 (2011)
23. Bonnefon, J.-F., Fargier, H.: Comparing sets of positive and negative arguments: Empirical assessment of seven qualitative rules. In: Proc. of 17th European Conf. on Artificial Intelligence. IOS Press (2006)
24. Triandis, H.C.: Individualism-collectivism and personality. Journal of Personality 69, 907–924 (2001)
25. Bricks, D.A.: Bunders in International Business, 4th edn. Blackwell (2006)
26. Tapia García, J.M., del Moral, M.J., Martínez, M.A., Herrera-Viedma, E.: A consensus model for group decision making problems with linguistic interval fuzzy preference relations. Expert Syst. Appl. 39(11), 10022–10030 (2012)
27. Isherwood, D., Coetzee, M.: Towards Trust and Reputation for E-Commerce in Collectivist Rural Africa. In: International Symposium on Human Aspects of Information Security & Assurance (HAISA 2012), Crete, Greece, June 6-8 (2012)

A Knowledge Integration Approach for Safety-Critical Software Development and Operation Based on the Method Architecture

Shuichiro Yamamoto

Nagoya University
syamamoto@acm.org

Abstract. It is necessary to integrate practical software development and operation body of knowledge to deploy development and operation methods for assuring safety. In this paper, an approach based on the method architecture is proposed to develop a Knowledge integration method for describing various software related bodies of knowledge and the safety case for assuring software life cycle and operation processes.

1   Introduction

Information technology (IT) systems have a profound effect on our modern society. In order to assure the safety of the software used in these systems, it is not sufficient to simply confirm the safety of the software that is developed and operated: we also need software development and operation processes that allow the safety of the processes themselves to be verified. Such development and operation processes may be employed in actual software development and operation projects, it is crucial that they are integrated with the development and operation bodies of knowledge already being used by software developers and operators. We, therefore, propose an approach to assure safety throughout all stages of software development and operation by specifying a method for integrating the safety case[1, 2, 3]—a technique used to assure safety both in software and its development and operation processes—with multiple bodies of knowledge based on the method architecture[4], which can be used to describe a variety of practices in a uniform manner.

2   Background

There are high expectations for the safety case in the assurance of system safety in fields such as aerospace, medical devices, and automobiles. In order to promote and support the adoption of this technique in the software development and operation workplace in Japan, the authors established the D-Case Validation & Evaluation Study Session (http://www.dcase.jp) in September 2012. On the international front, meanwhile, we have participated in efforts aimed at proposing the Assured Architecture Development Method (AADM)[6] to the international standards organization

S. Teufel et al. (Eds.): CD-ARES 2014, LNCS 8708, pp. 17–28, 2014.

The Open Group (TOG) as a technique for highly safe development of architectures in relation to TOGAF[5]—the group's enterprise architecture framework. As a result of this work, *Open Dependability through Assuredness* (O-DA) became the first standard originating in Japan to be adopted by TOG in July 2013. However, this standard is still quite new, and the safety case approach has not yet made sufficient inroads into the development and operation workplace.

Our experience in the promotion and standardization of the safety case has shown the following to be the main factors behind slow progress in the pickup of this technique at home and overseas:

(1) Software developers and operators, as well as managers at IT and user companies, have no clearly defined objectives for the introduction of the safety case due to insufficient awareness of the approach itself;

(2) The safety case has not yet been sufficiently integrated with bodies of knowledge currently being used by software developers and operators, such as SoftWare Engineering Body Of Knowledge (SWEBOK)[7], Project Management Body Of Knowledge (PMBOK)[8], Capability Maturity Model Integration (CMMI)[9], Business Analysis Body Of Knowledge (BABOK)[10], Requirements Engineering Body Of Knowledge (REBOK)[11], IT Infrastructure Library (ITIL)[12,13], and SQuARE[14]; and

(3) As a result of the above, no clearly defined methods for introduction of the safety case into development and operation processes have been established, and therefore, organization capabilities for effective application of this approach have yet to be realized.

The application of the safety case to safety-critical systems is obligatory in the United States and Europe, and in much the same way as the O-DA standard has been accepted, the safety case is now recognized as an effective and important tool for building consensus between stakeholders such as the client, the software developer, the operator, and supervisory authorities. However, O-DA has just been integrated with TOGAF, and this standard has yet to see full-fledged application by developers and operators; in addition, the safety case has not been sufficiently integrated with development and operation bodies of knowledge other than TOGAF. Other impediments to introduction into the workplace also exist—for example, the relationships between the safety cases for development and operation process and those for the software deliverables have yet to be clearly defined, and no specific methods have been developed for integrating the safety case with conventional approaches such as Fault Tree Analysis (FTA), Failure Mode and Effect Analysis (FMEA), and Hazard and Operability (HAZOP). As a result, there has been limited crossover between knowledge bases for development and operation and safety-case development knowledge, and practices for analysis and evaluation of the safety of system development and operation processes have been inadequate.

Overseas research aimed at reshaping software development practices in a theoretical fashion has led to the proposal of Software Engineering Method and Theory (SEMAT)[15] based on the method architecture, and a Japan subdivision has been set up by this research project's participants. In its current form, however, SEMAT does not incorporate the safety case or any other operation or project-management knowledge bases. The applicability of the safety case must be enhanced by leveraging a method-architecture perspective in order that the compound bodies of knowledge described above can be put to effective use.

The team leaders and participants in this research project are working to promote the safety case and SEMAT in Japan so that their benefits may be felt in the software development workplace. While certain corporations do appear to be taking steps towards this end, little progress has been made in this country in terms of the integration and advancement of these techniques.

We propose a comprehensive approach to assure safety in all stages of the software development and operation life cycle by combining multiple bodies of knowledge with the safety case based on the concept of the SEMAT method architecture. Furthermore, in consideration of the findings of this research project's team leaders and participants in relation to patterns, editors, and other elemental safety-case techniques, introduction training activities, knowledge engineering techniques, and the reuse of development practices, we also propose an approach to efficiently assure software safety throughout the entirety of the software development and operation life cycle on the basis of the method architecture and plan to verify its benefit through case studies.

The aim of this wide-ranging, advanced research is to facilitate highly safe development and operation of software based on the concept of the method architecture by proposing an approach whereby (1) a range of bodies of knowledge are integrated with the safety case and (2) multiple knowledge bases are efficiently combined and applied at each stage of the software life cycle.

3   Related Work

This section provides a description of the method architecture, the safety case, and software-related bodies of knowledge.

3.1   Method Architecture[4]

In the method architecture, multiple practices can be combined to define a method. These practices are described using both the Essence Kernel—a fundamental practice—and the Essence Language. In this way, a practice can be safely combined with many others in order to create super-ordinate methods. The fundamental concept of the method architecture is as follows.

Method: A method comprises multiple practices. Configured from plans and results, methods are dynamic descriptions that support the daily work of developers by describing not only what is expected, but what is actually done.

Practice: A practice is a repeatable approach for achieving a specified objective. It provides a systematic and verifiable procedure for addressing a specific aspect of a work task. Each practice can be a component element of multiple methods.

Essence Kernel: This kernel constitutes the essential elements for software development techniques. It can be used to define kernels for other domains.

Kernel Language: This domain-specific language is used to define methods, practices, and kernels.

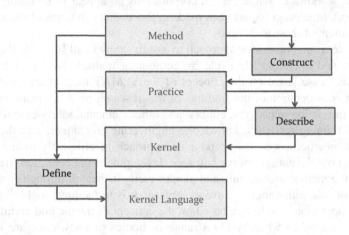

Fig. 1. The Method Architecture

3.2   The Safety Case

The component elements of the safety case are claim, strategy, context, evidence, and undeveloped nodes[1][2]. These nodes can be connected to one another in two different ways—namely, by an arrow with a solid head, which is used for claim, strategy, and evidence association, or an arrow with an empty head, which associates a context with a claim or strategy. A typical example of a safety case in Goal Structuring Notation (GSN) is shown in Figure 2.

Claim: A rectangular claim node defines a required property of the system, and it can be decomposed into sub-claims and strategies.

Strategy: A strategy node takes the form of a parallelogram describing an argument required to support the claim. Each strategy can be decomposed into sub-claims or other strategies.

Context: Displayed as a rounded rectangle, a context node provides external information required for correctly interpreting the associated claim or strategy.

Evidence: These nodes provide support for a sub-claim or strategy.

Undeveloped: Shown using a hollow diamond, undeveloped nodes indicate that the corresponding sub-claim or strategy has not been argued.

The authors are working to promote establishment of the O-DA standard within TOGAF[6]. AADM—the O-DA method for assured architecture development—proposes that the following must be established: (1) a management technique for evidence documents and safety cases using an architecture repository; (2) a consensus building technique reflecting claim priorities; (3) a technique for defining the scope of the safety case; (4) a technique for defining quantitative evaluation scales for claims; (5) an evaluation technique for safety-case development capabilities; (6) a safety-case review technique; (7) a technique for combining safety cases; (8) techniques for developing safety cases for the development and operation processes; (9) a technique for combining safety cases with failure-analysis and risk-management techniques; and (10) a tracking technique for safety-case claims and system requirements. In order to achieve this, the authors are studying the formulation of safety case patterns as well as methods for developing safety cases for the development and operation processes [16-20].

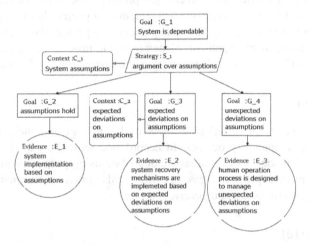

Fig. 2. Typical Safety Case

Sections 3.3 through 3.10 provide an overview of software-related bodies of knowledge; Section 3.11 presents the results of a comparison thereof focusing on commonality and identifies research tasks to be undertaken going forward.

3.3   SWEBOK[7]

For each knowledge area, the *Guide to the Software Engineering Body of Knowledge* (SWEBOK® Guide V3.0) provides (1) an introduction, (2) component elements (topics), (3) a correspondence table of topics reference documents, (4), recommended reference documents, and (5) a list of related documents.

SWEBOK knowledge areas are decomposed into two or three hierarchical levels comprising topics. This hierarchical decomposition is configured so as not to include any dependency on specific fields of application, business uses, development techniques, and the like. However, SWEBOK recommends that necessary information be directly acquired from reference documents, and therefore, it does not itself describe knowledge in detail.

The SWEBOK knowledge fields are: (1) software requirements, (2) software design, (3) software construction, (4) software testing, (5) software maintenance, (6) software configuration management, (7) software engineering management, (8) software engineering process, (9) software engineering tools and methods, and (10) software quality.

3.4   PMBOK[8]

PMBOK recognizes that processes can fall into different knowledge areas and different process groups. The PMBOK knowledge areas are: (1) project integration management, (2) project scope management, (3) project time management, (4) project cost management, (5) project quality management, (6) project human resource management, (7) project communications management, (8) project risk management, and (9) project procurement management. Meanwhile, the process groups are (1) initiating, (2) planning, (3) executing, (4) monitoring and controlling, and (5) closing.

3.5   CMMI[9]

CMMI models are systematized collections of knowledge that help organizations improve their development processes. In accordance with the CMMI for Development, Version 1.3 model, process areas are described using purpose statements, introductory notes, related process areas, specific goals, practice summaries, example work products, generic goals, and generic practices.

3.6   BABOK[10]

BABOK 2.0 systematically describes business analysis knowledge in the form of three hierarchical levels—(1) knowledge areas, (2) tasks, and (3) techniques. Knowledge areas are described in the form of (1) a knowledge area definition, (2) related tasks, (3) related techniques, (4) inputs to the knowledge area, and (5) outputs from the knowledge area. Meanwhile, each task is presented in the form of (1) its purpose, (2) a description of its content, (3) relevant stakeholders, (4) inputs, (5) outputs, (6) task elements, and (7) techniques for performing the task.

3.7   REBOK[11]

REBOK is a body of knowledge intended to support practical requirements engineering in regard to requirements negotiated by users and vendors. Its principal features are as follows:
(1)   It is common to both users and vendors;
(2)   It organizes standards and knowledge areas that may need to be acquired not only by requirements analysts, but also by end users, managers, and all other stakeholders participating in requirements engineering;

(3)   It reflects the scope of business requirements, system requirements, and software requirements; and

(4)   It covers techniques common to requirements engineering for enterprise systems and embedded systems (although domain-specific knowledge is defined separately).

3.8   ITIL[12,13]

ITIL is a body of knowledge for best practices in service management that allows organizations to provide customers with services that are safe, highly reliable, and meet their objectives, and to also become trusted providers. As a process-based framework covering the entire service life cycle, it comprises five individual processes—namely, service strategy, service design, service transition, service operation, and continual service improvement.

3.9   TOGAF[5,6]

TOGAF Version 9 comprises seven parts. Part 1 provides an explanation of the main concept and definitions of terms used. The Architecture Development Method (ADM), which is a step-by-step approach to developing enterprise architectures is described in Part 2 in terms of purposes, objectives, processes, inputs, and outputs. Part 3 provides guidelines and describes techniques for application of the ADM. The TOGAF architecture content framework, which includes a metamodel, architecture building blocks for re-use, and the deliverables of the various ADM phases, is described in Part 4. Part 5 describes the Enterprise Continuum—a categorization system for storing the deliverables of enterprise architecture activities—as well as related tools. The Enterprise Continuum can be seen as a mechanism for categorizing, associating, and storing all information produced in relation to an enterprise architecture. Part 6 provides a description of architectural reference models primarily in terms of the TOGAF Foundation Architecture and the Integrated Information Infrastructure Reference Model. Using the Enterprise Continuum and these reference models, the state of practical implementation of the enterprise architecture can be elicited from business capabilities and the current state of business can be presented with respect to the business vision. Finally, Part 7 describes the organization, processes, skills, roles, and responsibilities required to manage enterprise-architecture activities in terms of the Architecture Capability Framework.

3.10   SQuaRE[14]

Software Product Quality Requirements and Evaluation (SQuaRE) is a new standard for evaluating the quality requirements of software products. The SQuaRE standard covers scope, conformance, normative references, terms and definitions, a software quality requirement framework, and requirements for quality requirements. The software quality requirement framework is described in terms of purpose, software and systems, stakeholders and stakeholder requirements, software properties, a software quality measurement model, software quality requirements, system requirements categorization, and a quality requirements life cycle model. Requirements for quality requirements take the form of general requirements, stakeholder requirements, and software requirements.

3.11 Comparison of Bodies of Knowledge

Table 1 shows the results of analysis of the common content of software bodies of knowledge. From this, we can see that certain content is shared by multiple bodies of knowledge, and therefore, that they should be integrated in an appropriate fashion. As stated in this paper, therefore, a technique based on the method architecture for describing bodies of knowledge in a cross-body manner and safely and efficiently integrating these descriptions is required.

Table 1. Analysis of Commonality of Software Bodies of Knowledge

	SWEBOK	PMBOK	CMMI	BABOK	REBOK	ITIL	TOGAF	SQuaRE
SWE BOK	Software development	Development projects	Development management	Requirements engineering	Requirements engineering	Design and transition	Solution deployment monitoring	Software quality
PM BOK		Project management	Development management	Requirements management	Risk management	Operation management	EA management	Quality improvement processes
CMMI			Development, procurement, and services	Process improvement	Process improvement	Service maturity	EA maturity	Quality improvement processes
BA BOK				Business analysis	Business requirements	Business requirements	Business architecture	Quality assurance
RE BOK					Requirements engineering	Operation requirements	Requirements management	Quality requirements
ITIL						Services	Operation monitoring	Service quality
TOGAF							EA	EA quality
SQuaRE								Software quality

4   Research Issues

We propose an approach to support efficient and high-quality development and operation of safety-critical software by making it easier for developers and operators to introduce the safety case, and furthermore, we plan to develop the associated support tools. The following three research tasks must be undertaken in order that the safety case may be implemented in all stages of the software life cycle from development through operation.

4.1 Enhancement of Safety in Software Development and Operation Processes with the Safety Case

Based on specific case studies of software development and operation, impediments to practical implementation of the safety case must be identified and effective solutions proposed. Using the O-DA AADM, for example, we must confirm that safety cases can be developed and that critical safety can be analyzed and assured for all data processed by information systems, beginning with the business vision; for the execution of application functionality and the information technologies utilized; and for system deployment and operation scenarios. Further, we also propose a safety extension similar to the O-DA for bodies of knowledge other than TOGAF, such as BABOK and ITIL.

In order to assure safety, we must confirm that safety countermeasures for mitigating system risk to the greatest possible extent have been implemented with software. We thus propose (1) an approach for enumerating risk factors related to system requirements and system design and reviewing the completeness of the safety case, and (2) an approach for confirming that safety requirements and designs are free of omissions by preparing an ontology and case-study basis for system failure.

4.2 Reconfiguration of Bodies of Knowledge with Method Architecture

We propose an approach whereby the above-described safety case and method for enhancing the safety of bodies of knowledge currently used in the workplace are integrated in a manner that spans multiple bodies of knowledge in order to facilitate smooth implementation by developers and operators. More specifically, we propose an approach for confirming and assuring the validity of highly safe software that—based on the method architecture—can systematically integrate a software-engineering body of knowledge, a requirements-engineering body of knowledge, a project-management body of knowledge, an operation body of knowledge, and so forth. In particular, this approach would allow for the assurance of safety-related intentions by software and its development and operation processes to be objectively explained and confirmed based on evidence from the safety case. Research into this approach with thus focus on (1) cross-body integration based on objective evidence common to multiple bodies of knowledge, and (2) verification of the effectiveness thereof on the basis of case studies.

4.3 Support Tool Development

We plan to design and prototype a tool that can provide highly effective support for this paper's proposed development and operation approach for safety-critical software based on the method architecture. Editors[21] and other tools for the development of safety cases allow safety-case patterns and failure patterns based on application case studies to be managed in repositories and reused. Furthermore, we hope to realize support functionality for analyzing safety confidence levels and the completeness of arguments. We will also develop ontologies for eliminating inconsistencies in terminology and other knowledge arising from the combination of different bodies of knowledge and the reuse of safety cases. These repositories and ontologies will contain guidelines and training materials for practical application of these bodies of knowledge with higher levels of safety due to implementation of the safety case, and they will also prove useful in training and promotion related to the development and operation approach employing the method architecture.

5   Considerations

5.1   Practice and Theory

In proposing an approach based on the method architecture for efficiently integrating the safety case with the various bodies of knowledge put to practical use by developers and operators of safety-critical software, this research project is highly practical in nature. Meanwhile, it also has an academic aspect in proposing a theory for cross-body integration of compound bodies of knowledge on software development and operation with the safety case.

5.2   Development Process for Proposed Approaches

We aim to contribute to greater levels of safety and security in software providing social infrastructure by collecting and reusing valuable knowledge through the study of case studies on actual software development and operation and also by publicizing and promoting the above-described approaches in the form of seminars, study sessions, and so forth.

5.3   Enhancing the Safety of Software Bodies of Knowledge

In terms of the practical development and operation of safety-critical software both in Japan and overseas, we also aim to contribute to higher levels of safety in these processes not only by enhancing the safety of the software itself based on principles and targets but by also systematically reconfiguring software development and operation knowledge bases according to the method architecture concept.

6   Summary and Future Issues

In this paper, we introduced efforts aimed at enhancing the safety of software-related bodies of knowledge utilized by the developers and operators of safety-critical software and efficiently integrating these bodies of knowledge using the method architecture and the safety case in order that this type of software may be developed and operated in a more practical fashion. We have examined eight specific bodies of knowledge in this regard, but in order to generalize our research, more must be evaluated. In regard to testing, for example, a method has been established for confirming sufficiency using the safety case (or, more precisely, the assurance case)[17], and therefore, it is necessary to integrate the bodies of knowledge considered in this research using the method architecture.

Figure 3 shows an overview of our proposal. Going forward, we plan to conduct research focusing on the tasks identified in Section 4. In terms of the technical knowledge contained in the various different bodies of knowledge, meanwhile, we will examine (1) how it can be integrated and (2) how a high level of safety can be achieved by means of the safety case.

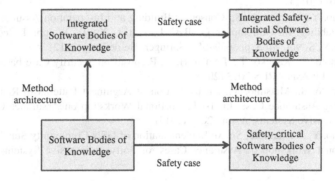

Fig. 3. Integration of Bodies of Knowledge for Safety-Critical Software

References

1. Kelly, T.P.: A Six-Step Method for the Development of Goal Structures. York Software Engineering (1997)
2. Kelly, T.P.: Arguing Safety, A Systematic Approach to Managing Safety Cases. PhD Thesis, Department of Computer Science, University of York (1998)
3. Bloomfield, P., Bishop, P.: Safety and Assurance Cases: Past, Present and Possible Future – an Adelard Perspective (2010)
4. OMG, Essence – Kernel and Language for Software Engineering Methods, ad/2013-02-01 (2013), http://www.omg.org/spec/Essence/1.0
5. The Open Group, TOGAF V.9 A Pocket Guide (2008)
6. The Open Group, The Open Group Real-Time & Embedded Systems Forum, Dependability through Assuredness™ Standard (O-DA) (2013)
7. Guide to the Software Engineering Body of Knowledge (SWEBOK V3), http://www.computer.org/portal/web/swebok/home
8. PMBOK Guide, http://www.pmi.org/
9. CMMI, CMU/SEI-2010-TR-033 (2010)
10. IIBA, Japan Chapter, A Guide to the Business Analysis Body of Knowledge (2009)

11. Japan Information Technology Services Industry Association, REBOK Working Group, Requirements Engineering Body of Knowledge,
    http://www.seto.nanzan-u.ac.jp/~amikio/NISE/eng/REBOK/
    REBOK-APSEC2011-Tutorial-2011-12-05.pdf
12. ITIL, itSMF Japan, http://www.itsmf-japan.org/itil
13. iTSMF, ITIL V3 Foundation Handbook (2009)
14. Boegh, J.: A New Standard for Quality Requirements. IEEE Software, 20–27 (January/February 2008)
15. Jacobson, I., Ng, P.-W., McMahon, P.E., Spence, I., Lidman, S.: The Essence of Software Engineering – Applying the SEMAT Kernel. Addison-Wesley Pearson Education (2013)
16. Yamamoto, S., Matsuno, Y.: d* framework: Inter-Dependency Model for Dependability. DSN (2012)
17. Yamamoto, S., Matsuno, Y.: A Review Method based on a Matrix Interpretation of GSN. JCKBSE (2012)
18. Matsuno, Y., Yamamoto, S.: Consensus Building and In-operation Assurance For Service Dependability? In: Quirchmayr, G., Basl, J., You, I., Xu, L., Weippl, E. (eds.) CD-ARES 2012. LNCS, vol. 7465, pp. 639–653. Springer, Heidelberg (2012)
19. Yamamoto, S., Kaneko, T., Tanaka, H.: A Proposal on Security Case based on Common Criteria. In: Asia ARES 2013 (2013)
20. Yamamoto, S., Matsuno, Y.: An Evaluation of Argument Patterns to Reduce Pitfalls of Applying Assurance Case. In: 1st International Workshop on Assurance Cases for Software-intensive Systems, Assure 2013 (2013)
21. Matsuno, Y., Yamamoto, S.: An Implementation of GSN Community Standard. In: 1st International Workshop on Assurance Cases for Software-intensive Systems, Assure 2013 (2013)

Metrics-Based Incremental Determinization
of Finite Automata

Sergiu I. Balan[1], Gianfranco Lamperti[1], and Michele Scandale[2]

[1] Dipartimento di Ingegneria dell'Informazione, Università degli Studi di Brescia (I)
[2] Dipartimento di Elettronica, Informazione e Bioingegneria, Politecnico di Milano (I)

Abstract. Some application domains, including monitoring of active systems in
artificial intelligence and model-based mutation testing in software engineering,
require determinization of finite automata to be performed incrementally. To this
end, an algorithm called *Incremental Subset Construction* (*ISC*) was proposed a
few years ago. However, this algorithm was recently discovered to be incorrect
is some instance problems. The incorrect behavior of *ISC* originates when the
redirection of a transition causes a portion of the automaton to be disconnected
from the initial state. This misbehavior is disturbing in two ways: portions of the
resulting automaton are disconnected and, as such, useless; moreover, a considerable amount of computation is possibly wasted for processing these disconnected
parts. To make *ISC* sound, a metrics-based technique is proposed in this paper,
where the distance between states is exploited in order to guarantee the connection of the automaton, thereby allowing *ISC* to achieve soundness. Experimental
results show that, besides being effective, the proposed technique is efficient too.

Keywords: Finite Automata, Incremental Determinization, Incremental Subset
Construction, Model-Based Reasoning.

1 Introduction

For efficiency reasons, determinization of finite automata is essential to a wide range of
applications, from pattern matching based on regular expressions [8] to analysis of protein sequences [4]. The determinization of a nondeterministic finite automaton (NFA)
into an equivalent deterministic finite automaton (DFA) is commonly performed by
Subset Construction (*SC*), an algorithm introduced several decades ago [18].

However, some application domains, including monitoring and diagnosis of active
systems [12, 15, 17] in artificial intelligence, and model-based mutation testing [1–3, 9]
in software engineering, require determinization to be carried out incrementally, where
the NFA expands over time and determinization is required at each expansion.

Specifically, in [12], principles and techniques of diagnosis of active systems are
presented. A technique for incremental processing of temporal observations in model-
based reasoning is proposed in [17]. Despite being specific for automata derived from
temporal observations, this technique contains the seeds of a more general-purpose algorithm for automata determinization. In [15], the notion of monotonic monitoring of
discrete-event systems is introduced, which is supported by specific constraints on the
fragmentation of the temporal observation, leading to the notion of stratification.

S. Teufel et al. (Eds.): CD-ARES 2014, LNCS 8708, pp. 29–44, 2014.

In model-based mutation testing, a test model is mutated for test case generation, thereby becoming a *mutant*. The resulting test cases are able to detect whether the faults in the mutated models have been implemented in the system under test. For this purpose, a conformance check between the original and the mutated model is required. An approach is proposed for conformance checking of action systems in [1], which relies on constraint solving techniques. This approach is extended in [2, 3] by two techniques: a strategy to efficiently handle a large number of mutants and incremental solving. An extensive approach to model-based mutation testing can be found in [9], where input-output conformance check [19] is shown to benefit from incremental determinization.

The rest of the paper is organized as follows. In Section 2, the classical technique for NFA determinization is recalled, and the problem of incremental determinization is defined. Section 3 provides some hints on the application domain in which incremental determinization originated. Section 4 introduces the basic notions of the metrics-based incremental determinization technique, while a detailed specification of the algorithm is outlined in Section 5. A discussion on why avoiding disconnection is provided in Section 6. Experimental results are shown in Section 7. Section 8 concludes the paper.

2   Determinization of Finite Automata

According to the *SC* algorithm, each state in the DFA is identified by a subset of the states of the NFA. *SC* yields the DFA starting from the ε-closure of the initial state of the NFA, which becomes the initial state of the DFA, and by progressively generating the successor states of each state $\mathbb{N}$ (subset of NFA states) as the ε-closure of the set of NFA states reached by a label ℓ from the NFA states in $\mathbb{N}$, called the ℓ-*closure* of $\mathbb{N}$.

Example 1. Traced in Figure 1 is the determinization of the NFA outlined in the left side. Gray states indicate that further processing is required. Next to the NFA is the sequence of intermediate DFAs leading to the equivalent DFA outlined in the right side.

1. The initial state of the DFA is the ε-closure of the initial state of the NFA, $\{0, 1\}$.
2. Considering $\{0, 1\}$, two transitions are created, $\{0, 1\} \xrightarrow{a} \{1, 2\}$ and $\{0, 1\} \xrightarrow{b} \{2, 3\}$, which are obtained by considering each symbol of the alphabet marking a transition exiting either 0 or 1. With a, two transitions are applicable in the NFA, $0 \xrightarrow{a} 1$ and $0 \xrightarrow{a} 2$. Thus, the target state for the transition exiting $\{0, 1\}$ and marked by a in the

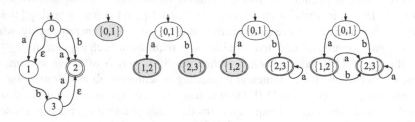

Fig. 1. Determinization by *SC*: the NFA on the left side is determinized into the equivalent DFA on the right side, starting from the initial state $\{0, 1\}$

DFA is the ε-closure of $\{1,2\}$, namely $\{1,2\}$. With b, we come up with transition $\{0,1\} \xrightarrow{b} \{2,3\}$.

3. Considering $\{2,3\}$, since we have $2 \xrightarrow{a} 3$ in the NFA (while no transition marked by a symbol in the alphabet exits state 3) and the ε-closure of $\{3\}$ is $\{2,3\}$, an auto-transition $\{2,3\} \xrightarrow{a} \{2,3\}$ is created. Notice how this transition does not cause the creation of a new state.

4. Considering $\{1,2\}$, since $1 \xrightarrow{b} 3$ and $2 \xrightarrow{a} 3$ are in the NFA and the ε-closure of $\{3\}$ is $\{2,3\}$, two transitions are created in the DFA, $\{1,2\} \xrightarrow{a} \{2,3\}$ and $\{1,2\} \xrightarrow{b} \{2,3\}$, without the generation of any new state.

The final states of the DFA are those including a state which is final in the NFA, in our example, $\{1,2\}$ and $\{2,3\}$.

Definition 1 (Incremental Determinization Problem). *Let $\mathcal{N}$ be an NFA and $\mathcal{D}$ the DFA equivalent to $\mathcal{N}$ (as generated by SC). Let $\Delta\mathcal{N}$ be an expansion of $\mathcal{N}$ yielding $\mathcal{N}'$, a new NFA. Generate the DFA $\mathcal{D}'$ equivalent to $\mathcal{N}'$ based on $\mathcal{N}$, $\mathcal{D}$, and $\Delta\mathcal{N}$.*

Definition 1 refers to a single determinization step, following a single expansion of the NFA. When the NFA expands over time, incremental determinization is required several (possibly many) times, after each expansion. In principle, the incremental determinization problem can be solved by means of *SC* by determinizing $\mathcal{N}'$ while neglecting $\mathcal{N}$, $\mathcal{D}$, and $\Delta\mathcal{N}$. However, this naive approach is bound to poor performances, especially when $\mathcal{N}'$ becomes increasingly large, as the incremental nature of $\mathcal{N}'$ is not exploited. To solve the incremental determinization problem efficiently, an *Incremental Subset Construction* algorithm (*ISC*) was proposed [16]. *ISC* was recently discovered to be incorrect in some instances, as it generates spurious states which are disconnected from the initial state, as shown in [10]. What may be problematic in the processing is not that the final DFA is disconnected (which is however unsound) but, rather, the possibly large amount of irrelevant processing uselessly wasted on the disconnected part. To cope with this problem, a revisitation of *ISC* is presented in [5], called *RISC*, where three variants of the algorithm are proposed. In this paper, we provide details on the most elegant variant, which exploits a specific metrics in the DFA.

3 Originating Application Domain

The need for incremental determinization stems from the domain of model-based diagnosis (MBD) of active systems [12], specifically, monitoring-based diagnosis [13, 14, 17]. MBD aims to diagnose a physical system based on the model of the system and relevant observations. The discrepancy between the normal behavior of the system and the observation allows the diagnostic engine to generate candidate diagnoses, where each candidate is a set of faulty components. MBD can be applied to discrete-event systems (DESs) [7], whose behavior is modeled as networks of components, with each component being a communicating automaton [6]. Active systems are a special class of asynchronous DESs, where components may exchange events to one another by means of links. During operation, the active system reacts to external events by performing system transitions, which possibly trigger new transitions by generating events toward neighboring components through links. The active system evolves according to its model, which incorporates both normal and faulty behavior, by performing a sequence of component transitions within its behavioral space. The evolution of the system is a sequence of transitions, called the trajectory of the system.

The problem lies in the ambiguity of the mode in which the system is evolving, because only a subset of component transitions are visible by the diagnosis engine. If the transition is visible, it generates an observable label. Consequently, the trajectory is perceived by the engine as a sequence of observable labels, called the trace.

The diagnosis engine performs consistent reasoning and eventually provides the candidate diagnoses, where each candidate is a set of faulty transitions, and corresponds to one or several candidate trajectories, each one equally possible. In large, distributed systems, the problem is complicated by the way observable labels are conveyed to the observer, which may involve multiple (possibly noisy) channels. This causes a distortion of the trace, where each label is perceived as a set of candidate labels, while the total temporal ordering among labels is relaxed to partial temporal ordering. The result is an uncertain temporal observation [11], which is represented by a directed acyclic graph, where nodes are marked by candidate labels, while edges define partial temporal ordering among nodes.

However, the observation graph, namely $\mathcal{O}$, is inconvenient for processing as is. A surrogate of it, namely $Isp(\mathcal{O})$, the index space of $\mathcal{O}$, is used instead. The index space is a DFA whose regular language is the whole set of candidate traces of the relevant observation. The point is, $Isp(\mathcal{O})$ is derived via subset-construction by an NFA called prefix space, denoted $Psp(\mathcal{O})$, which is directly derived from $\mathcal{O}$. Thus, three transformations occur for a trace $\mathcal{T} : \mathcal{T} \rightsquigarrow \mathcal{O} \Rightarrow Psp(\mathcal{O}) \Rightarrow Isp(\mathcal{O})$, where the former ($\rightsquigarrow$) depends on the nature of both the communication channels and the observer, and, as such, is beyond the scope of the diagnostic engine, while the others ($\Rightarrow$) are artificially performed by the diagnostic engine for computational purposes.

In monitoring-based diagnosis, candidate diagnoses must be generated each time a piece of observation is received. Typically, the observation graph is received as a sequence of fragments, with each fragment carrying information on one node and the arcs coming from its parents. These are called fragmented observations. At the reception of each fragment, the index space is to be updated based on the extension of the prefix space. Since generating the sequence of index spaces via SC may become computationally prohibitive in real applications, as each index space is generated from scratch at each new fragment, a better solution is to make SC incremental, so that each index space in the sequence is generated as an update of the previous one, thereby pursuing computational reuse.

4   Metrics-Based Incremental Subset Construction

According to the incremental determinization problem (Definition 1), based on an NFA $\mathcal{N}$, the equivalent DFA $\mathcal{D}$, and an expansion $\Delta\mathcal{N}$ of $\mathcal{N}$, the determinization $\mathcal{D}'$ of the expanded NFA $\mathcal{N}' = \mathcal{N} \cup \Delta\mathcal{N}$ is required. What makes intriguing the problem is the possible exploitation of $\mathcal{D}$ instead of starting from scratch the determinization of $\mathcal{N}'$. Rather than applying SC to $\mathcal{N}'$ (disregarding altogether $\mathcal{N}$, $\mathcal{D}$, and $\Delta\mathcal{N}$), $\mathcal{D}'$ is determined by updating $\mathcal{D}$ based on $\Delta\mathcal{N}$. This idea is substantiated by algorithm ISC.

Let d be the identifier of a state of the automaton $\mathcal{D}$ being processed by *ISC*, ℓ a symbol of the alphabet, and $\mathbb{N}$ the ℓ-closure of the NFA states incorporated in d. The triple $(d, \ell, \mathbb{N})$ is a *bud* for $\mathcal{D}$. A bud indicates that further processing needs to be performed to update the transition exiting d and marked by ℓ in $\mathcal{D}$.

ISC produces the same results as *SC* by exploiting a stack of buds. Roughly, the bud-stack parallels the stack of DFA states in *SC*. Just as new DFA states are inserted into the stack by *SC* and thereafter processed, so are the new buds accumulated into the bud-stack of *ISC* and processed one by one. In *SC*, the first state pushed onto the stack is the initial state of the DFA. In *ISC*, the bud-stack is initialized by a number of buds relevant to the states exited by the new transitions in the NFA.

The algorithm loops, by popping a bud at each iteration, until the bud-stack becomes empty. While processing each bud, new buds are possibly inserted into the bud-stack. The processing of each bud depends on both the bud and the current DFA.

In order to make the algorithm sound by avoiding the disconnection of the DFA, a metrics is introduced, as formalized in Definition 2, where $\mathcal{D}$ is the DFA being processed by *ISC*.

Definition 2 (Distance). *Let d be a state in $\mathcal{D}$ and d_0 the initial state of $\mathcal{D}$. The distance of d, written $\delta(d)$, is the minimal number of transitions connecting d_0 with d.*

Example 2. Considering the DFA displayed in the right side of Figure 1, we have $\delta(\{0, 1\}) = 0$ (for the initial state), and $\delta(\{1, 2\}) = \delta(\{2, 3\}) = 1$.

Note that, even if the DFA is cyclic, the distance of each state d is always less than the (finite) number of states of the DFA, as the minimal path of transitions connecting the initial state to d cannot include cycles.

5   Detailed Specification of Metrics-Based *ISC*

A pseudo-coded formalization of metrics-based *ISC* is outlined below (lines 1–90). *ISC* takes as input an NFA $\mathcal{N}$, the equivalent DFA $\mathcal{D}$ (as being generated by *SC*), and an extension $\Delta\mathcal{N}$ of $\mathcal{N}$. $\mathcal{D}$ is updated based on $\Delta\mathcal{N}$ so as to make it equivalent to the extended NFA $\mathcal{N}' = \mathcal{N} \cup \Delta\mathcal{N}$ (as if it were generated by *SC*). We assume that each state d in $\mathcal{D}$ is qualified by the relevant distance $\delta(d)$, as specified in Definition 2.

ISC is supported by bud-stack $\mathcal{B}$. Buds in $\mathcal{B}$ are implicitly grouped by the first two fields: if a new bud $B = (d, \ell, \mathbb{N})$ is pushed onto $\mathcal{B}$ and a bud $B' = (d, \ell, \mathbb{N}')$ is already in $\mathcal{B}$, then B' will be absorbed by B, thereby becoming $B = (d, \ell, \mathbb{N} \cup \mathbb{N}')$.

Throughout the pseudo-code, we keep a distinction between the identifier of a state in $\mathcal{D}$ and its content, where the former is a symbol (e.g. d), while the latter is a set of nodes in $\mathcal{N}'$ (e.g. $\mathbb{N}$). The content of a node d is written $\|d\|$. During execution, the content may change, while the identifier cannot.

The algorithm makes use of two auxiliary procedures, *Relocate* and *Expand*. Procedure *Relocate* (lines 8–26) takes as input a state d and a distance $\bar{\delta}$, and possibly updates the distance of d and the distance of a finite set of states reached by d. Specifically, $\bar{\delta}$ represents the upper bound for the distance of d as a consequence of an update in the topology of $\mathcal{D}$, typically by the creation of a new transition entering d.

Example 3. Outlined in the left side of Figure 2 is a fragment of $\mathcal{D}$ where states are associated with relevant distances before the insertion of transition from d_1 to d (while transition labels are omitted). Since $\delta(d_1) = 2$ and $\delta(d) = 5$ (we assume other transitions entering d but not displayed in the figure), the distance of d cannot be larger than $\bar{\delta} = \delta(d_1) + 1 = 3$. Since $\delta(d) > \bar{\delta}$, the distance $\delta(d)$ becomes $\bar{\delta}$, while the distances of successive states d_2, d_3, and d_4 change as shown in the right side of the figure.

After the possible change of $\delta(d)$ (lines 12–13), relocation of distances of successive nodes of d is required. This is accomplished by means of breadth-first distance-propagation. First a list $\mathbb{D}$ of candidate states is initialized by the singleton $[d]$ (line 14). Then, a loop is iterated until $\mathbb{D}$ becomes empty (lines 15–24). At each iteration, the first candidate h (head) is removed from $\mathbb{D}$ and the children $\mathbb{D}_c$ of h are considered. For each child $d_c \in \mathbb{D}_c$, the relevant distance is possibly updated (lines 19–20) and, if so, d_c is appended to $\mathbb{D}$ (line 21), in order to propagate this change to its successors.

Example 4. In Example 3, the update of the distance of d is propagated as follows:

1. Initial configuration: $\mathbb{D} = [d]$, $\delta(d) = 3$, $\delta(d_2) = 6$, $\delta(d_3) = 6$, and $\delta(d_4) = 7$.
2. First iteration: d is removed from $\mathbb{D}$ and the distance of the children of d are updated, thereby $\delta(d_2) = \delta(d_3) = 4$, while $\mathbb{D} = [d_2, d_3]$.
3. Second iteration: d_2 is removed from $\mathbb{D}$, however the distance of d_3 (the only child of d_2) is not updated, as $\delta(d_3) \not> \delta(d_2) + 1$, in fact $\delta(d_2) = \delta(d_3) = 4$.
4. Third iteration: d_3 is removed from $\mathbb{D}$ and the distance of child d_4 is updated, $\delta(d_4) = 5$. Since d_4 has no child, $\mathbb{D}$ remains empty and the propagation terminates.

Procedure *Expand* (lines 30–50) takes as input a state d in $\mathcal{D}$ and adds to its content the subset $\mathbb{N}$ of states in $\mathcal{N}'$. The bud-stack $\mathcal{B}$ is extended by the buds relevant to d and the labels exiting nodes in $(\mathbb{N} - \|d\|)$ in $\mathcal{N}'$. If the content of the extended node d equals the content of a node d' already in $\mathcal{D}$, then the two nodes are merged into a single node (lines 36–49). Before the merging, if the distances of d and d' differ, the distance of the state with maximal distance is updated with the distance of the other state by means of *Relocate* (which also propagates the distance change to successor nodes). Then, all transitions entering (exiting) d are redirected to (from) d'. Finally, after the removal of d, all buds relevant to d are renamed to d'. The redirection of transitions exiting d may cause nondeterminism exiting d' (two transitions exiting d' that are marked by the same label ℓ). However, such nondeterminism is transient and disappears at the end of the processing.

Considering the body of *ISC* (lines 51–90), after determining the subset $\bar{\mathbb{N}}$ of states in $\mathcal{N}$ that are exited by transitions in $\Delta\mathcal{N}$, $\mathcal{N}$ is extended by $\Delta\mathcal{N}$. Bud-stack $\mathcal{B}$ is initialized with buds $(d, \ell, \mathbb{N})$, where $\mathbb{N}$ is the ℓ-closure of $\|d\| \cap \bar{\mathbb{N}}$. A loop is then iterated

Fig. 2. Relocation of distances after the insertion of the new transition entering d

until $\mathcal{B}$ becomes empty (lines 55–89). At each iteration, a bud $(d, \ell, \mathbb{N})$ is popped from $\mathcal{B}$. Depending on the content of the bud, one of seven *action rules*, $\mathcal{R}_1 \cdots \mathcal{R}_7$, is applied, in the form of [*Condition*] $\Rightarrow$ *Action*, as specified below.

($\mathcal{R}_1$) [$\ell = \varepsilon$] $\Rightarrow$ d is expanded by $\mathbb{N}$ (line 58).

($\mathcal{R}_2$) [$\ell \neq \varepsilon$, no ℓ-transition exits d, $\exists d'$ such that $\|d'\| = \mathbb{N}$] $\Rightarrow$ A transition $d \xrightarrow{\ell} d'$ is inserted into $\mathcal{D}$ and distance relocation is applied to d' (lines 61–62).

($\mathcal{R}_3$) [$\ell \neq \varepsilon$, no ℓ-transition exits d, $\nexists d'$ such that $\|d'\| = \mathbb{N}$] $\Rightarrow$ An empty state d' and a transition $d \xrightarrow{\ell} d'$ are created; then, after assigning the distance of d', the latter is expanded by $\mathbb{N}$ (lines 64–66).

($\mathcal{R}_4$) [$\ell \neq \varepsilon$, an ℓ-transition t exits d, the state d' entered by t is not the initial state, no other transition enters d'] $\Rightarrow$ d' is expanded by $\mathbb{N}$ (line 71).

($\mathcal{R}_5$) [$\ell \neq \varepsilon$, an ℓ-transition t exits d, either the state d' entered by t is the initial state or another transition different from t enters d' from a state d_{p} such that $\delta(d_{\mathrm{p}}) \leq \delta(d)$, $\exists d''$ such that $\|d''\| = \|d'\| \cup \mathbb{N}$] $\Rightarrow$ t is redirected toward d'' and distance propagation is applied to d'' (lines 74–75).

($\mathcal{R}_6$) [$\ell \neq \varepsilon$, an ℓ-transition t exits d, either the state d' entered by d is the initial state or another transition different from t enters d' from a state d_{p} such that $\delta(d_{\mathrm{p}}) \leq \delta(d)$, $\nexists d''$ such that $\|d''\| = \|d'\| \cup \mathbb{N}$] $\Rightarrow$ d' is duplicated into d'' (along with exiting transitions and buds), t is redirected toward d'', distance propagation is applied to d'', the latter is expanded by $\mathbb{N}$ (lines 77–80).

($\mathcal{R}_7$) [$\ell \neq \varepsilon$, an ℓ-transition t exits d, either the state d' entered by t is the initial state or another transition different from t enters d' and the distances of the states exited by these other transitions entering d'' are all greater than $\delta(d)$] $\Rightarrow$ all transitions entering d' other than t are removed and surrogated by newly created buds, d' is expanded by $\mathbb{N}$ (lines 83–85).

Rules $\mathcal{R}_4$, $\mathcal{R}_5$, $\mathcal{R}_6$, and $\mathcal{R}_7$ correspond to a single bud (line 56), but may be applied several times, depending on the number of ℓ-transitions exiting d (as stated above, a temporary nondeterminism in $\mathcal{D}$ may be caused after merging two states by *Expand*).

Rules $\mathcal{R}_5$, $\mathcal{R}_6$, and $\mathcal{R}_7$ requires some additional explanation as far as the connectivity of $\mathcal{D}$ is concerned, as they all remove at least one transition entering d', which in principle may cause a disconnection. Considering $\mathcal{R}_5$ and $\mathcal{R}_6$, since there exists a transition, other than t, entering d' from d_{p} such that $\delta(d_{\mathrm{p}}) \leq \delta(d)$, if the removal of t from d' causes a disconnection, also d_{p} will be disconnected, but in this case, being a successor of d, we will have $\delta(d_{\mathrm{p}}) > \delta(d)$, a contradiction. Hence, no disconnection occurs. Moreover, the distance of d' cannot increase, as it is at most $\delta(d) + 1$.

Considering $\mathcal{R}_7$, since all other transitions entering d' are such that the state they exit has distance greater than $\delta(d)$, the removal of t from d' is not safe because all parent states of d' other than d might be connected to the initial state by means of t. On the other hand, based on the same reasoning adopted for $\mathcal{R}_5$ and $\mathcal{R}_6$, all these other transitions entering d' can be safely removed because they are not essential to the connection of d (which has shorter distance). Hence, the removal of all other entering transitions leaves d' still connected to the initial state. Moreover, the distance of d' cannot increase, as it is $\delta(d) + 1$.

```
1.    algorithm ISC (N, D, ΔN)
2.        N = (N, Σ, T_n, n_0, F_n): an NFA,
3.        D = (D, Σ, T_d, d_0, F_d): the DFA equivalent to N (as generated by SC),
4.        ΔN = (ΔN, ΔT_n, ΔF_n): an extension of N;
5.        side effects
6.            N is extended by ΔN,
7.            D is updated, becoming the DFA equivalent to (N' = N ∪ ΔN) (as by SC);
8.        auxiliary procedure Relocate(d, δ̄)
9.            d: a state in D,
10.           δ̄: the upper-bound distance for d;
11.       begin ⟨Relocate⟩
12.           if δ(d) > δ̄ then
13.               δ(d) := δ̄;
14.               D := [d];
15.               repeat
16.                   Remove the first element h (head) from D;
17.                   Let D_c be the set of child states of h in D;
18.                   foreach d_c ∈ D_c do
19.                       if δ(d_c) > δ(h) + 1 then
20.                           δ(d_c) := δ(h) + 1;
21.                           Append d_c to D
22.                       endif
23.                   endfor
24.               until Empty(D)
25.           endif
26.       end ⟨Relocate⟩;
27.       auxiliary procedure Expand (d, N)
28.           d: a state in D,
29.           N: a subset of states in N';
30.       begin ⟨Expand⟩
31.           if N ⊄ ||d|| then
32.               B' := {(d, ℓ, N') | ℓ ∈ Σ, N' = ℓ-closure(N − ||d||), N' ≠ ∅};
33.               Push buds B' onto B;
34.               Enlarge ||d|| by N;
35.               if d ∉ F_d, N ∩ F_n ≠ ∅ then Insert d into F_d endif;
36.               if D includes a state d' such that ||d'|| = ||d|| then
37.                   if δ(d) > δ(d') then
38.                       Relocate(d, δ(d'))
39.                   elsif δ(d) < δ(d') then
40.                       Relocate(d', δ(d))
41.                   endif;
42.                   Redirect to d' all transitions entering d and remove duplicates;
43.                   Redirect from d' all transitions exiting d and remove duplicates;
44.                   if d is the initial state d_0 then d_0 := d' endif;
45.                   if d ∈ F_d then Remove d from F_d endif;
```

46.   Remove d from $\mathcal{D}$;
47.   Convert to d' the buds in $\mathcal{B}$ relevant to d
49.   **endif**
49.   **endif**
50.   **end** $\langle Expand \rangle$;
51.   **begin** $\langle ISC \rangle$
52. $\bar{\mathbb{N}} :=$ the set of states in $\mathcal{N}$ exited by transitions in ΔT_{n};
53.   Extend $\mathcal{N}$ by $\Delta \mathcal{N}$;
54. $\mathcal{B} := \{(d, \ell, \mathbb{N}) \mid d \in D, n \in \|d\| \cap \bar{\mathbb{N}}, n \xrightarrow{\ell} n' \in \Delta T_{\mathrm{n}}, \mathbb{N} = \ell\text{-}closure(\|d\| \cap \bar{\mathbb{N}})\}$;
55.   **repeat**
56.   Pop bud $(d, \ell, \mathbb{N})$ from the top of bud-stack $\mathcal{B}$;
57. $(\mathcal{R}_1)$ **if** $\ell = \varepsilon$ **then**
58. $Expand\,(d, \mathbb{N})$
59.   **elsif** no ℓ-transition exits d **then**
60. $(\mathcal{R}_2)$ **if** $\mathcal{D}$ includes a state d' such that $\|d'\| = \mathbb{N}$ **then**
61.   Insert a new transition $d \xrightarrow{\ell} d'$ into $\mathcal{D}$;
62. $Relocate(d', \delta(d) + 1)$
63. $(\mathcal{R}_3)$ **else**
64.   Create a new state d' and insert $d \xrightarrow{\ell} d'$ into $\mathcal{D}$;
65. $\delta(d') := \delta(d) + 1$;
66. $Expand\,(d', \mathbb{N})$
67.   **endif**
68.   **else**
69.   **foreach** transition $t = d \xrightarrow{\ell} d'$ such that $\mathbb{N} \nsubseteq \|d'\|$ **do**
70. $(\mathcal{R}_4)$ **if** $d' \neq d_0$ **and** no other transition enters d' **then**
71. $Expand\,(d', \mathbb{N})$
72.   **elsif** $\mathcal{D}$ includes a transition $d_{\mathrm{p}} \xrightarrow{\ell'} d' \neq t$ such that $\delta(d_{\mathrm{p}}) \leq \delta(d)$ **then**
73. $(\mathcal{R}_5)$ **if** $\mathcal{D}$ includes a state d'' such that $\|d''\| = \|d'\| \cup \mathbb{N}$ **then**
74.   Redirect t toward d'';
75. $Relocate(d'', \delta(d) + 1)$
76. $(\mathcal{R}_6)$ **else**
77.   Create a copy d'' of d' along with the buds relevant to d'';
78.   Redirect t toward d'';
79. $\delta(d'') := \delta(d) + 1$;
80. $Expand\,(d'', \mathbb{N})$
81.   **endif**
82. $(\mathcal{R}_7)$ **else**
83.   Remove all transitions entering d' other than t;
84.   Update $\mathcal{B}$ with the buds for the starting state of the removed transitions;
85. $Expand\,(d', \mathbb{N})$
86.   **endif**
87.   **endfor**

88.   **endif**
89.   **until** bud-stack $\mathcal{B}$ becomes empty
90.   **end** $\langle ISC \rangle$.

Definition 3 (Configuration). *Let $\mathcal{D}_i$ be the automaton $\mathcal{D}$ after the processing of i buds, and $\mathcal{B}_i$ the corresponding instance of $\mathcal{B}$. The pair $\alpha_i = (\mathcal{D}_i, \mathcal{B}_i)$ is a* configuration, *where $\alpha_0 = (\mathcal{D}_0, \mathcal{B}_0)$ is the initial configuration, with $\mathcal{D}_0$ being the DFA in input and $\mathcal{B}_0$ the initial instance of $\mathcal{B}$. The* path *of ISC is the sequence $[\alpha_0, \ldots, \alpha_i, \alpha_{i+1}, \ldots]$ of configurations.*

Example 5. Outlined in plain lines in the left side of Figure 3 is an NFA $\mathcal{N}$. An expansion of $\mathcal{N}$, namely $\mathcal{N}' = \mathcal{N} \cup \Delta\mathcal{N}$, is represented in dashed lines, where $\Delta\mathcal{N}$ includes a new state and three transitions. The DFA $\mathcal{D}'$ equivalent to $\mathcal{N}'$ (generated by *SC*) is shown in the right side of Figure 3. We now show how the same result is generated by means of *ISC*, starting from $\mathcal{N}$, $\mathcal{D}$, and $\Delta\mathcal{N}$. Depicted in Figure 4 is the corresponding path of *ISC*, namely $[\alpha_0, \alpha_1, \ldots, \alpha_7]$ (the last configuration $\alpha_8 = \mathcal{D}'$, not shown in Figure 4, equals the DFA placed on the right-hand side of Figure 3). Distance of each state is indicated, while each bud $(d, \ell, \mathbb{N})$ is represented as a dashed arc exiting d, marked by ℓ, and entering a filled node marked by $\mathbb{N}$.

Initially, according to *ISC* (line 54), four buds are generated for $\alpha_0 = (\mathcal{D}_0, \mathcal{B}_0)$, where $\mathcal{D}_0 = \mathcal{D}$ and $\bar{\mathbb{N}} = \{2\}$ (line 52). Therefore, the initial buds are relevant to nodes incorporating state 2, namely $\{1,2\}$ and $\{2,3\}$, giving rise to bud-stack $\mathcal{B}_0 = [B_1, B_2, B_3, B_4]$, where $B_1 = (\{2,3\}, b, \{2,3,4\})$, $B_2 = (\{2,3\}, a, \{0,1,2,3\})$, $B_3 = (\{1,2\}, b, \{2,3,4\})$, and $B_4 = (\{1,2\}, a, \{0,1,2,3\})$. Then, the main loop (lines 55–89) is started and buds are precessed one by one. Each processed bud is indicated in Figure 4 by a dashed filled node. The path of *ISC* is described below.

(α_0) $B = (\{1,2\}, a, \{0,1,2,3\}) \Rightarrow$ rule $\mathcal{R}_6$: since transition $\{1,2\} \overset{a}{\to} \{2,3\}$ is not essential to the connectivity of state $\{2,3\}$, state $\{2,3\}$ is duplicated (along with exiting transitions and buds), transition $\{1,2\} \overset{a}{\to} \{2,3\}$ is redirected toward the new state, with the latter being expanded to $\{0,1,2,3\}$.

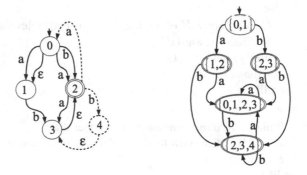

Fig. 3. Determinization of the expanded NFA $\mathcal{N}' = \mathcal{N} \cup \Delta\mathcal{N}$ by *SC* (the dashed part is $\Delta\mathcal{N}$)

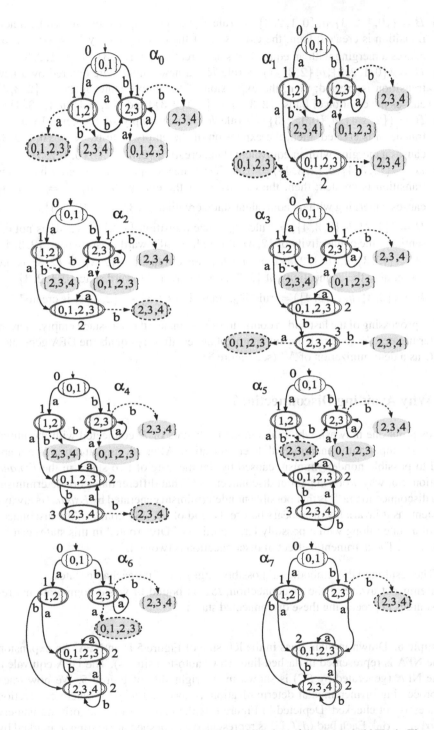

Fig. 4. Path of algorithm *ISC* for incremental determinization of the expanded NFA in Figure 3

(α_1) $B = (\{0,1,2,3\}, a, \{0,1,2,3\}) \Rightarrow$ rule $\mathcal{R}_3$: a new empty state entered by a new transition is created; then, the expansion of the empty state by $\mathbb{N} = \{0,1,2,3\}$ causes a merging with an equivalent state, creating $\{0,1,2,3\} \overset{a}{\rightarrow} \{0,1,2,3\}$.

(α_2) $B = (\{0,1,2,3\}, b, \{2,3,4\}) \Rightarrow$ rule $\mathcal{R}_3$: a new empty state entered by a new transition is created; then, the expansion of the empty state by $\mathbb{N} = \{2,3,4\}$ causes the creation of buds $(\{2,3,4\}, a, \{0,1,2,3\})$ and $(\{2,3,4\}, b, \{2,3,4\})$.

(α_3) $B = (\{2,3,4\}, a, \{0,1,2,3\}) \Rightarrow$ rule $\mathcal{R}_3$: a new empty state entered by a new transition is created; then, the expansion of the empty state by $\mathbb{N} = \{0,1,2,3\}$ causes a merging with an equivalent state, creating $\{2,3,4\} \overset{a}{\rightarrow} \{0,1,2,3\}$.

(α_4) $B = (\{2,3,4\}, b, \{2,3,4\}) \Rightarrow$ rule $\mathcal{R}_3$: a new empty state entered by a new transition is created; then, the expansion of the empty state by $\mathbb{N} = \{2,3,4\}$ causes a merging with an equivalent state, creating $\{2,3,4\} \overset{b}{\rightarrow} \{2,3,4\}$.

(α_5) $B = (\{1,2\}, b, \{2,3,4\}) \Rightarrow$ rule $\mathcal{R}_5$: since transition $\{1,2\} \overset{b}{\rightarrow} \{2,3\}$ is not essential to the connectivity of $\{2,3\}$, it is redirected toward existing state $\{2,3,4\}$.

(α_6) $B = (\{2,3\}, a, \{0,1,2,3\}) \Rightarrow$ rule $\mathcal{R}_5$: since transition $\{2,3\} \overset{a}{\rightarrow} \{2,3\}$ is not essential to the connectivity of $\{2,3\}$, it is redirected toward state $\{0,1,2,3\}$.

(α_7) $B = (\{2,3\}, b, \{2,3,4\}) \Rightarrow$ rule $\mathcal{R}_2$: transition $\{2,3\} \overset{b}{\rightarrow} \{2,3,4\}$ is created.

The processing of the last bud in configuration α_7 makes the bud-stack empty, thereby *ISC* terminates. As required, the automaton obtained after α_7 equals the DFA generated by *SC* as a determinization of $\mathcal{N}'$ (see Figure 3).

6   Why Avoiding Disconnection?

At this point one may ask why maintaining each state of $\mathcal{D}$ connected with the initial state is so important in incremental determinization. After all, this attention is not applied to possible nondeterminism caused by the merging of two states in the *Expand* function. So, why worrying about disconnection? What differentiates nondeterminism from disconnection in $\mathcal{D}$ is that possible nondeterminism generated by *Expand* is always transient, as it invariably disappears before the end of *ISC*. By contrast, the disconnection of a state (along with a possibly large portion of DFA rooted in this state) can be permanent. The detrimental effect of disconnection is twofold:

1. The resulting DFA embodies a (possibly large) set of unreachable states;
2. Being not aware of the disconnection, *ISC* is bound to waste computational resources in processing these disconnected states.

Example 6. Drawn in plain lines in the left side of Figure 5 is an NFA. An expansion of the NFA is represented in dashed lines (four auto-transitions). The DFA equivalent to the NFA (generated by *SC*) is shown in the right side of Figure 5. We now trace the processing of incremental determinization as specified in [16], where connection of states is not checked. Depicted in Figure 6 is the path of of the algorithm, namely $[\alpha_0, \alpha_1, \ldots, \alpha_9]$. Each bud $(d, \ell, \mathbb{N})$ is represented as a dashed arc exiting d, marked by ℓ, and entering a filled node marked by $\mathbb{N}$.

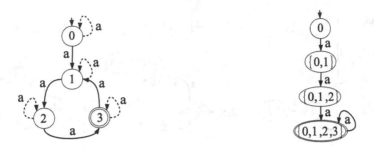

Fig. 5. Determinization of the expanded NFA by *SC*, with the dashed part being the expansion

At the beginning, four buds are generated for $\alpha_0 = (\mathcal{D}_0, \mathcal{B}_0)$, where $\mathcal{D}_0 = \mathcal{D}$ and $\mathcal{B}_0 = [(\{0\}, a, \{0,1\}), (\{1\}, a, \{1,2\}), (\{2\}, a, \{2,3\}), (\{3\}, a, \{1,3\})]$. The next processed bud is dashed in the figure. Intermediate configurations are described below.

(α_0) $B = (\{3\}, a, \{1,3\})$: since state $\{1\}$ is also entered by transition $\{0\} \overset{a}{\to} \{1\}$, the latter is removed and surrogated by bud $(\{0\}, a, \{0,1\})$ (which is already in the bud stack), while state $\{1\}$ is expanded to $\{1,3\}$, accompanied by the update of the relevant bud, which becomes $(\{1,3\}, a, \{1,2,3\})$. Note how $\mathcal{D}$ is now disconnected.

(α_1) $B = (\{1,3\}, a, \{1,2,3\})$: state $\{2\}$ is expanded to $\{1,2,3\}$, causing the expansion of the relevant bud to $(\{1,2,3\}, a, \{1,2,3\})$.

(α_2) $B = (\{1,2,3\}, a, \{1,2,3\})$: state $\{3\}$ is expanded to $\{1,2,3\}$, causing the merging with the equivalent state and the generation of the new bud $(\{1,2,3\}, a, \{1,2,3\})$.

(α_3) $B = (\{1,2,3\}, a, \{1,2,3\})$: since two relevant transitions exit $\{1,2,3\}$, based on $\{1,2,3\} \overset{a}{\to} \{1,3\}$, state $\{1,3\}$ is extended to $\{1,2,3\}$, thereby causing a merging and the generation of bud $(\{1,2,3\}, a, \{2,3\})$; at this point, the second transition is $\{1,2,3\} \overset{a}{\to} \{1,2,3\}$, therefore no other expansion of state $\{1,2,3\}$ is generated.

(α_4) $B = (\{1,2,3\}, a, \{2,3\})$: no effect is produced by the processing of this bud.

(α_5) $B = (\{0\}, a, \{0,1\})$: transition $\{0\} \overset{a}{\to} \{0,1\}$ is created along with state $\{0,1\}$, and bud $(\{0,1\}, a, \{0,1,2\})$ is generated.

(α_6) $B = (\{0,1\}, a, \{0,1,2\})$: transition $\{0,1\} \overset{a}{\to} \{0,1,2\}$ is created along with state $\{0,1,2\}$, and bud $(\{0,1,2\}, a, \{0,1,2,3\})$ is generated.

(α_7) $B = (\{0,1,2\}, a, \{0,1,2,3\})$: transition $\{0,1,2\} \overset{a}{\to} \{0,1,2,3\}$ is created along with state $\{0,1,2,3\}$, and bud $(\{0,1,2,3\}, a, \{0,1,2,3\})$ is generated.

(α_8) $B = (\{0,1,2,3\}, a, \{0,1,2,3\})$: transition $\{0,1,2,3\} \overset{a}{\to} \{0,1,2,3\}$ is created.

(α_9) Since the bud stack is empty, this is the final configuration of $\mathcal{D}$.

Note how the resulting DFA in α_9 is still disconnected, although the part connected with the initial state equals the expected DFA generated by *SC* and displayed in the right side of Figure 5. As anticipated, what is disturbing in the resulting DFA is not only the disconnection, which may be removed by eventual garbage collection: the real disturbing point is the wasted processing on the disconnected part, which may cause considerable expenditure of computational resources.

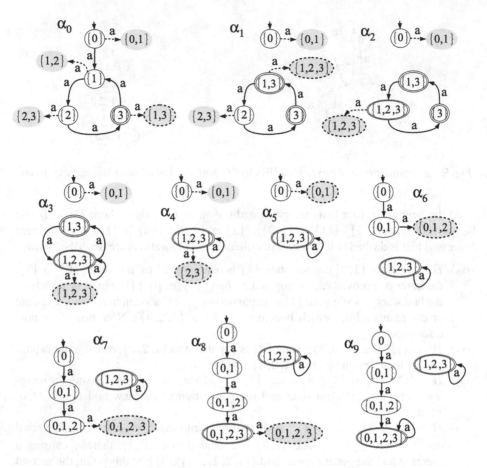

Fig. 6. Incremental determinization with disconnection

7   Implementation and Results

Both algorithms *SC* and *ISC* were implemented in C++ on a laptop, under GNU/Linux. In the first stage of the project, we adopted a more naive approach based on classical search techniques. Before removing (redirecting) a transition entering state d' we test the essentiality of such a transition: the transition is essential if, after its removal (redirection), d' is no longer connected with the initial state. If essential, the transition is not removed (redirected); instead, all other transitions entering d' are removed and surrogated by buds. By contrast, if not essential, the transition can be removed (redirected). The problem with this technique lies in the complexity of the connectivity check: in the worst case, a complete traversing of the processed automaton is required. Early experimentation showed that an overwhelming percentage of the processing time was devoted to connectivity checking, in many cases with the result of making *ISC* and *SC* comparable, thereby nullifying altogether the advantage of incrementality. That is why we started searching for a more efficient alternative approach, which led us to

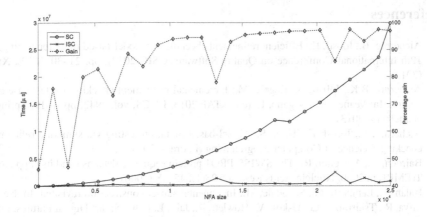

Fig. 7. Comparison between *SC* and *ISC*. Outlined in the diagram is also the gain, defined as $((time(SC) - time(ISC))/time(SC)) * 100$.

the metrics-based technique presented in this paper. Based on this new technique, we can efficiently check the inessentiality of a transition based on the distance of involved states: we removed (redirect) the transition only if it is *not* essential.

Results from subsequent experimentation based on metrics-based *ISC* show that memory allocation is equivalent in the two algorithms. Instead, in CPU time, *ISC* outperforms *SC*: the larger the NFA, the more favorable the performances of *ISC*. Hereafter we present average results, based on one reference experiment, with the following parameters: the initial NFA includes 1000 states, the alphabet includes 30 labels, and the percentage of ε-transitions is 10%. The NFA is extended up to 25000 states by 1000 states each time. Outlined in Figure 7 is the graphical representation of the comparison between *SC* and *ISC*. Besides, the *gain* is indicated (right-side *y*-axis), that is, the percentage of time saving when using lazy *ISC* rather than *SC*, defined as $((time(SC) - time(ISC))/time(SC)) * 100$. The gain grows with the size of the NFA: in the last determinization, the gain is 97.00% (0.89" for *ISC* vs. 29.89" for *SC*).

8 Conclusion

In contrast with the first algorithm introduced in [16], metrics-based *ISC* is sound in the sense that it generates the same DFA which is produced by *SC*, with the additional advantage of being considerably more efficient than *SC*. To do so, *ISC* exploits a metrics based on the distances of states from the initial state. This metrics allows *ISC* to efficiently check the connectivity of the processed automaton when conflicts arise in removing (or redirecting) transitions.

A goal for future research is the proof of formal correctness (termination, soundness, and completeness) of *ISC*. The extension of the incremental approach to minimization of DFAs, where the DFA equivalent to the NFA is required to include a minimal set of states at each expansion, is a further interesting research topic.

References

1. Aichernig, B., Jöbstl, E.: Efficient refinement checking for model-based mutation testing. In: 12th International Conference on Quality Software (QSIC 2012), pp. 21–30. IEEE, Xi'an (2012)
2. Aichernig, B.K., Jöbstl, E., Kegele, M.: Incremental refinement checking for test case generation. In: Veanes, M., Viganò, L. (eds.) TAP 2013. LNCS, vol. 7942, pp. 1–19. Springer, Heidelberg (2013)
3. Aichernig, B., Jöbstl, E., Tiran, S.: Model-based mutation testing via symbolic refinement checking. Science of Computer Programming (in Press, 2014)
4. Bairoch, A., Apweiler, R.: The SWISS-PROT protein sequence database and its supplement TrEMBL in 2000. Nucleic Acids Research 28(1), 45–48 (2000)
5. Balan, S., Lamperti, G., Scandale, M.: Incremental subset construction revisited. In: Neves-Silva, R., Tshirintzis, G., Uskov, V., Howlett, R., Jain, L. (eds.) Smart Digital Futures, Frontiers in Artificial Intelligence and Applications, vol. 262, pp. 25–37. IOS Press, Amsterdam (2014)
6. Brand, D., Zafiropulo, P.: On communicating finite-state machines. Journal of ACM 30(2), 323–342 (1983)
7. Cassandras, C., Lafortune, S.: Introduction to Discrete Event Systems. The Kluwer International Series in Discrete Event Dynamic Systems, vol. 11. Kluwer Academic Publishers, Boston (1999)
8. Friedl, J.: Mastering Regular Expressions, 3rd edn. O'Reilly Media, Sebastopol (2006)
9. Jöbstl, E.: Model-based mutation testing with constraint and SMT solvers. Ph.D. thesis, Institute for Software Technology, Graz University of Technology, Austria (2014)
10. Lamperti, G., Scandale, M.: From diagnosis of active systems to incremental determinization of finite acyclic automata. AI Communications 26(4), 373–393 (2013)
11. Lamperti, G., Zanella, M.: Diagnosis of discrete-event systems from uncertain temporal observations. Artificial Intelligence 137(1-2), 91–163 (2002)
12. Lamperti, G., Zanella, M.: Diagnosis of Active Systems – Principles and Techniques. The Kluwer International Series in Engineering and Computer Science, vol. 741. Kluwer Academic Publishers, Dordrecht (2003)
13. Lamperti, G., Zanella, M.: A bridged diagnostic method for the monitoring of polymorphic discrete-event systems. IEEE Transactions on Systems, Man, and Cybernetics – Part B: Cybernetics 34(5), 2222–2244 (2004)
14. Lamperti, G., Zanella, M.: Monitoring and diagnosis of discrete-event systems with uncertain symptoms. In: Sixteenth International Workshop on Principles of Diagnosis, DX 2005, Monterey, CA, pp. 145–150 (2005)
15. Lamperti, G., Zanella, M.: Monitoring of active systems with stratified uncertain observations. IEEE Transactions on Systems, Man, and Cybernetics – Part A: Systems and Humans 41(2), 356–369 (2011)
16. Lamperti, G., Zanella, M., Chiodi, G., Chiodi, L.: Incremental determinization of finite automata in model-based diagnosis of active systems. In: Lovrek, I., Howlett, R.J., Jain, L.C. (eds.) KES 2008, Part I. LNCS (LNAI), vol. 5177, pp. 362–374. Springer, Heidelberg (2008)
17. Lamperti, G., Zanella, M., Zanni, D.: Incremental processing of temporal observations in model-based reasoning. AI Communications 20(1), 27–37 (2007)
18. Rabin, M., Scott, D.: Finite automata and their decision problems. IBM Journal of Research and Development 3(2), 114–125 (1959)
19. Tretmans, J.: Test generation with inputs, outputs and repetitive quiescence. Software – Concepts and Tools 17(3), 103–120 (1996)

Towards Developing Secure Software
Using Problem-Oriented Security Patterns

Azadeh Alebrahim and Maritta Heisel

Paluno - The Ruhr Institute for Software Technology,
University of Duisburg-Essen, Germany
{firstname.lastname}@paluno.uni-due.de

Abstract. Security as one essential quality requirement has to be addressed during the software development process. Quality requirements such as security drive the architecture of a software, while design decisions such as security patterns on the architecture level in turn might constrain the achievement of quality requirements significantly. Thus, to obtain sound architectures and correct requirements, knowledge which is gained in the solution space, for example from security patterns, should be reflected in the requirements engineering. In this paper, we propose an iterative method that takes into account the concurrent development of requirements and architecture descriptions systematically. It reuses security patterns for refining and restructuring the requirement models by applying problem-oriented security patterns. Problem-oriented security patterns adapt existing security patterns in a way that they can be used in the problem-oriented requirements engineering. The proposed method bridges the gap between security problems and security architectural solutions.

Keywords: Requirements engineering, security requirements, problem frames, security patterns, digital signature.

1 Introduction

Many software systems fail to achieve their quality objectives due to neglecting quality requirements at the beginning of the software development life cycle [1]. In order to obtain a software that achieves not only its required functionality but also the desired quality properties, it is necessary to consider both types of requirements, functional and quality ones, early enough in the software development life cycle. Security is one essential quality requirement to be considered during the software development process.

Architecture solutions provide a means to achieve quality requirements. While requirements are supposed to be the architectural drivers, architecture solutions represent design decisions on the architecture level that in turn affect the achievement of quality requirements significantly. Decisions made in the design phase could constrain the achievement of initial requirements, and thus could change them. Hence, requirements cannot be considered in isolation. They should be co-developed with the software architecture iteratively known as *Twin Peaks* as proposed by Nuseibeh [2] to support the creation of sound architectures and correct requirements [3]. The sooner architectural knowledge becomes involved in the process of the requirements analysis, the less costly are the changes to be made. Hence, there is a need for a method that systematically takes into account the development of both artifacts, concurrently.

S. Teufel et al. (Eds.): CD-ARES 2014, LNCS 8708, pp. 45–62, 2014.

There exist solutions to security problems represented as patterns [4] that can be applied during the design and implementation phases of software development processes. In order to reuse the knowledge which is gained in the solution space such as security patterns, we make use of *problem-oriented security patterns* [5]. Problem-oriented security patterns reuse existing security patterns and mechanisms and adapt them in a way that they can be used in the problem-oriented requirements engineering.

In this paper, we follow the concept of the twin peaks [2] that advocates the concurrent and iterative development of requirements and software architecture descriptions, as requirements and software architecture cannot be developed in isolation. We propose a method on how to exploit the knowledge gained in the solution domain systematically in the problem space considering the intertwining nature of requirements engineering and architectural design. Our method provides an instantiation of the twin-peaks model for developing secure software systems. We make use of the problem-oriented security patterns to refine and restructure the requirement models.

The proposed method relies on problem frames [6] as a requirements engineering approach. It is important that the results of the requirements analysis with problem frames can be easily re-used in later phases of the development process. Since UML [7] is a widely used notation to express analysis and design artifacts, we make use of a specific UML profile [8] for problem frames that carries over problem frames to UML. We use the problem frames approach, because 1) it allows decomposing the overall software problem into subproblems, thus reducing the complexity of the problem, 2) it makes it possible to annotate problem diagrams with quality requirements, such as security requirements, 3) it enables various model checking techniques, such as requirements interaction analysis and reconciliation [9] due to its semi-formal structure, and 4) it supports a seamless transition from requirements analysis to architectural design (e.g. [10]).

The benefit of the proposed method is manifold. First, it provides guidance for refining security problems located in the problem space using problem-oriented security patterns. Second, the elaborated security requirement models can easily be transformed into a particular solution at the design level. Thus, it bridges the gap between security problems and security solutions. Third, it supports the concurrent and iterative development of requirements and architectural descriptions systematically. Fourth, it supports less experienced software engineers in applying solution approaches early in the requirements engineering phase in a systematic manner.

The remainder of the paper is organized as follows. We present the background on which our approach builds in Sect. 2, namely problem frames and problem-oriented security patterns. In Sect. 3, we describe our method. Section 4 is devoted to illustrating the applicability of our method by taking into account digital signature as a specific problem-oriented security pattern. Related work is discussed in Sect. 5, and conclusions and future work are given in Sect. 6.

2   Background

In this section, we give a brief overview on basics our approach relies on. We first describe the concepts of the problem frames approach in Sect. 2.1. Then, we introduce problem-oriented security patterns in Sect. 2.2.

2.1 Problem Frames

Requirements analysis with problem frames [6] proceeds as follows: to understand the problem, the environment in which the *machine* (i.e., software to be built) will operate must be described first. To this end, we set up a *context diagram* consisting of *machines*, *domains* and *interfaces*. Domains represent parts of the environment which are relevant for the problem at hand. Then, the problem is decomposed into simple subproblems that fit to a *problem frame*. Problem frames are patterns used to understand, describe, and analyze software development problems. An instantiated problem frame is a *problem diagram* which basically consists of one *submachine* of the machine given in the context diagram, relevant domains, interfaces between them, and a *requirement* referring to and constraining problem domains. The task is to construct a *(sub-)machine* that improves the behavior of the environment (in which it is integrated) in accordance with the requirement.

We describe problem frames using UML class diagrams [7], extended by a specific UML profile for problem frames (UML4PF) proposed by Hatebur and Heisel [11]. A class with the stereotype ≪machine≫ represents the software to be developed. Jackson distinguishes the domain types biddable domains (represented by the stereotype ≪BiddableDomain≫) that are usually people, causal domains (≪CausalDomain≫) that comply with some physical laws, and lexical domains (≪LexicalDomain≫) that are data representations. To describe the problem context, a *connection domain* (≪ConnectionDomain≫) between two other domains may be necessary. Connection domains establish a connection between other domains by means of technical devices. Figure 5 shows a problem diagram in the context of our case study *smart grids* (see Sect. 4.1). It describes that smart meter gateway submits meter data to an authorized external entity. The submachine *SubmitMD* is one part of the smart meter gateway. It sends the *MeterData* through the causal domain *WAN* to the biddable domain *AuthorizedExternalEntity*.

When we state a requirement we want to change something in the world with the machine to be developed. Therefore, each requirement expressed by the stereotype ≪requirement≫ constrains at least one domain. This is expressed by a dependency from the requirement to a domain with the stereotype ≪constrains≫. A requirement may refer to several domains in the environment of the machine. This is expressed by a dependency from the requirement to these domains with the stereotype ≪refersTo≫. The requirement *RQ4* constrains the domain *WAN*, and it refers to the domains *MeterData* and *AuthorizedExternalEntity*.

2.2 Problem-Oriented Security Patterns

We make use of the concept of *problem-oriented security patterns* [5], which are described as problem diagrams. Security patterns and mechanisms have been reused and adapted in a way that they can be used in the problem-oriented requirements engineering as problem-oriented security patterns. A problem-oriented security pattern consists of a three-part graphical pattern and a template. The graphical pattern involves one problem diagram that describes the structure of the generic functional requirement and the involved domains. It is annotated with a specific security requirement, for which

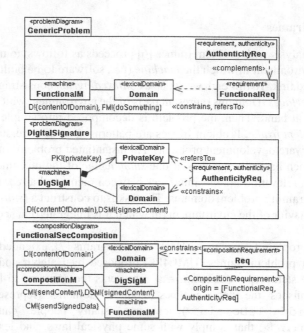

Fig. 1. Problem-oriented digital signature pattern (graphical pattern)

we provide a solution approach. The second part of a problem-oriented security pattern is a problem diagram that describes the particular solution approach for the security requirement. Conclusively, we provide a problem diagram that describes how the problem diagram describing the functional problem and the problem diagram describing the security solution can be composed to solve the overall problem.

The proposed template consists of two parts documenting additional information related to the domains in the graphical pattern. Such information is not observable in the graphical pattern. The first part accommodates information about the security mechanism itself such as name (*Name*), purpose (*Purpose*), description (*Brief Description*), and the quality requirement which will be achieved when applying this pattern (*Quality Requirement to be achieved*). Moreover, a security solution may affect the achievement of other quality requirements. For example, improving the security may result in decreasing the performance. Hence, the impact of each security solution on other quality requirements has to be captured in the first part of the template (*Affected Quality Requirement*). A security pattern not only solves a problem, but also produces new functional and quality problems that have to be addressed either as *Requirements* to be elicited or as *Assumptions* needed to be made in the second part of the template. We elicit new functional and quality problems as requirements if the software to be built shall achieve them. Assumptions have to be satisfied by the environment [12]. They do not guarantee to be true in every case. For the case that we assume the environment (not the machine) takes the responsibility for meeting them, we capture them as assumptions. This should be negotiated with the stakeholders and documented properly.

Digital signature is an important means for achieving integrity and authenticity of data. Using the digital signature, the receiver ensures that the data is created by the

Table 1. Problem-oriented digital signature pattern (template)

Security Solution	
Name	Digital Signature
Purpose	For *Domain* constrained by the requirement *FunctionalReq*
Brief Description	Sender produces a signature using the private key and the data.
Quality Requirement to be achieved	Security (integrity and authenticity) *IntegrityReq, AuthenticityReq*
Affected Quality Requirement	Performance *PerformanceReq*
Necessary Conditions	
Requirement ☐ Assumption ☐	Confidentiality of private key during storage shall be/is preserved.
Requirement ☐ Assumption ☐	Integrity of private key during storage shall be/is preserved.
Requirement ☐ Assumption ☐	Confidentiality of signature machine shall be/is preserved.
Requirement ☐ Assumption ☐	Integrity of signature machine shall be/is preserved.

known sender. We present the *problem-oriented digital signature pattern* by its corresponding graphical pattern depicted in Fig. 1 and its corresponding template shown in Table 1. The graphical pattern first describes the functional problem expressed as the problem diagram *GenericProblem*. It describes the functional requirement *Functional-Req* and the involved domains. The functional requirement *FunctionalReq* has to be met by the functional machine *FunctionalM*. The functional requirement is complemented by the security requirement *AuthenticityReq* demanding "the verification of genuineness of data". The first problem diagram in Fig. 1 depicts the functional problem. Depending on the functional requirement, the problem diagram might contain other domains that are not relevant for the security problem. Hence, they are not represented in the pattern. The digital signature as a solution for the authenticity problem is expressed as the problem diagram *DigitalSignature* in the middle of Fig. 1. It consists of all domains that are relevant for the solution. The machine *DigSigM* should achieve the authenticity requirement *AuthenticityReq* by signing the *Domain* using the *PrivateKey* which is part of the machine *DigSigM*. The third part composes the functional machine *FunctionalM* with the security machine *DigSigM* by introducing a new machine *CompositionM* that has to meet the requirement *CompositionReq* composed of the requirements *FuncitonalReq* and *AuthenticityReq*.

Note that the *problem-oriented digital signature pattern* can be used to achieve integrity as well. In Fig. 1, we only showed the use of *problem-oriented digital signature pattern* to achieve the integrity requirement *AuthenticityReq* in order to keep the figure clear and readable. One can apply the same pattern and only replace the authenticity requirement with the integrity requirement to achieve integrity.

The template shown in Table 1 represents the additional information corresponding to the graphical part of the problem-oriented pattern *digital signature*. New requirements and assumptions to be considered are represented in the second part of the template.

3 Problem-Oriented Secure Software Development

As we mentioned earlier, problem descriptions and architectural descriptions should be considered as intertwining artifacts influencing each other. We therefore take the Twin Peaks model [2] into account and illustrate our problem-oriented software development method embedded in the context of the Twin Peaks model (see Fig. 2).

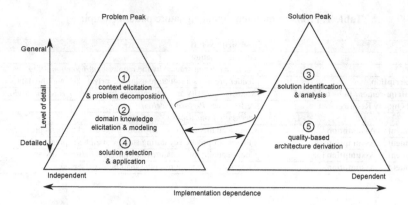

Fig. 2. Overview of our method embedded in the Twin Peaks Model

Our problem-oriented software development method consists of five phases. Phases 1 and 2 are introduced in details in [13,14]. Thus, we describe them briefly here. In this paper, our focus is on identification, selection, and application of appropriate security patterns which refine and restructure the requirement models. So refined problem descriptions can easily be transformed into architectural descriptions.

Phase 1- Context Elicitation and Problem Decomposition. This phase (see 1 in Fig. 2) involves understanding the problem and its context, decomposing the overall problem into subproblems, and annotating security requirements. In order to understand the problem, we elicit all domains related to the problem to be solved, their relations to each other and the software to be constructed. Doing this, we obtain a *context diagram* consisting of the machine (software-to-be), related domains in the environment, and interfaces between these domains. Then, we decompose the overall problem into subproblems, which describe a certain functionality, as expressed by a set of related functional requirements. We set up *problem diagrams* representing subproblems to model functional requirements.

To analyze and integrate quality requirements in the software development process, quality requirements have to be modeled and integrated as early as possible in the requirement models. Modeling quality requirements and associating them to the functional requirements is achieved by annotating them in problem diagrams. For more information about context elicitation and problem decomposition, see [13].

Phase 2- Domain Knowledge Elicitation and Modeling. The system-to-be comprises the software to be built and its surrounding environment such as people, devices, and existing software [12]. In requirements engineering, properties of the environment and constraints about it, called *domain knowledge*, need to be captured in addition to exploring the requirements [6,15]. Hence, the second phase (see 2 in Fig. 2) involves *domain knowledge elicitation & modeling*. We elicit the relevant information that has to be collected when dealing with specific software qualities such as security and document them as structured templates called *Domain Knowledge Templates*. To guarantee security, we need domain knowledge about the type of possible attackers that influence the

Fig. 3. Relationship between security requirements, tactics, and security patterns

restrictiveness of a security requirement. It depends on the abilities of the attacker how much resources and effort to spend on a requirement, how much influence security has on the behavior of the overall system-to-be, and which solution to fulfill the requirement has to be chosen later on. Different types of attackers can be considered. For example, a software attacker targets at manipulating the software, whereas a network attacker aims at manipulating the network traffic. To describe the attacker we use the properties as described by the Common Methodology for Information Technology Security Evaluation (CEM) [16] for vulnerability assessment of the TOE (target of evaluation i.e., system-to-be). These properties are used to instantiate the domain knowledge templates. For more information regarding eliciting, modeling, and using domain knowledge, we refer to [14].

Phase 3- Solution Identification and Analysis. The first two phases are concerned with the activities accommodated in the requirements engineering (known as *problem peak* in the Twin Peaks model). Exploring the solution space for finding security strategies to achieve security requirements is the aim of the third phase (see 3 in Fig. 2). Tactics proposed by Bass et al. [17] provide first basic approaches for the achievement of quality requirements, in particular, security requirements. Such general solutions are proved and recognized as coarse-grained solutions that help the achievement of quality requirements to some extent. Figure 3 shows a synopsis of the relationship between the artifacts in requirements engineering, namely requirements, and the artifacts in architectural design, namely coarse-grained solutions (tactics) and more specific solutions (patterns). It depicts how security requirements are mapped to security tactics (arrows on the left-hand side)[1]. Each security requirement is mapped to one or more tactics. From the tactics, we select the one that can realize the security requirement in a high-level manner. Furthermore, Figure 3 represents the mapping of tactics to more specific ones, namely security patterns. We make use of such mapping to refine the selected tactic further by selecting the appropriate security pattern in the next phase.

Phase 4- Solution Selection and Application. This phase (see 4 in Fig. 2) is concerned with selecting the appropriate security pattern such as *encryption* and *digital signature*

---

[1] Note that the figure does not provide a complete list of security requirements, security solutions, and security patterns. It only serves as an example to show how these artifacts are related to each other.

that supports the achievement of security requirements. To this end, we make use of the relationship between tactics and security patterns depicted on the right-hand side of Fig. 3. Each tactic is mapped to one or more security patterns. The selected security pattern implements the corresponding tactic. After selecting the appropriate security pattern, we look for the counterpart *problem-oriented security pattern* such as *problem-oriented digital signature pattern*, which can be applied to refine the requirement models.

Phase 5- Quality-Based Architecture Derivation. In the previous phases, we refined and restructured the problem descriptions by applying problem-oriented security patterns. The so enhanced requirement models contain first security solution approaches. This facilitates deriving a high-level architecture description from the requirement models, which can be further refined by applying appropriate security and design patterns.

In this phase (see 5 in Fig. 2), we define an architecture description that is oriented on the decomposition of the overall software development problem into subproblems represented as problem diagrams. The architecture consists of one component for the overall machine, with the stereotype ≪machine≫. For a distributed architecture, we add the stereotype ≪distributed≫ to the architecture component. For client-server architectures, there are two components representing client and server, respectively, inside the overall machine. Each component has to be annotated with the stereotype ≪local≫. Then we make use of the problem diagrams. The derivation of the software architecture is achieved by mapping domains from problem diagrams to components in the software architecture. Each submachine in the problem diagrams becomes a component in the architecture. We annotate components with the stereotype ≪component≫. This provides support for a seamless integration of security patterns into software architecture.

4   Application Example

To illustrate the application of our method, we use the real-life example of smart grids. As sources for real functional and quality requirements we consider diverse documents such as "Application Case Study: Smart Grid" and "Smart Grid Concrete Scenario" provided by the industrial partners of the EU project NESSoS[2] and the "Protection Profile for the Gateway of a Smart Metering System" [18] provided by the German Federal Office for Information Security[3] and "Requirements of AMI" [19] provided by the EU project OPEN meter[4].

4.1   Introduction to the Case Study "Smart Grid"

To use energy in an optimal way, smart grids make it possible to couple the generation, distribution, storage, and consumption of energy. Smart grids use Information and Communication Technologies (ICT), which allow for financial, informational, and electrical transactions. Figure 4 shows the simplified context of a smart grid system based on [18].

---

[2] http://www.nessos-project.eu/
[3] www.bsi.bund.de
[4] http://www.openmeter.com/

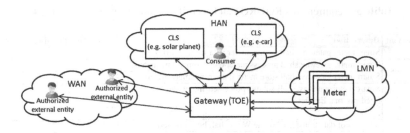

Fig. 4. The context of a smart grid system based on [18]

Table 2. An excerpt of relevant terms for the smart grid

Gateway	represents the central communication unit in a *smart metering system*. It is responsible for collecting, processing, storing, and communicating *meter data*.
Meter data	refers to meter readings measured by the meter regarding consumption or production of a certain commodity.
Smart meter	represents the device that measures the consumption or production of a certain commodity and sends it to the gateway.
Authorized external entity	could be a human or IT unit that communicates with the gateway from outside the gateway boundaries through a *Wide Area Network (WAN)*.
WAN	WAN provides the communication network that interconnects the gateway with the outside world.

To achieve the goals of the system, 20 use cases are necessary, from which we consider only the use case *Meter Reading for Billing*, as treating all 20 use cases would go beyond the scope of this paper. This use case is concerned with gathering, processing, and storing meter readings from smart meters for the billing process. Table 4.1 shows an excerpt of terms specific to the smart grid domain taken from the protection profile that are relevant to understand the requirements. Detailed description of the example smart grid is described in [9].

The protection profile states that "the Gateway is responsible for handling Meter Data. It receives the Meter Data from the Meter(s), processes it, stores it and submits it to external parties". Therefore, we define the requirements *RQ1-RQ3* to receive, process, and store meter data from smart meters. The requirement *RQ4* is concerned with submitting meter data to authorized external entities.

In the smart grids case study, security requirements have to be taken into account. A smart grid involves a wide range of data that should be treated in a secure way. Protection profile defines security objectives and requirements for the central communication unit in a smart metering system. To ensure security of meter data, the protection profile [18, pp. 18, 20] demands protection of data from unauthorized disclosure while transmitted to the corresponding external entity via the WAN (*RQ11*). The gateway shall provide the protection of authenticity and integrity when sending processed meter data to an external entity, to enable the external entity to verify that the processed meter data have been sent from an authentic gateway and have not been changed during transmission (*RQ10, RQ12*). Requirements with their descriptions are listed in Table 3.

Table 3. Requirements RQ1-RQ4 and security requirements related to RQ4

Requirement	Description	Related functional requirement
RQ1	Smart meter gateway shall receive meter data from smart meters	-
RQ2	Smart meter gateway shall process meter data from smart meters	-
RQ3	Smart meter gateway shall store meter data from smart meters	-
RQ4	Smart meter gateway shall submit processed meter data to autho-rized external Entities	-
...	...	...
RQ10	Integrity of data transferred in the WAN shall be protected	RQ4
RQ11	Confidentiality of data transferred in the WAN shall be protected	RQ4
RQ12	Authenticity of data transferred in the WAN shall be protected	RQ4
...	...	...

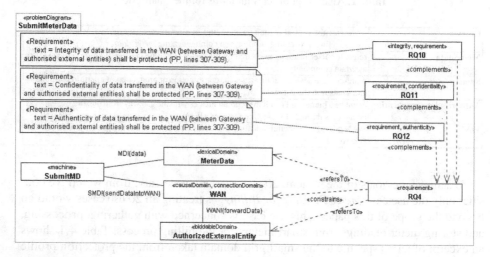

Fig. 5. Problem diagram for the requirement RQ4 and its related security requirements

4.2   Application of Our Method to the Smart Grid

Applying our method to the case study smart grids implies the following activities and working results.

Phase 1- Context Elicitation and Problem Decomposition. In this phase, we set up a *context diagram* to understand the problem and its context and *problem diagrams* to decompose the overall problem into subproblems, and annotate them with required security requirements. Due to the lack of space, we do not show the context diagram here. Figure 5 illustrates the problem diagram for describing the functional requirement *RQ4* annotated by the security requirements *RQ10*, *RQ11*, and *RQ12*.

In the original problem frames approach, the focus is on functional requirements. We extended the UML-based problem frames approach by providing a way to attach quality requirements to problem diagrams [13]. We represent quality requirements as annotations in problem diagrams. Since UML lacks notations to specify and model quality requirements, we use specific UML profiles to add annotations to the UML models. We use a UML profile for dependability [11] to annotate problem diagrams with

Table 4. Instantiated domain knowledge template for security

Quality: Security, Requirement: RQ10			
Elicitation Template			Mapping to profile
Domain Knowledge Description	Possible Values	Value	Property (Dependability profile)
Preparation time	one day, one week, two weeks, ...	more than six months	Attacker.preparationTime
Attack time	one day, one week, two weeks, ...	more than six months	Attacker.attackTime
Specialist expertise	laymen, proficient, expert, ...	multiple experts	Attacker.specialistExpertise
Knowledge of the TOE	public, restricted, sensitive, critical	public	Attacker.knowledge
Window of opportunity	unnecessary/unlimited, easy, ...	difficult	Attacker.opportunity
IT hardware/software or other equipment	standard, specialized, bespoke, ...	multiple bespoke	Attacker.equipment

security requirements. For example, we apply the stereotypes ≪integrity≫, ≪confidentiality≫, and ≪authenticity≫ to represent integrity, confidentiality, and authenticity requirements as it is illustrated in Figure 5. In the problem diagram for submitting meter readings (Figure 5), the functional requirement *RQ4* is complemented by the following quality requirements: *RQ10* (integrity), *RQ11* (confidentiality), and *RQ12* (authenticity). For further phases of our method, we consider the security requirements *RQ10* and *RQ12*.

Phase 2- Domain Knowledge Elicitation and Modeling. The achievement of security requirements requires additional resources such as computational power, which might affect the achievement of other quality requirements such as performance requirements negatively. The resource usage is affected by the strength of the security mechanism to be selected to achieve the corresponding security requirement. The kind of attacker and its characteristics determine the strength of the security mechanism. Therefore, we elicit and model the attacker and its characteristics as domain knowledge. For eliciting security-relevant domain knowledge, we have to instantiate the *Domain Knowledge Template* for each identified attacker once. We identify two network attackers for the two security requirements *RQ10* and *RQ12*. The reason is that the meter data to be transmitted through the network WAN can be manipulated by a network attacker. There is no information in the Protection Profile [18] about the attacker that the system must be protected against. Therefore, we assume that the system must be protected against the strongest attacker. Hence, we select for each property in the domain knowledge template for security the strongest one to obtain values for the column "Value". Table 4 shows the instantiated domain knowledge template for the integrity requirement *RQ10*. We model the network attacker explicitly as a biddable domain. Then, we apply the stereotype ≪attacker≫. We assign the attributes of the stereotype ≪attacker≫ using mapping provided by Table 4.

Phase 3- Solution Identification and Analysis. We introduced Fig. 3 in the previous section to show how security requirements, tactics, and security patterns are related to each other. This relationship allows us to identify the possible tactics and patterns for satisfying the security requirements *RQ10* and *RQ12*. For example, one tactic for supporting the achievement of the authenticity requirement is *Authenticate Users* which can be realized by applying the security patterns *Identification & Authentication* and

Digital Signature. To achieve the integrity requirement, the tactics *Authorize Users* and *Maintain Integrity* can be selected. The tactic *Authorize Users* can be implemented by applying the security pattern *Access Controls*, whereas the tactic *Maintain Integrity* can be achieved by applying the security pattern *Digital Signature*. We decide for the security pattern *Digital Signature* as it can achieve both integrity and authenticity requirements. In the next phase, we apply the counterpart to the *Digital Signature* pattern for the requirements engineering phase, namely the *problem-oriented digital signature pattern*.

Phase 4- Solution Selection and Application. In phase four, we instantiate the *problem-oriented digital signature pattern*. First, we map the problem diagram shown in Fig. 5 to the first part of the graphical pattern described in Sect. 2.2. Figure 5 represents an instance of the first part of the *problem-oriented digital signature pattern*, in which the machine *SubmitMD* represents the machine *FunctionalM*, the domain *MeterData* represents the domain *Domain*, the functional requirement *RQ4* represents the functional requirement *FunctionalReq*, and the authenticity requirement *RQ12* represents the authenticity requirement *AuthenticityReq*. As mentioned in Sect. 2.2, depending on the functional requirement, the problem diagram might contain other domains that are not relevant for the security problem at hand. Hence, they are not represented in the pattern. The causal domain *WAN* and the biddable domain *AuthorizedExternalEntitiy* in Fig. 5 are examples for such a case.

Figure 6 illustrates the solution *digital signature* for the authenticity/integrity problem (second part of the pattern) and the composition problem diagram (third part of the pattern). We instantiate the second part of the pattern. Doing this, we obtain the upper problem diagram, in which the domain *MeterData* represents the domain *Domain*, the domain *PrivateKey* represents the domain *PrivateKey*, the authenticity requirement *RQ10* represents the authenticity requirement *authenticityReq*, and the machine *SigningMachine* represents the machine *DigSigM* in the pattern. As described in Sect. 2.2, the problem-oriented digital signature pattern provides a solution for the integrity problem as well. Thus, we model the authenticity requirement *RQ12* as well as the integrity requirement *RQ10* in Fig. 6. In this problem diagram, the machine *SigningMachine* receives the key (*privateKEy*) from the domain *PrivateKey* and the data (*contentOfMeterData*) from the domain *MeterData* and signs it by producing the *signedMeterData* using a signing algorithm in the machine *SigningMachine*.

We instantiate the third part of the pattern by mapping the domain *Domain* to the domain *MeterData*, the machine *DigSigM* to the machine *SigningMachine*, the machine *FunctionalM* to the machine *SubmitMD*, the composition requirement *Req* to the composition requirement *RQ4+RQ10+RQ12*, and the composition machine *CompositionM* to the composition machine *SecurityManager*. Doing this, we obtain the lower problem diagram, in which the problem diagram represented in Fig. 5 and the upper problem diagram in Fig. 6 are combined. The machine *SecurityManager* receives the *contentOfMeterData* from the domain *MeterData* and sends it to the machine *SigningMachine*. The machine *SigningMachine* signs the data and sends the *signedMeterData* back to the machine *SecurityManager*. This machine sends the signed data to the machine *SubmitMD*, which sends the data to the *AuthorizedExternalEntity* through the connection domain *WAN*.

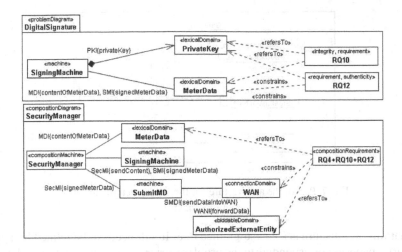

Fig. 6. Instance of the second and third parts of the *problem-oriented digital signature pattern*

In this way, we successfully instantiated and applied the problem-oriented digital signature pattern in phase four of our method in order to achieve the integrity requirement *RQ10* and the authenticity requirement *RQ12* for the functional requirement *RQ4*. We only showed the instantiation of the graphical part of the pattern. The corresponding template can be easily filled out using the information obtained from the solution space and according to the responsibility for the achievement of necessary conditions. As mentioned before, the templates as part of the problem-oriented security patterns describe the effect of each pattern on the requirement models. According to this part of the templates, we have to update the requirement models including domain knowledge (first and second phases of the method) by selecting and applying a problem-oriented security pattern. Therefore, our method has to be conducted as a recursive one to obtain correct requirements and a sound architecture.

Phase 5- Quality-Based Architecture Derivation. In phase five, we set up an architecture by transforming the machines in the problem diagrams into components in the architecture. The architecture represented as a composite structure diagram in UML is shown in Fig. 7. The component for the overall machine *Gateway* has the stereotype ≪machine≫. Within this component, there exist components *SubmitMD*, *Security-Manager*, and *SigningMachine*, which are machines in the problem diagram *Security-Manager* shown in Fig. 6. In addition, we have to transform the lexical domains in the problem diagrams into components in the architecture. The reason is that lexical domains usually are data representations, thus they have to be part of the architecture. The component *MeterData* is such an example. The component *SubmitMD* is connected via *WAN* to outside of the smart meter gateway to *AuthorizedExternalEntity* as it is illustrated in the problem diagram *SecurityManager* shown in Fig. 6. Figure 7 represents only the part of the overall architecture which corresponds to the functional requirement *RQ4* and its related security requirements. For other requirements, we follow the same principle. Doing this, we obtain a full architecture for the smart meter gateway.

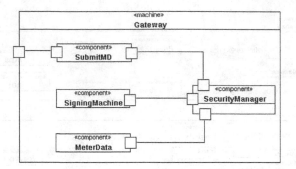

Fig. 7. Part of the architecture for the smart meter gateway

Note that this architecture is a coarse-grained one. It still needs to be refined by applying security patterns corresponding to the problem-oriented security patterns and design patterns.

Benefits. The proposed method allows software engineers not only to think about security problems as early as possible in the software development life cycle, but also to think about solution approaches solving such security problems. By exploring the solution space, we find appropriate solution mechanisms and patterns, which can be used as *problem-oriented security patterns* for refining security requirement models in the requirement engineering phase. The corresponding templates represent consequences of applying such solution approaches by providing new assumptions and/or requirements to be considered when deciding on a specific pattern. The elaborated security requirement models can easily be transformed into a particular security pattern at the design level. Thus, problem-oriented security patterns support bridging the gap between security problems and security solutions. Note that *problem-oriented security patterns* do not replace the application of "classical" security patterns. *Problem-oriented security patterns* are located in the problem space aiming at restructuring and elaborating security problems while "classical" security patterns are accommodated in the solution space aiming at solving security problems. *Problem-oriented security patterns* in the requirements engineering phase represent the counterpart to "classical" security patterns in the design phase.

5   Related Work

Investigating early phases of software development, namely requirements analysis and architectural design, has been subject to research in related work for many years. This investigation however has been conducted for each phase separately and in isolation. Little attention has been given to investigating the relationship between requirements phase and architecture phase. Hence, as related work, we discuss approaches that relate requirements and architectures with regard to security.

The security Twin Peaks model [20] provides a framework for developing security in the requirements and the architectural artifacts in parallel. Taking architectural security patterns into account, the model supports the elaboration of the problem and the solution artifacts by considering feedback coming from the counterpart peak. This framework, which is an elaboration of the original Twin Peaks model [2] in the context of security, is similar to our approach regarding the refinement of security requirements in the problem domain. However, the authors make use of the existing methods for each peak separately, namely the goal-oriented requirements engineering approach KAOS [21] to represent security requirements in the problem peak and Attribute Driven Design [17] for the solution peak.

Haley et al. [22] propose an approach to derive security requirements, which are expressed as constraints on the functional requirements. Threat descriptions are treated as crosscutting concerns that impact functional requirements represented as problem frames. Composing threat descriptions with problem diagrams reveal vulnerabilities that can be reduced by adding appropriate security requirements to the corresponding problem diagram. This approach uses problem frames as a basis for identifying vulnerabilities and deriving security requirements. Hence, it can be used complementary to our method as a step prior to our method.

Similar to our work, a method to bridge the gap between security requirements and the design is proposed in [23]. This method introduces new security patterns at the requirements and the design level, in contrast to our approach that reuses the existing security design patterns at the requirements level by applying problem-oriented security patterns. Alebrahim et al. [24] provide an aspect-oriented method for developing secure software. It treats security requirements as crosscutting concerns and refines them by using security patterns. Similar to our approach in this paper, it uses problem frames as a basis for requirements engineering. In contrast, we apply problem-oriented security patterns in this paper, which systematically adopt the notion of security patterns for requirements engineering.

Rapanotti et al. [25] propose an approach similar to our work by introducing *Architectural Frames*. They use architectural styles [26] located in the solution space to support the decomposition and recomposition of functional models within the problem frames framework. The *Pipes and filters* is selected to solve the transformation problems, represented in the problem frame approach by the *transformation frame*. Another architectural style is the Model-View-Controller (MVC) that is considered to solve the control problem, captured by the *commanded behaviour frame*.

Hall et al. [27] present an extension of the problem frames approach allowing design concerns. They suggest to benefit from architectural support in the problem domain by annotating the machine domain with them. However, it does not become clear how the architectural descriptions can be used explicitly in order to structure the machine domain.

These two approaches provide suggestions to use architectural knowledge in the problem domain based on the problem frames concept. However, they do not propose a systematic method on how to find the appropriate architectural solution and how to integrate it in the problem domain explicitly. Further, they only consider functional requirements and not security requirements. From this point of view, these approaches can be considered as complementary to our work.

6 Conclusions and Future Work

We have proposed a systematic method based on the problem frames approach for the iterative development of requirements analysis and software architectures with focus on achieving security requirements. The method provides an instantiation of the Twin Peaks model in the context of security proposing explicit steps that takes into account the intertwining nature of requirements and architectures. The iterative nature of our method as an instance of the Twin peaks model facilitates considering the feedback, which arise in one peak, in the another peak. Our method exploits the knowledge gained in the solution domain in a systematic way to refine the security requirements in the problem space by applying *problem-oriented security patterns*.

To summarize, we have proposed a pattern-based method that

- provides guidance on how requirements analysis and software architectures can be developed incrementally and iteratively to achieve security requirements.
- allows software engineers not only to think about security problems as early as possible in the software development life cycle, but also to think about solution approaches solving such security problems.
- bridges the gap between security problems and security solutions.

In the present work, we applied problem-oriented security patterns, which support the achievement of security requirements as early as possible in the software development life cycle. But not all kinds of security requirements can be achieved by enforcing security patterns. For example, there exist no patterns for *non-repudiation, anonymity*, and *privacy* in literature [28]. In the future, we will extend our method to also support the systematic selection of security mechanisms to refine all security requirements in the problem domain. Additionally, we strive for extending our method to support the achievement of not only security requirements in an iterative software development process, but also other quality requirements such as performance by using the architectural knowledge such as generic solutions, patterns, and mechanisms.

References

1. Chung, L., Nixon, B.A., Yu, E., Mylopoulos, J.: Non-functional requirements in software engineering. Klewer Academic (2000)
2. Nuseibeh, B.: Weaving together requirements and architectures. IEEE Computer 34(3), 115–117 (2001)
3. Whalen, M., Gacek, A., Cofer, D., Murugesan, A., Heimdahl, M., Rayadurgam, S.: Your "What" Is My "How": Iteration and Hierarchy in System Design. IEEE Software 30(2), 54–60 (2013)
4. Schumacher, M., Fernandez-Buglioni, E., Hybertson, D., Buschmann, F., Sommerlad, P.: Security patterns: integrating security and systems engineering. John Wiley & Sons (2005)
5. Alebrahim, A., Heisel, M.: Problem-oriented Security Patterns for Requirements Engineering. In: Proc. of the 19th European Conf. on Pattern Languages of Programs (EuroPLoP). Universitätsverlag Konstanz (accepted, 2014)
6. Jackson, M.: Problem Frames. Analyzing and structuring software development problems. Addison-Wesley (2001)

7. UML Revision Task Force, OMG Unified Modeling Language (UML), Superstructure, http://www.omg.org/spec/UML/2.3/Superstructure/PDF
8. Hatebur, D., Heisel, M.: Making Pattern- and Model-Based Software Development more Rigorous. In: Dong, J.S., Zhu, H. (eds.) ICFEM 2010. LNCS, vol. 6447, pp. 253–269. Springer, Heidelberg (2010)
9. Alebrahim, A., Choppy, C., Faßbender, S., Heisel, M.: Optimizing functional and quality requirements according to stakeholders' goals. In: System Quality and Software Architecture (SQSA), pp. 75–120. Elsevier (2014)
10. Alebrahim, A., Hatebur, D., Heisel, M.: A method to derive software architectures from quality requirements. In: Thu, T.D., Leung, K. (eds.) Proc. of the 18th Asia-Pacific Software Engineering Conf (APSEC), pp. 322–330. IEEE Computer Society (2011)
11. Hatebur, D., Heisel, M.: A UML profile for requirements analysis of dependable software. In: Schoitsch, E. (ed.) SAFECOMP 2010. LNCS, vol. 6351, pp. 317–331. Springer, Heidelberg (2010)
12. Lamsweerde, A.: Requirements Engineering: From System Goals to UML Models to Software Specifications. Wiley (2009)
13. Alebrahim, A., Hatebur, D., Heisel, M.: Towards systematic integration of quality requirements into software architecture. In: Crnkovic, I., Gruhn, V., Book, M. (eds.) ECSA 2011. LNCS, vol. 6903, pp. 17–25. Springer, Heidelberg (2011)
14. Alebrahim, A., Heisel, M., Meis, R.: A structured approach for eliciting, modeling, and using quality-related domain knowledge. In: Murgante, B., et al. (eds.) ICCSA 2014, Part V. LNCS, vol. 8583, pp. 370–386. Springer, Heidelberg (2014)
15. van Lamsweerde, A.: Reasoning about alternative requirements options. In: Borgida, A.T., Chaudhri, V.K., Giorgini, P., Yu, E.S. (eds.) Mylopoulos Festschrift. LNCS, vol. 5600, pp. 380–397. Springer, Heidelberg (2009)
16. International Organization for Standardization (ISO) and International Electrotechnical Commission (IEC), Common Evaluation Methodology 3.1, ISO/IEC 15408 (2009)
17. Bass, L., Clements, P., Kazman, R.: Software Architecture in Practice. SEI Series in Software Engineering. Addison Wesley (2003)
18. Kreutzmann, H., Vollmer, S., Tekampe, N., Abromeit, A.: Protection profile for the gateway of a smart metering system. BSI, Tech. Rep. (2011)
19. Remero, G., Tarruell, F., Mauri, G., Pajot, A., Alberdi, G., Arzberger, M., Denda, R., Giubbini, P., Rodrguez, C., Miranda, E., Galeote, I., Morgaz, M., Larumbe, I., Navarro, E., Lassche, R., Haas, J., Steen, A., Cornelissen, P., Radtke, G., Martnez, C., Orcajada, A., Kneitinger, H., Wiedemann, T.: D1.1 Requirements of AMI. OPEN meter project, Tech. Rep. (2009)
20. Heyman, T., Yskout, K., Scandariato, R., Schmidt, H., Yu, Y.: The security twin peaks. In: Erlingsson, Ú., Wieringa, R., Zannone, N. (eds.) ESSoS 2011. LNCS, vol. 6542, pp. 167–180. Springer, Heidelberg (2011)
21. van Lamsweerde, A.: Requirements Engineering: From System Goals to UML Models to Software Specifications. John Wiley & Sons (2009)
22. Haley, C.B., Laney, R.C., Nuseibeh, B.: Deriving security requirements from crosscutting threat descriptions. In: Proc. of the 3rd Int. Conf. on Aspect-oriented Software Development (AOSD), pp. 112–121. ACM, USA (2004)
23. Okubo, T., Kaiya, H., Yoshioka, N.: Effective Security Impact Analysis with Patterns for Software Enhancement. In: Proc. of the 6th Int. Conf. on Availability, Reliability and Security (ARES), pp. 527–534 (2011)
24. Alebrahim, A., Tun, T.T., Yu, Y., Heisel, M., Nuseibeh, B.: An aspect-oriented approach to relating security requirements and access control. In: Proc. of the CAiSE Forum, CEUR Workshop Proceedings, vol. 855, pp. 15–22. CEUR-WS.org. (2012)

25. Rapanotti, L., Hall, J.G., Jackson, M., Nuseibeh, B.: Architecture-driven problem decomposition. In: Proc. of the 12th IEEE Int. Requirements Engineering Conf. (RE), pp. 80–89 (2004)
26. Shaw, M., Garlan, G.: Software Aechitecture: Perspectives on an emerging discipline. Prentice Hall (1996)
27. Hall, J., Jackson, M., Laney, R., Nuseibeh, B., Rapanotti, L.: Relating software requirements and architectures using problem frames. In: Proc. of the IEEE Joint Int. Conf. on Requirements Engineering, pp. 137–144 (2002)
28. Yskout, K., Heyman, T., Scandariato, R., Joosen, W.: A system of security patterns. K.U. Leuven, Department of Computer Science, Report CW 469 (2006)

Visual Analytics for Detecting Anomalous Activity in Mobile Money Transfer Services

Evgenia Novikova[1] and Igor Kotenko[1,2]

[1] Laboratory of Computer Security Problems
St. Petersburg Institute for Informatics and Automation (SPIIRAS)
39, 14 Liniya, St. Petersburg, Russia
{novikova,ivkote}@comsec.spb.ru
[2] St. Petersburg National Research University of Information Technologies,
Mechanics and Optics, 49, Kronverkskiy prospekt, Saint-Petersburg, Russia

Abstract. Mobile money transfer services (MMTS) are currently being deployed in many markets across the world and are widely used for domestic and international remittances. However, they can be used for money laundering and other illegal financial operations. The paper considers an interactive multi-view approach that allows describing metaphorically the behavior of MMTS subscribers according to their transaction activities. The suggested visual representation of the MMTS users' behavior based on the RadViz visualization technique helps to identify groups with similar behavior and outliers. We describe several case studies corresponding to the money laundering and behavioral fraud. They are used to assess the efficiency of the proposed a pproach as well as present and discuss the results of experiments.

Keywords: Mobile money transfer services, fraud detection, visual analytics, RadViz visualization.

1 Introduction

The field of Mobile Money Transfer service (MMTS) is a growing market segment, particularly in developing countries, where banking systems may not be as dense or available as in developed countries. For example, M-Pesa, which was launched in 2007 in Kenya, displayed in December 2011 about 19 million subscribers, namely 70% of all mobile subscribers in Kenya [29]. Orange Money is deployed in 10 countries and gathers around 14% of the mobile subscribers of these countries [23]. In such services, transactions are made with electronic money, called mMoney. The users can convert cash to mMoney through distributors and use it to purchase goods at merchants, pay bills or transfer it to other users [16].

The risks inherent to all payment systems are present in the mobile environment. However, the usage of mobile technologies introduces additional risks caused by the large number of non-bank participants, rapidity of transactions and higher level of anonymity compared to traditional banking systems [16, 18]. Therefore, it is required to determine new approaches to detect frauds in mobile money transfer services.

S. Teufel et al. (Eds.): CD-ARES 2014, LNCS 8708, pp. 63–78, 2014.

The aim of this paper is to show how visual analytics can provide better insight in the large data sets describing MMTS activity and can assist in fraud detection. Visual data exploration can be considered as a hypothesis generation and verification process which is intuitively clear and does not require explicit application of complex mathematical and statistical methods [11, 13, 21]. We suggest an interactive multi-view approach allowing the analyst to get a global overview of the MMTS subscribers' activity and then focus on users of the particular interest drilling down into their transactions. It is based on RadViz-based [3] visualization of the MMTS users that helps to determine similarity groups and outliers among them and is supported by graph-based and table views assisting in analyzing structural links of the user.

Specifically, our main contribution is the interactive RadViz-based visual representation of MMTS subscribers allowing detection of groups of users with similar behavior. To the best of our knowledge, our work is the first to exploit RadViz visualization technique to visualize MMTS subscribers. To demonstrate and evaluate the usefulness of the proposed approach we investigated several case studies corresponding to the money laundering and behavioral fraud, which take place when the mobile device is used to carry out illegitimate transactions without its owner's consent.

The rest of the paper is structured as follows: *Section 2* overviews mobile money transfer service and its structure, and discusses related work in the field of fraud detection techniques in mobile payments as well as visualization techniques used to detect financial frauds. *Section 3* describes the approach suggested, including visual models and interactions with them. *Section 4* presents the case studies used to demonstrate the proposed approach for financial fraud detection in mobile payments using visual analytics techniques, discusses the results and presents ideas about further developments of the approach. *Section 5* sums up our contributions.

2   Background

2.1   Mobile Money Transfer Service

The paper is based on the MMTS use case detailed in [1, 25]. This section outlines the major points to understand the use case. MMTS are systems where electronic money, called *mMoney* or *m*, is issued to different roles such as regular users, retailers, merchants, in order to perform various types of transactions which range from merchant payments to transfers between individuals.

Fig. 1, which is adapted from [10], shows the economic principle of mMoney and the roles of various actors. As depicted, the Mobile Network Operator (MNO) emits mMoney in partnership with a private bank. The MNO regularly produces compliancy reports, including suspicious activity reports, to the Central Bank, responsible for the country's monetary policy. The emitted mMoney can only be used among the MNO's clients subscribing to the MMT service. The subscribers are end-users, service providers or retailers. They hold a prepaid account stored on a platform and accessible via the MNO's network and an application on their mobile device. Some users, such as retailers or service providers, can use computers to access their account. This account contains mMoney which can be acquired from the retailers. End-users can either transfer money to other end-users or purchase goods.

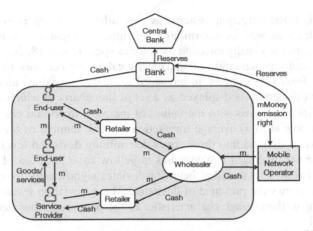

Fig. 1. Economic environment of Mobile Money Transfer services [10]

2.2   Fraud Detection Techniques in Mobile Payments

In the Kenyan MMT service M-Pesa, fraud detection is carried out by the Minotaur tool which uses neural networks [19, 22]. Apart from this system, there is not much publicly available information about fraud detection in MMT services. However, to our knowledge, the most widely deployed tools are based on rules, linear regression and neural networks.

If we consider other payment systems, several fraud detection techniques have been applied. For example, in the field of credit card fraud detection, Al-Khatib [2] identifies several studies which use neural networks, expert systems, case-based reasoning, genetic algorithms, inductive logic programming and regression. Another illustration is the use of graphs proposed by Ron and Shamir [26] to explore the data related to the transactions in the Bitcoin payment system in order to highlight awkward transactions schemes.

3   Related Work

Due to the complexity of financial data (often with multidimensional attributes), many sophisticated visualization and interaction techniques have been proposed (to analyze the financial market as a whole, or single assets in particular), which support visually decision making [15]. Parallel coordinates, scatter-plot matrices, survey plots, special glyphs [28], treemaps [31], stacked and iconic displays, dense pixel-displays [33], dendrograms, fish-eye views [14] are applied to explore financial data.

However, the visualization techniques applied in fraud detection systems are rather limited. The most of commercial software products [8, 20, 27] extensively use trends, pie charts and histograms and gauge-based glyphs to display characteristics of financial flows, number of registered alerts, their type and criticality, etc. The choice of these visual models is explained by their simplicity and ability to communicate the most important information at glance. They can be easily included in the reports of any level and purpose. Apart from the standard visual models, geographical maps are often present in fraud detection systems as they allow detecting regions with high financial risk level as well as determining the limits of organization responsibility. Such kind of metrics is usually encoded by color or specific icon [8, 20].

In [8] the visual representation of statistically calculated behavior of a peer group and deviations from it is used as an advanced technique to reduce alert generation. The behavior of the group is displayed as a set of line charts in which x-axis corresponds to the time and y-axis – to the values of the most important characteristics of the transaction flow such as average transaction amount, number of transactions, etc. The vertical axis is divided into three zones determining deviation level in users' behavior. The normal (average) behavior lies in yellow zone, location of the charts in the red colored zone indicates that behavior deviates significantly from the average one and orange shows the presence of deviation. These deviation levels could be adjusted according to the average characteristics of the peer group thus decreasing alert triggering level.

In order to support alert investigation the most of the fraud detection systems implement flexible querying mechanism that allows the analyst to extract all data associated with a given key value, i.e. account or credit card number [8, 27]. However, identifying hidden relationships, based on data from multiple sources, and tracking the movement of money made between a variety of entities is difficult using tabular methods. For this reason the graph-based representation of users' financial contacts are applied in fraud detection systems [20, 27] and adopted by different forensic companies [6, 32]. Usually graph vertexes represent different entities such as accounts, user IDs, phones, credit cards, addresses, organizations, etc. The edges between them indicate the usage or participation of the corresponding entity in financial operations, and the line thickness displays the frequency of the transactions between entities. The graph-based representation of transaction activity helps to discover connections between customers, to identify suspicious communication patterns, revealing thus organized group of fraudsters.

Korczak et al. [12] address the problem of graphical representation of sequential financial operations in readable manner. Exploration of transaction chains assists the analyst to detect money laundering operations. However, the major concern when designing a visualization algorithm of sequential operations is the complexity of the resulting graph. In order to solve this problem the authors propose the evolutionary algorithm that minimizes the number of edge intersections.

Chang et al. [4] present the WireVis tool for the analysis of financial wire transactions for fraud protection. It is based on transaction keyword analysis and built in collaboration with the Bank of America. All the textual elements contained in transaction data records are seen as keywords. WireVis uses a multi-view approach including a keyword heatmap and a keyword network graph to visualize the relationships among accounts, time and keywords within wire transactions. The keyword heatmap characterizes the usage frequency of the keyword in the users' groups. Authors suggest an interesting modification of the clustering algorithm applied to form groups of similarities. They treat each account as a point in the k-dimensional space (where k is the number of keywords), and group the accounts based on their distances to the average point of all accounts. This approach significantly decreases the complexity of clustering procedure having complexity $O(3n)$. In order to support the visualization of transaction activity over time, authors propose the Strings and Beads view in which the strings refer to the accounts or cluster of accounts over time, and the beads refer to specific transactions on a given day. The x-axis of the view corresponds to the progression of time, and the y-axis shows a transaction attribute selected form the predefined list.

4   Data, Models, and Techniques

4.1   Data

The data from existing MMTS are not publicly available and in the most cases confidential. A possible solution of this problem can be usage of artificially generated data. This approach is widely used to train automatic fraud detection techniques based on pattern recognition and machine learning [9]. In our work we use MMTS log synthetic simulator [9] to generate test data containing different fraudulent scenarios. The MMTS log synthetic simulator was developed within the FP7 project MASSIF to assess efficiency of the proposed intrusion detection techniques for the mobile money transfer scenario [25]. It models the mobile money transfer platform and the behavior of its legitimate or fraudulent users.

These data describe only transaction logs and contain such information as the phone number of the customer (sender/receiver), their account ID and role (customer, retailer, merchant, operator, etc.), transaction ID, its timestamp, type (money transfer between individuals, cash in or cash out of the mobile wallet, etc.), transaction amount, status as well as sender's and receiver's balance before and after transaction.

In order to assess the suggested approach we generated various case studies, including money laundering activities and mobile botnets, using this simulator. In generated scenarios each MMTS subscriber has only one account and role associated with him (her).

4.2   Visual Models and Interaction Techniques

When designing main form of the MMTViewer, a tool demonstrating the approach, we followed Shneiderman's information seeking mantra [30] that consists in having the overview first and then focusing on particular areas of interests.

Thus, the main window is divided into three subviews: (A) RadViz-based view, (B) graph-based view and (C) table view, designed to inspire the analyst to dive into data, generate hypotheses and verify them (Fig. 2).

The goal of the RadViz-based view (A) is to provide the general overview of the transaction activity in the MMTS. It allows identification of the existence of patterns in subscribers' behavior, while the graph-based view (B) helps to focus on the links of a particular user or a group of users. The table view (C) gives detailed information on the selected MMTS entity (subscriber or transaction). These three views are coordinated together, so selecting a user in view A results in highlighting corresponding user and his/her transactions in view B and refreshing detailed information in view C.

With these three tightly linked views the analyst can interact with users and transactions in order to understand how the data correlate. We suppose such approach is significantly more powerful that using the views separately.

The tool described in the paper is written in Java. All visual models are implemented using Prefuse Toolkit [24], which allows development of highly interactive visualizations. It can be easily integrated into Swing applications or Java applets.

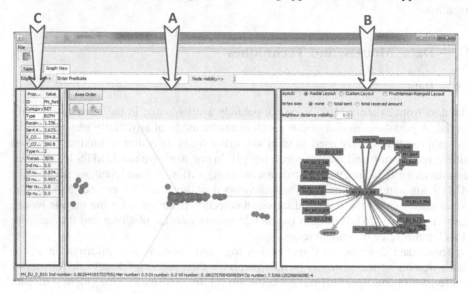

Fig. 2. The main window of MMTViewer

4.2.1.   The RadViz-Based View

The main view is a RadViz visualization [3] of the MMTS users. Its goal is to highlight groups of users with similar "transaction" behavior.

The Radviz is a non-linear multi-dimensional visualization technique that can map n-dimensional data into 2-dimensional space. The analyzed attributes are represented as dimension nodes placed around the perimeter of a circle. Then the objects are displayed as points inside the circle, with their positions determined by a metaphor from physics: each point is connected by n springs to the n respective dimension nodes. The stiffness of each spring is proportional to the value of the corresponding attribute. Thus, the point is located at the position where the spring forces are in equilibrium. Prior to visualization, all used attribute values are normalized. The objects set close to some dimension node have higher values for the corresponding attribute then for the others. For example, analyzing Fig. 3 it is possible to conclude that the merchant payments and individual transfers are prevailing among all other end user's financial operations, furthermore their quantity is comparable. The important feature of the Radviz technique is that it supports visualizing all dimensions of a dataset at once and is very useful when searching for clusters and outliers in multidimensional data. It can be effectively used as clustering tool that is characterized by low complexity $O(n)$.

We suggest using the following attributes of the user as dimension anchors because these properties are commonly used in detecting anomalous activity both in financial systems and scientific research tools [2, 6, 8, 20] and can rather exactly describe the "transaction" behavior of the user:

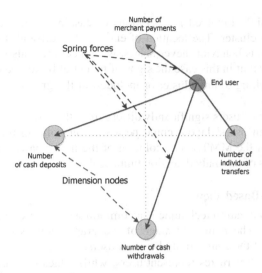

Fig. 3. Schema of the RadViz-based visualization of user transaction-based behavior

- a number of individual transfers for a given period of time;
- a number of cash deposit operations for a given period of time;
- a number of cash withdrawal operations for a given period of time;
- average amount of individual transfers for a given period of time;
- average amount of cash deposit operations for a given period of time;
- average amount of cash withdrawal operations for a given period of time;
- minimum and maximum amount of individual transfers for a given period of time;
- minimum and maximum amount of cash deposit operations for a given period of time;
- minimum and maximum amount of cash withdrawal operations for a given period of time.

As the major problem of the RadViz visualization is an appropriate selection of the dimension nodes' layout which determines the quality of the posterior visualization and ability to detect clusters [7], we use the arrangement of the anchors given in Table 1 as default. However, we implemented a mechanism that enables a user to adjust the layout of dimension nodes by selecting them from the predefined list and setting their order.

Table 1. Default order of dimension nodes in RadViz-based view

Order	Dimension node
0	a number of individual transfers for a given period of time
1	a number of deposit operations for a given period of time
2	a number of withdrawal operations for a given period of time

The MMTS subscribers are displayed as colored points inside the unit circle. The color is used to encode their role in the MMTS. We suppose that users having the same role should merge in clusters, showing thus similar behavior. For example, retailers who are mainly involved in operations of cashing in/out customers mobile wallet should form a cluster. The location of end users is difficult to predict as they can show rather various behavior, nevertheless, we expect them also to be grouped in clusters. We consider that in this case the signs of potential fraud could be as follows:

• a user does not belong to any cluster or included in the group of the users having another role;

• location of a group of users significantly differs from the rest.

These anomalies in users' layout could be a starting point in the analysis of the transaction activity in the MMTS. The coloring of the nodes based on the users' role simplifies the process of anomaly detection immensely.

4.2.2.   The Graph-Based View

The graph-based visualization technique is a common way for presenting transactions in financial systems. The main advantage of the graph view is that it emphasizes structural properties of the connectivity between users.

In the tool the graph vertexes represent users, while edges – transactions between them. As mentioned above in our case studies, a user has only one mobile account associated with him, therefore we do not display mobile account as a separate vertex connected with the user. However, if the user has several accounts we suggest to aggregate them into one meta-node preserving all input and output links in order to improve readability of the generated image.

Color is used to encode the role of the user in the MMTS as well as the transaction type. Both color schemes were created using Color-Brewer2 [5]. The transaction types that are frequently used in detection of suspicious activity such as cash withdrawal, deposit and individual money transfers are encoded with color-blind safe colors. The shape of the vertex depends on whether the user is only transaction sender (diamond), receiver (ellipse) or both (rectangle). This feature can simplify the detection of subscribers whose accounts are used only for cash withdrawal or deposit operations. If the user is linked with another user by a set of transactions of the same type then they are displayed as one edge, whose thickness is determined by their quantity. The size of the graph vertex could be determined by a sum of received and sent amounts for a given period of time. We consider that this option helps to discover subscribers, who participate in large cash flows.

To support visual exploration of the data, we implemented the following interaction techniques. Flexible *filtering* mechanism allows specifying different complex logical expressions to filter data. *Linking and brushing* effect can be applied in order to highlight contacts of the MMTS user. When switched to this mode, it is possible to select the user by clicking on the corresponding node, this will make all input and output links visible while the rest will be hidden. The combination of this technique with filtering mechanism allows focusing on particular user transactions with given characteristics. Apart from *tooltip* that gives only brief information about the object, i.e. transaction type, its sender and receivers, etc., the user can get detailed information on every element of the graph (node or vertex) shown in table view by clicking on it. This information includes subscriber's id, role, number of transactions, total amount, minimum and maximum transaction amounts, transaction time, etc. This informational display is updated whenever a particular graph node or edge is selected.

We also implemented two graph layouts: radial and based on scatter plot (Fig. 4).

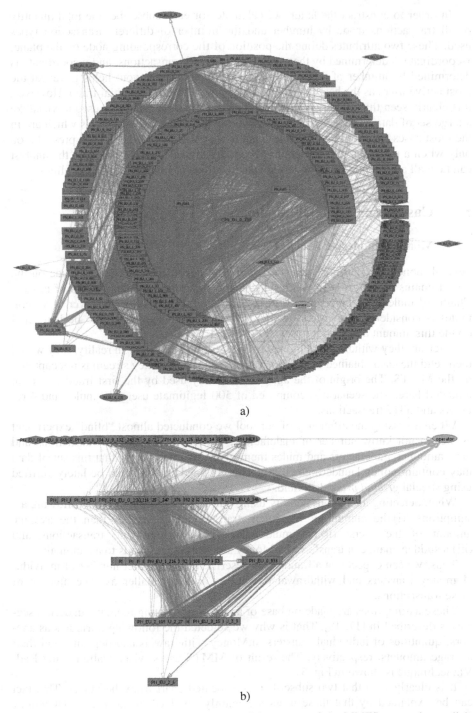

a)

b)

Fig. 4. Graph-based representation of the financial contacts of the MMTS user using radial layout (a) and scatter plot-based layout (b)

In order to construct the latter, we calculate for each subscriber the total quantity of all transactions made by him/her and the number of different transaction types used. These two attributes define the position of the corresponding node on the plane: x-coordinate is determined by the total quantity of all transactions, and y-coordinate is determined by number of different transaction types. This layout helps to reveal the most active users as the heightened activity can be a sign of potential fraud. However, it is clearly seen that these two graphical data presentation cannot be used to visualize a large set of data as generated image is overloaded with lines and labels which are in the most cases are simply unreadable. That is why we suggest using such presentation only when a particular set of users has been already selected. In this case the analyst can take all advantages of graph-based visualization for investigating users' links.

5   Case Studies and Discussion

5.1   Money Laundering Misuse Case

Several money laundering schemes exist. In this paper, the emphasis is made on the use of chains of mules. Using *mules* enables to hide the fraudulent origin of money. Chains of mules may be composed of several layers. Here, only one layer of several mules is considered. Fraudsters owning a certain amount of money to be laundered divide this amount and send it to several mules.

Later on, they withdraw this money from a complicit retailer. In reality, they would then send the cash obtained to another fraudster, but this money stream is not captured by the MMTS. The origin of the amount of money used by the first fraudster is not modeled here. The scenario is composed of 500 legitimate users, 10 mules and 4 retailers and 5317 transactions.

When assessing the efficiency of our tool we conducted almost "blind" experiment as we do not know number of malefactors, number of fraudulent transactions and their amounts, malefactors and mules themselves. We only know that this set of data may contain money laundering activity. The obtained results could be lately verified using special *ground proof* data field.

When detecting anomalous activity using our tool, we considered the following assumptions: (i) the amount of fraudulent transactions is smaller than the average amount of the users; (ii) the mules also perform legitimate transactions and (iii) a sudden change in transferred mMoney amounts corresponds to an anomaly.

Thus, we can expect that a fraudster is described by (i) greater number of individual money transfers and withdrawal operations and (ii) smaller average amount of these transactions.

These assumptions are made on base of analysis of existing money laundering scenarios described in [17, 18]. That is why we selected the following attributes as anchors: quantities of individual transfers, mMoney withdrawals and deposits, and their average amounts, respectively. The result of MMTS users' visualization using RadViz technique is shown in Fig. 5.

It is clearly seen that two subscribers are located apart from the others. This fact can be explained by that these users are mainly involved in the individual money transfers.

Additionally, from the graph-based view we see that one of them only sends money and another - only receives money. Further analysis of their contacts shows that these two subscribers (PN_FR1 and PN_FR2) are connected with each other via a set of users (Fig. 6). According to this, we can conclude that PN_FR1 and PN_FR2 could be potential fraudsters and the subscribers connected with them are the mules.

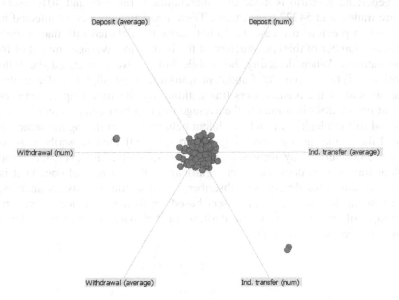

Fig. 5. RadViz visualization of MMTS users in money laundering scenario

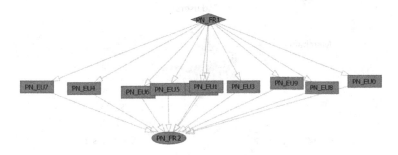

Fig. 6. RadViz visualization of MMTS users in money laundering scenario

5.2   Behavioral Fraud Case Study

Behavioral frauds occur when the behavior of the fraudster is superimposed on the legitimate user's one. Both actors use the mobile device to carry out transactions in the same window of time. In this paper, we consider two types of such fraud. The first one corresponds to a botnet which is deployed on several mobile devices. The malicious program carries out several transfers towards mules who withdraw the money within 72 hours after its reception. This scheme is rather similar to the money laundering scheme except that the amounts involved are not the same, there is no complicit retailer, and the mules are used here to hide the destination of the stolen money and not its origin. Moreover, the fraudulent transactions are initiated by the malicious programs. The second case corresponds to a theft. The mobile device is stolen and the fraudster then tries to withdraw money several times during a short range of time before the phone's theft is reported and the phone is deactivated.

The generated scenario is made of 2 merchants, 6 retailers and 4010 users, 4 of which are mules, and 54222 transactions. There are 3 thieves and 39 infected mobile devices. As in previous use case we do not know the detailed information on simulated frauds: number of thieves, structure of the botnet and average amount of fraudulent transactions. When detecting the mobile botnet, we considered the following assumptions: (i) the amount of fraudulent transactions is slightly inferior than the average amount of the regular users transactions, (ii) the time elapsed between two fraudulent transactions is similar to the average interval between two legitimate transactions and (iii) the legitimate and fraudulent behavior occur during the same window of time. Like in the money laundering scenario, the infected subscribers as well as mules are characterized by increased transaction quantity. However, the amount of fraudulent transactions does not differ significantly from a normal one. That is why we use only attributes describing subscriber's transaction activity as anchors. The RadViz visualization of the MMTS users based on their transaction activity reveals four groups of users exposing similarities in behavior - *Retailers, Merchants, End users 1, End users 2* (Fig. 7).

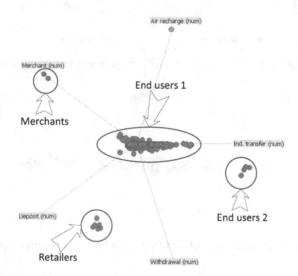

Fig. 7. RadViz visualization of MMTS users in the behavior fraud scenario

Groups *Retailers* and *Merchants* consist of retailers who are involved only in withdrawal and deposit operations, and merchants, respectively; group *End users 1*, the most numerous, consists of the subscribers who mostly uniformly make transactions of different types. Users belonging to the fourth group *End users 2* have individual money transfers significantly prevailing over transactions of other types. The link analysis of the users shows that apart from individual transfers they make numerous withdrawal operations (Fig. 8a). These two facts allow us to conclude that these users are mules whose accounts are used to cash out mMoney from the mWallets. In order to detect a set of subscribers with infected mobile devices we filtered out all transactions that are not sent to the mules and this enabled us to detect the botnet. Its structure is presented in Fig. 8b.

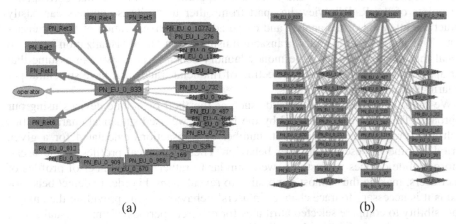

(a)   (b)

Fig. 8. Detection of mobile botnet: contacts of the mule (a) and botnet structure (b)

However, we failed to detect the theft of mobile devices. The detailed analysis of the raw data showed that the values of attributes selected as RadViz anchors of the compromised users are comparable to the ones of the subscribers using the MMTS comparatively rare during the selected period of time. And as the result their behavior is similar to the behavior of legal end users and they are in the group *End users 1*. Meanwhile it changes dramatically if observing his/her behavior in dynamics as legal activity fully stops.

5.3   Discussion

When choosing visualization technique for representation of the MMTS users and their transactions we aimed to produce a rather compact generalized view on users and their behavior, to divide them into relatively small groups uniting according to the similarities in their behavior and, thus, to decrease the amount of data to be investigated. We assumed that MMTS users could have similar behavior described in terms of average transaction amount, number of transactions and their types for a given period of time. Uniting them into groups allows focusing on these characteristics and determining subgroups or users in the group exposing anomalous behavior. Therefore, analysis of such groups could be a starting point in the investigation of the financial frauds of any type. The RadViz technique could be considered as a clustering tool that may be effectively used to solve this task. Its advantages such as low computational complexity ($O(n)$) and obvious representation of results of clustering procedure overweight its disadvantages which could be partly eliminated by providing a security officer a flexible mechanism for axis setup and layout.

Our experiments showed that the approach for analysis of the MMTS user behavior based on RadViz visualization used in conjunction with graph-based presentation of their transactions can be used effectively for money laundering scheme and botnet detection. These financial frauds are characterized by usage of mules, whose behavior usually significantly differs from ordinary users. Their accounts are used only as receivers of individual transfers and withdrawal operations, that means that corresponding points of the RadViz view lie apart from other users. These outliers can easily attract the attention of the analyst and cause additional investigation of their transactions. The analysis of the mules' transaction using graph-based visualization is able to reveal the botnet structure or the money-laundry scheme. Thus, we can assume that our approach can be effective in detection of financial frauds that have structural peculiarities involving usage of mules.

We failed to detect behavior frauds such as the theft of mobile devices using our approach. This failure is explained by the fact that we used statistical characteristics such as average transaction amount, number of transactions calculated for a given period of time to describe the user behavior. These statistical profiles of the users, whose mobile devices were stolen, were similar to rather large number of profiles of other users, making thus almost impossible to reveal them. In order to detect behavior frauds it is necessary to trace changes in users' behavior in time providing the analyst a possibility to compare selected attributes for different periods of time. Visualization techniques with time axes such as timelines or heat map with time axes enables historical analysis of data and could be used to monitor dynamics in users' behavior. However, the graphical representation of sufficiently large number of the MMTS users on one screen can cause certain difficulties in the analysis of their behavior due to illegible details of the generated image. Application of clustering techniques based on analysis of users' attributes and used to reduce data dimension can face the same difficulties as our approach. The possible solution of the problem within our approach is the usage of animated graphical data representation. Animation of user's location on RadViz visualization of the users and highlighting its trace if the changes in his/her behavior are significant can assist the analyst to spot a strange behavior.

6   Conclusions

The analysis of the state-of-art in fraud detection techniques in the mobile money transfer services showed that link analysis of subscribers' transactions using interactive graph-based data presentation is the most widely used visualization technique. It allows the analyst implementing link analysis of the user's contacts visually as well as applying graph-theoretic algorithms in order to discover structural peculiarities such as bridges and cliques. We proposed to form metaphoric presentation of the MMTS subscriber behavior according to his/her transaction activity. The user's activity is assessed using average amount of transactions, their quantity and usage of transactions of different type. This approach allows determining clusters of users exhibiting similar behavior and outliers. The latter is considered as a starting point of transaction analysis supported by traditional graph-based presentation of subscribers' transactions. However, the experiments implemented using the special synthetic simulator showed that our approach is able to detect fraud schemes that cause long term changes in the average behavior of the MMTS subscribers or characterized by the specific behavior of the fraud scheme participants. In order to improve the efficiency of the proposed approach we defined future directions of the research concerning with exploration of the appropriate selection and arrangement of the dimension nodes in RadViz visualization and elaboration of the dynamic data presentation.

Acknowledgements. This research is being supported by grants of the Russian Foundation of Basic Research (projects 13-01-00843, 13-07-13159, 14-07-00697, 14-07-00417), the Program of fundamental research of the Department for Nanotechnologies and Informational Technologies of the Russian Academy of Sciences (2.2), by Government of the Russian Federation, Grant 074-U01, the State contract #14.604.21.0033, and the project ENGENSEC of the TEMPUS program.

References

1. Achemlal, M., et al.: Scenario requirements. Technical report. MASSIF FP7-257475 project (2011)
2. Al-Khatib, A.: Electronic Payment Fraud Detection Techniques. World of Computer Science and Information Technology Journal (WCSIT) 2, 137–141 (2012)
3. Ankerst, M., Berchtold, S., Keim, D.A.: Similarity Clustering of Dimensions for an Enhanced Visualization of Multidimensional Data. In: 1998 IEEE Symposium on Information Visualization (INFOVIS 1998), pp. 52–60. IEEE Computer Society (1998)
4. Chang, R., Ghoniem, M., Kosara, R., Ribarsky, W., Yang, J., Suma, E., Ziemkiewicz, C., Kern, D., Sudjianto, A.: WireVis: Visualization of Categorical, Time-Varying Data From Financial Transactions. In: IEEE Symposium on Visual Analytics Science and Technology (VAST 2007), pp. 155–162 (2007)
5. ColorBrew2, http://colorbrewer2.org
6. Delloite. Visual Analytics: Revealing Corruption, Fraud, Waste, and Abuse. Presentation of the Forensic Center,
   http://www.slideshare.net/DeloitteForensicCenter/visual-analytics-revealing-corruption-fraud-waste-and-abuse-13958016
7. Di Caro, L., Frias-Martinez, V., Frias-Martinez, E.: Analyzing the Role of Dimension Arrangement for Data Visualization in Radviz. In: Zaki, M.J., Yu, J.X., Ravindran, B., Pudi, V. (eds.) PAKDD 2010. LNCS, vol. 6119, pp. 125–132. Springer, Heidelberg (2010)
8. Fiserv. Financial Crime Risk Management solution,
   http://www.fiserv.com/risk-compliance/
   financial-crime-risk-management.htm
9. Gaber, C., Hemery, B., Achemlal, M., Pasquet, M., Urien, P.: Synthetic logs generator for fraud detection in mobile transfer services. In: Int. Conference on Collaboration Technologies and Systems (CTS 2013), pp. 174–179 (2013)
10. Jack, W., Tavneet, S., Townsend, R.: Monetary Theory and Electronic Money: Reflections on the Kenyan Experience. Economic Quarterly 96-1, 83–122 (2010)
11. Keim, D.A., Andrienko, G., Fekete, J.-D., Görg, C., Kohlhammer, J., Melançon, G.: Visual Analytics: Definition, Process, and Challenges. In: Kerren, A., Stasko, J.T., Fekete, J.-D., North, C. (eds.) Information Visualization. LNCS, vol. 4950, pp. 154–175. Springer, Heidelberg (2008)
12. Korczak, J., Łuszczyk, W.: Visual Exploration of Cash Flow Chains. In: The Federated Conference on Computer Science and Information Systems, pp. 41–46 (2011)
13. Kotenko, I., Novikova, E.: VisSecAnalyzer: A Visual Analytics Tool for Network Security Assessment. In: Cuzzocrea, A., Kittl, C., Simos, D.E., Weippl, E., Xu, L. (eds.) CD-ARES Workshops 2013. LNCS, vol. 8128, pp. 345–360. Springer, Heidelberg (2013)

14. Lin, L., Cao, L., Zhang, C.: The fish-eye visualization of foreign currency exchange data streams. In: Asia-Pacific Symposium on Information Visualisation, pp. 91–96 (2005)
15. Marghescu, D.: Multidimensional Data Visualization Techniques for Financial Performance Data: A Review, TUCS Technical Report No 810, University of Turku, Finland (2007)
16. Merrit, C.: Mobile Money Transfer Services: The Next Phase in the Evolution in Person-to-Person Payments. Technical report. Retail Payments Risk Forum (2010)
17. [FinTRAC] Money Laundering and Terrorist Financing Trends in FINTRAC Cases Disclosed Between 2007 and 2011. FINTRAC Typologies and Trends Reports (2012)
18. [FATF] Money Laundering using New Payment Methods. FATF Report (2010)
19. Neural-technologies. MinotaurTM Fraud Detection Software - Finance Sector, http://www.neuralt.com/fraud_detection_software.html
20. Nice Actimize Integrated Fraud Management, http://www.niceactimize.com/index.aspx?page=solutionsfraud
21. Novikova, E., Kotenko, I.: Analytical Visualization Techniques for Security Information and Event Management. In: 21st Euromicro International Conference on Parallel, Distributed and Network-Based Processing (PDP 2013), pp. 519–525. IEEE Computer Society, Belfast (2013)
22. Okutyi, E.: Safaricom tightens security on M-Pesa with fraud management system (2012), http://www.humanipo.com/news/1341/Safaricom-tightens-security-on-M-Pesa-with-Fraud-Management-system
23. Orange Money dépasse les 4 millions de clients et lance ses services en Jordanie et à Maurice (2012) (in French), http://www.orange.com/fr/presse/communiques/communiques-2012/Orange-Money-depasse-les-4-millions-de-clients-et-lance-ses-services-en-Jordanie-et-a-l-Ile-Maurice
24. Prefuse Information Visualization toolkit, http://prefuse.org/
25. Rieke, R., Coppolino, L., Hutchison, A., Prieto, E., Gaber, C.: Security and Reliability Requirements for Advanced Security Event Management. In: Kotenko, I., Skormin, V. (eds.) MMM-ACNS 2012. LNCS, vol. 7531, pp. 171–180. Springer, Heidelberg (2012)
26. Ron, D., Shamir, A.: Quantitative Analysis of the Full Bitcoin Transaction Graph. In: Sadeghi, A.-R. (ed.) FC 2013. LNCS, vol. 7859, pp. 6–24. Springer, Heidelberg (2013)
27. SAS Fraud detection solutions, http://www.sas.com/offices/europe/uk/industries/banking/fraud-detection.html (viewed on the October 10, 2013)
28. Schreck, T., Tekusova, T., Kohlhammer, J., Fellner, D.: Trajectory-based visual analysis of large financial time series data. ACMSIGKDD Explorations Newsletter 9(2), 30–37 (2007)
29. Second quarter of the financial year 2012/2013. Quarterly sector statistics report. Communications Commission of Kenya (2012)
30. Shneiderman, B.: Dynamic queries for visual information seeking. In: The Craft of Information Visualization: Readings and Reflections, pp. 14–21. Morgan Kaufman (2003)
31. Wattenberg, M.: Visualizing the stock market. In: CHI Extended Abstracts on Human Factors in Computing Systems, pp. 188–189 (1999)
32. Westphal, C.R.: Patterns for Financial Intelligence Units (FIUs) and Anti-Money Laundering (AML) Operations, http://support.visualanalytics.com/technicalArticles/whitePaper/pdf/VAI%20AML%20FIU%20Patterns%20Presentation.pdf
33. Ziegler, H., Jenny, M., Gruse, T., Keim, D.A.: Visual Market Sector Analysis for Financial Time Series Data. In: IEEE Symposium on Visual Analytics Science and Technology (VAST), October 25-26, pp. 83–90 (2010)

A Review of Security Requirements Engineering Methods with Respect to Risk Analysis and Model-Driven Engineering

Denisse Muñante, Vanea Chiprianov, Laurent Gallon, and Philippe Aniorté

LIUPPA University of Pau, France
{denisseyessica.munantearzapalo,laurent.gallon,
vanea.chiprianov,philippe.aniorte}@univ-pau.fr

Abstract. One of the most important aspects that help improve the quality and cost of secure information systems in their early stages of the development lifecycle is Security Requirements Engineering (SRE). However, obtaining such requirements is non-trivial. One domain dealing also with eliciting security requirements is Risk Analysis (RA). Therefore, we perform a review of SRE methods in order to analyse which ones are compatible with RA processes. Moreover, the transition from these early security requirements to security policies at later stages in the lifecycle is generally non-automatic, informal and incomplete. To deal with such issues, model-driven engineering (MDE) uses formal models and automatic model transformations. Therefore, we also review which SRE methods are compatible with MDE approaches. Consequently, our review is based on criteria derived partially from existing survey works, further enriched and specialized in order to evaluate the compatibility of SRE methods with the disciplines of RA and MDE. It summarizes the evidence regarding this issue so as to improve understanding and facilitate evaluating and selecting SRE methods.

Keywords: Security requirements engineering, risk analysis, model-driven engineering, review.

1 Introduction

Millions of dollars in losses are the result of attacks on unsecured systems. Many security breaches occur in software because errors and misspecifications in analysis, design and implementation [1]. Hence, information security is gaining more and more emphasis in recent years. In this sense, security requirements engineering (SRE) is an appropriate means to elucidate and model security requirements in the analysis stage in software development. Moreover, some works, such as UMLsec [7], SecureUML [8], MODELO [22] ..., allow us to define security aspects (policies) in the design and the software architecture stages. However, the transition from security requirements to security policies is generally non-automatic, unstructured and informal causing information loss, and thus the generation of incorrect security policies. To avoid these negative consequences, an automatic generation of

S. Teufel et al. (Eds.): CD-ARES 2014, LNCS 8708, pp. 79–93, 2014.

security policies starting from KAOS [11] is proposed in [25]. Despite of the fact that this work helps obtaining security policies of access control in a more formal way, it does not formalise its process of generation of security policies.

Model-driven engineering (MDE) encourages efficient use of models in several domains. Model-driven architecture (MDA) [20] uses model in the software development process and proposes three levels of abstraction: computation independent model (CIM), platform independent model (PIM) and platform specific model (PSM). A CIM presents what the system is expected to do (i.e. requirements), a PIM represents how the system reach its requirements out technical details (i.e. design and architecture) and a PSM combines the specification in PIMs with details required to stipulate how a system uses a particular type of platform. To build a software system, a series of transformations is performed: transformation from CIM to PIM, transformation from PIM to PSM, and transformation from PSM to code. To benefit from MDE advantages, some works have already been done to model Requirements Engineering (RE) as CIM. Tao et al. [21] review such approaches with respect to MDE principles, in particular on the possibility of (semi)automatic transformation from RE definition to PIM. In contrast, in this paper, we focus our study on SRE, i.e. regarding specific security concerns in requirement engineering, in order to analyse the compatibility of SRE methods with MDE approaches.

SRE methods often offer in practice just a general list of security features, which are implementation mechanisms rather than security requirements [26]. On the other hand, risk analysis (RA) is the activity of analyzing threat, vulnerability and impact on each component of the system. Therefore, RA could be used to elicit a more complete list of security requirements. So it is necessary to combine SRE methodologies with RA methodologies. Several works have already been proposed this: KAOS [25], Secure Tropos [24] [27], CORAS [15] [28].

To sum up, we investigate three disciplines. RA comprises processes that can help identify security requirements early in the development lifecycle of information systems. The definition of these security requirements is dealt with by the discipline of SRE. To enable automatic, formal transition from early stage requirements to later-stage security policies, we investigate the field of MDE. Therefore, the paper's contribution is a summary and a comparison of state of the art security requirements engineering methods according to risk analysis demands and model-driven exigencies. Consequently, this survey helps to improve understanding and facilitates the evaluation and selection of SRE methods as part of an MDE approach based on a RA process.

The remainder of this paper is organized as follows. Section 2 presents method of review. An analysis and discussion is presented in Section 3. Finally, Section 4 concludes this paper and gives perspectives.

2   Method of Review

Our method of review is based on two steps. Firstly, we identify and select criteria to classify SRE methods, related to MDE and RA points of view. Secondly, we identify and select SRE methods which we classify using our criteria.

As basis, we start by selecting from Karpati paper [2] criteria which are related to MDE. Karpati paper is a tertiary study (i.e. review of review papers) which defines groups of criteria, called dimensions, to categorize SRE methods. These criteria are extracted from all of those SRE review papers, up to 2010, they find in their study. We enrich this set of criteria with new criteria selected from more recent papers, in particular Salini paper [5] (2012). Salini is a review paper that analyses and compares SRE methods in order to guide developers to adopt SRE methods for software systems. None of these papers are MDE-oriented. Despite of this, after an analysis, we succeded to identify some criteria which are related to MDE principles (5 criteria). They are detailled in section 3.3.

We also indentify and select RA criteria mainly based on Fabian review paper [3]. Fabian paper defines a conceptual framework (CF) in order to categorize SRE methods. This CF establishes a vocabulary and the interrelations between the different notions used in security engineering. Among these different security notions, we select those which are related to a RA process (8 criteria). They are detailled in section 3.2.

Then, we select the list of SRE methods that we review starting from three SRE methods review papers: Fabian [3], Mellado [4] and Salini [5]. Fabian and Mellado are the most recent review papers taken into account by Karpati. Salini is a review paper more recent than Karpati paper. Fabian paper present a comparison of 18 fully developed SRE methods, classified using its conceptual framework. Mellado performs a systematic review on the SRE litterature of the period 2004 - 2009. It identifies 22 initiatives, and compares them using an analytical framework. Finaly, Salini classifies 11 different methods. Therefore, we are confident that our list contains most of SRE methods.

From these 32 distinct methods, we considered only the SRE methods that focus strictly on requirements. Although, some works considered UMLsec [7] and SecureUML [8] as SRE methods, we did not consider them because they are used in the system design. We employ the same reasoning for all the methods focus on later stages of the system development. In the same way, we did not study SRE methods that do not generate any analysis artifact such as agile methods, capability maturity model (CMM) methods, etc. Finally, the result of this selection is represented by 13 SRE methods. We evaluate these selected SRE methods and present an analysis of them in the next section.

3   Analysis and Discussion

In this section, we present our analysis and discussion of SRE methods. This analysis is divided in three parts. The first part introduces *the reviewed SRE methods*. The second one presents an evaluation of these SRE methods with respect to criteria corresponding to *risk analysis*. And, the third one presents an evaluation of these SRE methods with respect to criteria corresponding to *model-driven engineering*. For each part of our analysis, we present the criteria we used, a comparative table between SRE methods according to these criteria and a discussion of this comparison.

Notice that a dash symbol (-) in cells of the comparative tables implies that the method does not consider the related criterion. In contrast, the mark symbol (x) in cells indicates that the related criterion is considered by the method. Some criteria are described in a textual manner. Moreover, a table entry labelled with ⊇ means that the notion defined in the considered method is used in a narrower sense than the related criteria.

3.1   The Security Requirements Engineering Methods Reviewed

In this section, we introduce the reviewed SRE methods. For this, we give a brief introduction of each SRE method. Then, we summarize these methods focussing on the main characteristics that are relevant to our study.

As we mentioned, we study 13 SRE methods:

(a) *Security quality requirements engineering methodology (SQUARE) [9]:* is a comprehensive methodology, which consists of 9 steps. Its aim is to integrate security requirements engineering into software development processes.
(b) *Misuse cases [10]:* extends use cases to represent behaviour not wanted in the system. Ordinary use cases represent requirements, security cases represent security requirements, and misuse cases represent security threats.
(c) *Keep all objectives satisfied (KAOS) [11] with anti-models:* extends KAOS to include the elaboration of security requirements using anti-models. An anti-model is constructed using obstacles. An obstacle negates existing goals of the system.
(d) *Secure Tropos [12]:* extends Tropos, which is a software development methodology, with new concepts to cover security modelling, such as the *security features* of the system-to-be.
(e) *Secure i* [13]:* extends i*-modeling framework with modeling and analysis of security trade-offs. Secure i* focuses on the alignment of security requirements with other requirements.
(f) *Goal-based req. analysis method (GBRAM) [14]:* allows to use goal- and scenario-driven req. engineering methods to formulate privacy and security policies.
(g) *CORAS [15]:* is a model-based method for security risk analysis. CORAS consists of eight steps, provides a customized language for threat and risk modelling, and comes with detailed guidelines explaining how the language should be used.
(h) *Tropos goal-risk framework [16]:* extends Tropos methodology to assess risk based on trust relations among actors. Risk analysis is used to evaluate alternative goals and to assess countermeasures to mitigate risks.
(i) *Model-based information system security risk management (ISSRM) [17]:* proposes a risk analysis process that consists of four steps.
(j) *Abuse Frames [29]:* is based on problem frame to define anti requirements (i.e. requirements for malicious users) and abuse frame to analyse security threats.

(k) *Security engineering process using patterns (SEPP) [30] [31]:* is a security engineering process based on security problem frames and associated solution approaches.They are defined using patterns.

(l) *Security requirements engineering framework (SREF) [32]:* is based on constructing a context for the system using a problem-oriented notation to represent security requirements as constraints, and to develop and evaluate satisfaction arguments for the security requirements.

(m) *Security requirements engineering process (SREP) [18]:* is an iterative and incremental process. Furthermore, SREP is asset-based, risk driven, and, following the Common Criteria (CC) supports the reuse of security requirements, as well as the reuse of knowledge on assets, threats, and countermeasures.

Following Fabian et al. [3], we classify the reviewed SRE methods using:

- *Type of method:* indicates the global/general type of a SRE method or a SRE process.
- *Method/Process:* corresponds to the name of a SRE method or a SRE process (hereinafter SRE method).

Following Fabian et al. [3], Mellado et al. [4] and Salini et al. [5], we give the main characteristics of these methods:

- *Contribution:* indicates the purpose of each selected SRE method. This characteristic is divided in *integration of standards* and *main contributions* [4].
- *Security Properties:* indicates the security properties accomplish by a SRE method [3]. This characteristic is divided in: *CIA* corresponding to confidentiality, integrity and availability security properties, and *Other* related to other security properties such as non-repudiation, authentication, and others.

In Table 1, the first, second and fourth columns summarize the reviewed SRE methods. According to the third column (integration standards criterion), three methods only consider the integration of a standard. CORAS considers the ISO 31000 standard, which is related to risk management. ISRRM uses the ISO 27001 standard, which is related to information security management. Abuse Frames considers the ISO 13335. And, SEPP and SREP include Common Criteria to propose a software lifecycle model.

According to this criterion, CORAS is only the method which are close to our analysis based on a risk analysis method.

Moreover, SQUARE is reported to be used by a few organizations [9]. It means that SQUARE is validated in the both academic and industrial context. Although we did not found a similar report for the other SRE methods, it does not imply that they are not employed for any organization (i.e. within an industrial context).

According to the fifth and sixth columns, almost all the SRE methods address security properties (8 SRE methods). SEPP and SREP address partially security properties, i.e. SEPP only addresses confidentiality and integrity security

Table 1. Relevant characteristics of security requirements engineering methods for our study

Type of method	Method / Process	Integration Standards	Main Contributions	CIA	Other
			Contribution	**Secu Props**	
Multilateral approaches	SQUARE	-	SQUARE: 9-step process for eliciting, categorizing and prioritizing security requirements.	x	x
UML-based approaches	Misuse cases	-	Executable misuse cases (UML extension for modeling threats in use case diagrams).	x	x
Goal-oriented approaches	KAOS	-	Use of antimodels to elaborate security requirements.	x	x
	Secure Tropos	-	Extension of Tropos methodology. Secure dependencies.	x	x
	Secure i*	-	i* framework for alignment of security requirements in organizations.	x	x
	GBRAM	-	Formulate privacy and security policies using heuristic activities.	-	-
Risk analysis-based approaches	CORAS	ISO 31000	Three artefacts (language, tool and process) to support a risk analysis activity.	-	-
	Tropos goal-risk	-	To assess risk based on trust relations among actors.	x	x
	ISSRM	ISO 27001	Security RE process: 4-step. It uses i* RE techniques.	x	x
Problem frame-based approaches	Abuse frames	ISO 13335	To define anti-requirements and abuse frames.	-	-
	SEPP	CC	To define Security Problem Frames (security requirements) and Concretized Security Proble Frames (security problem solutions).	-	x
	SREF	-	To analyse security goals, argumentation and software evolution.	x	x
Common Criteria	SREP	CC	Sw lifecycle model with multiple stages based on CC.	x	-

properties, whilst SREP only addresses confidentiality, integrity and availability (CIA) security properties. And, GBRAM, CORAS and Abuse Frames do not address security properties. Therefore, in terms of security properties, these 8 methods are the most compatible.

3.2 SRE Methods and Risk Analysis

In this section, we analyse the reviewed SRE methods with respect to criteria corresponding to a risk analysis process. For this, we present a set of criteria

Table 2. Correspondence between ISO 27005 terms and terms of the CF

ISO 27005 terms	CF Fabian et al.
Security objectives	Security goal
Security mechanism control	Security requirement
Interested parties	Stakeholder
Criteria definition (risk evaluation, impact and risk acceptance criteria)	Domain Knowledge
Asset	Asset
Threat	Threat
Vulnerability	Vulnerability
Risk	Risk

related to risk analysis, which are used to elaborate a comparative table. Finally, an analysis of this table is presented.

1) Criteria of comparison

As mentioned, our objective is to evaluate current SRE methods according to risk analysis. Among existing risk analysis approaches, we focus on the ISO 27005 [19] standard. ISO31000 talks about Risk Management covering concepts, definitions and methodology for a Risk Management process to be applied to any industry or activity. It is broad enough to be used by any activity touching the management of risks. ISO27005 talks about IT Risk Management. It uses the same framework described in 31000 and applies it to IT needs. It supports the general concepts specified in ISO/IEC 27001. It also revised and superseded ISO 13335. Common criteria defines concepts and principles of IT security evaluation. Security requirements can be defined, but mainly for an evaluation purpose. ISO 27005 takes into account Common Criteria. To sum up, ISO 27005 is the most recent IT Risk Management standard.

To choose our criteria, we employ the following method: Fristly, we select ISO 27005 terms as criteria using the list of terms resulting from the metrics analysis proposed by Mayer et al. [6]. This list of terms populates the first column of Table 2. Secondly, to reuse the analysis of SRE methods proposed by Fabian, we define a mapping between the previous selected criteria and the Fabian conceptual framework (CF). The terms of Fabian CF populates the second column of Table 2.

2) Comparison

Table 3 gives the result of the evaluation of SRE methods related to risk analysis criteria. Whe consider that a SRE method is totally compatible (or related) to the ISO 27005 risk analysis analysis process if it addresses all its concepts (i.e. all the criteria of Table 3). According to this table, the most compatible methods are *GBRAM* and *ISSRM* . So, these methods are compatible with ISO 27005 process.

Table 3. Evaluation of SRE methods related to Risk Analysis criteria

Method/ Process	Security goal	Security requirement	Stakeholder	Domain Knowledge	Asset	Threat	Vulnerability	Risk
				ISO 27005 criteria				
SQUARE	x	System req.	⊇ Client	-	-	x	-	x
Misuse cases	x	-	⊇ Actor	-	x	x	-	x
KAOS	x	x	⊇ Agent	Domain properties, expectation	-⊇ Object	x	x	-
Secure Tropos	Softgoal	cf. Security goal	⊇ Actor	-	-	x	x	x
Secure i*	Softgoal	cf. Security goal	⊇ Actor	-	x	x	x	-
GBRAM	x	x	x	-	Information	x	x	x
CORAS	x	-	-	Assumption	x	x	x	x
Tropos goal-risk	Softgoal	cf. Security goal	⊇ Actor	-	-	Event	-	x
ISSRM	Softgoal	cf. Security goal	⊇ Actor	Context	x	x	x	x
Abuse Frames	Sec. objective	Negated anti-req.	⊇ Biddable domain	-	x	x	x	-
SEPP	-	x	⊇ Biddable domain	Fact, assumption	⊇ Lexical domain, Phenomenon	x	-	-
SREF	x	x	⊇ Biddable domain	⊇ Fact, trust assumption	x	x	-	x
SREP	Sec. objective	x	-	Sec. objective	x	x	x	x

Moreover, the almost compatible methods are *KAOS, Secure Tropos, Secure i*, Abuse Frames, SREF* and *SREP*. Secure i* includes almost all the terms, risk is not considered as entity but this term is considered as an evaluated value of *risk level*, so we consider that Secure i* is compatible with ISO 27005. KAOS is similar to Secure i* because it does not consider the *risk* term. In contrast to Secure i*, KAOS and Abuse Frames do not quantify the *risk level* of a system. So, they are a little bit less compatible than Secure i*. However, KAOS can improve its compatibility by including a quantification method that adds information related to risks (such as impact and exploitability) in contrast to Abuse Frames. On the other hand, SREF does not include the *vulnerability* term, but this term can be included to improve this SRE method.

On the other hand, Secure Tropos does not specify assets, thus security goals are related only to system goals. In ISO 27005, the asset identification is an important activity because the later stages use the valuable assets in order to evaluate and to protect them. Consequently, Secure Tropos is not clearly compatible with ISO 27005.

Despite of stakeholders are interested parties to perform a risk analysis in ISO 27005 (i.e. they establish the context composed of risk analysis objectives, criteria of estimation risk, ..), the conceptual representation of stakeholders is not essential in ISO 27005. Therefore, SREP is compatible with ISO 27005 in spite of it does not consider stakeholders as a conceptual entity.

In our evaluation, we find that SQUARE, misuse cases, Tropos Goal-Risk and SEPP do not fulfill enough criteria to be compatible with ISO 27005. Notice that, for misuse cases and CORAS security requirement criterion is not included according to the Fabian analysis [3]. This criterion is important because it corresponds to the target resulting from a requirement engineering process. Finally, from our comparison, KAOS, Secure i*, GBRAM, ISSRM, SREF and SREP are compatible with risk analysis approaches.

3.3   SRE Methods and Model-Driven Engineering

In this section, we analyse the reviewed SRE methods with respect to criteria corresponding to model-driven engineering. For this, we present a set of criteria related to a model-driven approach, these criteria are used to elaborate a comparative table. Finally, an analysis of this table is presented.

1) Criteria of comparison
As mentioned, our objective is to evaluate current SRE methods according to model-driven concepts. For this, we identify and select some model-driven criteria with the aim of analysing the possibility of the selected SRE methods to be part of a model-based approach. Therefore, we selected the criteria proposed in [3], [4] and [5]:

- *Security RE tools (language, profile, technique, etc.):* describes the means to identify or elucidate security requirements [4]. Criterion included to analyse if Security RE tools can be formalized.
- *Model/Standard of Development:* indicates if there is a formal language as the basis of the method [4]. This criterion is used to analyse if there is a model or standard used by a SRE method.
- *Support for other development stages:* indicates which later stages in software development are supported by security requirements [4]. This criterion allows to analyse if it is possible to define a transition (e.g. an MDE automatic model transformation) between artifacts in different stages of software development.
- *Formality:* corresponds to formal validation of the method, i.e. if a method can evaluate its outputs [3].

Table 4. Evaluation of SRE methods related to Model-Driven Engineering criteria

Method / Process	Security RE tool (language, profile, technique, etc.)	Model/Standard of Development	Support for other development stages	Formality	Prototype
		MDE criteria			
SQUARE	Use/misuse cases, etc. (selection of elicitation technique)	-	Design, Testing	-	P-SQUARE tool (web application)
Misuse cases	Use/misuse cases	UML	Design		-
KAOS	KAOS + anti-models	Goal-oriented requirements	Not used	x	Objectiver (XML as the output format)
Secure Tropos	Tropos language, Secure Tropos	Agent oriented software development	Later requirements	x	SecTro (export diagram to XML)
Secure i*	Strategic Dependency and Strategic Rationale models	Agent oriented software development	Not used	x	Sistar and Serenity
GBRAM	Identify, elaborate, refine operationalized goals	Goal and scenario-driven requirements	Not used	-	SMaRT
CORAS	CORAS method	Modeling QFTP [1]	Not used	-	Coras
Tropos goal-risk	Risk analysis is used to evaluate alternative goals	Goal model	Later requirements	-	GR-tool
ISSRM	Risk analysis method	ISSRM domain model	Not used	-	
Abuse Frames	Anti-requirements and abuse frames	-	Not used	-	-
SEPP	Security problem frames and concretized security problem frames	UML profile	Not used	-	UML4PF support tool
SREF	System context and satisfaction arguments	ESR (Evolving Security Requirements) metamodel	Not used	-	OpenPF / De-creasoner
SREP	Use/misuse cases	-	Not used	-	-

[1] Quality Of Service and Fault Tolerance Characteristics And Mechanisms

– *Prototype:* indicates if there is a prototype (tool) that implements the corresponding SRE method [5]. Criterion used to know if the SRE method is not only conceptual.

We elaborate a comparative table, which is presented and analysed in the next section.

2) Comparison

In Table 4 gives the result of the evaluation of SRE methods related to a model-driven approach. We consider that a SRE method is totally compatible to a MDE approach if the requirement it produces can be described as a model (CIM). It means that the SRE method addresses all the criteria of Table 4. The first column shows the security requirement engineering tool, which considers languages, profiles, techniques or others, used by a SRE method to elucidate security requirements. The second column shows if a formal model/standard of development is proposed by SRE methods. These two first columns allow to analyse if it is possible to represent the SRE method's elements through formal models. As we can see, SQUARE, Abuse Frames and SREP do not have their own model or standard because they are processes that use existing techniques such as use/misuse cases or problem frames. Consequently, they can be compatible with MDE whether the used technique is compatible with MDE.

Moreover, the third column in Table 4 shows which later stages in systems development are supported by SRE methods. For a model-driven approach, this criterion allows to analyse if there is a way to derive from security requirements to another concepts corresponding to later stages, i.e. if a model transformation process is feasible. As we can see, security requirements derived from SQUARE, misuse cases, Secure Tropos or Tropos goal-risk can be used by the later stages such as design, testing and later requirements. Therefore, they are good candidates for being compatible with MDE approaches. However, this does not mean that the other methods have to be excluded. There are works that define a transition between development stages, for example, a correspondence between KAOS and SecureUML is proposed in [23] to define security policies related of access control. And, in [24] a mapping between Secure Tropos and UMLsec is proposed.

In an object-oriented environment, later requirements stage presents the system-to-be, as a part of the design stage. Hence, Secure Tropos and Tropos goal-risk are not the most appropriate but they propose some evidences to define model transformations. In contrast, SQUARE and misuse cases give means to define model transformations, whilst, for the other methods, we have to find a correspondence between security requirements and others artifacts from later stages of an object-oriented system development.

Moreover, we use the *formality* criterion to determine if an SRE method is validated formally. KAOS, Secure Tropos and Secure i* are validated formally. In a model-driven approach, we can say that these SRE methods are appropriate thanks to their level of formality. Additionally, the majority of methods implement a prototype (tool). It implies that they have been implemented and tested except misuse cases, ISSRM, Abuse Frames and SREP.

Finally, we can conclude, KAOS, Secure Tropos, Secure i* and Tropos goal-risk are the most compatible methods with MDE approaches. That is because, Secure Tropos accomplishes all the MDE criteria, and KAOS, Secure i* and Tropos goal-risk consider all but one criterion, the *support for other development stages* criterion for KAOS and Secure i* and the *formality* criterion for Tropos goal-risk. However, these SRE methods can be extended to included elements in order to improve their compatibility with MDE.

3.4 General Discussion

Returning to previous analysis, CORAS is close to our analysis because it is based on ISO 31000. However, CORAS, GBRAM and Abuse Frames do not address security properties while SEPP and SREP address partially security properties. Hence, the 8 others methods are the most compatible in terms od security properties. On the other hand, KAOS, Secure i*, GBRAM, ISSRM and SREP are compatible with risk analysis approaches, whilst KAOS, Secure Tropos, Secure i* and Tropos goal-risk are compatible with model-driven approaches. As we can see, KAOS and Secure i* are compatible with security properties, RA and MDE approaches. Therefore, we conclude that they can be integrated into a model-driven approach based on a risk analysis. Notice that, this result does not imply limiting the selection of SRE methods to KAOS or Secure i*. KAOS and Secure i* are the most compatible, but some other SRE methods can be adapted to improve their compatibility. For example, Secure Tropos or Tropos goal-risk could be extended to include elements related to ISO 27005. Similarly, GBRAM, ISSRM, SREF or SREP could be extended to include elements related to MDE approaches. Moreover, notice that, GBRAM does not address security properties. This could be a real drawback if we want to be able to model the security policy of a system.

Despite KAOS and Secure i* being the most compatible SRE methods for our study, these methods do not consider any technique to derive from security requirements at an early stage of the system development to security policies at later stages (e.g. design, architecture and implementation stages). Hence, in order to reach a totally compatibility, it is necessary to study this derivation technique and define a (semi)automatic model transformation. Such a model transformation will allow to prevent an incorrect, incomplete or informal definition of security policies.

4   Conclusions

We compared and discussed various types of Security Requirements Engineering (SRE) methods and processes. Our perspective of comparison and evaluation uses some criteria defined by previous works found in the literature. We have selected criteria according to a risk analysis process (namely, we use the ISO 27005 standard) and a model-driven approach. One objective of these criteria is to analyse which SRE methods can be used to (semi)automatically derive from security requirements at an early stage of system development lifecycle to later stages security policies. Another objective is to analyse which SRE methods can be used to evaluate/quantify the security/protection level of a system against attacks. Then, our analysis shows which SRE methods are suitable to be part of a model-based approach based on a risk analysis.

We conclude that *KAOS* and *Secure i** are the most compatible SRE methods with a model-driven approach because they use a model/standard of development and they are validated formally. Despite these methods not presenting all the risk analysis terms, we consider that extending the method to these concepts is feasible.

For future works, we will use this review to choose an SRE method, which will be part of a model-driven approach based on the risk analysis ISO 27005. Namely, we want to integrate this SRE method with MODELO [22], which is a UML profile that we proposed to build access control policies (i.e. OrBAC) at an abstract level. More precisely, we want to derive (semi)automatically the access control policy from the definition of these security requirements.

References

1. Anderson, R.: Security Engineering: A Guide to Building Dependable Distributed Systems. John Wiley and Sons (2001)
2. Karpati, P., Sindre, G., Opdahl, A.L.: Characterising and analysing security requirements modelling initiatives. In: Proceedings of the International Conference on Availability, Reliability and Security (ARES), pp. 710–715. IEEE Computer Society (2011)
3. Fabian, B., Gürses, S., Heisel, M., Santen, T., Schmidt, H.: A comparison of security requirements engineering methods. Requir. Eng. 15(1), 7–40 (2010)
4. Mellado, D., Blanco, C., Sánchez, L.E., Fernández-Medina, E.: A systematic review of security requirements engineering. Computer Standards & Interfaces 32(4), 153–165 (2010)
5. Salini, P., Kanmani, S.: Survey and analysis on Security Requirements Engineering. Computers & Electrical Engineering 38(6), 1785–1797 (2012)
6. Mayer, N., Dubois, E., Matulevicius, R., Heymans, P.: Towards a Measurement Framework for Security Risk Management. In: Modeling Security Workshop (MODSEC 2008), in conjunction with the 11th International Conference on Model Driven Engineering Languages and Systems (MODELS 2008), Toulouse, France (September 2008)
7. Jurjens, J.: UMLsec: Extending UML for secure systems development. In: Fifth International Conference on the Unified Modeling Language, Model Engineering, Languages Concepts and Tools (2002)
8. Lodderstedt, T., Basin, D., Doser, J.: SecureUML: A UML-Based Modeling Language for Model-Driven Security. In: Fifth International Conference on the Unified Modeling Language, Model Engineering, Languages Concepts and Tools (2002)
9. N. Mead, E. Houg, T. Stehney: Security quality requirements engineering (SQUARE) Methodology. Technical report CMU/SEI-2005-TR-009. Software Eng. Inst., Carnegie Mellon Univ. (2005)
10. Sindre, G., Opdahl, A.L.: Capturing security requirements by misuse cases. Presented at 14th Norwegian Informatics Conference (NIK 2001), Tromsø, Norway (2001)

11. van Lamsweerde, A.: Elaborating security requirements by construction of intentional anti-models. In: Proceedings of the 26th International Conference on Software Engineering, May 23-28, pp. 148–157 (2004)

12. Mouratidis, H., Giorgini, P.: Secure tropos: A security-oriented extension of the tropos methodology. Int. J. Softw. Eng. Knowl. Eng. 17(2), 285–309 (2007)

13. Elahi, G., Yu, E.: A goal oriented approach for modeling and analyzing security trade-offs. University of Toronto, Department of Computer Science. Technical report (2007)

14. Anton, A.I., Earp, J.B.: Strategies for developing policies and requirements for secure electronic commerce systems. Department of Computer Science, North Carolina State University. Technical report (2000)

15. Braber, F., Hogganvik, I., Lund, M.S., Stolen, K., Vraalsen, F.: Model-based security analysis in seven steps-a guided tour to the CORAS method. BT Technol. J. 25(1), 101–117 (2007)

16. Asnar, Y., Giorgini, P., Massacci, F., Zannon, N.: From trust to dependability through risk analysis. In: Proceedings of the International Conference on Availability, Reliability and Security (AReS), pp. 19–26. IEEE Computer Society (2007)

17. Mayer, N., Rifaut, A., Dubois, E.: Towards a risk-based security requirements engineering framework. In: Proceedings of the 11th International Workshop on Requirements Engineering: Foundation for Software Quality (REFSQ 2005), in conjunction with the 17th Conference on Advanced Information Systems Engineering, CAiSE 2005 (2005)

18. Mellado, D., Fernandez-Medina, E., Piattini, M.: Applying a security requirements engineering process. In: Proceedings of the 11th European Conference on Research in Computer Security, Hamburg, Germany, September 18-20, pp. 192–206 (2006)

19. Hervé Schauer Consultants. ISO/IEC 27005:2011 Information technology – Security techniques – Information security risk management (2010)

20. Kleppe, A., Warmer, J., Bast, W.: MDA explained the model driven architecture: Practice and promise. Addison-Wesley, Boston (2003)

21. Yue, T., Briand, L.C., Labiche, Y.: A systematic review of transformation approaches between user requirements and analysis models. Requirements Engineering 16(2), 75–99 (2011)

22. Muñante, D., Gallon, L., Aniorté, P.: An approach based on Model-driven Engineering to define Security Policies using the access control model OrBAC. In: The Eight International Workshop on Frontiers in Availability, Reliability and Security (FARES 2013), in conjonction with the 8th ARES Conference (ARES 2013), September 2-6. University of Regensburg, Germany (2013)

23. Ledru, Y., Richier, J., Idani, A., Labiadh, M.: From KAOS to RBAC: A Case Study in Designing Access Control Rules from a Requirements Analysis. In: 6 me Conference sur la Scurit des Architectures Rseaux et des Systmes d'Information (SARSSI 2011). La Rochelle, France (2011)

24. Mouratidis, H., Jürjens, J., Fox, J.: Towards a comprehensive framework for secure systems development. In: Martinez, F.H., Pohl, K. (eds.) CAiSE 2006. LNCS, vol. 4001, pp. 48–62. Springer, Heidelberg (2006)

25. Graa, M., Cuppens-Boulahia, N., Autrel, F., Azkia, H., Cuppens, F., Coatrieux, G., Cavalli, A., Mammar, A.: Using Requirements Engineering in an Automatic Security Policy Derivation Process. In: Garcia-Alfaro, J., Navarro-Arribas, G., Cuppens-Boulahia, N., de Capitani di Vimercati, S. (eds.) DPM 2011 and SETOP 2011. LNCS, vol. 7122, pp. 155–172. Springer, Heidelberg (2012)

26. Mead, N.R., Allen, J.H., Barnum, S.J., Ellison, R.J., McGraw, G.: Software Security Engineering: A Guide for Project Managers. Addison-Wesley Professional (2004)
27. Matulevicius, R., Mayer, N., Mouratidis, H., Dubois, E., Heymans, P., Genon, N.: Adapting Secure Tropos for Security Risk Management in the Early Phases of Information Systems Development. In: Bellahsène, Z., Léonard, M. (eds.) CAiSE 2008. LNCS, vol. 5074, pp. 541–555. Springer, Heidelberg (2008)
28. Braber, F., Dimitrakos, T., Gran, B.A., Lund, M.S., Stolen, K., Aagedal, J.O.: The CORAS methodology: Model-based risk assessment using UML and UP. In: UML and the Unified Process, pp. 332–357. IGI Publishing (2003)
29. Lin, L., Nuseibeh, B., Ince, D., Jackson, M.: Using Abuse Frames to Bound the Scope of Security Problems. In: Proceedings of the 12th IEEE International Conference on Requirements Engineering (RE 2004), pp. 354–355. IEEE Computer Society (2004)
30. Hatebur, D., Heisel, M., Schmidt, H.: A security engineering process based on patterns. In: Proceedings of the International Workshop on Secure Systems Methodologies Using Patterns (SPatterns), pp. 734–738. IEEE Computer Society (2007)
31. Beckers, K., Hatebur, D., Heisel, M.: A problem-based threat analysis in compliance with Common Criteria. In: Proceedings of the International Conference on Availability, Reliability and Security (ARES 2013), pp. 111–120 (2013)
32. Haley, C.B., Laney, R., Moffett, J., Nuseibeh, B.: Security requirements engineering: A framework for representation and analysis. IEEE Trans. Softw. Eng. 34(1), 133–153 (2008)

Adaptive User-Centered Security

Sven Wohlgemuth

Center for Advanced Security Research Darmstadt (CASED)
Mornewegstr. 32, 64293 Darmstadt, Germany
sven.wohlgemuth@trust.cased.de
http://www.cased.de

Abstract. One future challenge in informatics is the integration of humans in an infrastructure of data-centric IT services. A critical activity of this infrastructure is trustworthy information exchange to reduce threats due to misuse of (personal) information. *Privacy by Design* as the present methodology for developing privacy-preserving and secure IT systems aims to reduce security vulnerabilities already in the early requirement analysis phase of software development. Incident reports show, however, that not only an implementation of a model bears vulnerabilities but also the gap between rigorous view of threat and security model on the world and real view on a run-time environment with its dependencies. Dependencies threaten reliability of information, and in case of personal information, privacy as well. With the aim of improving security and privacy during run-time, this work proposes to extend *Privacy by Design* by adapting an IT system not only to inevitable security vulnerabilities but in particular to their users' view on an information exchange and its IT support with different, eventually opposite security interests.

Keywords: Security, privacy, usability, resilience, identity management.

1   Data-Centric Society and Security

One future challenge in computer science is the integration of humans in an infrastructure supported by Big Data Analytics and Cyber-Physical Systems (CPS) for promising innovative IT services aiming at sustainable and improving welfare of a society [1,45]. Their IT services should automatically predict, prepare for, response to, and recover from incidents in real-time. This flexibility requires availability of a sufficient amount of authentic personal data from different origins for the analyzing services implying disclosure of personal data and derived information to third parties, their aggregation, and secondary usage. Such IT services are data-centric as seen for business applications relying on information exchange as basic activity [42].

Data-centric services raise severe privacy concerns not only in well aware applications domains as eHealthcare [31], but also on areas where one would not expect these challenges, e.g., as in Archaeology [25]. While collection of personal data is of no real concern to most, their cross-domain usage is. Current studies shows that the majority of a population refrains from participating in data-centric services due to this

S. Teufel et al. (Eds.): CD-ARES 2014, LNCS 8708, pp. 94–109, 2014.

concern [14]. The key issue to be resolved is usage of (personal) data in compliance with agreed-upon social and business rules. This is necessary to achieve acceptable quantity and quality of required information [36], which reduces error rate of data-centric services and so a vulnerability by misuse of (personal) information.

1.1 Privacy by Design and User-Centered Security

Beside citizens as participants in an information exchange service providers of data-centric services become attractive for cyber-attacks [20]. Incidents arise mainly via third parties [12], i.e. dependencies between IT systems participating in an informa-tion exchange. *Privacy by Design* postulates to consider IT security requirements in all phases of software development to reduce vulnerabilities [5,16]. Software engi-neering process models are enriched by threat and risk modeling, which combine functional requirements as *liveness* properties with IT security requirements as *safety* properties [4]. An equilibrium of the participant's individual security interests [40] specifies a privacy policy, which formalizes 'balanced' *safety* and *liveness* require-ments as security properties [10]. Isolation separates then trustworthy from non-trustworthy participants as well as reliable IT systems from failed ones. Irrespective of a software development process, the scope of implementing *Privacy by Design* ends at present after the release of an IT system. Its enforcement of a privacy policy holds as long as events and executions of the IT system during run-time correspond to its security model. Data-centric services, however, constantly changes their depen-dencies due to information exchanges with other users.

User-Centered Security extends *Privacy by Design* by integrating users' require-ments and view on the IT system of an information exchange into the threat model and IT security architecture [54]. Even though an iterative software development process model with short cycles might reduce the consequences of a security incident, it reacts on a vulnerability instead of preventing its exploitation. In addition, enforceability of a privacy policy, and in general of a security policy, is at present decided by rigorous enforceability of *safety* properties. Security mechanisms are statistical program analy-sis, signaling with equivalent security policies as detectors, monitoring control traces with enforcement monitors, and re-writing control traces. The result is that enforce-ment of *safety* properties can violate required *liveness* properties and it is not decidable in case of vulnerabilities by non-observable traces [27], e.g. covert channels. This is as well the challenge for enforcing the 'right to be forgotten' as granted to European citi-zens as a countermeasure against misuse of personal information [11].

1.2 Contribution

The contribution of this work is *Adaptive User-Centered Security* in adapting the threat model, IT security model, and its enforcement to users as participants in an informa-tion exchange, dependencies, and incidents of an IT system during run-time. In con-trary to the rigorous aim of strictly enforcing *safety* properties, Adaptive User-Centered Security aims at an acceptable enforcement of an equilibrium between *safety* and *live-ness* requirements according to the risk tolerance of the given user. An adaptation component configures and enforces individual security interests on behalf of the user as far as desired and possible. Starting point is the electronic identity (eID) of a user as his electronic representation in the Internet.

2   Adaptation to the User

Security mechanisms need to be used and configured without loss of information according to the privacy policy of an information exchange. The basics are a *user model* supporting the target user groups, establishment of *trust domains* with specific *safety* and *liveness* requirements, and a *measurement on authenticity of information* of an exchange. An adaptive user interface should prevent privacy vulnerabilities due to an interaction with the given user as far as possible according to the user model and privacy policy of an information exchange. It considers user interactions for the security configuration of an IT system and scale its enforcement according to the privacy expectations of the user and properties of the security mechanisms. Depending on the results of a measurement, a change in the privacy policy for the isolation and the usage of security mechanisms should improve security and privacy and remain the information exchange acceptable or at least brittle, which means that an additional incident will turn the IT risk to be unacceptable for the affected user.

2.1   Security-Relevant User Interactions

The user interface of security tools must fulfil two requirements. On the one hand, it should offer the user all the necessary information about the configuration of security mechanisms, and on the other hand the user should interact with it as few as possible for achieving the goal of his activity with an IT service. Usability studies for security tools [46,49] show that their current user interfaces threaten an enforcement of a policy, since the user interfaces are driven by IT security concepts. A user has to learn these technical concepts and adapt to it.

In order to configure all IT security protection goals, a user needs to explicitly configure *accountability* and *unobservability* by his eID. Due to dependencies of IT security protection goals, *confidentiality* can be controlled by the IT system. Integrity can be automatically controlled so that a user interaction needs only take place in case of a non-acceptable anomaly of *integrity* [28]. In addition to this configuration by *safety* requirements of a privacy policy, its *liveness* requirements define obligations on the availability of data according to the purpose of data processing, storage, their further disclosure and removal [30].

In case of *accountability* and *unobservability*, an IT security situation depends on the user's configuration, otherwise it is user-independent. If the current vulnerability is part of the system's threat model, the IT security situation is independent on a manual user's decision, otherwise dependent. If an information exchange depends on the context, the IT system can control enforcement of the privacy policy as long as the threat model considers the current security vulnerability under investigation. If the context has no dependency to the privacy policy, e.g. integrity can always be assured without raising an additional vulnerability, the situation is context-independent. These dependencies result in the definition of an IT security situation by four classes (Table 1).

Table 1. Classes of IT security situations

	Context-independent Privacy Policy	Context-dependent Privacy Policy
User-independent Configuration	**Class 1:** No user interaction necessary, totally controlled by the IT security system	**Class 2:** Controlled by the IT security system, if situation can be detected; otherwise user interaction necessary
User-dependent Configuration	**Class 3:** User interaction necessary for initial configuration, then totally controlled by the IT security system	**Class 4:** User interaction necessary, controlled by the user

2.2   Scalability for Enforcement of a Privacy Policy

Starting point for a user-centered enforcement of a privacy policy is identity management to achieve *accountability* with the digital representation of a user [43]. Identity management systems according to Chaum [9] and with anonymous credentials [23] are suitable for the enforcement of an adaptable user-centered security model, since they support *accountability* and *unobservability* by authentication with pseudonyms without raising any vulnerability by contradicting with a *liveness* requirement of an information exchange. Even though identity management supports end-to-end security of an information exchange by authentication to an intermediary, dependencies between the IT systems of participants in a data-centric service imply at the same time a vulnerability of non-observable traces between these IT systems. A compromise of participants and their IT system can thus not be ruled out. Dependencies need to be considered for the user, threat, and IT security model as well as for enforcement.

Regarding enforcement, these vulnerabilities relate to the threat model of Dolev and Yao [15], in which security is based on perfect security of cryptographic public key protocols, secure and available public directory of cryptographic public keys, and confidentiality of cryptographic secret keys. Since identity management ensures authenticity of identity but not of exchange information, e.g., such as the necessary cryptographic public key for cryptographic protection of an information exchange, either an authentic pre-key sharing or an authentic key exchange via a third party is required to enforce IT security. A third party as an intermediary in information exchanges is in particular threatened by hidden dependencies, as IT security analysis for IT systems of data-centric services show. The concluding approach is *ICT Resilience*, which takes dependencies and incidents of any kind for IT security into account [53]. So that additional vulnerabilities don't arise when formalizing the IT security model and its policies for an information exchange, the privacy policy model for adaptive user-centered security in general is usage control. Usage control considers obligations and does not raise additional vulnerabilities by its concept.

Enforcement of privacy and security policies, respectively, differs according to their enforceability in static analysis of the IT system, enforcement by a monitor, and by re-writing [27] whereas the approach differs in preventing, tolerating, removing, or forecasting vulnerabilities [6]. According to different security interests of the participants, their self-protection requires *Privacy-Enhancing Technologies (PET)*, *Transparency-Enhancing Technologies (TET)*, or a mixed mode of their operation.

Scalability for IT security requires a semantically accurate mapping of the required *safety* and *liveness* properties to different user interfaces for configuring privacy policies and their enforcement by the IT security architecture with its different security mechanisms PETs and TETs. Thereby, scalability may not raise by itself a vulnerability across these IT security abstraction layers. Dependencies between these layers should be minimized so that changes within one layer does not affect internals of the other layers. The Model-View-Controller (MVC) software pattern for user interfaces [21] to enhance usability for non-experts, e.g., as deployed for film production processes [29], is suitable for *Adaptive User-Centered Security*. It considers dependencies only between abstraction layers but not across their internal state transitions.

2.3   System Evolution Cycle

The system evolution cycle aims at adapting an IT security system to changes, vulnerabilities, and incidents during run-time. Figure 1 shows the process of adaptation.

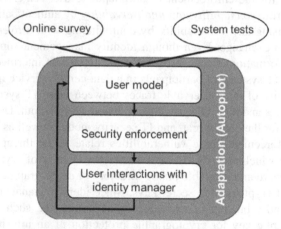

Fig. 1. Procedure for continuous adaptation of IT security enforcement

User modeling gets input from two sources: From the initial evaluation and modelling by a user survey and from system tests. For the Internet usage in Germany, the study on trust and security on the Internet [14] is a starting point for the user modelling. System tests during run-time derive an evidence on anomalies of a policy violation on isolation and their *information accountability* [48] in combination for using security mechanisms for *unobservability*. In order to detect evidence on anomalies in information, a system test predicts and re-constructs the provenance on this information to be derived or on derived information, respectively. The idea is to classify information and their provenance to patterns, since this kind of monitoring does not change the state of the observed IT system. Patterns represent categories of enforcement with isolation patterns and vulnerabilities as well as incidents by anti-isolation patterns with machine learning algorithms. This requires log data as observation by sensors on the provenance of the information under investigation. The adaptation component initializes this system evolution cycle and continuously re-configures the IT security architecture while evaluating evidences of system tests and user's interactions.

2.4   Adaptive System Model for IT Security

The MVC software pattern allows a scalable adaptation of the IT security architecture to the given user model, system model, and available security mechanisms. According to the current approach of *Privacy by Design*, the IT security architecture with its security mechanisms for controlling isolation follows immediately after the specification of the IT security model. The consequence is a direct dependency between the state transitions of the model with a security mechanisms for their enforcement. A change of such a dependency requires a change in the model or security architecture with a re-validation of its security. The adaptation component aims exactly at a continuous re-validation of isolation. This give a view to the user on his privacy during run-time. According to the MVC software pattern, the adaptation component is an abstraction layer between then concrete IT system architecture and state of the isolation and the adaptive user interface with its UI elements (Figure 2).

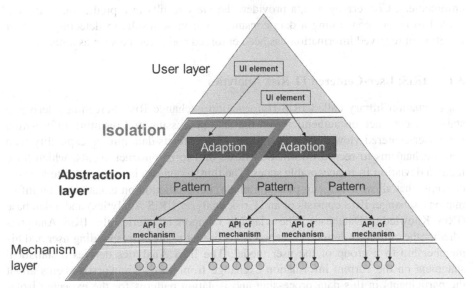

Fig. 2. 3-Layer-Security-Model introducing abstraction for user-centered isolation

This model introduces user-centered isolation for an information exchange across the layers and isolation patterns on combining suitable, available security mechanism according to different classes of isolation and its expected results. Isolation refers to an information exchange between a user and his trust relationships to the other participants and their IT systems according to a 'balanced' IT privacy policy of their interests. In this context, isolation of an information exchange is seen as a special sort of privacy, which refers to a controllable data processing for this information exchange [44]. Measurement of accountability of information derives an evidence on enforcement of a given isolation.

A certified isolation pattern can then be used for an equivalent scenario of an information exchange as well as for an exchange with other users. This allows the adaptation component to re-configure the IT system configuration according to a given user. System-centered isolation patterns complements it. They formalize a deployment of security mechanisms to enforce an isolation with acceptable risk according to the current and possible future states of the given IT system. If a previously unknown requirement, vulnerability, or incident occurs, the adaptation component can simulate deployment of known isolation patterns on this new situation, improve them, or develop a new isolation pattern. This results in a new view on the required isolation.

3   Adaptive User-Centered View on Information Exchange

A view on isolation derives a statement on the likelihood for authenticity and accountability of information, i.e. anomalies in the specified isolation and accountability of the data processing. A view differs in the model of a user including his trust assumptions and knowledge about suitable isolation patterns as well as evidence on their enforcement. Concerning a data provider, the view results in a prediction of the expected isolation; concerning a data consumer, the view results in detecting whether isolation of received information has been enforced and it can be seen as authentic.

3.1   IRiS: User-Centered IT Risk Analytics

An evaluation library called IRiS (Information exchange Risk Screening) derives a statistical evidence on authenticity on the data processing and resulting information for a user-centered view on this IT system. IRiS extends data mining capability with two mechanisms to record information flows and to reconstruct events, which have led to a deviation from acceptable states. The third extension is to incorporate *liveness* concepts that allow a usage in planning mode, i.e. prediction on isolation of an information exchange. IRiS consists of an IT risk analyzer (IRiS Analytics) and a database (IRiS Knowledge Database). The adaption component queries the IRiS Analytics whether the current isolation is acceptable according to the corresponding user and his membership to a group of the user model. The IRiS Analytics derives a statistical statement on the current information exchange from user's known statements about the participants in this data processing and isolation patterns for the expected isolation. The IRiS Knowledge Database stores this knowledge of the user and extends it with discovered isolation patterns and anomalies during run-time.

The challenge for IRiS IT risk analyzer whether information and, in turn, its data processing can be seen as being authentic is the same as in a PKI in providing a statement on the authenticity of a cryptographic public key. Irrespectively on the organizational model of a PKI, the evaluation model of Maurer [33] derives with propositional logic a user-centered view. Trust assumptions of a user A in other participants' enforcement of certification of the PKI, here isolation of the information exchange, is taken into account. Statements of a view refer to the cryptographic key of another participant X ($Aut_{A,X}$) known to the user A and taken as being authentic as well as on his belief in X, that is expressed by a trust statement ($Trust_{A,X,i}$).

Still, cryptographic key certificates and recommendations need to be considered to obtain the user's trust in this view on an information exchange. A cryptographic key certificate issued by a participant X in the role of a certification authority (CA) on enforcement of isolation and this, in turn, on the reliability of the IT system of another participant Y ($Cert_{X,Y}$). A recommendation expresses a belief i of a participant X in a participant Y ($Rec_{X,Y,i}$) in that Y enforces the certification policy and, hence, can be trusted, i.e. privacy policy for this information exchange. Figure 3 illustrates an exemplary view of a user $X=Alice$ on the exchange of information from a user $Y=Bob$ with the intermediaries and statements of user $C=System\ 3$ and $D=System\ 4$. The red arrow represents the requested statement whether $Alice$ can consider the information from Bob as being authentic ($Aut_{Alice,Bob}$). The blue arrows represent the statements for the information exchange via $System\ 3$ on authenticity of data processing ($Aut_{Alice,System\ 3}$), certification ($Cert_{System\ 3,Bob}$), and trust ($Trust_{Alice,\ System\ 3,2}$). The black arrows represent statements known to $Alice$ on an exchange of the same information via participant $System\ 4$: $Aut_{Alice,System\ 4}$, $Cert_{System\ 4,Bob}$, $Cert_{System\ 3,System\ 4}$, and $Trust_{Alice,System\ 4,1}$.

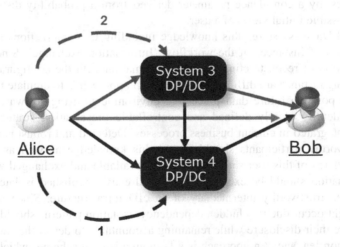

Fig. 3. Exemplary view of a user Alice on an information exchange according to [Maurer 1996]

The aim of IRiS Analytics is to derive the statement $Aut_{A,B}$, here $Aut_{Alice,Bob}$, by the following rules [33] from the view of $A=Alice$.

- $\forall X,Y: Aut_{A,X}, Trust_{A,X,1}, Cert_{X,Y} \rightarrow Aut_{A,Y}$ (1)
- $\forall X,Y,i\geq 1: \ Aut_{A,X}, Trust_{A,X,i+1}, Rec_{X,Y,i} \rightarrow Trust_{A,Y,i}$ (2)
- $\forall X,Y,1\leq k<i: \ Trust_{A,X,i} \rightarrow Trust_{A,X,k}$ (3)
- $\forall X,Y,1\leq k<i: \ Rec_{A,X,i} \rightarrow Rec_{A,X,k}$ (4)

Concerning the example, *Alice* considers the information from *Bob* as authentic, since $Aut_{Alice,Bob}$ can be derived by one of the data traces in the directed graph of the data traces for this information. Afterwards IRiS Analytics checks whether the received information matches with acceptable probability to a cluster of expected valid information or is valid in case this information is the cryptographic public key of *Bob* or a certified statement of a credential. In case of information, a data clustering scheme should assign this information to a cluster of expected results according to the privacy policy and isolation patterns known to *Alice*. In case of a cryptographic public key, its validity will be checked according to the privacy policy on its authorized usage, timeliness, and revocation to grant access on *Alice*'s IT system [7].

IRiS Analytics checks security vulnerabilities as dependencies of the given instance of the workflow 'Information exchange' between the participating IT systems as a Black Box [3] and, if necessary and possible, additionally their internal data traces with a White Box test scheme [17]. The former evaluation results in $evidence_{INFORMATION}$; the evaluation of the workflow instance results in $evidence_{DATA\ TRACE}$. Their combination contributes together with the statement $Aut_{A,X}$ on $evidence_{ISOLATION}$ [52]. However, even though if a data trace between nodes or a node itself is faulty, a data trace of another information exchange might be acceptable correct. Taking several data traces for exchanging the same information into account results, in turn, in a consensus on $Aut_{A,X}$. The evaluation model of [33] considers dependencies and incomplete knowledge about enforcement, which is the case for data traces of hidden dependencies, by a confidence parameter derived from a probability distribution on the set of possible initial views of a user.

The IRiS Database stores this knowledge including user interactions and system configurations of instances of the workflow 'Information exchange'. Since the outcome and costs of reconstructing archived information with the configuration of the corresponding instance are difficult to estimate, an approach is to emulate their reconstruction in possible future data processing environments using software [41]. The aim is to identify clearly defined and controllable preservation strategies, which should be integrated in current business processes. Detected and robust patterns from other trustworthy participants should extend this knowledge as well as the robust isolation patterns of this user should be publicly available and exchanged with others. This information should be exchanged via an already established isolated channel, e.g. a proven trustworthy intermediary of an eID infrastructure. Since information leakage might occur due to a hidden dependency, isolation patterns should be anonymized before their disclosure while remaining accountable to detect the cause of such an information leakage. An approach is a k-anonymization scheme, which tags anonymized information by the procedure of their anonymization [32]. This evaluation considers colluding data consumers, as given by an incident propagation, with the aim of non-authorized re-identification of the related identity to this information.

3.2   Retrieving and Re-Writing Data Traces

IRiS Analytics derives a view on an IT system and exchange of personal information, which is built with the IT systems of the participants in an information exchange and eventually needs to be modified or dissolved during run-time. If a non-acceptable evidence on an anomaly derived by a system test or a new requirement from the user model occurs, a re-writing of the workflow [47], the IT system [27], or both is required in advance or during an information exchange, respectively, to prevent more severe incidents. Retrieving and re-writing data traces may not raise an additional vulnerability in enforcing the user's security interests on *accountability* and *unobservability*. Since these mechanisms consider isolation as a kind of privacy, they are called *Privacy Foren*sics and *Privacy Control*.

Privacy Forensics aims at detecting evidence on isolation by the most probable data provenance history and its classification to an anomaly pattern. Information is tagged with a label, which represents the data providing and data consuming parties together with the corresponding privacy policy for this isolation. The provenance of information, and in general data, d consists of the data provider's, data consumer's, and the user's identity as well as a pointer to the privacy policy. The privacy policy is indirectly part of a tag by a link to it. This, in turn, allows the user to modify the privacy policy and the IT system, if the purpose of the data's usage changes or a severe vulnerability and incidents occurs. The tag should stick to d, so that $d^*=(d, tag)$ can be disclosed further while assuring the integrity of the relationship within d^*. If d^* is disclosed further, the tag has to be updated by adding the new role of this now data providing participant and adding the identity of the new data consumer. The sequence of tags for the same personal information thus constitutes its data trace.

Tagging of data requires authentic information for testing and to reduce the statistical error rate of the applied machine learning scheme. So that the necessary (personal) data as log data don't violate the protection goal *unobservability*, each log data is encrypted and related log data for deriving an evidence on isolation of a given information exchange are linked by a chain of cryptographic hash values. Linked log data represent a log view on a data provider's information. Each log view is individualized to the identity of the corresponding data provider. Collection and retrieval log views depend on a trusted execution environment to which the data provider or an authorized participant, e.g. an auditor, authenticates with his identity to get access [2]. Since internal traces of a sub IT system are not known, but labeled evidence exists by the specification of this data processing, supervised machine learning can be useful for deriving $evidence_{DATA\ TRACE}$. Since not all kind of data can be annotated, mechanisms of unsupervised machine learning should also be researched to establish their suitability. The derived data provenance has some safety and liveness properties, which are expressed by a policy as its *detector* [27]. If this policy is not equivalent to the privacy policy of the expected isolation, an anomaly has been detected.

Privacy Control aims at re-writing the 'code' according to changes in the privacy policy and supporting at the same time self-protection against information leakage. The main identity of users as data providers remains unobservable, when the eID infrastructure supports pseudonymity as well as non-linkable delegation and revocation of rights [44]. Pseudonymity should be revocable should provable fraud have occurred. According to distributed trust management [7], an orchestration according to authorizations can be done by delegation and revocation of rights with credentials. Credentials are a representation of access rights, which are delegated to service providers to obtain access to personal data in agreement with the individual in question. Anonymized credential schemes achieves unobservability in the issuing and showing protocols [8]. The individual (in the role of the data subject) specifies these access decisions by delegating the access rights together with obligations or using these access rights to the requesting service provider (in the role of a data consumer). To obtain a user's agreement for each disclosure of his personal data to a third party, it should be possible to delegate and revoke rights for isolating an information exchange. Thereby, a delegation of rights defines a collaboration between service providers including the exchange of given user's personal data between them.

4   Adaptive Identity Management System

Preliminary work of the author exists as partial identities for security-relevant user interactions, *Privacy Control*, and *Privacy Forensics*.

4.1   *iManager*: User Interactions and Personal IT Security Tool

iManager as an eID client for mobile use introduces partial identities for user interaction and a concept for automatic configuration of security mechanisms [50]. It offers interfaces to the user, security mechanisms, and applications of a mobile device. The access to personal data and to cryptographic keys is exclusively possible by using the identity manager. An application's request to these data will be checked by the identity manager to see whether the user has granted authorization to this access on personal data. Based on a *security platform* with the necessary security mechanisms in order to protect the communication, the personal data and the privacy of the user, the components *identity configuration*, *identity negotiation*, and *confirmation of action* are responsible for managing partial identities. The concept of partial identities for security-relevant user interactions and its implementation for the *iManager* has been developed according to the software development process model of *User-Centered Security Engineering (UCSec)* [22]. *UCSec* combines usability engineering for development of user interfaces with security engineering.

4.2   *DREISAM*: Non-Linkable Delegation of Rights for *Privacy Control*

DREISAM extends an eID infrastructure for an unobservable delegation and revocation of rights to third parties [44]. The higher cryptographic protocols of *DREISAM* combine the mechanisms for delegation of rights by credentials with mechanisms for enforcing non-linkability for unobservability when using credentials. Anonymous credentials make use of a cryptographic commitment scheme for binding authorizations to a cryptographic key and of zero-knowledge proofs for showing this relationship without revealing any identifying data. Since a user would lose control on his identity, if he would use anonymous credentials for delegation, a proxy credential replaces sharing of individual's master identity. It represents to the certification authority (CA) the individual's delegation request for a certain right to a service provider.

If the service provider gets a proxy credential, he has the individual's authorisation to get the requested access right by means of an anonymous credential. The CA logs requests from users and service providers with the issued proxy and anonymous credentials in the delegation list. The CA uses this list for checking service providers' requests for anonymous credentials and for resolving disputes between participants.

4.3   DETECTIVE: Data Provenance Protocols for Privacy Forensics

DETECTIVE is an experimental data provenance system with the aim of privacy-preserving tracing disclosure of data to third parties even in case of covert channels [51]. *DETECTIVE* makes use of cryptographic commitments and of a symmetric digital watermarking algorithm but without the need of a trustworthy data provider or a TTP regarding the embedding and checking of data provenance information. Cryptographic commitments link the identities of the participating service providers in any disclosure of personal data. Digital watermarking is used to tag the corresponding personal data with this link. Since users do not take part in the disclosures of personal data, users give their authorization in advance, e.g. by using *DREISAM*. *DETECTIVE* operates in the three phases (1) definition of the collaborating service providers of a business process by obligations and their delegation according to the privacy policy, (2) documenting disclosures of personal data to third parties by adding data provenance as a digital watermark, and (3) checking the enforcement of the obligations by comparing the delegated rights with the data provenance information of the found personal data.

5   Related Work

Adaptation of IT security enforcement is considered for user interfaces and on getting access on data, but without proposing a concept for adaptation in general and in case of an information exchange. Recent work configures screen locking of a device for non-authorized access via the GUI according to the current physical environment of the (mobile) device. The physical environment represent the context on which a machine learning scheme derives a classification and classify the current context. The focus is on data disclosure, i.e. on data collection, of location data [34].

Adaptation of security-relevant user interactions on IT security considers the design of a GUI, which addresses different level of user risk [12]. A dialogue adaptation engine tracks user's behavior, generates security dialogues, and provides feedback to the user. It uses collected security information to alter the behavior of the dialogs. Security information is stored in data stores, which is decision risk, user performance, and environmental data. Decision risk data are executions with high risks, user performance data refers whether a user differentiates between non-risk and risky operations, and environmental data are other external data. However, there is no assurance that this system runs as expected, since it assumes an IT system without vulnerabilities. It has been shown that a misuse of GUI elements by introducing hidden GUI elements is possible and an exploit of this vulnerability results in information leakage.

Approaches for detecting security vulnerabilities by assessing a GUI consider certain classes of vulnerabilities and user group, but not a general user and threat model [29,35].

6   Conclusion

Adapting an IT system of an information exchange to security vulnerabilities during run-time to acceptable enforce individual security interests would improve security and privacy by reducing security vulnerabilities in an isolation. However, this inherits a *privacy paradoxon*. Whereas PETs should impede a privacy violation by restricting availability personal information, they impede at the same time a detection of security vulnerabilities in isolation of an information exchange and, hence, threaten privacy as understood by isolation of an information exchange. On the one side, accountability of information with *TETs*, as demanded with transparent, accountable data flow tracking by the *Big Data and Privacy 90-day review* of The White House [19], requires authentic personal information to reduce the error rate of an adaptation. On the other side, usage of personal information according to an isolation, hence security and privacy, is threatened by hidden dependencies such as an exploit of a covert channel for an information leakage and modification of information. The proposal for *Adaptive User-Centered Security* should contribute to identify and enforce an equilibrium in such a multilateral settings between the individual security and privacy interests of participants in an information exchange, among others on security incidents.

Acknowledgement. Basics of this work was funded by the German Research Foundation (DFG) within the priority program 'Security in the Information and Communication Technology' (SPP 1079) under coordination of Günter Müller. I would like to thank all members of the corresponding project group 'ATUS – A Toolkit for Usable Security', Isao Echizen and Stefan Sackmann for the discussions on resilience and IT risk in social infrastructures, and the reviewers of CD-ARES 2014 for their valuable comments.

References

1. acatech. Cyber-Physical Systems. Driving force for innovation in mobility, health, energy and production. acatech - National Academy of Science and Engineering, acatech POSITION PAPER (2011)
2. Accorsi, R.: A secure log architecture to support remote auditing. Mathematical and Computer Modelling 57, 1578–1591 (2013)
3. Accorsi, R., Lehmann, A., Lohmann, N.: Information leak detection in business process models: Theory, application, and tool support. Information Systems (2014)
4. Alpern, B., Schneider, F.B.: Defining Liveness. Information Processing Letters 21(4), 181–185 (1985)
5. Anderson, R.J.: Security Engineering: A Guide to Building Dependable Distributed Systems, 2nd edn. John Wiley & Sons (2008)

6. Avižienis, A., Laprie, J.-C., Randell, B., Landwehr, C.: Basic Concepts and Taxonomy of Dependable and Secure Computing. IEEE Transactions on Dependable and Secure Computing 1(1), 11–33 (2004)
7. Blaze, M., Feigenbaum, J., Lacy, J.: Distributed Trust Management. In: IEEE Symposium on Security and Privacy, pp. 164–173. IEEE Computer Society (1996)
8. Camenisch, J.L., Lysyanskaya, A.: An Efficient System for Non-transferable Anonymous Credentials with Optional Anonymity Revocation. In: Pfitzmann, B. (ed.) EUROCRYPT 2001. LNCS, vol. 2045, pp. 93–118. Springer, Heidelberg (2001)
9. Chaum, D.: Security without Identification: Transaction Systems to make Big Brother Obsolete. CACM 28(10), 1030–1044 (1985)
10. Clarkson, M.R., Schneider, F.B.: Hyperproperties. Journal of Computer Security 18(6), 1157–1210 (2010)
11. Court of Justice of the European Union. Judgment of the Court (Grand Chamber) of 13 May 2014 (request for a preliminary ruling from the Audiencia Nacional – Spain) – Google Spain SL, Google Inc. v Agencia Espanola de Proteccion de Datos (AEPD), Mario Costeja Gonzalez, Case C-131/12 (2014)
12. De Keukelaere, F., Yoshihama, S., Trent, S., Zhang, Y., Luo, L., Zurko, M.E.: Adaptive Security Dialogs for Improved Security Behaviors of Users. In: Gross, T., Gulliksen, J., Kotzé, P., Oestreicher, L., Palanque, P., Prates, R.O., Winckler, M. (eds.) INTERACT 2009. LNCS, vol. 5726, pp. 510–523. Springer, Heidelberg (2009)
13. Dekker, M., Karsberg, C., Lakka, M.: Annual Incident Reports 2012 – Analysis of Article 13a incident reports. European Union Agency for Network and Communication Security, ENISA (2013)
14. DIVSI Deutsches Institut für Vertrauen und Sicherheit im Internet. DIVSI Milieu Study on Trust and Security on the Internet – Condensed version (2012)
15. Dolev, D., Yao, A.C.: On the Security of Public Key Protocols. In: SFCS 1981, pp. 350–357. IEEE Computer Society (1981)
16. Eckert, C.: IT-Sicherheit: Konzepte, Verfahren, Protokolle, 8th edn., Oldenbourg (2013)
17. Enck, W., Gilbert, P., Chun, B.-G., Cox, L.P., Jung, J., McDaniel, P., Sheth, A.N.: TaintDroid: An Information Flow Tracking System for Real-Time Privacy Monitoring on Smartphones. CACM 57(3), 99–106 (2014)
18. European Commission. Directive 2009/140/EC of the European Parliament and of the Council of 25 November 2009 amending Directives 2002/21/EC on a common regulatory framework for electronic communications networks and services, 2002/19/EC on access to, and interconnection of, electronic communications networks and associated facilities, and 2002/20/EC on the authorisation of electronic communications networks and services. Official Journal of the European Communities, L 337, 37–69 (2009)
19. Executive Office of the President. Big Data: Seizing Opportunities, Preserving Values. The White House (2014)
20. Federal Office for Information Security (BSI). The IT Security Situation in Germany in 2011 (2011)
21. Gamma, E., Helm, R., Johnson, R.E., Vlissides, J.: Design Patterns. Elements of Reusable Object-Oriented Software. Prentice Hall (1994)
22. Gerd tom Markotten, D.: User-Centered Security Engineering. In: 4th EurOpen/USENIX Conference – NordU (2002)
23. Gerd tom Markotten, D., Wohlgemuth, S., Müller, G.: Mit Sicherheit zukunftsfähig. PIK Sonderheft Sicherheit 26(1), 5–14 (2003)

24. Gilliot, M., Matyas, V., Wohlgemuth, S.: Privacy and Identity. In: Rannenberg, K., Royer, D., Deuker, A. (eds.) The Future of Identity in the Information Society (FIDIS) – Challenges and Opportunities. Springer, Heidelberg (2009)
25. Holzinger, K., Holzinger, A., Safran, C., Koiner, G., Weippl, E.: Use of Wiki Systems in Archaeology: Privacy, Security and Data Protection as Key Problems. IEEE ICE-B 2010 - ICETE, 120–123 (2010)
26. Holzinger, A., Struggl, K.-H., Debevc, M.: Applying Model-View-Controller (MVC) in Design and Development of Information Systems: An example of smart assistive script breakdown in an e-Business Application. In: IEEE ICE-B 2010 - ICETE, pp. 63–68 (2010)
27. Hamlen, K.W., Morrisett, G., Schneider, F.B.: Computability Classes for Enforcement Mechanisms. ACM Transactions on Programming Languages and Systems 28(1), 175–205 (2006)
28. Jendricke, U., Gerd tom Markotten, D.: Usability Meets Security – the Identity-Manager As Your Personal Security Assistant for the Internet. In: ACSAC 2000, pp. 344–354. IEEE Computer Society (2000)
29. Kajiyama, T., Echizen, I.: Evaluation of an Improved Visualization System for Helping Children Identify Risky Websites. In: ARES 2012, pp. 495–498. IEEE Computer Society (2012)
30. Karjoth, G., Schunter, M.: A Privacy Model for Enterprises. In: Proceedings of the 15th IEEE Workshop on Computer Security Foundations, CSFW 2002, pp. 271–281. IEEE Computer Society (2002)
31. Kieseberg, P., Hobel, H., Schrittwieser, S., Weippl, E., Holzinger, A.: Protecting Anonymity in the Data-Driven Medical Sciences. In: Holzinger, A., Jurisica, I. (eds.) Knowledge Discovery and Data Mining. LNCS, vol. 8401, pp. 301–316. Springer, Heidelberg (2014)
32. Kieseberg, P., Schrittwieser, S., Mulazzani, M., Echizen, I., Weippl, E.: An algorithm for collusion-resistant anonymization and fingerprinting of sensitive microdata. Special issue Security and Privacy in Business Processes 24(2) (2014)
33. Maurer, U.: Modeling a Public-Key Infrastructure. In: Martella, G., Kurth, H., Montolivo, E., Bertino, E. (eds.) ESORICS 1996. LNCS, vol. 1146, pp. 325–350. Springer, Heidelberg (1996)
34. Miettinen, M., Heuser, S., Kronz, W., Sadeghi, A.-R., Asokan, N.: ConXsense – Context Profiling and Classification for Context-Aware Access Control. In: ASIACCS 2014. ACM (2014)
35. Mulliner, C., Robertson, W., Kirda, E.: Hidden GEMs: Automated Discovery of Access Control Vulnerabilities in Graphical User Interfaces. In: IEEE Symposium on Security and Privacy 2014, pp. 149–162. IEEE Computer Society (2014)
36. Otto, B., Lee, Y.W., Caballero, I.: Information and data quality in business networking: a key concept for enterprises in its early stages of development. Electronic Markets 21(2), 83–97 (2011)
37. Orman, H., Schroeppel, R.: Positive Feedback and the Madness of Crowds. In: Proceedings of the 1996 Workshop on New Security Paradigms, pp. 134–138 (1996)
38. Patrick, A.S., Briggs, P., Marsh, S.: Designing Systems That People Will Trust. Security and Usability: Designing Secure Systems that People Can Use. O'Reilly (2005)
39. Pineda, L.A., Meza, I.V., Salinas, L.: Dialogue Model Specification and Interpretation for Intelligent Multimodal HCI. In: Kuri-Morales, A., Simari, G.R. (eds.) IBERAMIA 2010. LNCS, vol. 6433, pp. 20–29. Springer, Heidelberg (2010)
40. Rannenberg, K., Pfitzmann, A., Müller, G.: IT Security and Multilateral Security. Multilateral Security in Communications – Technology, Infrastructure, Economy, 21–29 (1999)

41. Rechert, K., von Suchodoletz, D., Valizada, I., Cardenas, T.J., Kulzhabayev, A.: Take care of your belongings today – securing accessibility to complex electronic business processes. Special issue Security and Privacy in Business Processes 24(2) (2014) (Electronic Markets)
42. Riemer, K., Steinfeld, C., Vogel, D.: eCollaboration: On the nature and emergence of communication and collaboration technologies. Electronic Markets 19(4), 181–188 (2009)
43. Saltzer, J.H., Schroeder, M.D.: The Protection of Information in Computer Systems. IEEE 63(9), 1278–1308 (1975)
44. Sonehara, N., Echizen, I., Wohlgemuth, S.: Isolation in Cloud Computing and Privacy-Enhancing Technologies – Suitability of Privacy-Enhancing Technologies for Separating Data Usage in Business Processes. Special focus Sustainable Cloud Computing of Business Information Systems Engineering (BISE) 3(3), 155–162 (2011)
45. Wahlster, W., Müller, G.: Placing Humans in the Feedback Loop of Social Infrastructures – NII Research Strategies on Cyber-Physical Systems. Informatik Spektrum 36(6), 520–529 (2013)
46. Waidner, M.: Open Issues in Secure Electronic Commerce (1998)
47. Wang, Q., Li, N.: Satisfiability and Resiliency in Workflow Authorization Systems. ACM Transactions on Information and System Security 13(4), 40:1–40:35 (2010)
48. Weitzner, D.J., Abelson, H., Berners-Lee, T., Feigenbaum, J., Hendler, J., Sussman, G.J.: Information Accountability. CACM 51(6), 82–87 (2008)
49. Whitten, A., Tygar, J.D.: Why Johnny can't encrypt: A Usability Evaluation of PGP 5.0. In: SSYM 1999. USENIX Association (1999)
50. Wohlgemuth, S., Gerd, D.: DFG-Schwerpunktprogramm Sicherheit in der Informations- und Kommunikationstechnik. IT – Information Technology 45(1), 46–54 (2003)
51. Wohlgemuth, S., Echizen, I., Sonehara, N., Müller, G.: Tagging Disclosures of Personal Data to Third Parties to Preserve Privacy. In: 25th IFIP International Information Security Conference Security & Privacy – Silver Linings in the Cloud, SEC 2010. IFIP AICT, vol. 330, pp. 241–252 (2010)
52. Wohlgemuth, S.: Resilience as a new Enforcement Model for IT Security based on Usage Control. In: 5th International Workshop on Data Usage Management, IEEE CS Security & Privacy Workshop (SPW 2014) within 35th IEEE Symposium on Security and Privacy, S&P 2014. IEEE Computer Society (2014)
53. Wohlgemuth, S., Sackmann, S., Sonehara, N.: Security and Privacy in Business Networking. Special issue 'Security and Privacy in Business Networking' of Electronic Markets 24(2) (2014)
54. Zurko, M.E.: User-Centered Security: Stepping Up to the Grand Challenge. In: Proceedings of the 21st Annual Computer Security Applications Conference (ACSAC 2005), pp. 187–202. IEEE Computer Society (2005)

Mobile Computing is not Always Advantageous: Lessons Learned from a Real-World Case Study in a Hospital

Andreas Holzinger[1], Bettina Sommerauer[1], Peter Spitzer[2], Simon Juric[3],
Borut Zalik[3], Matjaz Debevc[3], Chantal Lidynia[4], André Calero Valdez[4],
Carsten Roecker[1,4], and Martina Ziefle[4]

[1] Research Unit Human–Computer Interaction,
Institute for Medical Informatics, Statistics and Documentation, Medical University Graz,
{a.holzinger,b.sommerauer,c.roecker}@hci4all.at
[2] Department of Pediadric Surgery, Graz University Hospital
peter.spitzer@klinikum-graz.at
[3] Faculty of Electrical Engineering and Computer Science, University of Maribor
{simon.juric,borut.zalik,matjaz.debevc}@um.si
[4] Human–Computer Interaction Center, RWTH Aachen University, Germany
{lidynia,calero-valdez,Ziefle}@comm.rwth-aachen.de

Abstract. The use of mobile computing is expanding dramatically in recent years and trends indicate that "the future is mobile". Nowadays, mobile computing plays an increasingly important role in the biomedical domain, and particularly in hospitals. The benefits of using mobile devices in hospitals are no longer disputed and many applications for medical care are already available. Many studies have proven that mobile technologies can bring various benefits for enhancing information management in the hospital. But is mobility a solution for every problem?

In this paper, we will demonstrate that mobility is *not* always an advantage. On the basis of a field study at the pediatric surgery of a large University Hospital, we have learned within a two-year long mobile computing project, that mobile devices have indeed many disadvantages, particularly in stressful and hectic situations and we conclude that mobile computing is not always advantageous.

Keywords: Mobile computing, real-world, user experience, hospital computing, medical informatics.

1 Introduction and Motivation for Research

As the role of technology has grown smart phones and tablet computers ensure that staying connected 24/7 is not only possible but often expected, accelerating the hype in mobile computing [1]. Since the advent of personal digital assistants, mobile devices (e.g., smart phones and tablet computers) have also been widely adopted by medical professionals. Especially for young health professionals, these devices are quickly

S. Teufel et al. (Eds.): CD-ARES 2014, LNCS 8708, pp. 110–123, 2014.
© IFIP International Federation for Information Processing 2014

becoming one of the main tools for accessing medical information, following the general trend: according to [2], 63% of *all* internet users get access to the World Wide Web via portable devices, e.g., laptop, tablet, or smart phone – with an increasing tendency; 88% of people between 16 and 24 years of age use portable devices for internet access instead of their desktop computers at home and/or at work. We may say that mobility has become an integral part of everything we do in our daily lives. With the introduction of newer and more powerful smart phones and tablets, mobile users have easy and immediate access to information everywhere and at any time, a recent discussion of the state-of-the-art can be found here [3].

There has been a tremendous surge in the number of available mobile health technologies around the world [4]. According to a recent study [5], already in 2009 about two out of three people worldwide owned a mobile phone. A 2011 global survey of 114 nations [6], carried out by the World Health Organization, found that mobile health initiatives have been established in many countries.

The most common purpose was the creation of health call centers that respond to patient inquiries. This was followed by the use of SMS for appointment reminders, the use of telemedicine, the access of patient records, measuring treatment compliance, the promotion of health awareness by conducting health surveys, patient monitoring, and creating a decision support system for physicians (see Fig. 1).

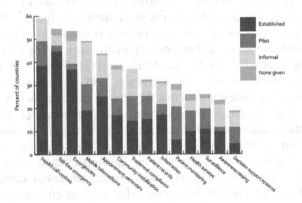

Fig. 1. Overview of mobile health applications worldwide in regard to type of service [5]

Based on previous work and based on the success story of a previous project [7] the primary goal of our project was to provide the benefits of such portable devices into the specific environment of emergency medicine: Every patient who requires medical care at the Department of Pediatric Surgery in Graz has to be recorded at the local medical information system (openMedocs), based on a SAP healthcare solution. In this system every patient has his own record with a patient report for each accident, including a collection of accident data (e.g. location, circumstances etc.). As this is a burdensome additional work for the clinicians, the idea was that the patients or their chaperons fill in this data. As an added bonus, this would also involve the patient at an even earlier stage of the treatment process. Unless in cases of life-threatening injuries, patients are always required to spend some time waiting until a doctor can see them.

Then they need to fill out forms and answer questions of a doctor or nurse who needs to write down the answers before the actual medical treatment can begin. This seems like a huge expenditure of time and our goal was to use the waiting period more efficiently and thereby free the doctors of work, so they can concentrate on the medical side of their profession, instead of them gathering data As an added bonus, this would also involve the patient at an even earlier stage of the treatment process. In the pigment lesion clinic this works in daily routine with excellent results [7].

2   Background and Related Work

Today, the health care industry is booming, which includes the need of handling large quantities of data [8], consequently, the necessity of computerized systems in the medical sector is indisputable, and much previous work is reporting on a multitude of benefits by the application of mobile computing in medicine and health care (see e.g. [6, 9-12].

2.1   Mobile Devices

Mobile devices such as Smartphones with advanced performance properties and especially tablet computers use a touch screen as main interaction method. For this reason, the design of applications running on these devices is crucial for the success of both the application and the device and particularly multi-touch interaction poses a lot of challenges but also possibilities for the developer [13]. The acceptance of mobile devices depends above all on their usefulness and their usability [14]. When using such devices it is quite apparent that the limited space on their screens involves significant challenges to the developers and usability engineers [15], [16],[17]. For example, one study demonstrated that a touch-based mobile device can be used successfully within the healthcare context only if it has an appropriate design [18]. For this reason, the necessity of usability engineering methods [19] is meanwhile commonly acknowledged for the development of medical mobile devices, as several studies show [20], [21], [14]. Mobile devices for medical contexts must always be created with the end user in mind and pay attention to the end user's expertise with both the technology as well as the domain (context) of its use [22], [23], [24].

The specifics of mobile devices pose special challenges in design and usage when they are to be used for mobile questionnaires, especially as they include multiple questions to be answered. Although several studies have already targeted this subject, e.g., [25], [26], [27], [28] and some solutions have been developed, there are no known tutorials on how to best develop mobile questionnaires as of yet. However, a user experience evaluation has found that the four most important things to keep in mind when developing questionnaires for mobile devices are the small screen size, the data entry method and interaction style, the mobile context, and the chosen implementation for the questionnaire [29].

2.2   Mobile Devices in Hospitals

There are several studies and reviews about the implementation of mobile computing in hospitals, including [26], [30], [31], [32], [33], [34], to mention only a few. The study of [26], e.g., gives a comprehensive picture of how to integrate handheld devices into health care and the possible applications of PDAs. Previous studies have clearly shown that the users' information satisfaction resulting from the use of a mobile electronic medication administration record is significantly higher than that observed with the benchmark paper-based workflow, see [35], or [36].

2.3   Touch and Gesture Inputs

In recent years, the use of gestural interface technology has become much more frequent in mass consumer products, especially products such as the Apple iPhone or the Nintendo Wii videogame console; both can be regarded as pioneering examples of this technology. An ever increasing number of consumer electronics manufactures have developed gesture control elements and included this technology in a whole range of mobile electronic devices such as laptops, cell phones, PDAs, remote controls, navigation systems, and digital cameras. It is not surprising that there are studies about, for example, the Nintendo Wii Remote Controller and its use in the area of e-Teaching. One study shows the design and development of a low-cost demonstrator kit for the Wiimote [37]. It concludes that gestures can enhance the quality of learning processes for children by adding another layer to the instructional discourse. Communication is not restricted to verbal speech and language alone. One cornerstone of human interaction lies in non-verbal communication, parts of which are gestures that are used to complement verbal messages.

Other studies indicate that touch interfaces and their use are much more natural to users than other input devices such as mouse, touchpad or trackball [38], [39], [40]. An added benefit of touch-screen devices is the easier maintenance in terms of cleanness and hygiene. A flat screen is much simpler to swipe clean and disinfect than the movable parts of the other input devices, an important aspect for the use in a hospital.

3   Experiment

The field of application for the questionnaire developed by us was the emergency department of the pediatric surgery in Graz. A mobile questionnaire can add value by replacing handwritten documentation, thereby providing more accurate and complete documentation with less risk of transcription errors or legibility issues. For this work, not all the features of a tablet PC were utilized, because only a single application, namely our questionnaire, was run on the device.

In this specific case, we could not draw on literature or previous studies about the best screen size, the ideal weight, or the optimal battery life for effective handling in a hospital scenario. There are no such sources yet. The only way to come to a definite solution as to which device is the best for the use in such an environment is to test possible candidates in real life. We began our test phase with an iPad as input device.

For this work, the handling, the practicability and the ease of use was most important. Especially, as an emergency department is a place of urgency and hectic activity, meaning cumbersome equipment or difficult or hard to use software defeat the purpose of easing the workload and providing quick and accurate information. Additionally, we designed this application with the idea that filling out the questionnaire should also provide the patients with a simple task to calm their nerves and help bridge the time spent waiting for the doctor to see them. Due to the fact that it is the pediatric surgery, also elements of play were under consideration, to keep the motivation for the input of the data.

3.1   System Architecture

For the experiment, a web application for tablet computers was developed. To understand the whole system, it is important to have a short look at the technical environment. In order to display heterogeneous IT-systems of numerous hospitals, a system was developed by the Styrian healthcare organization (KAGes) and governing body of Styrian hospitals. This countrywide hospital information system (HIS), called open-Medocs , is a customized software product designed by the commercial company SAP. The core of openMedocs is the electronic patient record (EPR) system which is used for patient management. All documents and patient data are stored in this system.

Because very sensitive information about every patient is stored here, there has to be high data security, guaranteed by strict privacy policies [41], [42]. Due to this fact, the questionnaire for the patient reports cannot be easily integrated in Medocs. Consequently, the questionnaire is designed and developed completely autonomously.

Therefore, the questionnaire will be a stand-alone system which operates only on the frontend side. For that reason, all necessary data for the development of the questionnaire, i.e., the questions, the answers, the structure, and the logical interconnection, are stored locally on the tablet.

3.2   User Interaction

The user interface of the tablet application was designed with the future users (parents or guardians and children) in mind. The visuals are based on the corporate identity of the clinic called "Bärenburg" (German for "bears castle", which is a child safety house, built as a center for injury prevention adjacent to the pediatric surgery) and have a child-friendly user interface with large text buttons (see Fig. 2). The interaction with the system is based on a linear sequence of questions that need to be answered one after another. The user fills in the questionnaire to record the individual accident data and then finishes the data input.

After all the questions have been answered, the completed questionnaire is transferred into Medocs, the hospital wide enterprise hospital information system. The integration of the patient data into the hospital information system is based on an existing system from cancer research [7]. Therefore, the same XML interface as the technical protocol can be used so that the data collected from the questionnaire can be transferred directly into the Medocs-System via remote function call. The XML file contains all the patient's answer as well as the corresponding questions. All the

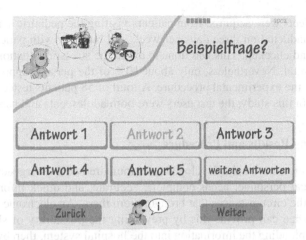

Fig. 2. Questionnaire screen shot of one version of an early prototype

obtained information is then stored in Medocs and the medical personnel, i.e., doctors and nurses, have access to the data of each patient at any given time and any place in the clinical workplace (see system architecture in Fig. 3).

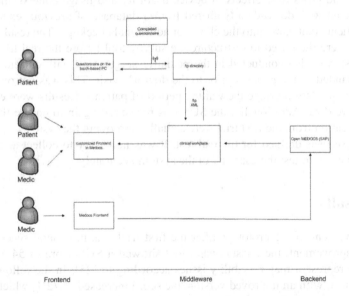

Fig. 3. System architecture of the Medocs system with our tablet solution

3.3 Test Users

As the application is used in a pediatric surgery, the target test users of this questionnaire are young patients and their escorts. With both injured children and their chaperons as users of this interface there cannot be any restrictions as to age or computer experience. All users were inexperienced with the system in the test.

The test subjects were acquired from patients visiting the pediatric surgery in Graz. The test was conducted on three days per week and but only with patients who were there for a second checkup. This was done to avoid the stressful situation of the initial visit to the hospital. Nevertheless, only about 10% of the persons approached agreed to participate in the experimental procedure. A total of 58 patients tested the system in the real-world. In this study, the test users were both adolescents and parents.

3.4   Collecting Results and Procedure

The field of application for the developed questionnaire is the emergency department. Here, the medical personnel needs complete, accurate, and quick information about the patient and the circumstances that brought them there. An electronic questionnaire on a mobile device can provide this by preventing the possibility of skipping questions and also uploading the information into the hospital system, thereby enabling the doctors or nurses to instantly access and, if necessary, edit the data.

For this work, only the handling and easy practicability were studied. The system was tested in two trials. The first trial was used to identify possible usability problems with the questionnaire tool. For this purpose, the system usability scale (SUS) was used. To avoid cross-over effects of device usability and usage context, the first test was conducted with demo-data (gathered from a database of previous examinations) but real patients that came into the clinic for additional checkups. The results from the initial trial were then used to restructure the survey tool before the real life test. This real life test was also conducted in the pediatric surgery but with current cases. An iPad was handed to the patients prior to the doctor's visit. This was not only done to collect data but also to bridge the waiting period of patients. Results were established as qualitative data. Additionally, the SUS was measured again to ensure the changes to the application from the first trial were actually improving the system.

No task set was defined for the real test. It was necessary to collect actual patient data of real cases to test the usability of the system accurately.

4   Results

The improvement of the prototype after the first trial was in general successful. Before the improvement, the questionnaire tool showed a SUS score of 54.4%. Scores under 60% represent major usability issues according to [25]. In the following iteration of the test, with an improved version, the score increased to 72%, which is a considerable improvement but still below the acceptable benchmark of approximately 80%. The individual results of the SUS can be seen in Fig. 4.

While most of the usability items yielded better results in the real test, two items dropped notably below the initial assessment of the pilot test. The first one, and also the strongest perceived hurdle of the mobile questionnaire, was the use of the system without assistance from an expert (question 4 – *"I believe I require help when using the system."*). This was followed by the assessment of the overall complexity of the topic at hand (question 6 – *"I find answering these questions hard."*).

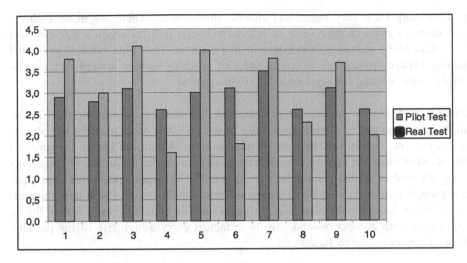

Fig. 4. SUS scores for the pilot and the real test for the questionnaire tool

Beyond the quantitative results, qualitative observations of the whole procedure were recorded. The following paragraphs report the findings from these observations.

4.1   Qualitative Observations

During the trial, several observations have been made about the general usage as well as the practicability of the mobile device in the environment of a hospital's emergency room. Due to agitation, anxiety, confusion, the continuous arrival of new patients as well as departure of already treated patients, the mobile solution showed several disadvantages during the experimental testing phase in real life.

Keeping Track of Tablets and Incidental Theft. Because new patients continuously arrive in the hospital, waiting patients are called into the doctor's office, or patients leave the emergency room after the treatment, it is very difficult to keep track of the distributed tablet computers. Although the secretary or nurse can hand the device to a particular patient, it is not impossible for another patient to take over the device after the initial patient has completed the questionnaire, and begin a new data entry session. The resulting constant change of persons handling the device and people moving around also makes the accidental removal of a tablet from the waiting room easier, either by absentmindedly bagging it or by taking it into another room of the hospital. Keeping track of the tablets is further challenged by the fact that many people bring a tablet or mobile device of their own to use while waiting in the anteroom or reception area.

Falling Down. A very big problem of the mobile solution is the possibility of the device falling down or being dropped. The tablet PC will be used in the department of pediatric surgery, a very hectic and chaotic environment. There are many children who cannot remain in their seats or fidget restlessly, particularly in a stressful and more than likely unfamiliar environment like a clinic. That plus medical personnel rushing between rooms due to emergencies or children running around increase the risk of a device being damaged by a drop to the ground.

Getting Wet. Due to the chaotic environment it is also easily possible that liquids might be spilled on the device. Especially in the pediatric hospital, there are always drinks present, mainly to soothe the young patients. Within the hectic environment and stressful situation of a visit to the emergency room, the frequency of the drinks being dropped or spilled is quite high. Additionally, hospitals, and in this case especially surgical or emergency departments, do have handle and deal with larger quantities of either li-quid medication, e.g., infusion bags or bottles, or even bodily fluids, e.g., blood from an open wound. All these factors carry a high risk of the portable device being damaged by liquids.

Usage Context. The flurry of activities and worry of the guardians and patients was a major obstacle when handling the device. In a stressful situation like the aftermath of an accident, participants were not able to concentrate on using a touch screen-based questionnaire tool. Hurting kids crying and wanting to be soothed presented a major hindrance for using the device. Additionally, as soon as the doctor called in a patient, the questionnaires were abandoned and left incomplete as patients rushed into the doctor's office.

Another disadvantage in this usage context is the small display size. With the application being designed mainly for children, i.e., using a larger font size, pictures, and big buttons, the presented text had to be short to avoid scrolling or overloading the screen. For an initial anamnesis and case history given by the patient, as was the idea behind this project, mobility is not a necessity in the end.

5   Discussion

Because in primary care, children, young people, and especially their guardians and chaperons are always under pressure, highly stressed, or even just concerned, we have decided to test our prototype only on patients who have come into the pediatric surgery for follow-up examinations. To advise children and their parents of the questionnaire, and to minimize inhibitions against this new system in the test run, they were assisted by a staff member of the Centre for Accident Research, in our case a pediatric nurse. Although this employee actively went to the patients and their parents and asked them to complete the questionnaire, only 10 percent actually did so.

In order to provide a complete collection of accident data and to permit the attending doctors to know how the accident happened shortly before the actual treatment, it has to be ensured that each patient fills out the questionnaire in the waiting room of the emergency department as completely as possible and to the best of their knowledge. However, as we have seen in the evaluation, both the children and young patients themselves but especially the accompanying persons, mostly parents, are too anxious and panicked to ultimately do so.

6   Conclusion

With the increasing spread and general usefulness of mobile devices, we had the idea to employ them in the context of initial patient assessment in an emergency room. Here, they were meant to gather important information about the patient and the accident as well as try and help shorten the waiting time by distracting the patients and their attendants.Medical doctors and nurses work in an environment that requires high mobility. The usefulness of handheld computers in the field of medicine is respected, even among patients. Consequently, it is not astonishing that mobile devices are already frequently used in medical care scenarios. Therefore, the new interface developed for this work should be implemented on a tablet computer. Inspiration for this project came from the successful implementation of a mobile solution in the dermatology clinic in Graz, a project in which a method was implemented that collects data by patients filling out a questionnaire on a touch-screen device. For this work, we then developed mock-ups for a mobile device and tested the idea in real life scenario. During the test phase, we found that in this case scenario a mobile solution is not the best option. These results support the opinion of the medical staff, confronted on a

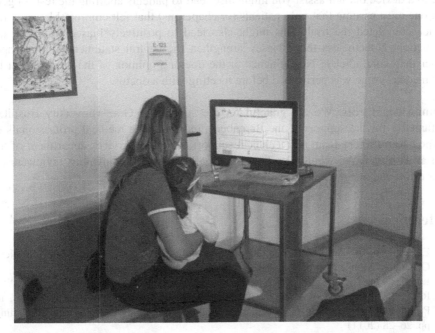

Fig. 5. Kiosk-based solution of the questionnaire tool. A mother and her child use the system in the waiting room.

daily basis with the hectic environment of the ER, who also advised against a mobile solution. For future applications of the questionnaire tool, a kiosk-based solution should be implemented, allowing the guardian to hold their child while clicking on the touch-screen solution (see Figure 5). The initial observations show that a non-mobile solution in this context is far superior to a mobile device. Furthermore, a standardized system can improve the data quality in patient records, but it must not necessarily be done by the patient alone; a cooperative usage of a questionnaire system with a doctor is feasible.

We can conclude, that in the hectic and turbulent environment with crying children around, a mobile solution is neither useful nor usable and poses a lot of unsolvable problems: mobile computing is not always an advantage in the hospital-world.

7   Limitations

The validity of the experiment can be challenged from a methodological and procedural angle. First comparing the results of a second return with an initial visit to the hospital is questionable. The idea to test in the second return of the patient came up, when patients were completely unwilling to take part in the study during the initial stressful visit after an accident. Not all patients necessary come back for a second visit, rendering the device non-useful for those who don't. Having an assistant direct you to a device but not assist you might also lead to patients aborting the test. In general one must assume that only patients (or chaperons) that felt comfortable using the device completed the trial. This might also lead to positively biased results in the evaluation. Nonetheless these biases strengthen the central statement of this paper rather than contradict it. No influence of the doctor's opinion of the device must be assumed, as usage was performed before meeting with a doctor.

Acknowledgements. We are grateful for the support of Graz University Hospital, particularly for the support of the Bärenburg and of all the medical professionals of the pediatric surgery team and technical support of the IT-Services department of the Styrian Hospital. We would also like to cordially thank all anonymous reviewers for their effort and insightful input on a previous version of this paper.

References

1. Edmondson, J., Anderson, W., Gray, J., Loyall, J.P., Schmid, K., White, J.: Next-Generation Mobile Computing. IEEE Software 31(2), 44–47 (2014)
2. http://www.statistik.at (last visited May 14, 2014)
3. Röcker, C.: Smart Medical Services: A Discussion of State-of-The-Art Approaches. In: Proceedings of the International IEEE Conference on Machine Learning and Computing, pp. 26–28 (2011)
4. Röcker, C., Ziefle, M., Holzinger, A.: From Computer Innovation to Human Integration: Current Trends and Challenges for Pervasive HealthTechnologies. In: Holzinger, A., Ziefle, M., Röcker, C. (eds.) Pervasive Health, pp. 1–17. Springer, London (2014)

5. Free, C., Phillips, G., Watson, L., Galli, L., Felix, L., Edwards, P., Patel, V., Haines, A.: The effectiveness of mobile-health technologies to improve health care service delivery processes: a systematic review and meta-analysis. PLoS Medicine 10(1), e1001363 (2013)
6. Kay, M., Santos, J., Takane, M.: mHealth: New horizons for health through mobile technologies. World Health Organization (2011)
7. Holzinger, A., Kosec, P., Schwantzer, G., Debevc, M., Hofmann-Wellenhof, R., Frühauf, J.: Design and Development of a Mobile Computer Application to Reengineer Workflows in the Hospital and the Methodology to evaluate its Effectiveness. J. Biomed. Inform. 44(6), 968–977 (2011)
8. Holzinger, A., Dehmer, M., Jurisica, I.: Knowledge Discovery and interactive Data Mining in Bioinformatics - State-of-the-Art, future challenges and research directions. BMC Bioinformatics 15(Suppl. 6), I1 (2014)
9. Waegemann, C.P.: mHealth: The Next Generation of Telemedicine? Telemedicine Journal and E-Health 16(1), 23–25 (2010)
10. Phillips, G., Felix, L., Galli, L., Patel, V., Edwards, P.: The effectiveness of M-health technologies for improving health and health services: a systematic review protocol. BMC Research Notes 3(1), 250 (2010)
11. Juric, S., Flis, V., Debevc, M., Holzinger, A., Zalik, B.: Towards a Low-Cost Mobile Subcutaneous Vein Detection Solution Using Near-Infrared Spectroscopy. The Scientific World Journal 2014 15 (2014)
12. Peischl, B., Ferk, M., Holzinger, A.: The Fine Art of User-centered Software Development on the example of Mobile Medical Apps. Softw. Qual. J. (in print, 2014), doi:10.1007/s11219-014-9239-1)
13. Holzinger, A., Ofner, B., Dehmer, M.: Multi-touch Graph-Based Interaction for Knowledge Discovery on Mobile Devices: State-of-the-Art and Future Challenges. In: Holzinger, A., Jurisica, I. (eds.) KnowledgeDiscovery andData Mining. LNCS, vol. 8401, pp. 241–254. Springer, Heidelberg (2014)
14. Harrison, R., Flood, D., Duce, D.: Usability of mobile applications: literature review and rationale for a new usability model. Journal of Interaction Science 1(1), 1–16 (2013)
15. Calero-Valdez, A., Ziefle, M., Schroeder, U., Horstmann, A., Herding, D.: Task performance in mobile and ambient interfaces. Does size matter for usability of electronic diabetes assistants? In: IEEE International Conference of the I-Society (2010) (in press) (Full paper at the IEEE)
16. Oehl, M., Sutter, C., Ziefle, M.: Considerations on efficient touch interfaces – how display size influences the performance in an applied pointing task. In: Smith, M.J., Salvendy, G. (eds.) HCII 2007. LNCS, vol. 4557, pp. 136–143. Springer, Heidelberg (2007)
17. Holzinger, A., Errath, M.: Mobile computer Web-application design in medicine: some research based guidelines. Universal Access in the Information Society International Journal 6(1), 31–41 (2007)
18. Sax, C., Lawrence, E.: Tangible Information: Gestures for a Portable e-Nursing touch screen interface. In: 11th International Conference on e-Health Networking, Applications and Services, pp. 1–8. IEEE (2009)
19. Holzinger, A.: Usability engineering methods for software developers. Communications of the ACM 48(1), 71–74 (2005)
20. Graham, M.J., Kubose, T.K., Jordan, D., Zhang, J., Johnson, T.R., Patel, V.L.: Heuristic evaluation of infusion pumps: implications for patient safety in Intensive Care Units. International Journal of Medical Informatics 73(11), 771–779 (2004)

21. Holzinger, A., Schlögl, M., Peischl, B., Debevc, M.: Optimization of a Handwriting Recognition Algorithm for a Mobile Enterprise Health Information System on the Basis of Real-Life Usability Research. In: Obaidat, M.S., Tsihrintzis, G.A., Filipe, J. (eds.) ICETE 2010. Communications in Computer and Information Science, vol. 222, pp. 97–111. Springer, Heidelberg (2012)
22. Calero Valdez, A., Ziefle, M., Horstmann, A., Herding, D., Schroeder, U.: Effects of Aging and Domain Knowledge on Usability in Small Screen Devices for Diabetes Patients. In: Holzinger, A., Miesenberger, K. (eds.) USAB 2009. LNCS, vol. 5889, pp. 366–386. Springer, Heidelberg (2009)
23. Ziefle, M., Klack, L., Wilkowska, W., Holzinger, A.: Acceptance of Telemedical Treatments – A Medical Professional Point of View. In: Yamamoto, S. (ed.) HCI 2013, Part II. LNCS, vol. 8017, pp. 325–334. Springer, Heidelberg (2013)
24. Ziefle, M., Rocker, C.: Human-centered design of e-health technologies: concepts, methods and applications. IGI Global (2011)
25. Richter, J.G., Nixdorf, M., Becker, A., Koch, T., Monser, R., Schneider, M.: Mobile Computing instead of paper based documentation in German Rheumatology. In: International Conference on Mobile Business, ICMB 2006, pp. 28–28. IEEE (2006)
26. Brewster, S., Lumsden, J., Bell, M., Hall, M., Tasker, S.: Multimodal'eyes-free'interaction techniques for wearable devices. In: Proceedings of the SIGCHI Conference on Human Factors in Computing Systems, pp. 473–480. ACM (2003)
27. Lam, H., Kirkpatrick, A.E., Dill, J., Atkins, M.S.: Effective display of medical laboratory report results on small screens: Evaluation of linear and hierarchical displays. International Journal of Human-Computer Interaction 21(1), 73–89 (2006)
28. Arhippainen, L., Tähti, M.: Empirical evaluation of user experience in two adaptive mobile application prototypes. In: Proceedings of the 2nd International Conference on Mobile and Ubiquitous Multimedia, pp. 27–34 (2003)
29. Väätäjä, H., Roto, V.: Mobile questionnaires for user experience evaluation. In: CHI 2010 Extended Abstracts on Human Factors in Computing Systems, pp. 3361–3366. ACM (2010)
30. Prgomet, M., Georgiou, A., Westbrook, J.I.: The Impact of Mobile Handheld Technology on Hospital Physicians' Work Practices and Patient Care: A Systematic Review. J. Am. Med. Inf. Assoc. 16(6), 792–801 (2009)
31. Holzinger, A., Hoeller, M., Bloice, M., Urlesberger, B.: Typical Problems with developing mobile applications for health care: Some lessons learned from developing user-centered mobile applications in a hospital environment. In: International Conference on E-Business (ICE-B 2008), pp. 235–240. INSTICC (2008)
32. Charlotte, T., Sheelagh, C.: Evaluating the deployment of a mobile technology in a hospital ward. In: Proceedings of the 2008 ACM Conference on Computer supported Cooperative Work, pp. 205–214. ACM (2008)
33. Jen, W.-Y., Chao, C.-C., Hung, M.-C., Li, Y.-C., Chi, Y.P.: Mobile information and communication in the hospital outpatient service. International Journal of Medical Informatics 76(8), 565–574 (2007)
34. Skov, M.B., Hoegh, R.T.: Supporting information access in a hospital ward by a context-aware mobile electronic patient record. Personal and Ubiquitous Computing 10(4), 205–214 (2006)
35. Geiger, A.M., Greene, S.M., Pardee III, R.E., Hart, G., Herrinton, L.J., Macedo, A.M., Rolnick, S., Harris, E.L., Barton, M.B., Elmore, J.G.: A computerized system to facilitate medical record abstraction in cancer research (United States). Cancer Causes & Control 14(5), 469–476 (2003)

36. Hsieh, S.-H., Hou, I.-C., Cheng, P.-H., Tan, C.-T., Shen, P.-C., Hsu, K.-P., Hsieh, S.-L., Lai, F.: Design and implementation of web-based mobile electronic medication administration record. Journal of medical systems 34(5), 947–958 (2010)

37. Holzinger, A., Softic, S., Stickel, C., Ebner, M., Debevc, M.: Intuitive E-Teaching by Using Combined HCI Devices: Experiences with Wiimote Applications. In: Stephanidis, C. (ed.) UAHCI 2009, Part III. LNCS, vol. 5616, pp. 44–52. Springer, Heidelberg (2009)

38. Holzinger, A.: Finger Instead of Mouse: Touch Screens as a Means of Enhancing Universal Access. In: Carbonell, N., Stephanidis, C. (eds.) UI4ALL 2002. LNCS, vol. 2615, pp. 387–397. Springer, Heidelberg (2003)

39. Siek, K.A., Rogers, Y., Connelly, K.H.: Fat finger worries: How older and younger users physically interact with pDAs. In: Costabile, M.F., Paternó, F. (eds.) INTERACT 2005. LNCS, vol. 3585, pp. 267–280. Springer, Heidelberg (2005)

40. Holzinger, A., Höller, M., Schedlbauer, M., Urlesberger, B.: An Investigation of Finger versus Stylus Input in Medical Scenarios. In: ITI 2008: 30th International Conference on Information Technology Interfaces, pp. 433–438. IEEE (2008)

41. Weippl, E., Holzinger, A., Tjoa, A.M.: Security aspects of ubiquitous computing in health care. Springer Elektrotechnik & Informationstechnik, e&i 123(4), 156–162 (2006)

42. Kieseberg, P., Hobel, H., Schrittwieser, S., Weippl, E., Holzinger, A.: Protecting Anonymity in Data-Driven Biomedical Science. In: Holzinger, A., Jurisica, I. (eds.) Interactive Knowledge Discovery and Data Mining in Biomedical Informatics. LNCS, vol. 8401, pp. 301–316. Springer, Heidelberg (2014)

Towards Interactive Visualization of Longitudinal Data to Support Knowledge Discovery on Multi-touch Tablet Computers

Andreas Holzinger[1], Michael Schwarz[1], Bernhard Ofner[1], Fleur Jeanquartier[1],
Andre Calero-Valdez[2], Carsten Roecker[1,2], and Martina Ziefle[2]

[1] Research Unit Human–Computer Interaction,
Institute for Medical Informatics, Statistics and Documentation,
Medical University Graz, Auenbruggerplatz 2, A-8036 Graz, Austria
{a.holzinger,m.schwarz,b.ofner,f.jeanquartier}@hci4all.at
[2] Human–Computer Interaction Center, RWTH Aachen University,
Campus-Boulevard 57, D-52074 Aachen, Germany
{calero-valdez,roecker,ziefle}@comm.rwth-aachen.de

Abstract. A major challenge in modern data-centric medicine is the increasing amount of time-dependent data, which requires efficient user-friendly solutions for dealing with such data. To create an effective and efficient knowledge discovery process, it is important to support common data manipulation tasks by creating quick, responsive and intuitive interaction methods. In this paper we describe some methods for interactive longitudinal data visualization with focus on the usage of mobile multi-touch devices as interaction medium, based on our design and development experiences. We argue that when it comes to longitudinal data this device category offers remarkable additional interaction benefits compared to standard point-and-click desktop computer devices. An important advantage of multi-touch devices arises when interacting with particularly large longitudinal data sets: Complex, coupled interactions such as zooming into a region and scrolling around almost simultaneously is more easily achieved with the possibilities of a multi-touch device than compared to a regular mouse-based interaction device.

Keywords: Data Visualization, Longitudinal Data, Time Series, Multi-Touch, Mobile Computing.

1 Introduction and Motivation for Research

One of the grand challenges in modern data-centric medicine is dealing with large, complex, heterogeneous and weakly structured data sets and large amounts of unstructured information. This calls for new, efficient and user-friendly solutions for handling such data – with raising expectations of end-users. Traditional approaches for data handling often cannot keep pace with demand, also increasing the risk of delivering unsatisfactory results. Consequently, to cope with this rising flood of data, new user-centered approaches are vital [1-4].

Particularly, the advent of mobile devices and ubiquitous smart sensors has led to an ongoing trend to record all sort of personal biomedical data over time [5, 6].

S. Teufel et al. (Eds.): CD-ARES 2014, LNCS 8708, pp. 124–137, 2014.

These recordings lead to a growing amount of so-called longitudinal data, in the engineering domain maybe better known as time series data [7].

A major challenge is how to deal with such time-dependent data, and not only to deal with it, but to *discover knowledge* from it.

Generally, there are two different ways to accomplish such tasks:

1) Applying *mathematical models* for description and prediction purposes [8, 9]; or

2) Using *visual inspection* to generate general assertions in regard to the properties of the underlying data set.

For the second kind of knowledge discovery, interactive data visualization plays an important role. As stated by Tufte (1983) [10], graphical representations of data sets are instruments for reasoning about quantitative information. A recent example for such analysis and sensemaking of complex biomedical data can be found in [11]. Therefore, often the most effective way to summarize a large set of quantitative information is to look at "pictures" of these numbers. However, during this visual information seeking process it is often necessary to *interact* with the displayed data: It is important to include the human expert into the data exploration process, and to combine the flexibility, creativity, general knowledge and pattern recognition abilities (in low dimensions) of the human with the enormous capacity, analytical power, and pattern recognition abilities (in high dimensions) of computer solutions.

A recent scientific approach is in combining the best of these two worlds [12] and a concrete topic is interactive visual data mining (VDM) [13, 14], which aims to integrate the human expert into the whole data exploration process and to effectively represent data visually, so to benefit from the human perceptual abilities and allowing the expert to get *insight* into the data by direct interaction with the data [15]. VDM can be particularly helpful when little is known about the data sets and/or the exploration goals are ill-defined or evolve over time [16]. The aspect of "time" in data visualization is generally most underrepresented in such approaches, yet, it is of vital importance, particularly in dealing with biomedical data [17].

Thereby, common tasks include: zooming into a portion of the overall data, changing the reference scale, comparisons with other data points and getting detailed, underlying information on some specific data points.

2   Theory and Background

2.1   Longitudinal Data

Longitudinal data (or time series data) arises when a certain random variable is recorded as a sequence over time, whereas the measurement of some characteristics at (roughly) one single point in time is called cross-section data. For a general introduction into time series data refer to [18-23].

Depending on the measurement, differentiated distinction can be drawn between *discrete* and *continuous* time series.

A discrete time series is one in which the set T_0 of times at which observations are made is a discrete set.

On the other hand, if observations are recorded continuously over a time interval, e.g. $T_0 = [0,1]$ a continuous time series arises [24]. In contrast to analog recording, the process of digital recording is inevitably connected to a discrete sample frequency. Therefore, strictly speaking, although the lag between two measurements may be in the magnitude of milliseconds, we always have discrete time series data in the electronic data processing domain.

The same is true for the recorded value. To be exact, we always record discrete variable values. Nevertheless, the underlying natures of, for instance, height, blood pressure, or weight of a person, are examples for continuous variables, whereas the number of patient visits on one day is an example for discrete ones. For continuous values it is therefore important to choose a recording sampling frequency that draws an adequate picture of the underlying process.

Furthermore, for discrete time series, we can differentiate between *evenly* and *unevenly* spaced time series. Evenly spaced time series have constant time intervals between measurement points, whereas time intervals for unevenly spaced series can vary over time. Unevenly spaced time series are also called event-based time series [25], while evenly spaced series are called time-based records.

Most of the long-term clinical longitudinal data falls in the category of discrete, unevenly spaced longitudinal data, as time intervals between medical checkups may vary in most of the cases [26].

An additional distinction regarding the recorded values can be made into *qualitative* and *quantitative* data.

Quantitative data is always numerical. It arises when certain characteristics are measured or counted. The number of patients in an ambulance is quantitative data, since it involves a count of the number of patients. Equally, the blood pressure of a patient is quantitative data, since the answer involves measuring the blood pressure.

Qualitative data is information that ranks or labels items, but does not measure or count them. For instance, if information about the drug name that is used for medication in a certain therapy is collected from patients, that data would be qualitative. If patients are asked during a medical checkup, whether they feel "very well", "well", "average", "bad" or "very bad", their subjective health status is converted into a ranking. Therefore, qualitative data is generated also in this case.

Furthermore, depending on the recorded variable, measured values can be assigned to different type classes, namely *nominal, ordinal, interval* or *ratio* [27]. Thereby, the type defines the recorded data's level of structure. In general, qualitative data is either nominal or ordinal, whereas quantitative data is either interval or ratio data.

Nominal data is the type with the least structure. Its values are simple labels that cannot be ordered or ranked in a meaningful way. The name of the drugs given to several patients would be such kind of data.

In contrast, ordinal data can be ordered or ranked, but does not measure or count any data characteristics. Questions about, e.g. the subjective health status or satisfaction level, generally involve a ranking.

Interval data does measure or count any characteristics, but ratios between two measured values have no intrinsic meaning. This applies for measurement scales, where the zero point does not describe a state of absence of a quantity (e.g. the absolute lowest value on a scale). Temperature measuring in degrees of Fahrenheit is an example of interval data.

Ratio data means that ratios between two measurement points have an intrinsic meaning. For instance, if one patient has a dosage of 400 mg and another patient a drug dosage of 200 mg, the former has a dosage that is twice as high as the second one.

Longitudinal data can also be classified by the number of independent quantities that are recorded for each observation. If a physician examines a patient and only records the heart rate, the data has just one independent quantity and is called univariate. On the other hand, data that involves more than one variable, is called multivariate. In special cases, when exactly two variables are measured, the data is called bivariate.

With regard to predictability of a time series we differentiate between *deterministic* and *stochastic* time series. If a time series can be predicted precisely, it is considered deterministic (e.g. if we look at the sinus wave). However, most of the time series fall in the category of stochastic time series [28]. Thereby, future events are only partly determined by past behavior and exact predictions are thus impossible and must be replaced by the idea that future values have a probability distribution that is conditioned by the knowledge of past values [21].

A time series is called *strictly stationary*, if the joint probability distribution does not change when shifted in time, i.e. $P_{t_1,...t_n}(x_1, ..., x_n) = P_{t_{1+c},...t_{n+c}}(x_{1+c}, ..., x_{n+c})$.

A time series is called *weakly stationary* if $\mathbb{E}(x_t) = \mu$ and for the autocovariances

$$\mathbb{E}[(x_t - \mu)(x_{t-c} - \mu)] = \gamma_i , \qquad c = 0, \pm 1, \pm 2, ...$$

This means, that the parameter mean and variance do not change over time, or follow any trends.

Insight can be gained from visualizations or from the hypothesis itself. This leads to the question: "What is interesting?" [29]. Closely connected is the approach of attention routing [30] to overcome one critical problem in visual analytics: to help end users locate good starting points for analysis. This may be achieved by application of longitudinal data visualization methods as described now.

3   Longitudinal Data Visualization

Nowadays, the most common visualization techniques for longitudinal data include point charts, bar charts, line graphs, sequence graphs and circle graphs [31]. For a general overview on visualization techniques refer to [32] and an excellent work on the visualization of time-oriented data is [33]. In the following paragraphs, longitudinal data visualization techniques are briefly introduced.

Sequence graphs represent time-dependent data on one dimension by indicating each data point with a mark on the axis. The distance between each mark on the axis represents the time span passing between the events. With sequence charts, it is not possible to visualize a second dimension for a data point.

Figure 1 shows a sequence graph. In this example the graph visualizes treatment frequency information.

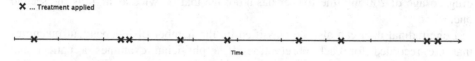

Fig. 1. - Sequence graph

This mode of presentation allows an easy recognition of treatment pilings and longer time frames without treatment. Nevertheless, it is not possible to add additional information, like a dosage quantity related to the treatment, to this visualization.

Therefore, **point graphs** extend sequence charts by using a second axis to display a further information dimension. The distance from the main axis thereby represents the second data dimension. Figure 2 shows a point chart. In this example the point chart visualizes treatment frequency and quantity information.

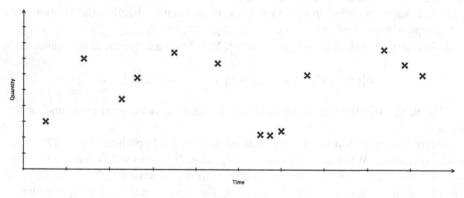

Fig. 2. - Point graph

The vertical distance to the origin represents the quantity information, whereas the horizontal distance to the origin stands for the elapsed time. Point charts are useful to detect pilings within two-dimensional data.

Bar graphs replace the points with bars, which increases the comparability between the data points. Figure 3 shows the same information as represented in Figure 2, visualized as a bar chart. A comparison of these two visualizations shows that the ability to compare data point quantities is enhanced by using bar charts.

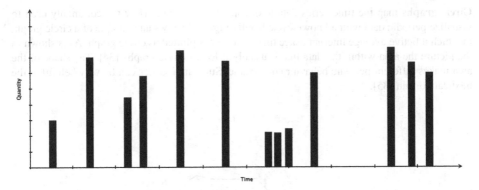

Fig. 3. - Bar graph

Line graphs extend point charts by connecting the dots with lines to emphasize the temporal aspect of data. Line charts are very helpful for indicating trends over time.

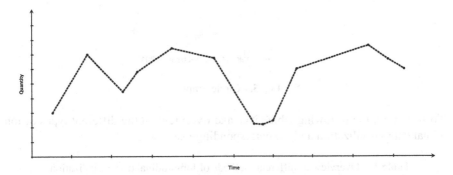

Fig. 4. - Line graph

According to Tufte [10], time series graphics are most suitable for big, complex data sets with real variability. Simple linear changes should better be summarized with one or two numbers. Tufte also introduced the following common guidelines that should be considered within every graphical display task:

- show the data
- induce the viewer to think about the substance, rather than about methodology, graphic design, the technology of graphic production, or something else
- avoid distorting what the data should express
- present many numbers in a small space
- make large data sets coherent
- encourage the eye to compare different pieces of data
- reveal the data at several levels of detail – from broad overview to fine structure
- serve a reasonably clear purpose: description, exploration, tabulation, or decoration.
- be closely integrated with the statistical and verbal descriptions of the data set.

Circle graphs map the time series data into a spherical domain. They are commonly used to visualize periodic data with a known cycle length. Figure 5 shows an example of a circle graph, in which a fictive average internet usage time of a user is plotted as circle graph. As is shown in the picture the area within the data line is usually filled in circle graphs [34]. The shape of the area makes different periodic behavior comparable. Such approaches can be very helpful in the medical domain [35].

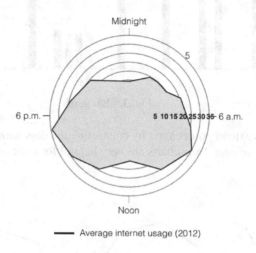

Fig. 5. - Circle graph

To sum it up, the following table gives and overview on the different types of longitudinal data visualization and the corresponding use cases.

Table 1. - Overview of different methods of longitudinal data visualization

Type	Use case
Sequence-Graph	For one dimensional data (time); for detecting pilings within the datasets
Point-Graph	Two dimensional data (e.g. time/quantity); detecting pilings within two dimensional datasets
Bar-Graph	Two dimensional data; special focus on comparison of nearby data-points
Line-Graph	Two dimensional data; Emphasizing the temporal aspect of the data
Circle-Graph	Two dimensional data; displaying periodicity

Plotting Value-Ranges

At times, it can be necessary to visualize not only a single point, but a range of values for each observation. This can be the case, if the observed data points comprise some margin of error or if multiple observations are merged into one time point of the plot. The latter is often done with stock market data. As stock market prices vary over a whole trading day, valuable information would be lost if only the closing price was plotted on a daily basis. Therefore, not just closing, but day-open, day-close, day-high and day-low are visualized.

In the following paragraph some techniques for visualizing such range information will be introduced. Although many of the techniques are most frequently used with stock-market data, they can easily be applied in other areas of use.

Figure 6 shows three common visualizations for range information. The first way of introducing range into a plot is the incorporation of **error bars [36]**. The horizontal bar symbols indicate some lower and upper threshold for each value. Error bars provide no possibility to introduce more information, like day-start and -end values, into the visualization.

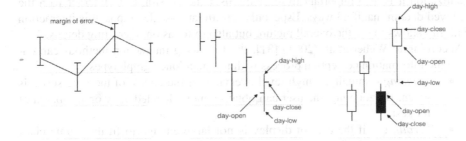

Fig. 6. - Different techniques to incorporate range information, from left to right: error bars, envelopes and candlesticks. The examples are typical for use in financial market analysis.

A second way to include range information is by using **envelopes**. As shown in Figure 6, envelopes provide information about the range as well as day -start and -end values.

The same kind of information can be visualized with **candlesticks [37]**. Whereas envelopes encode the information about start and end values by adding a small line to the left and right of the range line, candlesticks use the coloring of a rectangle. Black coloring means that the top line of the rectangle is the start- and the bottom line is the end-value. White coloring inverts this convention.

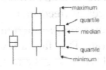

Box Plots

Fig. 7. - Box plot

Figure 7 shows a box plot visualization. **Box plots** [38] can provide information about the basic distribution properties of the data. The bottom and top of the box are first and third quartiles, and the band inside the box is the median. The ends of the lines, extending the box, are called whiskers. They can represent several possible alternative values. In this example, they stand for the minimum and maximum of the data set.

4   Longitudinal Data Interaction

As already emphasized in the introduction, besides choosing the right data-visualization it is also important to offer the user the possibility to interact with the displayed data in manifold ways. Especially within large-scale graphs, this interaction capability allows to see the overall picture but also to focus on interesting details.

According to Weber et al. (2001) [31], the following interaction methods can enhance the information perception process with the mentioned graph types.

- *Zooming* – initially, a high level overview of the course of the time series is given. By zooming, the user can obtain a more detailed view on a subarea of interest.
- *Scrolling* – if the area of display is not large enough to fit the whole chart (e.g. after zooming in), the user can scroll through areas.
- *Focusing and linking* – extends the idea of zooming by providing not only a zoomed-in version of the data, but also applying different, more effective visualization techniques to the zoomed-in dataset.
- *Brushing* – provides the idea of extended data visualization by automatically displaying pop-ups as a roll-over effect.
- *Filtering* – taking away (ignoring) irrelevant data objects.

When it comes to implementing these interaction methods, touch input has advantages compared to traditional point-and-click interfaces. This result from the fact that compared to mouse-based devices multi-touch devices provides a greater richness of interaction possibilities. Richness of interaction refers in this case to the degrees of freedom in interaction supported by the technology [39], [40]. Conventional mouse-based interfaces (the WIMP – Windows Icons Menu Pointers) rely heavily on a single 2D-cursor, which results in 2 degrees of freedom (not counting the state of the mouse-button). Sensing multiple fingers on a multi-touch display, however, results in a multiplication of the degrees of freedom. This fact allows the UI designer to encapsulate the various graph interaction methods into easy to learn and quickly executable gestural commandos.

Moreover, multiple tests with end users have yielded the confirmed result that complex mouse tasks, such as rotating an object and scaling, are faster done with multi-touch than with mouse-based devices [41]. Furthermore, well-designed gestural interfaces can shorten the learning curve by replacing a maze of menus and controls with simple actions, gestures, affordances and feedback [42]. Precondition to capture the benefits of the greater degree of freedom in interaction is a set of established gestural interaction guidelines. Nowadays, there are already some de facto gesture standards established for common tasks (see table 2).

Table 2. - Overview of gestural commandos for graph interaction

Gesture	Use case
Pinch gesture	Continuous zooming-out/in
Double-tap gesture	Discrete zooming-in and discrete zooming-out (fast overview and detail)
One-finger drag	Scrolling continuous back and forth
Cut-Gesture	Zooming into a discrete portion of the graph (market by the two fingers executing the cut)
Long-Press	Focusing on a data-point, showing detailed information

These gestural commandos are defined as follows [47]:

1.   *Pinch*: Touching down two fingers and either close or open both fingers without releasing from the touch device. The gesture ends when both fingers are removed from the device. "Pinch open" is usually used for zooming into an area, whereas "pinch closed" is used for zooming out.

2.   *Double Tap*: Fast, repeated tap with one finger at a single display location. Depending on the current state this action triggers discrete zooming in/out.

3.   *One finger drag*: Touching down with one finger and moving into an arbitrary direction, while keeping contact with the screen. Releasing the finger from the device stops the gesture.

4.   *Cut Gesture*: Touching down with two fingers and moving parallel into vertical direction, while keeping contact with the screen (Figure 8). Releasing both fingers from the device after moving a predefined distance triggers a cut gesture. A zooming action into the area defined by the "cut" is triggered.

5.   *Long Press*: Tapping down with one finger and keeping contact with the device for a predefined amount of time without movement.

Fig. 8. Cut Gesture

Another avenue for improvement would be to include the various other sensor inputs offered by multi-touch devices into the UI concept. Sensors like gyroscope and accelerometer allow the interface designer to create multiple state-dependent interface concepts. One easily integrated example would be to include the device orientation into the visualization approach. As stated by Widgor & Wixon, 2011 [42] a good user interface should be tailored to device properties and should take use of as much input information as possible.

5   Open Problems

Some open problems which we discovered during our work include:

- How to select the appropriate axis parameters? This is maybe the grand major challenge when dealing with interactive visualizations of longitudinal data sets.
- How to deal with missing data sets? Uncertainty is another crucial issue, particular in the medical domain.
- With the increasing amount of data we also have to find solutions for scalability and platform issues, especially when dealing with big data analysis on mobile devices.
- Another issue to name is dealing with high-dimensional longitudinal data.
- Combining the visualization of changes over time as well as showing trends, predictions and correlations is an open problem, too.
- A further open problem is to find methods for choosing optimal data resolutions (sampling frequencies) for the recording process as well as for the visualization step. The resolution should be chosen in dependence of the anticipated data variability and the expected cycle length of patterns within the set.
- Furthermore, it must be discussed how to handle changing visualization resolutions when continuously zooming in or out. Especially, methods for merging multiple data points into one.
- Bridging the gap between mathematical analyzing and visual inspection of longitudinal datasets is another issue, more concise: Create a user interface, which supports end users to utilize visual information for adjusting model parameters.

6   Conclusion and Future Work

Dealing with large longitudinal data sets is a hot and promising topic and the application of advanced multi-touch interaction, e.g. graph-based interactions [43] are a starting point for a number of unsolved problems, particularly in the visualization of complex, multidimensional and multivariate data sets, e.g. in summarizing and showing statistics and correlation of specific time sections; to get more insight into the applicability of such approaches in the real-world, some work on information perception would also be needed, e.g. to answer the question on what is a meaningful maximum number of simultaneously displayed plots for comparison purposes.

Acknowledgements. We are grateful for fruitful discussions within our meetings of the hci4all.at Group, and for the valuable reviewer' comments.

References

1. Holzinger, A., Dehmer, M., Jurisica, I.: Knowledge Discovery and interactive Data Mining in Bioinformatics - State-of-the-Art, future challenges and research directions. BMC Bioinformatics 15(Suppl. 6), I1 (2014)
2. Holzinger, A., Stocker, C., Ofner, B., Prohaska, G., Brabenetz, A., Hofmann-Wellenhof, R.: Combining HCI, Natural Language Processing, and Knowledge Discovery - Potential of IBM Content Analytics as an Assistive Technology in the Biomedical Field. In: Holzinger, A., Pasi, G. (eds.) HCI-KDD 2013. LNCS, vol. 7947, pp. 13–24. Springer, Heidelberg (2013)
3. Holzinger, A.: On Knowledge Discovery and Interactive Intelligent Visualization of Biomedical Data - Challenges in Human–Computer Interaction & Biomedical Informatics. In: DATA 2012, pp. 9–20 (2012)
4. Holzinger, A.: Weakly Structured Data in Health-Informatics: The Challenge for Human-Computer Interaction. In: Proceedings of INTERACT 2011 Workshop: Promoting and Supporting Healthy Living by Design, pp. 5-7. IFIP (2011)
5. Culler, D.E., Mulder, H.: Smart sensors to network the world. Scientific American 290(6), 84–91 (2004)
6. Ghrist, R., de Silva, V.: Homological sensor networks. Notic. Amer. Math. Soc. 54(1), 10–17 (2007)
7. Esling, P., Agon, C.: Time-series data mining. ACM Computing Surveys (CSUR) 45(1), 12 (2012)
8. Enright, C.G., Madden, M.G., Madden, N., Laffey, J.G.: Clinical time series data analysis using mathematical models and DBNs. Artificial Intelligence in Medicine, pp. 159–168. Springer (2011)
9. Sriyudthsak, K., Iwata, M., Hirai, M.Y., Shiraishi, F.: PENDISC: A Simple Method for Constructing a Mathematical Model from Time-Series Data of Metabolite Concentrations. Bulletin of Mathematical Biology, 1–19 (2014)
10. Tufte, E.R.: The Visual Display of Quantitative Information. Graphics Press, Chesire (1983)
11. Mueller, H., Reihs, R., Zatloukal, K., Holzinger, A.: Analysis of biomedical data with multilevel glyphs. BMC Bioinformatics 15(Suppl. 6), S5 (2014)
12. Holzinger, A.: Human-Computer Interaction and Knowledge Discovery (HCI-KDD): What Is the Benefit of Bringing Those Two Fields to Work Together? In: Cuzzocrea, A., Kittl, C., Simos, D.E., Weippl, E., Xu, L. (eds.) CD-ARES 2013. LNCS, vol. 8127, pp. 319–328. Springer, Heidelberg (2013)
13. Grinstein, G., Ankerst, M., Keim, D.: Visual Data Mining: Background. Applications, and Drug Discovery Applications. Tutorial at ACM SIGKDD2002, Edmonton, Canada (2002)
14. Keim, D.A.: Information visualization and visual data mining. IEEE Transactions on Visualization and Computer Graphics 8(1), 1–8 (2002)
15. Beale, R.: Supporting serendipity: Using ambient intelligence to augment user exploration for data mining and Web browsing. International Journal of Human-Computer Studies 65(5), 421–433 (2007)
16. Otasek, D., Pastrello, C., Holzinger, A., Jurisica, I.: Visual Data Mining: Effective Exploration of the Biological Universe. In: Holzinger, A., Jurisica, I. (eds.) Interactive Knowledge Discovery and Data Mining in Biomedical Informatics. LNCS, vol. 8401, pp. 19–33. Springer, Heidelberg (2014)

17. Gschwandtner, T., Gärtner, J., Aigner, W., Miksch, S.: A taxonomy of dirty time-oriented data. In: Quirchmayr, G., Basl, J., You, I., Xu, L., Weippl, E. (eds.) CD-ARES 2012. LNCS, vol. 7465, pp. 58–72. Springer, Heidelberg (2012)
18. Harvey, A.C., Harvey, A.: Time series models. Harvester Wheatsheaf, New York (1993)
19. Hamilton, J.D.: Time series analysis. Princeton university press, Princeton (1994)
20. Box, G.E., Jenkins, G.M., Reinsel, G.C.: Time series analysis: forecasting and control, 4th edn. John Wiley & Sons, Hoboken, NJ (2008)
21. Chatfield, C.: The analysis of time series: an introduction, 6th edn. CRC Press, Boca Raton (2009)
22. Brockwell, P.J., Davis, R.A.: Time series: theory and methods. Springer (2009)
23. Shumway, R.H., Stoffer, D.S.: Time series analysis and its applications: with R examples, 3rd edn. Springer, Heidelberg (2011)
24. Brockwell, P.: Time Series. In: Lovric, M. (ed.) International Encyclopedia of Statistical Science, pp. 1601–1605. Springer, Heidelberg (2011)
25. Warner, R.M.: Spectral analysis of time-series data. Guilford Press (1998)
26. Simonic, K.M., Holzinger, A., Bloice, M., Hermann, J.: Optimizing Long-Term Treatment of Rheumatoid Arthritis with Systematic Documentation. In: Proceedings of Pervasive Health - 5th International Conference on Pervasive Computing Technologies for Healthcare, pp. 550–554. IEEE (2011)
27. Stevens, S.S.: On the theory of scales of measurement. Science 103, 677–680 (1946)
28. Gradišek, J., Siegert, S., Friedrich, R., Grabec, I.: Analysis of time series from stochastic processes. Physical Review E 62(3), 3146–3155 (2000)
29. Dervin, B.: Sense-making theory and practice: an overview of user interests in knowledge seeking and use. J. Knowl. Manag. 2(2), 36–46 (1998)
30. Chau, D.H., Myers, B., Faulring, A.: What to do when search fails: finding information by association. In: Proceeding of the Twenty-sixth Annual SIGCHI Conference on Human Factors in Computing Systems, pp. 999–1008. ACM (2008)
31. Weber, M., Alexa, M., Müller, W.: Visualizing time-series on spirals. In: IEEE Symposium on Information Visualization, pp. 7–7. IEEE Computer Society (2001)
32. Turkay, C., Jeanquartier, F., Holzinger, A., Hauser, H.: On Computationally-Enhanced Visual Analysis of Heterogeneous Data and Its Application in Biomedical Informatics. In: Holzinger, A., Jurisica, I. (eds.) Interactive Knowledge Discovery and Data Mining in Biomedical Informatics. LNCS, vol. 8401, pp. 117–140. Springer, Heidelberg (2014)
33. Aigner, W., Miksch, S., Schumann, H., Tominski, C.: Visualization of Time-Oriented Data. Human-Computer Interaction Series. Springer, London (2011)
34. Harris, R.L.: Information graphics: A comprehensive illustrated reference. Oxford University Press (1999)
35. Holzinger, A., Hoeller, M., Bloice, M., Urlesberger, B.: Typical Problems with developing mobile applications for health care: Some lessons learned from developing user-centered mobile applications in a hospital environment. In: International Conference on E-Business (ICE-B 2008), pp. 235–240. INSTICC (2008)
36. Cumming, G., Fidler, F., Vaux, D.L.: Error bars in experimental biology. The Journal of Cell Biology 177(1), 7–11 (2007)
37. Lee, K., Jo, G.: Expert system for predicting stock market timing using a candlestick chart. Expert Systems with Applications 16(4), 357–364 (1999)
38. Williamson, D.F., Parker, R.A., Kendrick, J.S.: The box plot: a simple visual method to interpret data. Ann. Intern. Med. 110(11), 916–921 (1989)

39. Hodges, S., Izadi, S., Butler, A., Rrustemi, A., Buxton, B.: ThinSight: Versatile Multi-touch Sensing for Thin Form-factor Displays. In: UIST 2007: Proceedings of the 20th Annual Acm Symposium on User Interface Software and Technology, pp. 259–268. ACM (2007)
40. Buxton, B.: A Touching Story: A Personal Perspective on the History of Touch Interfaces Past and Future. In: SID Symposium, pp. 444–448. Wiley (2010)
41. Benko, H., Wilson, A.D., Baudisch, P.: Precise selection techniques for multi-touch screens. In: Proceedings of the SIGCHI Conference on Human Factors in Computing Systems, pp. 1263–1272. ACM (2006)
42. Wigdor, D., Wixon, D.: Brave NUI world: designing natural user interfaces for touch and gesture. Morgan Kaufman, Burlington, MA (2011)
43. Holzinger, A., Ofner, B., Dehmer, M.: Multi-touch Graph-Based Interaction for Knowledge Discovery on Mobile Devices: State-of-the-Art and Future Challenges. In: Holzinger, A., Jurisica, I. (eds.) Knowledge Discovery and Data Mining. LNCS, vol. 8401, pp. 241–254. Springer, Heidelberg (2014)

Semantic-Aware Mashups for Personal Resources in SemanticLIFE and SocialLIFE

Sao-Khue Vo, Amin Anjomshoaa, and A. Min Tjoa

Institute of Software Technology and Interactive Systems,
Vienna University of Technology, Vienna, Austria
{saokhue,anjomshoaa,amin}@ifs.tuwien.ac.at

Abstract. SemanticLIFE is a Semantic Desktop system, which deals with the personal lifetime data. However, SemanticLIFE is limited to local storage, which is an isolated data repository. In the recent years, people have the tendency to share their resources, which are not only stored locally on their personal computers, but also hosted on social networking sites (SNSs). We propose and use the term 'SocialLIFE' to denote one's lifetime information in SNSs, in which personal resources are his/her activities, interests, and related connections. In this paper, we also propose a mashup language and a semantic-based mashup framework. The final goal of this research is to provide a semantic-based way for bridging the gap between SemanticLIFE and SocialLIFE in order to integrate and reuse existing personal resources of existing applications such as information resources of Semantic Desktops and SNSs. The proposed mashup system also aims to supports non-expert users to create data mashups based on semantic-aware mashup dataflow.

Keywords: Semantic Desktop, Semantic Web, Social Networks, Linked Data, Linked Data Services, Semantic Mashup.

1 Background and Motivation

Business objectives are accomplished successfully when human resource management systems are developed and implemented according to organizational goals, particularly if personal information management (PIM) is adopted to utilize all employee information productively [1]. Some PIM systems use Semantic Desktop approach, which create a semantic layer for integrating applications and personal life items, as the means to support users in information management.

Today, an increasing number of organizations/enterprises are taking advantage of mashups, which support users in fast integration of heterogeneous data from multiple sources [2][3]. Furthermore, they also benefit from the collaborative principles of Web 2.0 technologies by using social networking sites (SNSs) to build their social activities/relations and support their knowledge management. As a result, the amount of heterogeneous data assets, which are distributed among personal and business domains, is increasing. In addition, those PIM systems are limited to isolated data repositories, and do not fulfill most of the requirements for a holistic collaborative

S. Teufel et al. (Eds.): CD-ARES 2014, LNCS 8708, pp. 138–154, 2014.

environment at the organizational level. Although enterprise knowledge management systems facilitate reusing and accessing of knowledge resources, these systems cannot work effectively unless knowledge workers contribute their knowledge resources and assets to organizations/enterprises.

In order to support users in exploiting the potential of sharing data on the web, the data should be managed in a machine-processable way by applying Semantic Web technologies. During designing and discussing issues around the Semantic Web, Tim Berners-Lee came up with the new term "Linked Data" that describes a method for publishing and interlinking structured data so that it can become more useful for people or machines in exploring the Web of Data [4]. In the meantime, we observe a number of contributions in the Enterprise 2.0 domain [5] that are aiming to apply Web 2.0 and SNSs principles to create an effective and collaborative community, and to explore the role of social computing in achieving the performance goals of enterprises. The potential of Enterprise 2.0 cannot be fully realized without an active support and an increased involvement of human resources [6]. Using SNSs in an enterprise environment, employees can share their data (e.g. skills, interests, or activities, etc.) with their groups or colleagues. From the enterprise perspective, employees can collect business information from customers and partners through SNSs by exploring the relationship of business establishments, professionals, or individuals.

From the above remarks, we can derive the need for a flexible and semantic–aware approach to bridge the gap between internal and external data sources, and especially bringing the relevant personal resources into enterprises. The ultimate goal of this paper is also to find the solution for semantic-aware mashups of personal resources from Semantic Desktops and SNSs following the trends of Enterprise 2.0.

2   Personal Resources in SemanticLIFE and SocialLIFE

SemanticLIFE is a prototype of a PIM system that has been developed in Vienna University of Technology to store, organize and manage various personal life items [7]. The architecture of SemanticLIFE framework is depicted in Fig. 1. It provides a repository of lifetime personal data from varied resources (e.g. email messages, web browser history, images, contacts, phone calls, life events, and other resources). However, the major limitation of Semantic Desktops approaches is that it is restricted to a personal computers and its precious semantic information is not yet effectively used in business processes and tasks that people deal with in their workplace and daily life [8].

With the advent of Web 2.0, many organizations/enterprises have started using the Web 2.0 techniques by applying SNSs in order to increase the effectiveness of their business by means of a tighter collaboration. People have the tendency to share their knowledge or resources, which are not only stored locally on their personal computer or isolated data repositories, but also hosted on SNSs on the web (e.g. Google documents, LinkedIn profiles, Flickr images, Twitter tweets, etc.).

In our research, we propose and use the term 'SocialLIFE' to denote one's lifetime information in SNSs, in which personal resources are user activities (messages, comments, twits, etc.), user interests (books, movies, etc.), and other related connections

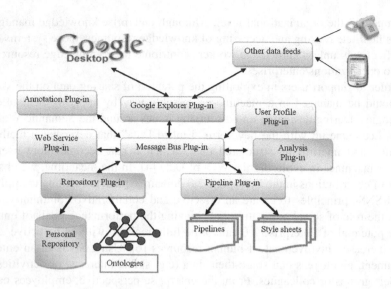

Fig. 1. SemanticLIFE framework [6]

(friends, colleagues, etc.). To be more specific, one's SocialLIFE consists of interconnections of people relations such as friendship or business/professional relationships on Facebook or LinkedIn; their interests such as video, image or music on YouTube, Flickr, MySpace and so on.

With the aim of interlinking data on the Semantic Web to support people or machines in exploring the Web of Data, Linked Data delivers an important mechanism for information management and information integration [2]. Linked Data extends the standard Web technologies such as HTTP, URIs, and RDF to share information in a machine-readable way. Besides, the term "Linked Open Data" (LOD), refers to a community project that is aiming to encourage people or organizations to follow the Linked Data principle and publish their raw data under open licenses [2]. The Semantic Web community has gained momentum with the widespread publishing of LOD and the big number of promising datasets with a high potential for further exploration. In order to bridge the gap between Semantic Desktops and Linked Data, several research projects are conducted [9], [10]. These researches have the common goals to combine resources from Linked Data and Semantic Desktops by using semantic metadata as a common denominator, and to enrich the data within the personal information as well as the enterprise spaces.

To benefit from the LOD cloud, it is crucial to put personal resources into a context that facilitates the interlinking of resources and enables powerful personal services. These personal resources are not just textual content but also multimedia content such as music, videos, pictures, etc. There are a number of well-known vocabularies such as FOAF, SIOC, DBPedia, etc., which empower data sharing and linking personal resources with LOD cloud. Furthermore, for the multimedia content, there are some application-specific exporters that allow users to export their data. For instance, Flickr's data can be exported via tools such as Flickr2RDF [11] and FlickrWrappr [12] that parse the user profile and image metadata in order to generate the RDF serialization which reuses the FOAF vocabulary. With a high potential for further exploration, SNSs have served as convincing and useful platforms for linking and reusing heterogeneous data of a user's SocialLIFE for performing further operations or aggregations.

As a result, the existing ontology models and exporters can be reused to extend the SemanticLIFE ontology and support information integration with one's SocialLIFE. Figure 2, depicts the linking of personal resources in SemanticLIFE and SocialLIFE with the LOD cloud.

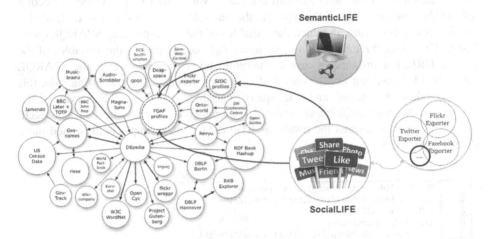

Fig. 2. Linking SemanticLIFE and SocialLIFE with LOD Cloud

To illustrate the potential of this approach, a motivating use case for personal financial data (such as bank statements) will be presented in Section 4.1. A number of financial institutions and banks allow their customers to access their financial statements via APIs or download their statements in standard formats such as Open Financial Exchange format. The Open Financial Exchange (OFX)[1] is a unified specification to exchange electronic financial information between financial institutions and consumers via the Internet. In order to turn personal financial data into mashable artifacts, personal financial data can be converted to RDF/N3 and linked with personal profile.

All gathered information in Semantic Desktops and SNSs platforms have to be parsed into semantic personal services or mashable semantic-based resources that provide a semantic way to express and exchange information from heterogeneous resources. In this context, there are a number of research efforts that try to combine the services and Web of Data. Linked Data Services (LIDS) [13] is one of these approaches that by definition provides HTTP URIs for entities. Dereferencing the LIDS' URIs returns an RDF description of the service input entity, its relation to the service output and the output data itself. This facilitates the transition from data silos to the Web of Data and enables the automatic integration of data resources.

---

[1] http://www.ofx.net/

The LIDS is applied as a suitable solution in our approach, in which we use the vocabulary of LIDS to define and describe the relevant services. The advantage of the LIDS is its capability to build semantic models of Web APIs semi-automatically. This includes the lowering and lifting processes that is converting RDF to the required input data of services and constructing semantic data out of a non-semantic API or service response, respectively.

To illustrate this by an example, consider a sample service for searching personal events in SocialLIFE, which has the URL *http://localhost/sociallife/thing*. This service is also used in the latter mashup use cases, which will be presented in Section 4.2. In the lowering side of this service, the variables are added to the URL of this service as a query string, in which the variables of the corresponding SPARQL query *"SELECT ?thing WHERE {?thing foaf:name ?q}"* are bound to the variables of the service URL. For instance in case of querying the *conference* events, the SPARQL query will be rewritten as *"?events foaf:name ?conference"*. In the lifting side, this service takes the name and the query variables to form the service URL *"http://localhost/sociallife?thing=events&q=conference"*. If the client accepts RDF format, the service returns the results as RDF data. This example is illustrated more details in Figure 3.

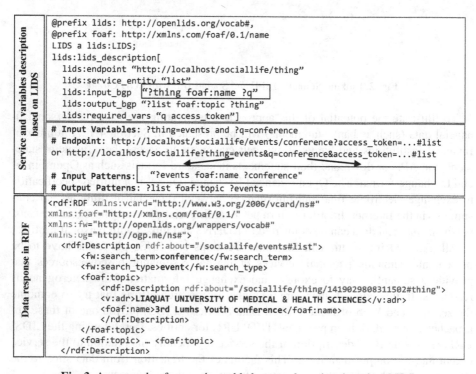

Fig. 3. An example of semantic-enabled personal services based on LIDS

3   Semantic-Based Mashup

Mashup is a web application that uses content from different data sources to generate a new service presented in a single graphical interface[2]. Based on the semantic approach, semantic mashup are mashups whose combined services and APIs are supported or annotated by a semantic layer for supporting (semi)-automatic service composition in mashup creation [14]. In this section, a semantic-based mashup architecture is proposed, which aims to: (i) facilitate the integration of heterogeneous personal resources from SemanticLIFE and SocialLIFE within organizations/enterprises; and (ii) improve the mashup usability by supporting the end users to choose the appropriate input data via mapping domain ontologies. This semantic-based mashup framework consists of the following four layers (as illustrated in Fig. 4):

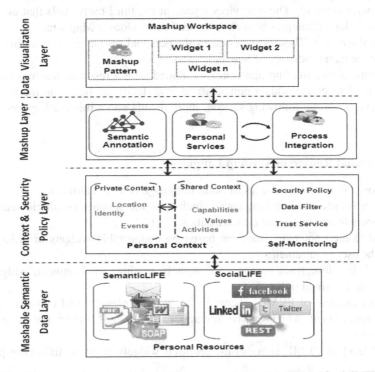

Fig. 4. Semantic-based mashup architecture for SemanticLIFE and SocialLIFE

— *Mashable semantic data layer*: focuses on the retrieval of personal resources from SemanticLIFE and SocialLIFE, and their converting them to RDF based on the relevant domain ontologies.
— *Context & Security Policy layer*: This layer is in charge of the efficient implementation of information security and privacy policies. More importantly, this layer includes context ontologies for describing personal services and the enforcement of

---

[2] http://en.wikipedia.org/wiki/Mashup_(web_application_hybrid)

privacy policies for self-monitoring of shared information in social networks [15]. Further details about this approach are provided in our previous article [16].

— *Mashup layer*: In this layer, the mashable semantic data of lower layers will be integrated and used in various use cases of data integration. To create mashup, the services of SemanticLIFE and SocialLIFE are referred in the mashup language that will be introduced in Section 3.1.

— *Data visualization layer*: This layer enhances the original contents by adding graphical representations like maps or images (e.g., Google Map, Flickr, etc.). This layer constitutes the main workspace that allows end-users to interact with the mashup platform.

In our framework, the following three groups of services are supported:

— *SPARQL-based services:* These services query the semantic data via dedicated SPARQL endpoints such as DBpedia[3], Events[4], etc.

— *Third party services:* These services represent the third party APIs that do not expose RDF data. Examples of such APIs are Flickr, Google Map, etc.

— *Personal services:* These services query the personal resources via custom personal services or data repository of Semantic Desktops.

Our semantic-aware mashup platform is equipped with a resource mashup language, which is used to create widget compositions and dataflows based on the aforementioned services. In the following section, more details about this mashup language is provided.

3.1   Personal Resources Mashup Language

The proposed Personal Resources Mashup Language (PRML) aims to:

— Create a simple mashup language, which uses the domain ontologies and helps developers to create semantic-aware data widgets.

— Formulate the composite solutions based on connectable widgets in order to address the user requirements.

The PRML has four main components, namely mashup, environment, widget, and parameter as described in Fig. 5.

The root element of PRML schema is the *mashup* element and contains an *environment* sub-element, which can be SemanticLIFE, SocialLIFE or any other predefined context.

The third level of PRML contains the required widgets with the following primary attributes:

— *context* and *type*: are the name and type of the required context respectively.

— *source*: indicates the service source of widgets (SPARQL endpoint, third party service, or personal service).

— *role*: indicates the role assigned to a specific user or a group of users who can use the widget.

---

[3] http://dbpedia.org/snorql/
[4] http://eventmedia.eurecom.fr/sparql/

— *mapping*: supports mapping to ontology resources or properties, for example, *mapping="rdf:type :Place"* is mapping the input/output with the Place concept of the target ontology.
— *parameters*: indicates the additional parameters of the target widget (input and output parameters).

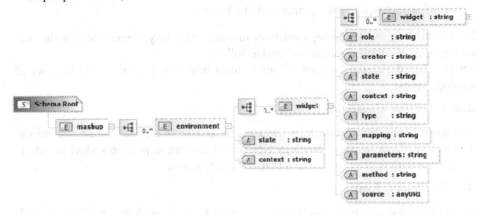

Fig. 5. The schema of personal resources mashup language (PRML)

The fourth level of PRML are *parameters* which contain one or more *input* and *output* elements with the following attributes:
— *type*: is the type of input/output parameters (String, Number, Array, Boolean, Date).
— *mapping*: supports mapping to the ontology resources or properties.
— *acceptedData/dataFormat*: is the type of data format that is accepted by the input ports. The data format can be JSON, XML, SPARQL-results or object.
— *operator*: identifies an operator to construct constraints (for instance: > , < , regular expression, etc.)
— *requireSource*: indicates the input of the target widget if required.

3.2 Semantic Mashup Formalization

In this section, the formal definition of mashup concepts and mashup rules based the proposed mashup language will be defined.

Definition 1. Widget

A widget is a tuple of <I, R, P> where I = {$i_1, i_2, \dots, i_p$} is a set of Input ports, R is the result set and P is the process (or web service) which is run internally in the widget to consume the inputs I and produce the result R. Each one of these elements has a set of metadata that describes the functions and properties of that element. The input ports and output results will have the previously defined attributes of *input* and *output* parameter of PRML (e.g. *type, mapping, acceptedData/dataFormat, etc.*).

The process may include further metadata such as additional parameters for the widget (e.g. id, name, width, height...), process description, and type of process (e.g., SPARQL, Javascript based, Web Service, etc.). In order to use widgets, they should be instantiated and called by the mashup framework.

Definition 2. Mashup

A mashup M is a set of 4-tuple, $M = \{<w_i, c_{ij}, w_j, I_{wj}> \mid \forall i,j=0...n, i \neq j\}$ where

— w_i, $w_j \in W$ are instances of widget (W is the set of available widgets)
— c_{ij} is the connector between two widgets that denotes the dataflow between output port of widget w_i and the I_{wj} input port of widget w_j.

In order to help users to design mashups in a semantic way, some rules for the mashup process are needed that are defined as follows.
Let $D = \{d_1, d_2, ..., d_q\}$ be a set of data formats, and $O = \{o_1, o_2, ..., o_r\}$ be a set of ontology types.

Rule 1: Feasible Connection

A feasible connection between two widgets w_i and w_j is a connection c_{ij} where the data format (d_i) or mapping ontology type (o_i) of the output port on widget w_i side is compatible with d_j or o_j on the input port at widget w_j side.

Rule 2: Avoiding loops

If the Mashup contains a 4-tuple $<w_i, c_{ii+1}, w_{i+1}, I_{wi+1}>$ then there should be no path $<w_{i+1}, c_{i+1\ i+2}, w_{i+2}, I_{wi+2}> ....<w_{i+n}, c_{i+n\ i+n+1}, w_{i+n+1}, I_{wi+n+1}>$ where $w_{i+n+1} = w_i$.

3.3   Widget-Based Query Generation

To query remote RDF resources, the corresponding query is constructed based on widget parameters as follows:

Suppose $I = \{i_1, i_2,..., i_n\}$ is a set of input parameters of a given widget and R is the resulting output of this widget. Each input parameter i_j (j=0...n) has also its optional properties (i.e., name, mapping, type, value and operator).

A query Q can be defined as: $Q = <S, W, F>$ where:
— $S = <SELECT, R, I>$: SELECT statement with relevant parameters
— $W = <WHERE, R, I>$: WHERE clause with relevant parameters
— $F = <FILTER, I>$: FILTER constrains with relevant required parameters
Query Q is generated in three steps as described below (depicted in Fig. 6):
— Step 1: The parameters' names are enumerated for creating the SELECT part. The SPARQL variables of SELECT statement are formed as "*SELECT ?R ?i$_{1[name]}$ ... ?i$_{n[name]}$*" by using output R and relevant parameters' names.
— Step 2: The output R and the parameter names and mappings are used to form the triple patterns of WHERE clause as follows: "*WHERE {?R ?i$_{1[mapping]}$?i$_{1[name]}$ · .... ?R ?i$_{n[mapping]}$?i$_{n[name]}$ }*".
— Step 3: The names, values, and operator of parameters are used to add filter constraints. Depending on relevant parameter's operator, the syntax of the FILTER will be formed differently. For example, if the operator of i_j is '*regex*', the string matching syntax must be "*FILTER (regex(?i$_{j[name]}$, ?i$_{j[value]}$))*"; otherwise, the syntax must "*FILTER (?i$_{j[name]}$?i$_{j[operator]}$?i$_{j[value]}$)*".

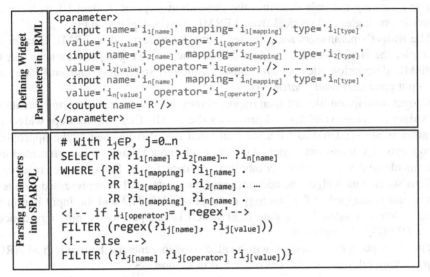

| Defining Widget Parameters in PRML | ```<parameter>
    <input name='$i_{1[name]}$' mapping='$i_{1[mapping]}$' type='$i_{1[type]}$'
    value='$i_{1[value]}$' operator='$i_{1[operator]}$'/>
    <input name='$i_{2[name]}$' mapping='$i_{2[mapping]}$' type='$i_{2[type]}$'
    value='$i_{2[value]}$' operator='$i_{2[operator]}$'/> … … …
    <input name='$i_{n[name]}$' mapping='$i_{n[mapping]}$' type='$i_{n[type]}$'
    value='$i_{n[value]}$' operator='$i_{n[operator]}$'/>
``` |
| Parsing parameters into SPARQL | ```# With $i_j \in P$, j=0…n
SELECT ?R ?$i_{1[name]}$?$i_{2[name]}$… ?$i_{n[name]}$
WHERE {?R ?$i_{1[mapping]}$?$i_{1[name]}$.
        ?R ?$i_{2[mapping]}$?$i_{2[name]}$. …
        ?R ?$i_{n[mapping]}$?$i_{n[name]}$.
<!-- if $i_{i[operator]}$= 'regex'-->
FILTER (regex(?$i_{j[name]}$, ?$i_{j[value]}$))
<!-- else -->
FILTER (?$i_{j[name]}$?$i_{j[operator]}$?$i_{j[value]}$)}``` |

Fig. 6. SPARQL query generation based on widget parameters

3.4   Widget UI Generation

In the proposed mashup system, UI Widgets are both a graphical user interface and a software component with a specific function. In PRML syntax, the UI Widgets can be described as a user interface with standard web form elements. In this section, a convenient and flexible UI generation mechanism for parsing and rendering the form widgets will be provided. This mechanism and the required steps for the UI Widget rendering process is described in the figure 7:

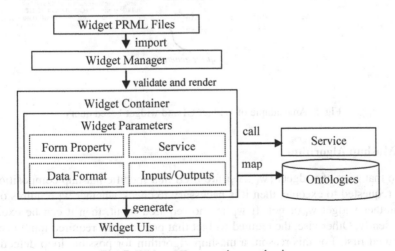

Fig. 7. Widget UI generation mechanism
```

The following example describes the generation steps of Widget UI with the appropriate ontologies and services from a PRML file (as depicted in Fig. 8):

— The widget's parameters are extracted from the corresponding PRML file: for example, the BankStatements widget defines the following input parameters in the PRML description file: *account, memo, amount, start_date, and end_date*; and output parameter *bank_statements*.

— Widget description files are then imported into the widget manager component. Widget container validates and processes the PRML files. In this step, widget parameters are rendered as form elements that are also mapped to the appropriate concepts of domain ontologies. As such, each input parameter is represented as a form element (e.g. textbox, combo box or date field). For example, in case of BankStatements widget, the account input parameter will be represented as a textbox and is mapped to the ontology concept *ofx:ACCTID* and the input parameter *start_date* is rendered as a date field which is mapped to the ontology concept *ofx:DTPOSTED*, and so on.

— The description of UI Widget will be also used to generate the required SPARQL query with relevant variables as described in section 3.3.

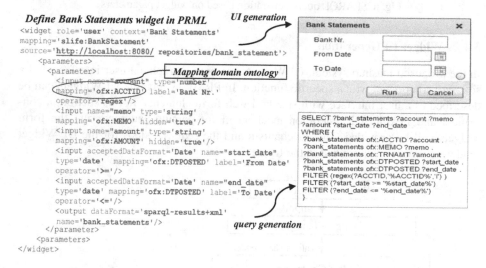

Fig. 8. An example of Widget UI and widget-based query

3.5   Mashup Algorithm

Suppose that a set of widgets $\{w_i...w_j\}$ are used in a specific mashup composition M. If w_j is requested to execute, then it is necessary to check whether wj requires output from another widget w_i or not. If w_j has no required input, then it can be executed independently. Otherwise, the requied widget that provides the required input needs to be executed first. For this reason, a mashup algorithm for possible loop detection is required.

The algorithm for mashup execution is based on the acyclic directed graphs, in which each widget of mashup is considered as a graph vertex, and each connection between two widgets is considered as a graph edge. For iterating through all widgets of a mashup (nodes of the graph), the Depth first-search (DFS) algorithm is used to visit the widgets. In case of mashup, the output value of any selected widget will be the input value of the connected widgets via the relevant port. The mashup M and the visited widget will be handled by a recursive function. Each visited widget will be asked to execute its internal process and return the value via its output port. The returned value will be then considered as the input value for the connected widgets. Instead of checking all edges at once in DFS algorithm, the edges are checked in two phases by differentiating discovery edges and back edges via input ports or output port respectively. Discovery edges are those edges that connect a vertex to another descendant node, and back edges are those edges that connect a vertex to another ancestor node. The mashup execution algorithm is described in the following recursive pseudo code:

```
Algorithm processWidget(M,widget)

Input: mashup M, an instance widget ∈ M
1:  if widget.inputPorts > 0 then
2:      for each inputPort ∈ widget
            //get connected widget
3:          previousWidget = inputPort.connectedWidget
4:          if previousWidget is executed then
                //get value of connected widget
5:              widget.inputPort.value = previousWidget.outputPort.value
6:          else
7:              //recursive-process connected widget
8:              widget.inputPort.isVisited = true
9:              processWidget(M,previousWidget)
10:     end for
11: end if
12: widget.isExecuted = true;
    //executeProcess function: execute process inside widget (SPARQL, service, etc)
13: widgetResult = executeProcess()
14: for each outputPort ∈ widget
15:     nextWidget = outputPort.connectedWidget
16:     if nextWidget.inputPort is visited then
17:         //get value of current widget
18:         nextWidget.inputPort.value = widgetResult
19:     else
            //recursive-process connected widget
20:         nextWidget.inputPort.isVisited = true
21:         processWidget(M,nextWidget)
22:     end if
23: end for
24: return widgetResult
```

Algorithm 1: Mashup algorithm

4   Use Cases

As a proof of concept of the proposed approach, some mashup use cases have been defined to prove the usefulness of our mashup platform and combine the personal resources of SemanticLIFE and SocialLIFE.

4.1   Use Case: Personal Finance Mashup

The first use case is dedicated to the Tim Berners-Lee's vision about combining different data resources [17]. He has formulated this vision as follows: *"The Semantic Web is a web of data. There is lots of data we all use every day, and it is not part of the web. I can see my bank statements on the web, and my photographs, and I can see my appointments in a calendar. But can I see my photos in a calendar to see what I was doing when I took them? Can I see bank statement lines in a calendar? Why not? Because we do not have a web of data. Because data is controlled by applications, and each application keeps it to itself"*. Besides, you might have many bank accounts and want to keep a record of different bank transactions from those accounts in a single view (i.e., a calendar view). For realizing this use case, we have created a specific data convertor that converts the financial data from OFX format into RDF triple and stored in the SemanticLIFE repository. Figure 9, depicts for the personal finance mashup. To illustrate and demonstrate the feasibility of this use case, two basic widgets are used:

— *Bank Statements widget*: which retrieves the bank statements of a given bank account in a specific period of time.
— *Calendar widget*: which shows the details of bank statements in a single and flexible view.

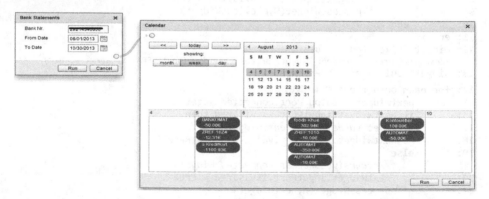

Fig. 9. Personal finance mashup for showing bank statements in calendar view

4.2   Use Case: Personalized Mashup

This use case is aiming to combine and enrich some personal data with relevant data from social networks and is formulated as follows: *I want to check the events in my local calendar as well as events from my SNSs in a specific time. For a specific event, show me some famous tourist attractions in the location of that event, including some photos (if available), other additional contextual information (weather condition, my friends, etc.).*

This use case can be realized via a personalized mashup that uses the following six widgets (as depicted in Fig. 10):

— *Calendar Events widget*: retrieves personal calendar events from SemanticLIFE or SocialLIFE (i.e., Facebook events as mentioned in Section 2). This widget will return the events with relevant information (e.g. locations or organizer).
— *Tourist attractions widget*: calls the third party service to return information about places based on the given input location. This service may be a query to DBpedia via its dedicated SPARQL Endpoint.
— *Geolocation converter*: is a widget that converts the place address into the geolocation format for viewing in Google map.
— *Google map widget*: shows the obtained places in a Google map.
— *Flickr widget*: is a third party service of Flickr to search photos that match some given criteria. In this use case, the matching condition will be the name of the place.
— *Weather widget*: shows the weather forecast of the given place.

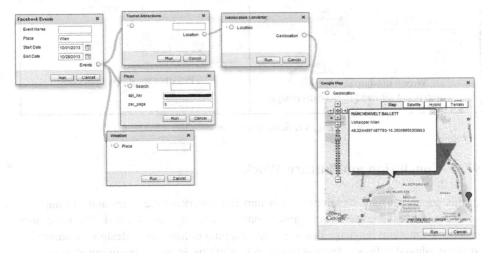

Fig. 10. Design personalized mashup

5   Related Work

There are a number of research works that deal with part of our proposed approach: (i) expanding the scope of Semantic Desktops with social community aspects, and (ii) building semantic mashup applications to support end-users integrate and reuse their heterogeneous personal life items. Nepomuk [18] is mainly enabling a more meaningful searching on the desktops and bridging the gap between Semantic Desktops and Linked Data, but does not support end-users in data mashups. DERI Pipes [19] have mainly focused on the data aggregation that aims at (semi-) automating mashup development, but end-users are still required to master a basic level of programming knowledge, such as specifying parameters for operators and widgets. Besides, some mashup languages (e.g. Yahoo Query Language[5], Enterprise Mashup Markup Language[6]) are proposed for the description of programming logic and presentation of data. However, these languages are mostly not easy to understand for end-users without prior knowledge of those languages or extensive programming skills. In addition, those languages does not support ontology or customized ontology mapping yet and support only the construction and formulation of service calls and their execution.

In our semantic-based mashup framework, end-users without programming skills can easily find the right and feasible widget connections on the fly. Fig. 11 depicts the semantic-aware dataflow between widgets and depicts how the mashup platform supports the end-users to find the appropriate input/output connections.

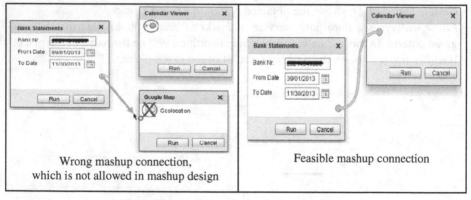

Wrong mashup connection,
which is not allowed in mashup design

Feasible mashup connection

Fig. 11. Semantic-aware dataflow

9   Conclusion and Future Work

In this paper, we have developed a mashup framework where users and mashup developers can collaborate to design personalized mashups on demand. We have also proposed a mashup language that supports mapping ontologies in designing semantic-aware mashup dataflows. The overall objective of this approach is aiming at overcoming the steadily increasing problem of information overload of Semantic Desktops and SNSs (i.e. SemanticLIFE and SocialLIFE in particular). To achieve this goal, the proposed solution expands the scope of our SemanticLIFE in particular and the Semantic Desktops systems in general into the Web of Data.

As future work, the development of the proposed system will be continued to further improve the mashup language and the mashup framework. In this context, we will extend our widget collection to include more third party services of well-known

---

[5] http://developer.yahoo.com/yql/
[6] http://en.wikipedia.org/wiki/EMML

SNSs in order to enrich both personal resources and the mashup repository. Furthermore, the development towards the automatic widget composition will be investigated. Another interesting issue is the mashup sharing which should be supported in order to enable end-users in building data mashups collaboratively in organizations/enterprises. In addition, further experiments for performance and usability evaluation should be conducted.

References

[1] Baird, L., Meshoulam, I.: Managing Two Fits of Strategic Human Resource Management. Academy of Management Review 13 (1988)

[2] Berners-Lee, T.: Linked Data (2006), http://www.w3.org/DesignIssues/LinkedData.html (accessed: September 22, 2012)

[3] Anjomshoaa, A., Tjoa, A.M., Hubmer, A.: Combining and integrating advanced IT-concepts with semantic web technology mashups architecture case study. In: Nguyen, N.T., Le, M.T., Świątek, J. (eds.) ACIIDS 2010. LNCS, vol. 5990, pp. 13–22. Springer, Heidelberg (2010)

[4] Bader, G., He, W., Anjomshoaa, A., Tjoa, A.M.: Proposing a context-aware enterprise mashup readiness assessment framework. Information Technology and Management 13(4), 377–387 (2012)

[5] Hinchcliffe, D.: 14 Reasons Why Enterprise 2.0 Projects Fail (2009), http://blogs.zdnet.com/Hinchcliffe/?p=718 (accessed: September 25, 2012)

[6] Metter, E., Perrin, T., Gyster, V., Lamson, R.: Enterprise 2.0 and HR - Realizing the Potential. IHRIM J. XII(5) (2008)

[7] Ahmed, M., Hoang, H.H., Karim, M.S., Khusro, S., Lanzenberger, M., Latif, K., Michlmayr, E., Mustofa, K., Nguyen, H.T., Rauber, A., Schatten, A., Nguyen, T.M., Tjoa, A.M.: 'SemanticLIFE' - A Framework for Managing Information of A Human Lifetime. In: iiWAS 2004, vol. 183 (October 2004)

[8] Anjomshoaa, A.: Integration of Personal Services into Global Business. Vienna University of Technology, Vienna (2009)

[9] Drăgan, L., Delbru, R., Groza, T., Handschuh, S., Decker, S.: Linking Semantic Desktop Data to the Web of Data. In: Aroyo, L., Welty, C., Alani, H., Taylor, J., Bernstein, A., Kagal, L., Noy, N., Blomqvist, E. (eds.) ISWC 2011, Part II. LNCS, vol. 7032, pp. 33–48. Springer, Heidelberg (2011)

[10] Groza, T., Drăgan, L., Handschuh, S., Decker, S.: Bridging the Gap between Linked Data and the Semantic Desktop. In: Bernstein, A., Karger, D.R., Heath, T., Feigenbaum, L., Maynard, D., Motta, E., Thirunarayan, K. (eds.) ISWC 2009. LNCS, vol. 5823, pp. 827–842. Springer, Heidelberg (2009)

[11] Kanzaki, Flickr photo info to RDF image description (2007), http://www.kanzaki.com/works/2005/imgdsc/flickr2rdf (accessed: September 25, 2012)

[12] Bizer, C.B.C.: Flickr wrappr (2009), http://wifo5-03.informatik.uni-mannheim.de/flickrwrappr/ (accessed: May 11, 2012)

[13] Bader, G., Anjomshoaa, A., Tjoa, A.M.: Privacy aspects of mashup architecture. In: Social Computing (SocialCom), pp. 1141–1146. IEEE (2010)

[14] Speiser, S., Harth, A.: Integrating Linked Data and Services with Linked Data Services. In: Antoniou, G., Grobelnik, M., Simperl, E., Parsia, B., Plexousakis, D., De Leenheer, P., Pan, J. (eds.) ESWC 2011, Part I. LNCS, vol. 6643, pp. 170–184. Springer, Heidelberg (2011)

[15] Malki, A., Benslimane, S.M.: Building Semantic Mashup. In: Proceedings ICWIT 2012, pp. 40–49 (2012)

[16] Anjomshoaa, A., Vo-Sao, K., Tahamtan, A., Tjoa, A.M., Weippl, E.: Self-monitoring in social networks. International Journal of Intelligent Information and Database Systems 6(4), 363 (2012)

[17] W3C, W3C Semantic Web Activity (2001), http://www.w3.org/2001/sw/ (accessed: August 15, 2013)

[18] Groza, T., Handschuh, S., Moeller, K., Grimnes, G.A., Sauermann, L., Minack, E., Mesnage, C., Jazayeri, M., Reif, G., Gudjónsdottir, R.: The NEPOMUK Project - On the way to the Social Semantic Desktop. In: Proceedings of I-MEDIA 2007 and I-SEMANTICS 2007, pp. 201–210 (2007)

[19] Le Phuoc, D., Polleres, A., Tummarello, G., Morbidoni, C.: DERI Pipes: Visual tool for wiring Web data sources (2009)

Trust Extension Protocol for Authentication in Networks Oriented to Management (TEPANOM)

Antonio J. Jara

University of Applied Sciences Western Switzerland (HES-SO)
Institute of Information Systems
3960, Sierre, Switzerland
jara@ieee.org

Abstract. Future Internet of Things is being deployed massively, since it is being already concerned deployments with thousands of nodes, which present a new dimension of capacities for monitoring solutions such as smart cities, home automation, and continuous healthcare. This new dimension is also presenting new challenges, in issues related with scalability, security and management, which require to be addressed in order to make feasible the Internet of Things-based solutions. This work presents a Trust Extension Protocol for Authentication in Networks Oriented to Management (TEPANOM). This protocol allows, on the one hand, the identity verification and authentication in the system, and on the other hand the bootstrapping, configuration and trust extension of the deployment and management domains to the new device. Thereby, TEPANOM defines a scalable network management solution for the Internet of Things, which addresses the security requirements, and allows an easy, and transparent support for the management, which are highly desirable and necessary features for the successful of the solutions based on the Internet of things. The proposed protocol has been instanced for the use case of a fire alarm management system, and successfully evaluated with the tools from the Automated Validation of Internet Security Protocols and Applications (AVISPA) framework.

Keywords: Sensor Networks Management, Security, Management Architecture, Internet of Things, Future Internet.

1 Introduction

The number and diversity of sensors and devices deployed is growing tremendously thanks to their capacities to offer low cost air-interfaces which allow an easy and quick deployment, the suitability of them to support an extended range of solutions, the infrastructure capacities to provide an Internet access to these networks, which is becoming ubiquitous to all the environments and users, and accessible for the sensors with the evolution of technologies such as IPv6 Low Power Wireless Personal Area Networks (6LoWPAN), and finally with the definition of In numerous this extension of the Internet to smart things is estimated for reaching by 2020 between 50 to 100 billion of devices defining the called Internet of Things.

S. Teufel et al. (Eds.): CD-ARES 2014, LNCS 8708, pp. 155–165, 2014.

A new generation of services where all the devices around the user are connected presents challenges for security management in aspects such as bootstrapping, privacy, confidentiality and trust.

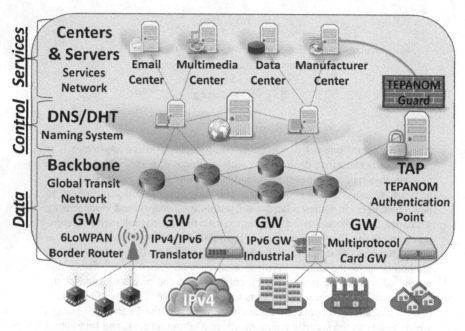

Fig. 1. TEPANOM Architecture

This security management cannot be addressed with the traditional out-of-band and centralized techniques, which are usually considered, designed and definitively added to the service in a final stage of the solution development. This requires a definition of the management issues at the design phase, since this requires a higher level of discussion, scalability and considerations in order to solve the requirements for scalability, which present the need of manage millions of devices, for that reason it is required a new management paradigm to cope with those new challenges, since out-of-band management is not able to setup a large number of device. It is required an in-band management, with semi-automatic configuration, bootstrapping online, assisted deployment of keys, i.e. key management protocols, and authentication of devices based on identity instead of simple identifiers.

For that reason, this work is focused on offer a scalable and secure management protocol, which allows, on the one hand, the identity verification and authentication of the new devices deployed in a network, and on the other hand, the extension of the trust domain to these new devices. Thereby, with this semi-automatic bootstrapping and configuration of the new devices is more feasible, scalable and extensible the deployments based on Internet of Things. This protocol addresses the requirements from the novel services, where security is highly required and desirable, such as authentication for home automation solutions.

The major novelty from this authentication protocol is that it is focused to the manufacturer, assuming that it is the common *trustable* previous "control point" to the initial installation for new devices. Therefore, it is the point where it can be pre-configured a set of credentials, which can be used after to verify the identity (type of device, family, features etc.) for the devices.

In addition, this kind of identity verification allows, on the one hand, make simpler and more automatic the bootstrapping, and on the other hand to authenticate the originality from a product face to guarantee the quality from an installation. This a high requirement assuming security deployments such as fire alarms.

2   TEPANOM Architecture

The architecture considered to extend for the entities defined by the Trust Extension Protocol for Authentication in Networks oriented to Management (TEPANOM) is based on the current Internet Architecture. The layout of the considered architecture is presented in the Fig 1.

The architecture is based on the domain names and locators of the current Internet. The role of the domain/device name and locator are:

- **Domain name** represents "whose it is", are usually denoted by Uniform Resource Locator (URL) such as the used for the WEB, e.g. lab.um.es.
- **Device name** represents "who it is", are usually denoted by variable-length strings e.g. Uniform Resource Name (URN), or a human readable and remembered name such as a Network Access Identifier (NAI), e.g. *temp_sensor- 2C91*@lab.hevs.ch, which represents a sensor called *temp_sensor- 2C91* inside the mentioned domain. This name is what can be used as a base-name to access specific web services and properties/methods with technologies such as by Simple Network Management protocol (SNMP) for management, or RESTFul from a more focused Internet of Things point of view, with the Web of Things.
- **Locator** is used to represent the location of an object in the network; it usually uses the IPv6 address.

The architecture is composed by the signaling control network, which mainly defines the mentioned mapping between the domain names and its locators, the interworking infrastructure with the routers and interconnection systems for the global transit networks, and the gateways, proxies and translators for the edge networks.

2.1   Signaling Control Network

The roles of the entities from the signaling control network are presented in Fig. 1.

- **Domain Name System (DNS):** This offers a mapping between the hostname and domain name which a particular host or device belongs to. This stores the binding between a domain and the manager of that domain, servers and resources centers. DNS have a hierarchical structure; thereby they can be effectively organized into a hierarchical logical network. As alternative to the

DNS, it can be found several solutions for the location of host and devices in the network such as Distributed Hash Tables, ID/Locator split architectures, and finally, in order to make the name/locator mapping more secure it can be also considered for this part of the architecture security extensions for DNS, i.e. DNSSEC (Domain Name System Security Extension), or for the mentioned ID/Locator architecture.

- **TEPANOM Authentication Point (TAP):** This entity is used to validate new devices/entities. This is a **Trust point**, following a similar idea to other entities such as the Trust Resolution Handlers (TRHs) defined in Data-Oriented Network Architecture (DONA) , where data needs to be registered in TRHs to validate the content and provider. In our approach, instead of data the registered entities are devices and the TAP is offered by the devices providers such as the manufacturer considered for the use case described in this work for security deployment of fire detection systems. Thereby, they can be dynamically registered and authenticated, where is presented the protocol proposed to reach this scalable security support.

2.2 Global Transit Network

This is a collection of networks and physical routers which interconnect the public organizations, research centers, and end users through Internet Service Providers around the entire world. This is composed of routers, backbones, servers, systems and agents of some of the entities mentioned from the signaling control network. The DNS and TAP are physically connected to this global transit network to store the records of host and device information, and make feasible a global access to the services of hostname resolution and provide global mobility capabilities.

2.3 Edge Networks

The edge networks provide access to the end systems such as hosts and clients through wired or wireless links. Examples can be any of the current industrial networks such as Control Area Networks (CAN), vehicular networks and hospital networks. These networks are connected to the Global Transit Network via one or more gateways. Thus a GW has at least two network interfaces, one connected to the edge network and the other to the global transit network, see Figure 1. Examples of gateways are:

- **Multiprotocol cards and adaptors:** The current situation of the Internet of Things can be compared to an archipelago, where the devices can interact with other devices from their own island, but not with devices from outside. A solution for this heterogeneity is found ins solutions such as Universal Device Gateway (UDG), or Multi-protocol cards which provide physical connectivity through various communication protocols, such as KNX and X10 from building automation.
- **Translators:** IPv4 to IPv6 translators for networks which are not adapted.
- **IPv6 gateways:** GW for networks with IPv6 support, it is the link between the ISP and the client/end user.

- **6LoWPAN Border Router:** Adapt the IPv6 packet to the defined in the 6LoWPAN standard (RFC 4494) for making IPv6 headers size feasible for constrained Low Power Wireless Personal Area Networks (LoWPANs).

3   TEPANOM Protocol

The Internet of Things deployments are being considered solutions with hundreds to thousands of nodes, what is defining a new dimension of the monitoring and control capabilities for solutions such as home automation, healthcare monitoring, and the use case considered in this work fire detectors monitoring, such as mentioned, this high capacity is presenting a critical challenge for managing in order to reach a scalable and safe management, offering a framework able to unify the functions of bootstrapping, configuration, set up, operation, check resource availability, administration and maintenance of all elements and services deployed.

The solution proposed on this work is TEPANOM, which is originally the gate guard in the temples in the islands of Thailand. It was chosen since the current internet is presented as an archipelago formed by several islands/networks with multi-technologies and multi-domains.

The three domains involved in the process for deployment, authentication, bootstrapping and configuration of a new device are presented in Fig. 1. They are, first, the factory domain, which is the domain for the provider or manufacturer from that device. Second, the manager domain for the remote monitoring station in solutions oriented to management, and finally the deployment domain, which refers to the domain where the new device to be monitored is being deployed.

The goals of TEPANOM protocol are:

- Verify that the new device belongs to an island, network or domain which is trustable from the gateway/platform where the new device is being deployed.
- Authenticate to the new device from its factory domain, e.g. provider or manufacturer.
- Optionally this also allows to send the identity of the device from the factory domain to the manager and deployment domains, e.g. technical specification and available resources/methods for consumer devices.
- Finally, this extends the trust domain from the deployment network to that new device.

The architecture defines two planes, on the one hand the signaling control plane composed by the DNS for naming resolution, and the servers and deployed platform, for the control, and on the other hand, the data plane, which is composed by the backbone and gateways, which offer the connectivity to the signaling control network and edge networks.

In the signaling control plane, it has been defined the existence of a trust relationship between the deployment platform and the manager server, this relationship is established during the deployment of the client/user side platform, e.g., the deployment of the residential platform for home automation solutions (see green tunnel in Fig. 2). In addition, it has been defined intra-domain trust relationships for each one of the domains, considering that the local communication between devices and its platform, and servers is safe (see blue tunnels in Fig. 2).

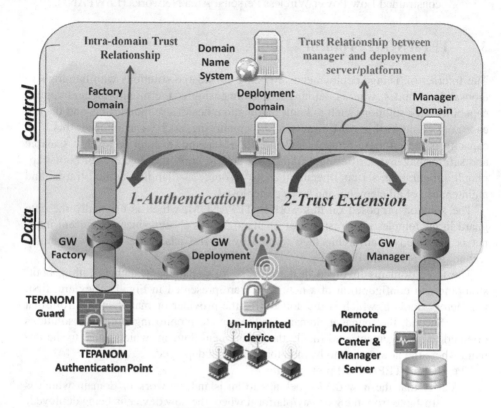

Fig. 2. TEPANOM environment and domains

The TEPANOM protocol defines two phases, a first phase for the authentication with the manufacturer, where the new device must prove to its gateway in the deployment environment that it is a proper device, with a profile, resources, services and quality adequate for the client and manager requirements, and a second phase for the trust extension and registration with the manager/remote monitoring center. The next subsections describe the protocol for each one of the phases.

3.1   Authentication Phase

The authentication of the device and its features is carried out with the services offered by the manufacturer through the manufacturer authentication agent, which has been denominated TEPANOM Authentication Point (TAP). The new device must prove to the TAP that it is the same entity they manufacture, requiring for that goal the use of cryptographic identities defined during the manufacturing phase, it is predefined the Factory Shared Key (SK0) in conjunction with the already defined devices such as MAC and Serial Number.

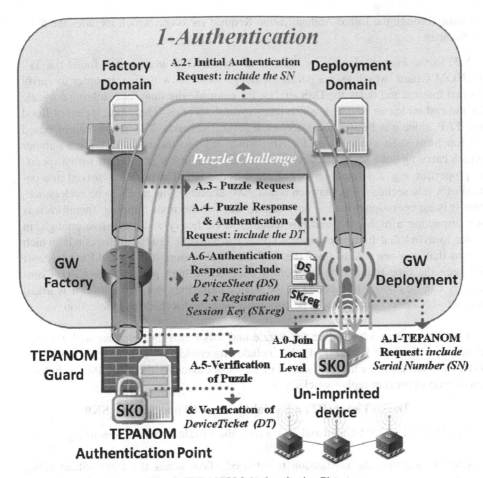

Fig. 3. TEPANOM Authentication Phase

The authentication is carried out with the Factory domain, where are deployed the TEPANOM Guard and TEPANOM Authentication Point.

The TEPANOM Guard protects of the Denial-of-Service (DoS) attacks to the TE-PANOM Authentication Point, since it is one of the most important challenges from the current Internet and Future Internet of Things, where the majority of the deployed protocols in Internet are vulnerable to DoS attacks.

The exchanged messages for the Authentication phase presented in the Fig. 3 are:

A.0) At the beginning the new device joins to the network in a local level.

A.1) Then this starts the TEPANOM protocol sending the TEPANOM Request, this includes the Serial Number, which can be required for the Puzzle election.

$$\text{DeviceTicket (DT)} = \{\text{Serial Number} \mid \text{Time Stamp}\}\_SK0$$

A.2) The gateway of the deployment, which is considered an intelligent platform such as the multiprotocol cards, starts the authentication process with the factory domain, through the Initial Authentication Request message, which includes the Serial Number.

A.3) In the Factory domain, in order to avoid the DoS attacks, it is found the TEPANOM Guard, which asks a puzzle challenge to the new device, in order to verify its real interest and delay the DoS attacks, for example the time for resolving a puzzle by the end node can be a task which takes several seconds. Therefore, it cannot flood the TAP, since it is limited to a query each several seconds. This puzzle can be based on functions such as the found for HIP, which asks to the node look for a number which carrying out a set of calculus with the offered number get a result with a specific properties, e.g. a defined number of zeros in the tail. The puzzle is solved in a period of a few seconds, e.g. between 5 and 300 seconds. This needs to be understood, that it is an operation which is only carried out for the bootstrapping, therefore it is not impacting a high time, and this requires to be heavy and expensive enough, in order to avoid that high performance CPUs can solve it is few milliseconds, which means that they are able to flood the TAP. For that reason, it is looked for a tradeoff between the time required for the sensor node and a high performance CPU. Complexity can be chosen in function of the device capacities, for that reason it is asked the Serial Number, since it could be optionally be used for the Puzzle selection.

A.4) The new device resolves the puzzle and this sends the response with the Authentication Request for the TAP, this includes its credential, i.e. DeviceTicket (DT). DT is a token used for the verification of the new device by the TAP; this includes a timestamp to prevent replay attacks.

DeviceTicket (DT) = {Serial Number | Time Stamp}_SK0

A.5) The TEPANOM Guard and TAP verify the Puzzle and DT respectively.

A.6) In case that the verification is satisfied, TAP sends the DeviceSheet (DS), which includes an extended description of the devices resources, methods and capabilities for its set up in the manager. This also includes the Registration Session Key (SKreg), which is sent in two versions, on the one hand, SKreg and a timestamp protected with SK0, which is sent to the new device in an unprotected medium in the deployment domain, because new device is not sharing any initial secret with the deployment GW, and this initial secret is required for the safe SK1 establishment.

SKreg_device = {SKreg | Time Stamp}_SK0

On the other hand, SKreg is sent protected with the public key of the deployment GW. Thereby, it cannot be intercepted in the originally unprotected route from the factory domain to the manager domain.

Finally, the deployment GW keeps the DS, SKreg, and SKreg_device, this last until that it is registered in the manager. The technique used for sending SKreg_device is comparable to the technique used to make the ticket in Kerberos, which permits to send SKreg encrypted end-to-end, being forwarded by intermediate nodes which cannot understand it.

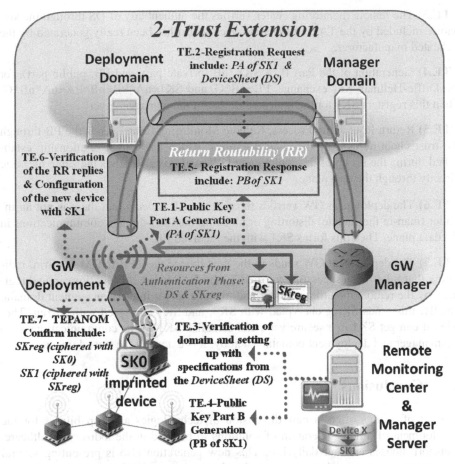

Fig. 4. TEPANOM Trust Extension Phase

3.2 Trust Extension Phase

The Trust Extension part is composed of the activities for the registration in the manager of the methods and resources from the new device specified in its DS, and the establishment of a new shared key between the manager, deployment domain and new device, which is SK1. For that purpose the deployment GW keeps the SKreg key in its two ciphered versions, and the DeviceSheet (DS) from the Authentication Phase.

The exchanged messages for the Trust Extension phase presented in the Fig. 4 are:

TE.1) At the beginning the deployment GW generates the Part A for the Diffie-Hellman Key exchange of SK1. (nA: private part, and PA: public part), PA=nA*G, where G is the generator of the curve.

TE.2) Then the deployment GW sends to the remote monitoring center the Registration Request with PA and DS.

TE.3) The remote monitoring center verifies the authenticity of DS through the signature included by the TAP, in order to check that it has been really generated by the indicated manufacturer.

TE.4) Generation of the Part B of SK1 (nB: private part, and PB: public part), for the Diffie-Hellman Key exchange, PB=nB*G, and SK1=nA*PB=nB*PA=nA*nB*G. Then this registers SK1 for the indicated device in the manager server.

TE.5) Return Routability Process. Remote Monitoring Center sends the PB through the trust chain defined by the control entities, which has a trust relationship established during the set up of the deployment GW, and this also sends the same message directly through the data plane.

TE.6) The deployment GW verifies through the RR process that there is not an intruder (man-in-the-middle) distorting or blocking the inter-domain communications in the data plane. Then this forms SK1 with the received PB.

TE.7) The deployment GW sends to the new device the TEPANOM confirm, indicating that it has been sucessfuly verified by the TAP in the Factory domain and registred by the remote monitoring center and manage server in the management domain. Finally, this sends SKreg encrypted with SK0, and SK1 encrypted with SKreg. Thereby, it can get SK1 in a secure way, and establish SK1 for its communications with the manager and deployment domain. Thereby, it is extended the trust domain.

4   Conclusions

Internet of Things offers a new dimension of technologies and capabilities for the development of a new generation of solutions to be used in the industry, healthcare, transport, houses and our daily life. This new generation also is presenting several challenges and open problems that need to be investigated. We have focused on, on the one hand, security and privacy for the authentication and protection of those networks, and on the other hand, management of those networks for configuration, bootstrapping addressing the scalability and security requirements.

There are several significant differences in the management of traditional networks and the defined by the Future Internet of Things. For that reason, it has been proposed a different management architecture, where are considered the found features, requirements and constrains.

Finally, with distributed resource repositories and the required functionalities such as: scalable look up, discovery of "Internet of Things" resources and services, context-awareness, reliability, self-management, self-configuration, self-healing properties.

Acknowledgements. The author would like to thank to the HES-SO and the Institute of Information Systems funding and support, and the European Project "Universal Integration of the Internet of Things through an IPv6-based Service Oriented Architecture enabling heterogeneous components interoperability (IoT6)" from the FP7 with the grant agreement no: 288445.

References

1. Sundmaeker, H., Guillemin, P., Friess, P., Woelfflé, S.: Vision and Challenges for Realising the Internet of Things. European cluster CERP-IoT, European Union (2010) ISBN: 978-92-79-15088-3
2. Atzori, L., Iera, A., Morabito, G.: The Internet of Things: A survey. Comput. Netw. 54(15), 2787–2805 (2010)
3. Rodrigo Roman sobre el impacto de Internet en Smart devices
4. Zamora, M.A., Santa, J., Skarmeta, A.F.G.: An integral and networked Home Automation solution for indoor Ambient Intelligence. IEEE Pervasive Computing 9, 66–77 (2010)
5. Kafle, V.P., Otsuki, H., Inoue, M.: An ID/locator split architecture for future networks. IEEE Communications Magazine 48(2), 138–144 (2010)
6. Koponen, T., Chawla, M., Chun, B.-G., Ermolinskiy, A., Kim, K.H., Shenker, S., Stoica, I.: A data-oriented (and beyond) network architecture. SIGCOMM Comput. Commun. Rev. 37(4), 181–192 (2007)
7. Mukhtar, H., Kim, K.-M., Chaudhry, S.A., Akbar, A.H., Kim, K.-H.: LNMP- Management architecture for IPv6 based low-power wireless Personal Area Networks (6LoWPAN). In: IEEE Network Operations and Management Symposium, NOMS 2008, April 7-11, pp. 417–424 (2008), doi:10.1109/NOMS.2008.4575163
8. Schonwalder, J., Fouquet, M., Rodosek, G., Hochstatter, I.: Future Internet = content + services + management. IEEE Communications Magazine 47(7), 27–33 (2009), doi:10.1109/MCOM.2009.5183469
9. Ruiz, L.B., Nogueira, J.M., Loureiro, A.A.F.: MANNA: A management architecture for wireless sensor networks. IEEE Communications Magazine 41(2), 116–125 (2003), doi:10.1109/MCOM.2003.1179560
10. Roman, R., Alcaraz, C., Lopez, J., Sklavos, N.: Key management systems for sensor networks in the context of the Internet of Things. Computers & Electrical Engineering, Modern Trends in Applied Security: Architectures, Implementations and Applications 37(2), 147–159 (2011), doi:10.1016/j.compeleceng.2011.01.009
11. Jara, A.J., Zamora, M.A., Skarmeta, A.F.G.: An internet of things–based personal device for diabetes therapy management in ambient assisted living (AAL). To be published in: Personal and Ubiquitous Computing (2011) (in press) doi:10.1007/s00779-010-0353-1
12. Papadimitriou, D., Tschofenig, H., Rosas, A., Zahariadis, S., et al.: Fundamental Limitations of Current Internet and the path to Future Internet, European Commission. FIArch. Group, Ver. 1(9) (2010)
13. Zorzi, M., Gluhak, A., Lange, S., Bassi, A.: From today's INTRAnet of things to a future INTERnet of things: A wireless- and mobility-related view. IEEE Wireless Communications 17(6), 44–51 (2010)
14. Jacobsson, M., Niemegeers, I., de Groot, S.H.: Personal Networks: Wireless Networking for Personal Devices. Wiley (June 2010) ISBN: 978-0-470-68173-2

Building an Initialization Cipher Block with Two-Dimensional Operation and Random Parameters

Yi-Li Huang[1], Fang-Yie Leu[1], Ilsun You[2], and Jing-Hao Yang[1]

[1] Department of Computer Science, TungHai University, Taiwan
{yifung,leufy,g01350036}@thu.edu.tw
[2] School of Information Science, Korean Bible University, South Korea
ilsunu@gmail.com

Abstract. In recent years, parallel computing capabilities have been more powerful than before. Consequently some block cipher standards, such as DES used to protect important electronic messages, have been cracked in the past years. Also due to the rapid development of hardware processing speeds, 3DES and AES may someday be solved by brute-force attacks. Basically, the common characteristics of these block cipher standards are that each time, when a standard is invoked, the same parent key is used to generate subkeys. The subkeys are then utilized in the standard's encryption rounds to encrypt data. In fact, the variability of the key values is quite limited. Generally, producing random parameters to encrypt data is an effective method to improve the security of ciphertext. But how to ensure the security level of using and delivering these random parameters and how to avoid information leakage have been a challenge. So in this paper, we propose a novel random parameter protection approach, called the Initialization Cipher Block Method(ICBM for short), which protects random parameters by using a two-dimensional operation and employs random parameters to change the value of a fixed parent key for block ciphering, thus lowering the security risk of a block cipher algorithm. Security analysis demonstrates that the ICBM effectively improve the security level of a protected system. Of course, this also safely protect our homeland, particularly when it is applied to our governmental document delivery systems.

Keywords: Cryptography, Block Cipher, random parameter, Two-Dimensional Operation, ICBM.

1 Introduction

In recent years, due to the rapid development of different network technologies, many government offices, private companies, banks, etc. for environmental protection purpose send electronic documents, rather than paper documents, to people or customers to save paper consumption, of course also reducing the resource consumption for our homelands. With this achievement, information on the contrary is easily spread, delivered and obtained. Today, the Internet has been the biggest information pool, from which users can access different kinds of required data. However, when people enjoy

S. Teufel et al. (Eds.): CD-ARES 2014, LNCS 8708, pp. 166–171, 2014.

the Internet access, attackers may also steal private information through the Internet for a variety of purposes. Currently, new attacks have been developed quickly and new vulnerabilities have been discovered frequently. So it is hard for us to completely protect private information by using IDS, IPS and firewall. Then how to use cryptographic techniques to protect such information has been a very serious and urgent issue.

In the field of data encryption, block cipher is one of the most common method to protect electronic documents from being known to hackers. The most famous and widely used block cipher standards are the Data Encryption Standard (DES)[1], Triple Data Encryption Standard (3DES)[2] and Advanced Encryption Standard(AES)[3] published by National Institute of Standards and Technology (NIST). However, in 1997, DES message has been broken for the first time in public. And in 1999, the security key of DES has been broken[4]. Due to the rapid advance of hardware speed and parallel computing, securely protecting this type of fixed-key cryptography has been a technical challenge[5]. Now the block cipher standards still used in many ways to protect personal privacy and confidential information. We hope to enhance their security levels without significantly changing their original structures.

Therefore, in this study, we propose a random number protection approach, named Initialization Cipher Block Method (ICBM for short), which strengthens the security of the block cipher standards by adding random parameters, which are themselves unpredictable, to them. Security analysis shows that the random parameters as security keys can effectively rise the security level of a system since only the user who has the legitimate keys can solve those messages protected by these random parameters.

The rest of this paper is organized as follows. Section 2 introduces the most popular block cipher standards. Section 3describesthe proposed method. The security of Initialization Cipher Block Method is analyzed in Section 4.Section5concludes this paper and outlines our future studies.

2   Related Work

In this section, we individually introduce DES, 3DES and AES.

2.1   DES and 3DES

DES algorithm was first developed between 1973 and 1974 by International Business Machines Corporation (IBM). This proposal was then accepted and published by National Bureau of Standards (NBS), the predecessor of National Institute of Standards and Technology (NIST). It is now one of the data encryption standards. Generally, its security key is used to customize the transformation from ciphertext to plaintext, i.e., only the user who has current key can solve the ciphertext. The original length of a key is 64 bits. But only 56 bits are used to encrypt data. Other 8 bits, employed to check data parity, are abandoned after encrypting data. Due to short key length, nowadays DES is no longer a secure block cipher standard.

The 3DES is then proposed to solve the short-key problem by repeating DES operations three times, as three phases, to complete its data encryption and decryption. Because users can choose different keys for each phase each time when 3DES is invoked, the length of a key is then $168(= 56 \times 3)$ bits.

The encryption process of 3DES does not really repeat DES encryption process. In the second phase, it decrypts the data, and in the third, it encrypts the data again. In other words, an integral 3DES encryption uses DES encryption-decryption-encryption process and its decryption employs DES decryption-encryption-decryption process. If the three keys utilized in the three phases of encryption and decryption are the same, 3DES is indeed a DES.

2.2   AES

AES algorithm was published by NIST in 2001 to substitute for the DES. Its block size is 128 bits. But the key length can be 128, 192 or 256 bits. Generally, a longer key can raise a system's security level.AES operation needs a 4×4matrix, in which an element is 8 bits long. Due to allowing different key lengths, the encryption / decryption algorithms will repeat 10, 12 or 14 rounds and each round includes 4 steps, except the last round. The 4 steps are as follows.

Step 1: AddRoundKey. When an encryption round starts, AES generates a round key by invoking the Rijndael key schedule[3], and the key is then XORed with the underlying plaintext block.

Step 2: SubByte. In this step, an element of the 4*4 matrix is moved to its designated position according to the content of the Rijndael S-box, which provides the matrix with a nonlinear transformation.

Step 3: ShiftRow. In this step, row i left shifts i bytes, i = 0, 1, 2, 3.

Step 4: MixColumns. In a column, the 4 bytes from bottom to top are treated as the coefficients of the 1, X, X^2 and X^3 in a $GF(2^8)$ polynomial. The column is first multiplied with $3X^3 + X^2 + X + 2$and moduloed by $X^4 + 1$.

3   Initialization Cipher Block Method (ICBM)

In the ICBM, there is a cipher block generated before the system starts encrypting data. The main function of this cipher block is protecting those random parameters used to encrypt the parent key. Of course, the length of the cipher block is changed if the lengths of the given key is different.

3.1   Parameters and Functions definition

In the following, we first define the parameters and functions used by the ICBM:

K: The key of block ciphering. Its length can be changed to meet the key length of the standard being concerned.

S-box: The S-box utilized when collaborating with DES or AES.

K_{01}: The first transient key generated by substituting for the bytes of K, following the content of S-box.

K_{02}: The second transient key generated by XORing K with K_{01}.

RND: The random parameter, the length of which is determined by the length of K. There are many methods to generate RND, e.g., invoking a random number generation function or using the One Time Password(OTP) system provided by a programming language, like Java/C++.

$+_2$: A binary adder, which is a logical operator defined in [6].

$-_2$: The inverse operation of $+_2$ [6].

K': The system key calculated by binary-adding RND and K_{02} for substituting for K to encrypt / decrypt data blocks.

ICB: Initialization Cipher Block, which when delivered is placed at the position in front of ciphertext.

3.2   Encryption Process of ICBM

Step 1. K is the parent key of block ciphering, i.e., 56 bits for DES, and 128, 192 or 256 bits for AES. After K is input, the proposed system will calculate the corresponding value, following the content of the S-box of the selected block cipher standard, and then generate the first transient key K_{01}.

Step 2. Calculating the second transient key K_{02} by XORing K_{01} with K.

Step 3. Generating RND by using the example method mentioned above and then encrypting it with K_{01} and K_{02} to generate two outputs. One is K' which substitutes for K in the following encryption and decryption processes. The other is ICB which is output with the ciphertext and as stated above, is placed at the position in front of the ciphertext. In decryption process, the ICB needs to be decrypted first to obtain the random parameter RND for the following decryption, i.e.,

$$K' = RND +_2 K_{02} \tag{1}$$

$$ICB = RND +_2 K_{01} \tag{2}$$

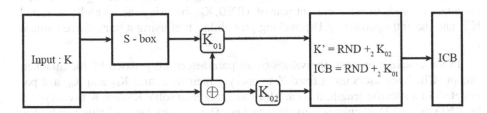

Fig. 1. Generation process of ICB

3.3   Decryption Process of ICBM

Step 1. As shown in Fig. 1, the first transient key K_{01} is obtained by substituting the bytes of K, following the content of DES / AES S-box.

Step 2. Calculating the second transient key K_{02} by XORing K_{01} with K.

Step 3. After the generation of K_{01} and K_{02}, RND and K' can be obtained by invoking the following formulas.

$$RND = ICB -_2 K_{01} \tag{3}$$

$$K' = RND +_2 K_{02} \tag{4}$$

4   Security Analysis

This section will describe the security of the Two-Dimensional Operation and Initialization Cipher Block Method.

4.1   Security of the Two-Dimensional Operation

Generally, the field of electronic cryptography only uses XOR($\oplus$) to encrypt / decrypt data because it is a fast and simple operation. If plaintext A and a key B are of the same length n, the probability of cracking $A \oplus B$ is $\frac{1}{2^n}$, which is also the cost of cracking a key by using a brute-force method.

In this study, we utilized another logic operator, the Binary Adder($+_2$), to enhance the complexities of the encryption / decryption processes of the ICBM. The security level of $+_2$ is the same as that of XOR [6]. If a key Y of m bits in length is employed to encrypt plaintext X of also m bits long, the probability of cracking $X +_2 Y$ is $\frac{1}{2^m}$ [7].

4.2   Security of Initialization Cipher Block Method

In the ICBM, we assume that (1) the system key K is X bits in length where X is determined by the block cipher standard invoked, i.e., a key is 56 bits for DES, 56 to 168 bits for 3DES and 128 to 256 bits for AES;(2) there is a random parameter RND which is also X bits long;(3) the attacker has invalidly acquired ICB with the goal of obtaining K.

In section 3.2, the ICB is calculated by adding K_{01} and RND with $+_2$. To crack K, the attacker needs to solve current pair of $\langle RND, K_{01} \rangle$ by using the invalidly acquired ICB and the anti-operator $-_2$. The cracking probability P of using a brute-force method is $\frac{1}{2^X}$.

In the cracking process, the values of all parameters are guessed by the attacker, except ICB. Even users use a fixed K to encrypt their data, and K_{01} and K_{02} are parameters of a specific length, it is hard for the attacker to solve K since K is encrypted by RND and RND is unknown to the attacker. The security level of this method is higher than that of only expanding the length of a key due to the unpredictability of RND.RND is different each time when it is generated for a session.

5   Conclusions and Future Studies

In this paper, we propose the ICBM which employs random parameters to increase the unpredictability of the generated ICB. This is a special design for encrypting keys before plaintext is encrypted.   So it can be widely applied to different block cipher standards, like DES, 3DES and AES. What we need to do is adjusting the length of RND to meet the key length of employed standard.

ICBM only uses the basic operators, like $\oplus$, $+_2$ and $-_2$, and one S-box. Its consumption time is short. In the future, we will apply this concept to block cipher algorithms and design an encryption system which has the characteristics of higher randomness, security and processing speed than those of the ICBM. We would also like to derive the reliability model and performance models for the ICBM and the newly designed system mentioned so that users can predict their reliability and performance before using them. These constitute our future studies.

Acknowledgements. This research was partially supported by TungHai University on GREENs project, and National Science Council, Taiwan, grants NSC 100-2221-E-029-018 and 101-2221-E-029-003-MY3. This research was also in part supported by Basic Science Research Program through the National Research Foundation of Korea (NRF) funded by the Ministry of Science, ICT & Future Planning (2014R1A1A1005915).

References

1. FIPS Publication 46-3, Data Encryption Standard (DES), U.S. DoC/NIST (October 25, 1999)
2. National Institute of Standards and Technology, NIST Special Publication 800-67, Recommendation for the Triple Data Encryption Algorithm (TDEA) Block Cipher, Reversion 1.1 (January 2012)
3. FIPS Publication 197, Advanced Encryption Standard (AES), U.S. DoC/NIST (November 26, 2001)
4. http://en.wikipedia.org/wiki/Data_Encryption_Standard
5. NIST Special Publication 800-57 Recommendation for Key Management — Part 1: General (Revised) (March 2007)
6. Wei, K.C., Huang, Y.L., Leu, F.Y.: A Secure Communication over Wireless Environments by Using a Data Connection Core. Computers and Mathematics with Applications (in press)
7. Huang, Y.-L., Leu, F.-Y., Dai, C.-R.: A Secure Data Encryption Method by Employing a Feedback Encryption Mechanism and Three-Dimensional Operation. In: Quirchmayr, G., Basl, J., You, I., Xu, L., Weippl, E. (eds.) CD-ARES 2012. LNCS, vol. 7465, pp. 578–592. Springer, Heidelberg (2012)

Crypto-Biometric Models for Information Secrecy

Marek R. Ogiela, Lidia Ogiela, and Urszula Ogiela

AGH University of Science and Technology
Cryptography and Cognitive Informatics Research Group
30 Mickiewicza Ave., PL-30-059 Krakow, Poland
{mogiela,logiela,ogiela}@agh.edu.pl

Abstract. In this paper will be presented some advances in crypto-biometric procedures used for encryption and division of secret data, as well as modern approaches for strategic management of divided information. Computer techniques for secret information sharing aim to secure information against disclosure to unauthorized persons. The paper will present algorithms dedicated for information division and sharing on the basis of biometric or personal features. Computer techniques for classified information sharing should also be useful in the process of shared information generation and distribution. For this purpose there will be presented a new approach for information management based on cognitive systems.

Keywords: Cryptographic protocols, bio-inspired cryptography, secret sharing algorithms.

1   Introduction

The important and vital information is very often secret. These information need to be protected using modern cryptographic procedures and techniques. To guarantee the highest level of protection needed to be applied special kinds of security. Sometimes it may be a personalized cryptography, which use some personal o biometric pattern for security purposes.

Many methods of information secrecy include secret splitting techniques, secret sharing, secure information, individual human biometrics analysis [7-11]. The last one – the biometrics analysis include personal features, which are different for each person. The most important in such type of analysis is the ability to take into account the individual characteristics, for example personal biometrical features. Of course we can consider for such purpose both standard as well as non-standard biometric patterns.

The most important personal biometrics are following [11]:

- the DNA code,
- face/hand/foot geometry,
- the shape of fingerprints, of hand/foot bones,
- anatomical features of the face, hand, foot, iris,
- anatomical feature of the body,
- the structure of blood vessels.

S. Teufel et al. (Eds.): CD-ARES 2014, LNCS 8708, pp. 172–178, 2014.
© IFIP International Federation for Information Processing 2014

The personal features are used to create crypto-biometrics secrecy. These type of secrecy is most important in many different kinds of IT systems [5, 6], but the particularly important in cognitive information systems, which may be applied for following tasks [11]:

- to sharing the secret information in enterprise,
- to splitting the strategic information in organization,
- to protection of confidential information.

The basic components of biometric analyses adopted in this paper are crypto-biometrics for the secrecy of information. The main content of this aspects can be a component for analysis, interpreting and mining managing processes [3, 4].

2   Data Security in Crypto-Biometrics Model

Data security in crypto-biometrics models may be achieved using of one of the following algorithm [4, 9, 13, 14] :

- Lagrange'a algorithm,
- vector algorithm,
- Asmuth-Bloom algorithm,
- Karnin-Greene-Hellman algorithm,
- Ong-Schnorr-Shamir algorithm,
- ElGamal algorithm,
- Fiat-Shamir algorithm.

These cryptographic algorithms are used for information sharing and information splitting, and also to secure data by asymmetric encryption [2]. Among these procedures in particular information sharing protocols may be divided into the following groups [9, 14]:

- information sharing without the involvement of a trusted person,
- message sharing without disclosing one's parts,
- message sharing with disclosure prevention,
- message sharing with cheaters,
- message sharing with testing,
- message sharing with a share withdrawal.

Cryptographic algorithms of data sharing and splitting are used to construct the data security model. Such models are used to secure of encrypted or divided data.

The essence of this kind of models is application of biometric features to sharing and reconstruction of information [9, 12]. Some of the data security algorithms are based on the use of linguistics algorithms for data interpretation, analysis, and understanding, before its encryption and distribution. Information sharing and information splitting approaches may use mathematical linguistics formalisms especially during coding processes. The main idea of this approach is used to linguistics formalism to process of data encryption [1, 7], especially sequence, tree and grammatical

formalisms. Such formalism are used to record and interpret the meaning of the analyzed biometric data.

Individual biometric features are used for example in DNA cryptography. DNA
cryptography may be used to generate keys based on DNA codes and personal information. It should be noted that DNA molecules, which have existed in nature as long
as known life forms, are beginning to play an increasing role in cryptography, but
it was only in the 21st century that science offered opportunities of using them as
information media, and the replication processes taking place in them as information
coding techniques. Recent years have seen increasingly frequent reports of further
discoveries, while the results of DNA research are becoming significant not just in
biology or genetics, but also in the field of steganography.

People have not realises the computational potential associated with molecules for
many years. The first ideas of combining computers with DNA chains appeared in
1973, when Charles Benett published a paper in which he proposed a model of a pro-
grammable molecular computer capable of executing any algorithm. However, the
first successful attempts were made 20 years after this idea publication. In 1993, Leo-
nard Adleman became the first to execute calculations using a DNA computer and
solved the Hamilton path problem for several cities [1].

Since then, many new proposals for using DNA sequences as an information medium have been made. Practically every such method of classifying data boils down,
at least at one stage, to storing this data in the appropriate DNA molecules. At this
level there are several available possibilities of using these acids as the medium for
coded information. The most obvious one is using the structure of particular nucleotides. As four types of them can be distinguished, one base can store 2 bits of information. We can thus assume that the coding will, for example, be executed as presented
in Fig 1. One can also start from the assumption that one pair of nucleotides (a single
bond) corresponds to one bit of information.

Such information coding methods are used in biological solutions which have in-
spired us to development of a new class of algorithms for secret splitting described in
[10]. However, presented algorithm, called a linguistic threshold scheme, operates in
a more general way and supports coding secret information (to be split) in longer
sequences, i.e. containing more than 2 bits of information. The purpose of this algorithm is a threshold split of strategic data managed within hierarchical structures, with
varied access capabilities dependent on the rights granted [9, 10, 11].

Thus, crypto-biometrics models based on DNA encoding and others biometric patterns are used to:

- secret sharing and secret splitting,
- secure information,
- encoding of information by individual biometrics feature,
- decoding information by personal biometrics feature,
- secure information prior to the disclosure to others person.

The secret and confidential information is analyzed and interpreted by way of cryptographic information analyses. The authors of this paper proposed to use the crypto-
biometrics analysis to strategic information management in enterprises.

DNA chains in information encoding

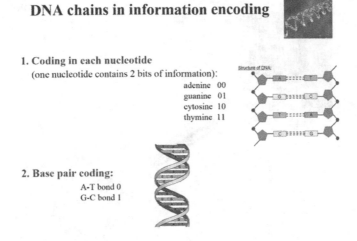

1. Coding in each nucleotide
   (one nucleotide contains 2 bits of information):

   adenine 00
   guanine 01
   cytosine 10
   thymine 11

2. Base pair coding:
   A-T bond 0
   G-C bond 1

Fig. 1. Possible methods of coding information using DNA molecules

3   Crypto-Biometrics Model for Strategic Information Management

Strategic business data require special protection, therefore they must be protected from disclosure. The methods of strategic data sharing in the enterprise presents Fig.2. Strategic data are splitting by used one of the cryptographic algorithms used to splitting processes. Consequently in this process information is divided into a number of parts of this information. Each of them is assigned to another holder. And no other person knows the other parts of strategic data. Therefore data are protected. To reproduce the strategic information is necessary to submit a certain number of them. Not necessarily all parts of divided strategic information. The number of necessary parts of strategic information needed to reproduced specifies the algorithm that was used to divide strategic information.

The strategic information management in enterprise present Fig. 3.

In this process the most important is stage of coding strategic information using personal biometrics feature. The biometrics features are different for different persons or kinds of biometrics. The encoded strategic information by one of the personal biometric is shared between the participants of procedure. In this way the information is not only divided, but also encoded. Reproduction of information therefore requires:

- submit an appropriate amount of parts shared information,
- disclosure of key biometric that was used to encode information.

Crypto-biometrics models therefore protected by algorithms of secret sharing and biometrics keys.

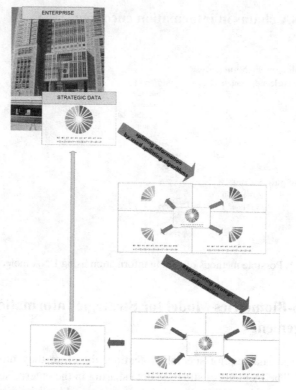

Fig. 2. The process of sharing strategic information in enterprise

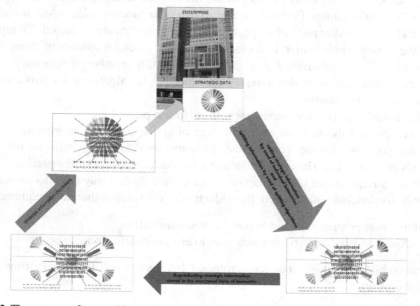

Fig. 3. The process of crypto-biometrics model for strategic information management in enterprise

4   Conclusions

Crypto-biometrics models are currently used to ensure security of different kinds of information, especially strategic information in organization. Strategic information management is often understood as management secret information. Ensure secrecy of strategic information is the responsibility of crypto-biometrics systems. The advantages of the proposed systems is:

- guarantee the security of strategic information,
- safety features during performing secret distribution,
- dividing important strategic data and assigning its shares to members of the authorized group,
- handle any digital data which needs to be intelligently divided among authorized persons and then possible to secretly reconstruct,
- used in different economical management structures e.g. hierarchical, divisional, functional etc.

Acknowledgments. This work has been supported by the National Science Centre, Republic of Poland, under project number DEC-2013/09/B/HS4/00501.

References

1. Adleman, L.M., Rothemund, P.W.K., Roweiss, S., et al.: On applying molecular computation to the Data Encryption Standard. Journal of Computational Biology 6(1), 53–63 (1999)
2. Blakley, G.R.: Safeguarding Cryptographic Keys. In: Proceedings of the National Computer Conference, pp. 313–317 (1979)
3. Chomsky, N.: Syntactic Structures, London Mouton (1957)
4. Menezes, A., van Oorschot, P., Vanstone, S.: Handbook of Applied Cryptography. CRC Press, Waterloo (2001)
5. Ogiela, L.: Cognitive Informatics in Automatic Pattern Understanding and Cognitive Information Systems. In: Wang, Y., Zhang, D., Kinsner, W. (eds.) Advances in Cognitive Informatics and Cognitive Computing. SCI, vol. 323, pp. 209–226. Springer, Heidelberg (2010)
6. Ogiela, L., Ogiela, M.R.: Advances in Cognitive Information Systems. In: COSMOS 17. Springer, Heidelberg (2012)
7. Ogiela, M.R., Ogiela, U.: Security of Linguistic Threshold Schemes in Multimedia Systems. In: Damiani, E., Jeong, J., Howlett, R.J., Jain, L.C. (eds.) New Directions in Intelligent Interactive Multimedia Systems and Services - 2. SCI, vol. 226, pp. 13–20. Springer, Heidelberg (2009)
8. Ogiela, M.R., Ogiela, U.: Shadow Generation Protocol in Linguistic Threshold Schemes. In: Ślęzak, D., Kim, T.-h., Fang, W.-C., Arnett, K.P. (eds.) SecTech 2009. CCIS, vol. 58, pp. 35–42. Springer, Heidelberg (2009)
9. Ogiela, M.R., Ogiela, U.: The use of mathematical linguistic methods in creating secret sharing threshold algorithms. Computers and Mathematics with Applications 60(2), 267–271 (2010)
10. Ogiela, M.R., Ogiela, U.: DNA-like linguistic secret sharing for strategic information systems. International Journal of Information Management 32, 175–181 (2012)

11. Ogiela, M.R., Ogiela, U.: Linguistic Protocols for Secure Information Management and Sharing. Computers and Mathematics with Applications 63(2), 564–572 (2012)
12. Peters, W.: Representing Humans in System Security Models: An Actor-Network Approach. Journal of Wireless Mobile Networks. Ubiquitous Computing, and Dependable Applications 2(1), 75–92 (2011)
13. Shamir, A.: How to Share a Secret. Communications of the ACM, 612–613 (1979)
14. Tang, S.: Simple Secret Sharing and Threshold RSA Signature Schemes. Journal of Information and Computational Science 1, 259–262 (2004)

One-Time Biometrics for Online Banking and Electronic Payment Authentication

Aude Plateaux[1], Patrick Lacharme[1],
Audun Jøsang[2], and Christophe Rosenberger[1]

[1] ENSICAEN, GREYC, F-14032 Caen, France
{aude.plateaux,patrick.lacharme,christophe.rosenberger}@ensicaen.fr
[2] Department of Informatics, University of Oslo, 0316 Oslo, Norway
audun.josang@mn.uio.no

Abstract. Online banking and electronic payment systems on the Internet are becoming increasingly advanced. On the machine level, transactions take place between client and server hosts through a secure channel protected with SSL/TLS. User authentication is typically based on two or more factors. Nevertheless, the development of various malwares and social engineering attacks transform the user's PC in an untrusted device and thereby making user authentication vulnerable. This paper investigates how user authentication with biometrics can be made more robust in the online banking context by using a specific device called OffPAD. This context requires that authentication is realized by the bank and not only by the user (or by the personal device) contrary to standard banking systems. More precisely, a new protocol for the generation of one-time passwords from biometric data is presented, ensuring the security and privacy of the entire transaction. Experimental results show an excellent performance considering with regard to false positives. The security analysis of our protocol also illustrates the benefits in terms of strengthened security.

Keywords: e-payment, biometrics, online banking security, strong authentication.

1 Introduction

Electronic commerce on the Internet is more and more used for online payment and online banking. In the same time, the fraud for these transactions is a major problem for financial institutions [11, 3]. Although the online payment only represents a small percentage of transactions, it concentrates a major loss for banks [19]. Many directives are related to online payments, such as the European directive 2000/31/EC on e-commerce security [6]. The Directive on Payment Services, [7], provides an european wide single market for payments and a legal platform for SEPA (Single Euro Payment Area, [8]). The 3D-Secure protocol is the payment protocol proposed by the industry and reduces the fraud in online payment.

S. Teufel et al. (Eds.): CD-ARES 2014, LNCS 8708, pp. 179–193, 2014.

In the usual case of e-commerce, the customer wants to purchase an online service, with a credit card, through a website. At a high level, the transaction generally begins with an authentication and a secure connection between the customer's client host and the service provider (SP) host, using a protocol such as SSL/TLS. In a second time, the user sends to the SP bank, through the SP host, his/her bank information: Personal Authentication Number (PAN), Card Verification Value (CVX2) and expiry date. SSL/TLS protocols enable to secure transaction between user's client host and the SP host. Nevertheless, there is no direct user's authentication in this scheme.

Security challenges in e-commerce are numerous, particularly related to user authentication, because the merchant and the cardholder are not in the same place during the transaction. So-called strong authentication is typically based on two-factor authentication. For example, an additional secret, sent by mobile phone, as for the 3D-Secure protocol [27] or an additional device as a CAP reader [12, 10] are required for electronic payments and online banking. The user's authentication system is traditionally realized by the user's bank (because the financial risk falls on the bank). Authentication should also take into account man-in-the-middle attacks (such as described in [3]). However, this paper is centered on user's authentication and such attacks are out of scope.

This paper presents an alternative method for user's authentication based on biometrics. The proposed system generates one-time passwords from fingerprints. The biometric data is not directly stored in the device and the generated password is different for each transaction in order to avoid replay attack.

The paper is organized as follows. Section 2 briefly presents state-of-the-art authentication solutions for e-payment. We define in Section 3 the security and privacy issues that the proposed solution should address. In Section 4, we present the OffPAD concept, a secure device to ensure secure Machine to Machine (M2M) transactions. We present in Sections the proposed authentication protocol. Some experimental results and security analysis are given in Section 6. Finally, we conclude and give some perspectives of this study.

2   E-payment Architectures

The Secure Electronic Transactions (SET, [24]) protocol, developed by VISA [1], and MasterCard [2], was a protocol for securing e-payment transactions by credit card. User authentication in SET was based on a public-key certificate installed on the client computer. VISA and MasterCard realised that the management of certificates was too complex for customers, so a simpler 3D-Secure protocol designed by VISA in 2001 was proposed as a solution to replace SET.

The 3D-Secure protocol [27] is the current authentication and payment architecture for credit cards on the web. It was first adopted by VISA, then other financial organizations developed their own implementations of VISA's 3D-Secure licensed architecture, such as MasterCard with its MasterCard SecureCode, American Express with SafeKey. A comparison between 3D-Secure and MasterCard SecureCode is proposed in [21]. The 3D-Secure protocol is composed of nine steps exchanged between five actors (Fig.1):

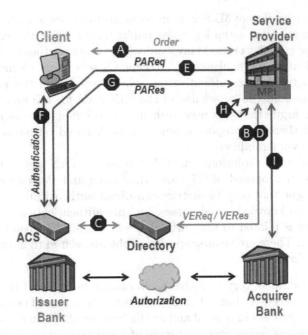

Fig. 1. The 3D-Secure protocol

A. The user sends to the SP his/her purchase intention, with his/her bank information: PAN (Personal Account Number), expiration date, CVV2 (Card Verification Value). These data are intended for a dedicated module called MPI (Merchant Plug In) implemented into the merchant website.

B. MPI queries the directory server with the VEReq (Verify Enrollment Request) message.

C. The directory server checks the SP identity, the card number and the user's bank and recovers the ACS (Access Control Server) managing the card.

D. The message VERes (Verify Enrollment result) contains the response of message. The ACS checks if the users's bank is enrolled in the 3D-Secure program and sends the cardholder authentication URL to the MPI.

E. MPI sends the PAReq (Payer authentication request) message to the given URL. This message contains the details of the authorized purchase. MPI also opens on the client computer a pop-up window to the ACS.

F. The user provides the necessary information for authentication from the bank.

G. ACS sends to MPI a confirmation of user authentication through PARes message.

H. MPI records PARes message as confirmation of user authentication by ACS.

I. SP authenticates to the bank. The bank verifies the nature of the transaction from the user's bank and confirms the payment authorization from the SP. The SP gets his/her payment and the users's bank stores payment information to ensure non-repudiation of the transaction.

The main security flaw of 3D-Secure implementations, underlined in [19], concerns user authentication (step F). Some banks have used in the past the date of birth or other trivial secrets. Many banks have replaced these solutions by a strong authentication mechanism (e.g. challenge is sent to user's mobile phone) which then is a two-factor authentication scheme (based on the possession of the mobile phone and the knowledge of the PIN code for the logical access to it). However we argue that this user authentication scheme has significant vulnerabilities. We therefore propose a new approach based on biometrics which eliminates these vulnerabilities.

User authentication solutions, as CAP readers, TAN generators or the lightweight system proposed in [17], are Knowledge and Possession based approaches. We argue that only biometrics can direct authenticate users, whereas solutions based on knowledge and possession only authenticate users indirectly. The main reason is related to the particular relationship between the user and its authenticator. There are f course specific problems related to biometrics, such as mentioned below:

- A biometric data is very sensitive as it cannot be revoked in general. Its encryption is necessary but not sufficient (as the data should be decrypted for the matching process in general and as the lifetime of this data is very high). For these reasons, using central storage of biometric data is problematic.
- The matching process could make errors for genuine users but also impostors could be falsely accepted. This is not the case for password verification as long as the correct password is typed (but there is no proof that it has been typed by the genuine user).
- Biometric data could be intercepted during its transmission. This could lead to security problems, such as replay attacks and privacy attacks based on linkability. For these reasons, the biometric data should be cancelable and dynamic (changing at each transaction).

In this paper, we propose a new solution that solves these problems. To achieve a security and privacy compliant solution, we combine two elements: the first one is a specific device owned by the user called OffPAD, and the second is a protocol using biometrics and cancelable algorithms. In the next section, we list the security and privacy requirements of the proposed solution.

3   Security and Privacy Requirements

In electronic payments, four main actors are present: The **user** C, who has an OffPAD, wants to purchase an online service with a credit card, through the website of a **service provider SP**. The user has an **issuer bank** and the SP has an **acquirer bank**. In this paper, we also call these payment providers: *user's bank* and *SP bank*. A fifth actor is often involved. It is the trusted party as a third-party cashier or the Directory used in 3D-Secure. The role of this fifth actor is various but generally allows to authenticate the banks. The proposed protocol is concentrated on user authentication and the user's registration with the SP.

During an online payment, numerous personal data are involved and must be protected against several threats, [4]. In order to preserve privacy and security properties, a list of ten requirements R_i is defined. These requirements should be taken into account during the user authentication/registration step in the e-payment architecture:

- R_1: **Confidentiality of transactions** requires that each exchanged data must be encrypted in order to protect these data against external entities.
- R_2: **Integrity of transmitted information** allows the accuracy of the content and so the non-alteration of data during transmission or storage.
- R_3: **User authentication** by a trusted party ensures the identity of the customer. Depending on the situation, the authentication can be realized thanks to a biometric data.
- R_4: **Authentication of the user's device** ensures the device is valid within the application. This authentication can be realized thanks to an identifier of the device.
- R_5: **Proof that the device belongs to the user** ensures the device prevents device replacement attacks.
- R_6: **SP authentication** by the user or by a trusted party ensures the identity of the SP.
- R_7: **Bank authentication** by a trusted party ensures the identity of SP bank and customer's bank.
- R_8: **Unlinkability** of realized transactions prevents linking different transactions of the same customer.
- R_9: **Confidentiality of customer information** CI (data minimization principle) ensures only authorized persons access to this information. This requires the user's biometric data are unknown to the banks and SP.
- R_{10}: **Data sovereignty** means that personal data associated with the customer can only be processed with his/her control and consent.

In the next section, we present the OffPAD concept as secure device for ensuring the security of sensitive operations.

4 OffPAd Concept

The PAD (Personal Authentication Device) is described by Jøsang and Pope [13] as a secure device external to the client computer platform. The PAD is the conceptual predecessor to the OffPAD. The OffPAD (Offline Personal Authentication Device) described by Klevjer et al. [16] and Varmedal et al. [26] is an enhanced version of the PAD, where an essential characteristic is to guarantee offline security (Machine to Machine communications). The OffPAD represents local user-centric identity management because it enables secure and user friendly management of digital identities and credentials locally on the user side. The OffPAD supports authentication of both user and service provider identities (i.e. mutual authentication) and can in addition support data authentication.

For access to the OffPAD, the user must unlock the device by using e.g. a PIN, pass phrase, biometrics or other adequate authentication credentials. A possible OffPAD design is illustrated in Figure 2.

Fig. 2. OffPAD concept [26]

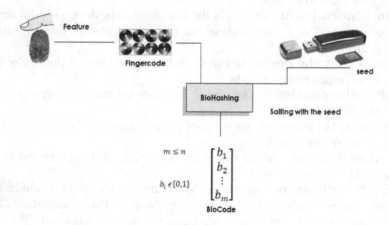

Fig. 3. BioHashing scheme

The OffPAD is a trusted device, meaning that it is assumed to function as intended and to be adequately protected against relevant attacks. The OffPAD has limited connectivity to client platforms. These communication channels must therefore be carefully controlled, e.g. by sanitizing the received data. Protection against attacks resulting from physical theft is to have traditional access control based on PIN and biometrics, combined with some level of physical tamper resistance. However, it is not necessary that the OffPAD operating system and applications are free from vulnerabilities that are typically found in online systems, because it is assumed that attackers will not be able to exploit such vulnerabilities since the OffPAD is offline most of the time. In that sense, a specific software bug which would have been a vulnerability in an online system is strictly speaking not a vulnerability in the OffPAD because it can not be exploited. The OffPAD may have several interfaces for communication. Microphone and camera may be used for voice and face recognition, and a fingerprint reader may be used for both authenticating to the device and elsewhere. The requirement of being offline does not exclude electronic communication with the OffPAD, but means

that the communication follows controlled formats and takes place in short, restricted time periods. This decoupling from networks improves security of the
device, as it is less vulnerable to outside attacks.

Any specific electronic communication should normally be disconnected, and
should only be connected whenever it is needed for authentication or for management of the device. NFC with a backup USB connection is a suitable for OffPAD
connectivity. This limits the threat of a man-in-the-middle attack when connecting an OffPAD to a computer. The first connection to the OffPAD builds upon
the concept of Trust-On-First-Use (TOFU). On first use, there is no cryptographic way to verify the connection between the device and the client platform,
the trust must simply be based on the physically observed set-up. On the first
connection, some kind of pairing between the device and computer occurs, so
that the subsequent connections can be verified to be between the same device
and computer.

We use this secure device for online banking and electronic payment following
an original protocol with biometrics. The following section explains the Biohashing algorithm used in the proposed protocol. Then, the section 6 details this new
original protocol.

5   BioHashing Algorithm

The BioHashing algorithm transforms a real-valued vector of length n (i.e. the
FingerCode, resulting from a feature extraction method) into a binary vector of
length $m \leq n$ (i.e. the BioCode), as first defined by Teoh et al. in [25].

It consists of projecting the FingerCode on an orthogonal basis defined by
a random seed (considered here as a secret), to generate the BioCode. The
template transformation uses the following algorithm, where the inputs are the
random seed and the FingerCode F and the output is the BioCode B:

1. For $i = 1, \ldots, m$, $m \leq n$ pseudorandom vectors v_i of length n are generated
   (from the random seed) and are gathered in a pseudorandom matrix.
2. The Gram-Schmidt algorithm is applied on the m vectors v_i of the matrix,
   for the generation of n orthonormal vectors $V_1, \ldots, V_m$.
3. For $i = 1, \ldots, m$, m scalar products $p_i = <F, V_i>$ are computed using the
   FingerCode F and the m orthonormal vectors V_i .
4. The m-bit biocode $B = (B_0, \ldots, B_m)$ is finally obtained, using the following
   quantization process:
$$B_i = \begin{cases} 0 & \text{if} \quad p_i < t \\ 1 & \text{if} \quad p_i \geq t, \end{cases}$$
   where t is a given threshold, generally equal to 0.

When used for authentication the *Reference BioCode* (computed from the
FingerCode after enrollment and after exhibiting the secret) is compared with
the *Capture BioCode* (computed from the FingerCode computed after a new
capture with the secret) with the Hamming distance. If this value is lower than

a specified threshold set by the system administrator, the identity of the user is verified. Roughly speaking, the first part of the algorithm, including the scalar products with the orthonormal vectors, is used for the performance requirements and the last step of the algorithm is used for the non-invertibility requirements of the BioHashing algorithm. As mentioned before, the random seed guarantees the diversity and revocability properties.

The user authentication protocol applies multiple times the BioHashing algorithm which we detailed in the next section.

6 Proposed Authentication Protocol

The proposed authentication protocol uses biometric data that must be protected through the capture with the OffPAD device and template protection algorithms. Biometric template protection schemes are a group of technologies, included in privacy enhancing technologies, used to enhance both privacy and security of biometric data. Therefore, any template protection approach should allow to revoke a biometric data in case of interception, and should be carefully designed, with a strong security analysis. Among the different solutions in the literature, template protection can be achieved using biometric cryptosystems [15, 14, 9, 20] or by transforming the biometric feature data [22, 5, 25, 23]. As detailed in the next section, BioHashing is one popular scheme that belongs to this second category and allows to revoke a biometric template.

The proposed protocol is detailed with fingerprints but could be used for any other biometric modality (face, iris...). As we use biometrics, two main steps are required: enrollment and authentication.

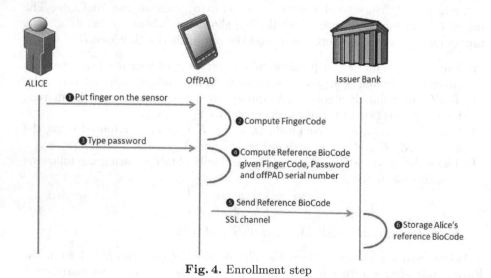

Fig. 4. Enrollment step

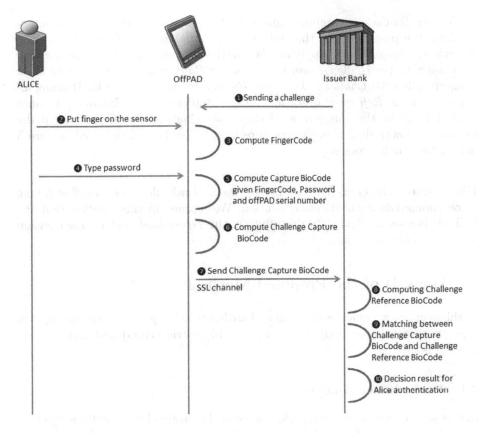

Fig. 5. Authentication step

Enrollment. This step has for objective to collect Alice's reference template. In our case, the template is given by a BioCode called *Reference BioCode* computed from a FingerCode (feature vector computed on the fingerprint) and a secret (user's secret concatenated with the serial number of the OffPAD device). User's secret could be a password or a random value stored in the OffPAD device (of course, it is protected by the biometric authentication to the device). Once the *Reference BioCode* has been computed, it is sent to the Alice's *Issuer Bank* through a SSL channel. Concerning an organizational point of view, this step could be done in a branch after identity checking by a physical person. Figure 4 details the enrollment process. There is no privacy issue to store the *Reference BioCode* by the *Issuer Bank* as this template is cancelable and as the BioHashing process is invertible.

Authentication. During an electronic payment, the *Issuer Bank* has to authenticate Alice (e.g. 3D-Secure process). A challenge is sent to Alice (number displayed on the computer or directly sent to her OffPAD). Alice has to provide her fingerprint and her password (that is not known by the *Issuer Bank*).

A *Capture BioCode* is computed given the FingerCode on the capture biometric data, the password and the OffPAD serial number. The *Challenge Capture Biocode* is computed by applying the BioHashing algorithm on the *Capture BioCode* with the challenge sent by the *Issuer Bank* as secret. The *Issuer Bank* computes also the *Challenge Reference Biocode* by applying the BioHashing algorithm on the *Reference BioCode* with the challenge. The Hamming distance is used to make the comparison of these two Challenge BioCodes and if the distance is lower than a predefined threshold, Alice is authenticated. Figure 5 details the whole process.

Discussion. The challenge sent by the *Issuer bank* allows us to define a One Time Biometrics authentication solution. We assume in this solution that the OffPAD is a secure device. In this solution, the *Issuer bank* controls the decision on Alice's authentication.

7   Analysis of the Proposed Method

In this section, we analyze the proposed authentication protocol considering two aspects: performance analysis (considering biometric errors) and security and privacy issues.

7.1   Performance Analysis

In this section, we analyze the performance of the protocol to avoid false rejection and false impostor. We start by defining the experimental protocol.

Experimental Protocol. In this study, we used three fingerprint databases, each one is composed of 800 images from 100 individuals with 8 samples from each user:

- FVC2002 benchmark database DB2: the image resolution is 296×560 pixels with an optical sensor "FX2000" by Biometrika ;
- FVC2004 benchmark database DB1: the image resolution is 640×480 pixels with an optical Sensor "V300" by CrossMatch ;
- FVC2004 benchmark database DB3: the image resolution is 300×480 pixels with a thermal sweeping Sensor "FingerChip FCD4B14CB" by Atmel.

   Figure 6 presents one image from each database. We can see that fingerprints are quite different and representative of the different types of fingerprint (acquired with sensors using different technologies).

   These databases have been used for competitions (Fingerprint Verification competition) in 2002 and 2004. Table 1 presents the performance of the best algorithms on these databases[1]. The Equal Error Rate (EER) computes the

---

[1] http://bias.csr.unibo.it/fvc2002

$$(a) \qquad\qquad (b) \qquad\qquad (c)$$

Fig. 6. One fingerprint example from each database: (a) FVC2002 DB2, (b) FVC2004 DB1, (c) FVC2004 DB3

Table 1. Performance of the best algorithm for each database (see `http://bias.csr.unibo.it/fvc2002`)

$Databases$	EER	$ZeroFMR$
$FVC2002\ DB2$	0.14%	0.29%
$FVC2004\ DB1$	0.61%	1.93%
$FVC2004\ DB3$	1.18%	4.89%

compromise error rate when genuine users have been falsely rejected and impostor falsely accepted. ZeroFMR is the value of False Non Match Rate (FNMR) when no impostor is falsely accepted. These values define the complexity of each database and give some elements of the performance what we can expect on these databases.

As FingerCode, we used Gabor features (GABOR) [18] of size n=512 (16 scales and 16 orientations) as template. These feature are very well known and permit a good texture analysis of a fingerprint. For each user, we used the first FingerCode sample as reference template. Others are used for testing the proposed scheme. BioCodes are of size m=256 bits. In order to quantify the performance of the One Time Biometrics approach, we computed 1000 comparisons (with the Hamming distance) between the challenge Reference BioCode and challenge Capture BioCode for each user. We obtained 100.000 intraclass and interclass scores for the performance analysis of the proposed scheme.

Experimental Results. We applied the previous protocol to the proposed authentication solution. On the three databases, we reach an EER value very close to 0%. In order to illustrate this efficiency, we show in Figure 7 the distribution of intraclass and interclass scores for each database. We clearly see that there is no overlap between the two distributions and a threshold near 60 (meaning maximal 60 different bits between the capture and Reference BioCodes is tolerated) could be used. In the last column of Table 2, we present the EER value by considering an impostor has in his/her possession the OffPAD device and the

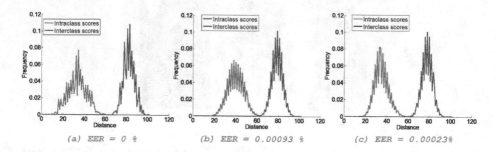

Fig. 7. Distribution of intraclass and interclass scores for each database: (a) FVC2002 DB2, (b) FVC2004 DB1, (c) FVC2004 DB3

Table 2. Performance of the proposed algorithm for each database

Database	EERwithoutattack	EERwithattack
FVC2002 DB2	0%	25.85%
FVC2004 DB1	0.00093%	23.95%
FVC2004 DB3	0.00023%	16.12%

user password (worst case). In this case, the impostor can apply the Zero effort attack by providing his/her biometric data to impersonate the genuine user. We tested 100.000 attacks for each database and this attack is successful from 16% to 25% of the cases. In classical approaches (two-factor authentication), this attack is always successful.

7.2 Security and Privacy Analysis

The proposed protocol is more respectful of the users' privacy than that of 3D-Secure protocol. We propose an analysis of the proposed protocol in this section.

Data Security and Authentication. The secure channel between actors and the encryption schemes ensure the confidentiality of exchanged data and the data integrity during the protocol. Consequently, the requirements R_1 and R_2 are ensured. Entities authentication is also realized through SSL for the SP (R_6) and the banks (R_7), whereas user authentication (R_3) is realized thanks to the strong authentication through Biohashing algorithm. Moreover, thanks to the challenges during user authentication, this authentication is an One Time Biometrics authentication solution. Consequently, the different transactions of a same user cannot be linked. The requirement R_8 is thus guaranteed. The device is also authenticated by its serial number and a proof of the user's device ownership is provided. Consequently, the requirements R_4 and R_5 are ensured. Moreover, for the user authentication solution, the user only needs to produce what he/she is (biometric data) and what is known (password).

Privacy Analysis. During our authentication process, several sensitive information items are exchanged and stored, such as biometric data and password. Their storage should not be centralized. However, thanks to the use of the BioHashing algorithm, the template is cancelable. Thus, the knowledge of the BioCode does not given knowledge concerning a user's personal information. In our case, the knowledge of the Reference BioCode does not involve the knowledge of the biometric data, the fingerprint. Only the relevant and necessary data are sent and stored. Thus, the minimization principle (R_9) is also respected. Moreover, for each user's authentication, the user must present his/her finger and give his/her password. These actions involve the user who gives his/her consent to use this data which he/she can control thanks to the computations of the Capture BioCode and the storage of the Reference BioCode. The data sovereignty principle (R_{10}) is consequently respected.

8   Conclusion and Perspectives

The proposed solution uses an extra device, which has a non negligible cost. Nevertheless, we consider the financial risk of on-line banking or payment is important and strongly increases. Consequently, this additional device is not a porblem for a real world deployment. In this paper, a new authentication protocol called "One Time Biometrics" for online banking and electronic payment authentication. We protocol consists of two main components. The first component is a specific device called OffPAD that ensures many security and privacy issues. The second component is the use of a biometric template protection algorithm to make possible the storage of a biometric data in a centralized way by the Issuer Bank. A challenge-based protocol is then proposed to prevent replay attacks. The user authentication scheme is usable for users as they do not have to remember different passwords. The protocol demonstrates very good performances on three benchmark fingerprint databases and good properties considering security and privacy issues.

Future perspectives of this study are numerous. We plan to use multiple biometric data in order to avoid the use of a password in the proposed protocol, and we also plan to design a biometric data authenticaiton protocol.

Acknowledgment. The authors would like to thank the Eurostars program for assistance to the project, as well as for financial support.

http://www.eurostars-eureka.eu/

References

[1] Visa corporate (1958), http://corporate.visa.com/index.shtml
[2] Mastercard worldwide (1966), http://www.mastercard.com/
[3] Adham, M., Azodi, A., Desmedt, Y., Karaolis, I.: How to attack two-factor authentication internet banking. In: Sadeghi, A.-R. (ed.) FC 2013. LNCS, vol. 7859, pp. 322–328. Springer, Heidelberg (2013)

[4] Antoniou, G., Batten, L.: E-commerce: protecting purchaser privacy to enforce trust. Electronic Commerce Research 11(4), 421–456 (2011)

[5] Bolle, R.M., Connell, J.H., Ratha, N.K.: Biometric perils and patches. Pattern Recognition 35(12), 2727–2738 (2002)

[6] European Commission. Directive 2000/31/ec of the european parliament and of the council of 8 june 2000 on certain legal aspects of information society services, in particular electronic commerce, in the internal market ('directive on electronic commerce') (2000)

[7] European Commission. Directive 2007/64/ec of the european parliament and of the council of 13 november 2007 on payment services in the internal market amending directives 97/7/ec, 2002/65/ec, 2005/60/ec and 2006/48/ec and repealing directive 97/5/ec (2007)

[8] European Payments Council. Sepa - single euro payment area (2007), http://www.sepafrance.fr/

[9] Daugman, J.: New methods in iris recognition. IEEE Transactions on Systems, Man, and Cybernetics, Part B: Cybernetics 37(5), 1167–1175 (2007)

[10] Drimer, S., Murdoch, S.J., Anderson, R.: Optimised to fail: Card readers for online banking. In: Dingledine, R., Golle, P. (eds.) FC 2009. LNCS, vol. 5628, pp. 184–200. Springer, Heidelberg (2009)

[11] Espelid, Y., Netland, L.-H., Klingsheim, A.N., Hole, K.J.: A proof of concept attack against norwegian internet banking systems. In: Tsudik, G. (ed.) FC 2008. LNCS, vol. 5143, pp. 197–201. Springer, Heidelberg (2008)

[12] MasterCard International. Chip authentication program functional architecture (September 2004)

[13] Jøsang, A., Pope, S.: User centric identity management. In: AusCERT Asia Pacific Information Technology Security Conference, p. 77. Citeseer (2005)

[14] Juels, A., Sudan, M.: A fuzzy vault scheme. In: ISIT, p. 408 (2002)

[15] Juels, A., Wattenberg, M.: A fuzzy commitment scheme. In: ACM Conference on Computer and Communications Security, pp. 28–36 (1999)

[16] Klevjer, H., Varmedal, K.A., Jøsang, A.: Extended http digest access authentication. In: Fischer-Hübner, S., de Leeuw, E., Mitchell, C. (eds.) IDMAN 2013. IFIP AICT, vol. 396, pp. 83–96. Springer, Heidelberg (2013)

[17] Li, S., Sadeghi, A.-R., Heisrath, S., Schmitz, R., Ahmad, J.J.: hPIN/hTAN: A lightweight and low-cost e-banking solution against untrusted computers. In: Danezis, G. (ed.) FC 2011. LNCS, vol. 7035, pp. 235–249. Springer, Heidelberg (2012)

[18] Manjunath, B.S., Ma, W.Y.: Texture features for browsing and retrieval of image data. IEEE Transactions on Pattern Analysis and Machine Intelligence 18, 37–42 (1996)

[19] Murdoch, S.J., Anderson, R.: Verified by visa and mastercard securecode: Or, how not to design authentication. In: Sion, R. (ed.) FC 2010. LNCS, vol. 6052, pp. 336–342. Springer, Heidelberg (2010)

[20] Osadchy, M., Pinkas, B., Jarrous, A., Moskovich, B.: Scifi - a system for secure face identification. In: IEEE Symposium on Security and Privacy (2010)

[21] Pasupathinathan, V., Pieprzyk, J., Wang, H., Cho, J.Y.: Formal analysis of card-based payment systems in mobile devices. In: Proceedings of the 2006 Australasian Workshops on Grid Computing and e-Research, vol. 54, pp. 213–220. Australian Computer Society, Inc. (2006)

[22] Ratha, N.K., Connell, J.H., Bolle, R.: Enhancing security and privacy in biometrics-based authentication system. IBM Systems J. 37(11), 2245–2255 (2001)

[23] Rathgeb, C., Uhl, A.: A survey on biometric cryptosystems and cancelable biometrics. EURASIP J. on Information Security, 3 (2011)

[24] S.E.T. Secure electronic transaction specification. Book 1: Business Description. Version, 1 (2002)

[25] Teoh, A.B.J., Ngo, D., Goh, A.: Biohashing: Two factor authentication featuring fingerprint data and tokenised random number. Pattern Recognition, 40 (2004)

[26] Varmedal, K.A., Klevjer, H., Hovlandsvåg, J., Jøsang, A., Vincent, J., Miralabé, L.: The offpad: Requirements and usage. In: Lopez, J., Huang, X., Sandhu, R. (eds.) NSS 2013. LNCS, vol. 7873, pp. 80–93. Springer, Heidelberg (2013)

[27] Visa. 3D secure protocol specification, core functions (July 16, 2002)

Expert Knowledge Based Design and Verification of Secure Systems with Embedded Devices

Vasily Desnitsky[1] and Igor Kotenko[1,2]

[1] Laboratory of Computer Security Problems
St. Petersburg Institute for Informatics and Automation (SPIIRAS)
39, 14 Linija, St. Petersburg, Russia
{desnitsky,ivkote}@comsec.spb.ru
[2] St. Petersburg National Research University of Information Technologies,
Mechanics and Optics, 49, Kronverkskiy prospekt, Saint-Petersburg, Russia

Abstract . The sweeping growth of the amount of embedded devices together with their extensive spread pose extensively new design challenges for protection of embedded systems against a wide set of security threats. The embedded device specificity implies combined protection mechanisms require effective resource consumption of their software/hardware modules. At that the design complexity of modern embedded devices, characterized by the proper security level and acceptable resource consumption, is determined by a low structuring and formalization of security knowledge. The paper proposes an approach to elicit security knowledge for subsequent use in automated design and verification tools for secure systems with embedded devices.

Keywords: Embedded security, embedded device design and verification, security components, expert knowledge.

1   Introduction

The sweeping growth of the amount of embedded devices and their extensive spread pose extensively the problem of design of their protection mechanisms against a wide range of information security threats. Mostly design complexity of secure embedded devices is determined by a low structuring and formalization of the embedded security knowledge. The specificity of the field is appearance of new expert knowledge, their obsolescence, information acquisition from various sources, such as embedded device industry, research and analytical works in information security and software engineering, experience in exploitation of existing information and telecommunication systems, through security and trust analysis of systems.

Embedded device specificity, leading to the need of specific approaches to their design and analysis, includes highly specialized purpose of devices and hence the domain specific character of their protection, considerable constraints on volumes of hardware resources, specific sets of vulnerabilities and possible attacks to compromise embedded device and its services, multi-component based approach [21] and therefore possible implicit connections and hidden conflicts between security components arising from the absence of their a priori joint conformity.

S. Teufel et al. (Eds.): CD-ARES 2014, LNCS 8708, pp. 194–210, 2014.

As a result, to solve security issues to the full extent information security experts of high qualification are required to be involved in the course of all stages of the design process. In general the search and involvement of such experts complicates the design process significantly, introducing new iterations, feedbacks between the developers, experts and other roles involved as well as increases financial costs to accomplish the development process. At that the current trend in the field of embedded device development is to delegate some part of expert duties to developers, owing to the application of specialized automated techniques and software tools for design, verification, testing, evaluation and implementation of embedded devices. That is knowledge on particular industry systems with embedded devices along with expert knowledge are subjected to generalization and transformed into particular techniques and tools for subsequent application by devices developers.

Another trend in embedded device development is to produce families of devices with a basic functionalities and different extra details determining peculiarities of the device exploitation and finally the cost of the device. As a result there is no necessity to fulfill the expert assisted design process fully for each device within a given family. Instead one should conduct some adaptation of already developed protection procedures and design protection procedures, taking into account the specificity of particular devices that mostly can be delegated to the developer.

The main goal is to form, structure and refine expert knowledge characterizing various design and verification aspects of embedded security mechanisms as well as to search new ones and adopt existing techniques and automated software tools for their subsequent use by developers with embedded devices. The main contribution of the paper is a proposed technique for design and verification on the base of the revealed expert knowledge. The technique is targeted on development of combined security mechanisms for embedded devices, considering resource consumption metrics, possible conflicts and anomalies of security components and information flows. The technique is characterized by engaged specific expert information on hardware resources, typical conflicts and anomalies.

Systems with embedded devices are getting spread in the sphere of home land defense and security. Such systems allow arrangement of collaborative coherent and secure operation of heterogeneous embedded and mobile devices, sensors, servers and other devices as well as various services and agents engaged. Development of security mechanisms for these systems taking into account specificity of particular devices and expert knowledge in the field will facilitate both global and national defense capability.

The paper represents a logical continuation of our published papers on design and analysis of secure systems with embedded devices [8, 6, 28]. Particularly, in the paper we (1) propose a heuristic to determine an order of consideration of hardware resources of the configurable device, depending on its functional and non-functional features, (2) extend the list of typical conflicts between security components of embedded devices, (3) reveal relevant types of information flow anomalies and the ways of their detection with reference to information flow analysis inside systems with embedded devices, (4) present the developed software prototype for detection of information flow anomalies, (5) fulfill an analysis of the proposed approaches. The rest of the paper is organized as follows. In section 2 the related works are surveyed. Section 3 encompasses the basic elements of the proposed technique, including configuring security components, detection of hidden conflicts, and verification of network information flows. Section 4 comprises the domain specific analysis of the field of embedded security. It outlines a fragment of the case study used as expert knowledge sources for the proposed technique. Section 5 exposes the revealed expert knowledge used in configuration and verification processes. Issues of software implementation and discussion are presented in section 6.

2   Related Works

A multi-component based approach to design systems with embedded devices got a relatively wide application [21] particularly within mobile operating systems Android. The protection system is represented as a set of interacting software and software/hardware components, each of them being in charge of particular functional security requirements. At that the process for combining security components, taking into account their peculiarities into a single mechanism is configuration of security components [8]. The drawbacks of the approach are possible implicit connections and hidden conflicts between security components arising from the absence of their a priori joint conformity. In [3, 17, 25, 13, 19] the core problems in the field of embedded device security are presented as particular security domain problems such as user identification, local secure data storage, software resistance to modifications, secure access, side channel attacks protection and others. Contemporary security mechanisms of embedded devices mostly are oriented to particular specific vulnerabilities. In [1, 18, 25, 28] various classifications of vulnerabilities, embedded device intruders are proposed, exposing intruder capabilities, competence and access type. At that combining various heterogeneous protection means within a single device, interrelations between them and issues of their integration correctness are not presented in existing works to the full extent.

The importance of the embedded device development, taking into account acceptable energy and computational expenses along with higher security level are uncovered in [9, 16, 27]. Besides granting necessary hardware and energy resources to the device and its services, a special issue is DoS attacks targeted on exhaustion of device energy resources [22, 33]. At that this kind of attacks is not detected by conventional antivirus solutions and other ones, but aimlessly waste energy resources through the use of the most energy expensive hardware components like Wi-Fi and Bluetooth modules or screens, complicating the further functioning of the device. Therefore a complex security mechanism should contain software and hardware modules against various relevant security vulnerabilities, taking into account possible implicit connections and inconsistencies between particular protection modules.

As a way to achieve a tradeoff between the security of the device and its resource consumption, Gogniat et al. [12] propose the usage of reconfigurable security primitives on the base of dynamic adaptation of the device architecture, depending on a state of the device and its environment. The adaptation suggested in [12] is based on, first, dynamic switching between a number of mechanisms integrated in the device and, second, update of these mechanisms.

Configuration processes along with analysis of hardware resource constraints and time expenses are of importance for development of end-products [15, 34, 35]. At that configuring facilitates a shift from development of a mass product to a customized one adjusted to the needs of a particular client [30].

As design case tools the specific UML profiles are used in the industry, holding relevant embedded security peculiarities, particular requirements, vulnerabilities, security components and their properties and connections between them. In particular in [28, 29, 31] Domain Specific Models are introduced to model and analyze security mechanisms for systems with embedded devices. In essence each domain is oriented to representation of the device or the whole system in the context of some particular security feature, such as secure storage domain, secure communication domain, user authentication one, etc. An advantage of the approach is delimitation of the design process tasks, responsibilities and roles involved as well as the use of expert knowledge in embedded security field to produce a device protection system. Software tool SPT (SecFutur Process Tool) [31] implementing the concept of domain specific models represents an extension to general purpose design environment MagicDraw. Model-driven design and analysis of embedded devices and real time systems are presented in MARTE framework [21] defining a complex UML based conception of software and hardware qualities of a device to support its specification, synthesis, verification, validation, performance evaluation, quantity analysis and device certification with the use of UML profiles. However UML based software tools for design and verification are oriented to development of static structure of devices, their specification and subsequent software/hardware implementation without evaluation of dynamically changing characteristics such as resource consumption laying beyond the scope of conventional UML apparatus.

3   Design and Verification Approaches

This section presents the basic elements of the proposed technique for design and verification of systems with embedded devices. The technique includes the following stages: (1) configuring security components of an embedded device; (2) verification of its protection system to reveal hidden conflicts; (3) verification of network information flows. The essence of the technique is in the use of specific heuristic based embedded security related knowledge as completed design and verification patterns along with the use of methods of model checking, discrete optimization and decision making.

A. Configuring Security Components

Correlation of security level of embedded devices and their various non-functional characteristics such as resource consumption represents a challenge in the field of secure embedded device development. Often the absence of effective design-time tools to develop combined security mechanisms complicates or even makes virtually impracticable the implementation of sound protection system. The proposed approach to design the protection systems for embedded devices is realized in accordance with multi-component based approach, taking into consideration both functional and non-functional requirements and limitations of the device and security components as well as resource consumption criteria to obtain the most effective solutions customized by non-functional constraints of a particular kind of devices. In essence a resource consumption criterion determines a sequence of hardware resources ordered by their criticality level. At that a discrete optimization problem is formed on a set of security configurations, while its solution allows getting the optimal configuration [8].

The goal of the proposed approach is to determine the most resource effective (optimal) configuration of the protection system on the base of input data on the device and its security components. The configuration is intended to be integrated into the protection system of the device. Finding the optimal configuration will allow ultimately improvement of device protection effectiveness. The choice of an optimal configuration depends on the following factors: (1) device hardware capabilities and volumes of resources to be allotted to support the protection system; (2) needs of the resources for particular security components. For instance asymmetric encryption as a rule requires significant computational expenses; a remote attestation component requires additional network bandwidth expenses leading to higher consumption of energy resources; (3) device peculiarities, scenario of the device, its autonomy, mobility as well as other characteristics and requirements to the device and protection.

Configuring is conducted in automated mode on the base of developed decision making tool to choose optimal configurations. At that, resource consumption criteria are set manually, depending on non-security requirements, peculiarities of the device and its protection system under configuration process. Therefore we propose to use a specific heuristic to determine an order of consideration of hardware resources in the configuration process, depending on functional and non-functional features of the device. Further in sections 4 and 5 in framework of a domain-specific analysis of the field of embedded security we survey shortly a case study as well as a heuristic based on the analysis of this case study. In essence configuring represents a discrete multicriteria optimization problem on the set of security components. Due to the finite and relatively small amount of security component alternatives available in the design process there is no need to look for or create any specific methods to solve the optimization problem in a short period of time. In fact the proposed heuristic should be used by the device developer to form particular optimization problem constraints and their order properly.

B. Detection of Hidden Conflicts between Security Components

Multi-component based approach to design of embedded devices and in particular their protection systems cause a problem of correct and secure combined use of several security components. Even assuming individually each security component has no internal inconsistencies and vulnerabilities, the combined protection mechanism nonetheless can be subject to hidden conflicts of different character.

Such conflicts may lead to security vulnerabilities in the protection system, incorrect work of the protection system and even business functions of the device. The main complexity is that these conflicts may appear at the exploitation stage of the device only. Therefore their elimination may require lots of financial costs and industrial expenses. Thus an important task is seen to detect known kinds of hidden conflicts between security conflicts in design-time. In section 4 we present a number of typical conflicts as a piece of expert knowledge and their examples. These conflicts were got heuristically through an analysis of existing systems with embedded devices and a range of papers on embedded security [5, 31].

C. Verification of Network Information Flows

The goal of network information flow verification is to evaluate security level of the developed information system with embedded devices. The verification is conducted through checking correctness of the security policy for the system and determine to what extent information flows in the real system correspond to the policy.

By information flow we mean summation of information passed between two or more interacting objects. Information flow security policy represents a set of rules determining which information flows in the system are permitted or prohibited.

Conventionally information flow analysis is conducted at three levels, (1) *hardware* – as an analysis of ties between the microcircuits [4], (2) *software* – as an analysis of the source code running on the device [24], and (3) *network* – as analysis of network connections in systems with embedded devices. Information flow analysis at these levels are covered in detail in existing literature [24, 14]. Amount of papers on verification of network information flows is significantly less than ones on software and hardware flows. The concept of information flow is widely used in security evaluation of a route and network effectiveness evaluation [2, 32]. Although these studies are not directly related to the types of data transmitted by information flows in the network, but nonetheless, they can be used for modeling information flows. Usually information flows between nodes are specified as a directed acyclic graph. Thus, to reveal covert channels the topological analysis described in [26] can be applied to this graph. In this paper we apply model checking to verify security policy rules for information flows. In general, checking correctness of network information flows is an integral part of the design process. Carrying out such verification at the initial design stages provides early detection of contradictions in the security policy and inconsistencies of the information system topology.

Verification of network information flows at the initial design stages represents the static analysis of a system. In contrast to the dynamic analysis including testing of end devices on the basis of attack vectors the proposed verification approach can reduce the number and complexity of actions that need to be repeated after the design errors become fixed. In general, the static approach is to analyze the structure of the information system and its characteristics as system models at different levels of abstraction [20] (security policies and business logic). To verify the security policy rules regarding checking network information flows we propose to apply model checking, using SPIN tool and PROMELA language. Checking information flows is carried out on a model of the system, since information flow verification on the real network would be much more difficult due to the need to involve specialized equipment, software tools and staff of qualification. Enumerating the policy rules is realized in order of decreasing priority until some rule holds. Prioritization allows organization of more complex management of interrelated policy rules.

4   Analysis of Expert Knowledge Sources

We used three industrial systems with embedded devices (case study) as a source of expert knowledge in the field of embedded systems [31], namely a system of remote automated control of energy consumption by consumers (*abr. MD*), a quickly deployable emergency management system (*abr. TMN*) and a system providing consumers with digital media services (*abr. STB*). The choice of these three case studies is determined by their different structure, purposes, functional and security features. The expert knowledge obtained through the analysis of these systems can be generalized and used as a completed design and verification patterns in the development of new systems.

The following patterns, forming the proposed technique, are related to expert knowledge. These are particular security requirements in the shape of functional protection properties and possible alternatives for choosing security components; information on non-security features and internal ties of both an embedded device and its security system to be the base of resource consumption construction; possible types of conflicts that security components are involved in; possible types of information flow anomalies and ways of their detection.

A brief description of the system *MD* developed by Mixed-mode [31] is presented below. The system represents a network containing digital trusted electricity meters on the client side, a trusted server and database as well as an infrastructure for communications between devices and their management. The system is characterized by a branched network topology, the presence of technical personnel roles in charge of installation, gauging and support of the system devices as well as a need to protect the devices and software services from malicious users and third parties trying to compromise the system. The system contains trusted sensor modules (TSM) to measure electricity of households (Fig. 1).

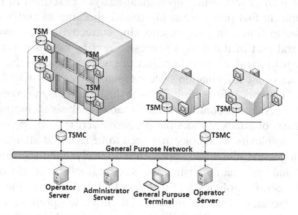

Fig. 1. The system of remote automated control of energy consumption [31]

Measurement data got from each TSM are sent, using the local data bus to a trusted sensor module collector (TSMC). For remote access and control of TSM and TSMC a general-purpose terminal belonging to a general purpose network is used. TSM and TSMC are considered as functional physical modules not necessarily standing alone. However they can be implemented within a single device [31].

On the base of the analysis of the system specification and models of embedded device intruders the developers have provided the following functional protection properties, each of them being associated with some security component [31]. These are the integrity of data transmitted to and from the device, in particular, the target data of the current energy consumption on the client side; the integrity of data stored locally on the device; the confidentiality of data transmitted to and from the device;

confidentiality of data stored locally on the device; data flow control in accordance with a given security policy; monitoring unauthorized and potentially dangerous action in the system; implementation of protection against unexpected data; presence of data protection from destruction and loss during their transmission or processing due to software failures; presence of a mechanism for safe update of security features; ability to identify compromised and alien devices and components; presence of a mechanism for detection of anomalies in the measured data received from the device; realization of local role based access to the device; continuous integrity monitoring software components of the device.

Non-security TSM related expert knowledge items are as follows: presence of a permanent power source; TSM does not store large amounts of data (only stores the measurement data), data loss is not critical; no complicated calculations (since the main function is reading and transfer of data from the sensor); requirement of timeliness of the business process function; importance of communication services, volumes of business data (measurement data) in the device are small.

The search of typical conflicts and anomalies in the system represents a heuristic analysis of specifications and system models, taking into account already known types of conflicts and anomalies listed in section 5. Specifically for the system *MD* the policy rules constituting a shadowing anomaly have been analyzed.

5   Expert Knowledge

A. Configuring security components

An optimal configuration choice is carried out using lexicographic ordering of speci-fied resource consumption criteria. The ordering is based on a heuristic to determine the order of consideration of hardware resources in the configuration process, depend-ing on the functional and non-functional features of the configurable device. The heuristic is based on expert knowledge derived from the analysis of three industrial systems with embedded devices (system *MD, TMN, STB*).

The heuristic represents a general algorithm for prioritization of hardware re-sources of an embedded device. A set of signs of embedded devices and the services they provide, having the influence on resource consumption is specified. We intro-duced a three-point ranking for resources according to their criticality to execution of the target device functions (*0 means the resource is noncritical, 1 means low criticali-ty and 2 means high criticality*). By experts a rank value is specified for each sign of the core device of each of the three systems in use. Table 1 shows the four types of hardware resources in accordance with the methodology MARTE [21], a set of signs for each of them, references to the analyzed systems that have devices with the re-garded signs and the corresponding ranks. Thus, the ranks obtained on the basis of expert evaluation of the analyzed systems are taken as ranks of the signs themselves. Hence these rank values can be used for express ranking of resources of the device by its developer without additional participation of experts.

Thus, in configuring process the device characteristic signs are identified from the list of available ones. After that each resource is assigned a maximum value of rank over all held signs corresponding to a given resource. As a result, the considered hardware resources are ordered according to decreasing their ranks. If two or more resources have the same rank value, the default order <HW_PowerSupply, HW_StorageManager, HW_Computing, HW_Communication> is used. It was defined BY experts as a priori and the typical for the most existing systems. It is assumed if necessary this heuristic may be refined by adding additional signs, resources, analyzed systems and devices to consider as expert knowledge.

Table 1. A heuristic for choosing resource consumption criteria

Resource type according to MARTE	Signs of embedded devices and its services	Abbreviation of the systems with devices of the sign	Rank
HW_PowerSupply (energy consumption resource)	The presence of a permanent power source	MD, STB	0
	Possibility of replacing the device or battery without damage to the provided services	TMN	1
	Sporadic access to a centralized power supply	TMN	1
	High dependency of the mission goal achievement on energy resources	TMN	2
HW_StorageManager (storage resource)	The device does not store large amounts of data, loss of data is not critical	MD	0
	Storing large amounts of data, loss of data is not critical	STB	1
	Storing large or unlimited amounts of data, the loss is critical	TMN	2
HW_Computing (computational resource)	No complex calculations, no requirements of message delivery timeliness	–	0
	No complex calculations, major timeliness	MD	1
	Complex calculations, minor timeliness	STB	2
	Complex calculations, major timeliness	TMN	2
HW_Communication (communicational resource)	No communications (or they are not obligatory for the device services)	–	0
	Importance of communications for the device services, minor data volumes	MD	1
	Importance of communications, large data	STB, TMN	2

B. Hidden Conflicts of Security Components

Analysis of hidden conflicts of security components is an integral part of the effective configuration selection process and is performed by embedded device developer during the protection system design. In essence this is a heuristic analysis aimed at identification of known kinds of hidden conflicts, which the security components of embedded devices are involved in [8].

Generally a conflict is regarded as a relationship between two or more security components and represents a contradiction between the functional of several security components, any their non-functional limitations and/or software/hardware platform of the device. The peculiarity of such conflicts is that as a rule they become apparent under certain conditions only and. Therefore, it is difficult to detect them during testing end devices by the use of attack vectors. Early design-time detection of conflicts in the process of integrating security components will help to reduce the number of iterations of the device development process. Besides for a conflict to be appeared not only the fact of integration of multiple security components with specified security functional is important, the way of their integration is significant as well. Specifically two components with opposite protection features can be in a conflict if they are performed simultaneously and interact within a common hardware/software context, for example, they use share data structure, memory, file, communication channel and so on. Knowledge of known types of conflicts is produced by expert analysis, modeling and development of new information systems with embedded devices. It seems appropriate to keep a list of previously discovered types of conflicts, regarding domain-specific nature of each particular system. As a consequence as the specification of the combined device protection system as well as specifications of considered security components should be analyzed together by the developers for the presence of conflicts from the list. Differences between the nature of each particular conflict, amounts of the involved security components and their protection functional, peculiarities of the components interactions and their integration as well as domain-specific character cause the development of comprehensive classification covering all possible hidden conflicts seems infeasible at the moment. However, in the design process a particular classification of conflicts (e.g. according to the type of the involved objects) can be used as an expert knowledge by the device developer of the protection system to realize a directional search of possible conflicts (Table 2).

Table 2. Types of conflicts between security components

Type 1 – conflict due to a lack of consistency between a security component and the device specification
Type 2 – conflict between the protection functions of several security components
Type 3 – conflict between several basic components within a complex security component

Fig. 2 schematically shows the three types of conflict discussed. Examples of each of the three above conflict types are presented in Table 3.

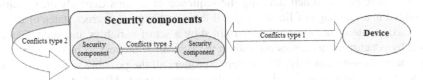

Fig. 2. Three types of security component conflicts

Resolving such conflicts is individual and determined by the specificity of a particular conflict and its security components involved. As resolution options a revision of one or several security components, changing the way their integration or correcting security requirements can be considered.

Table 3. Examples of expert knowledge on conflicts

Conflict type	Conflict example
Type 1	*Security_component* = "TPM based secure module for storing confidential customer data"; *Safity_requirement* = "to double customer data by an extra hardware storage module"; *Conflict* = "assuming the only TPM in the device the unprotected doubling violates data confidentiality"
Type 2	*Security_component_1* = "backup component for critical customer data"; *Security_component_2* = "component for secure guaranteed deletion of critical customer data after some specific event happens"; *Conflict* = "inconsistent application of the both components to the same data causes a conflict due to a logical opposite of the their security features"
Type 3	*Security_requirement* = "to implement RAID based redundant and high-performance storage of business data by two (or more) secure hardware units"; *Assumption* = "the inconsistent parameters of the units (e.g. different capacity of the units or their writing speeds)"; *Conflict* = "the units are correct themselves, but they do not implement RAID"

C. Network Information Flow Verification

For verification of network information flows the expert knowledge includes instances of security policy anomalies and methods for their detection. Consider one type of anomalies more in detail, "shadowing" anomaly. The presence of this anomaly supposed that a rule never works because there are one or more rules with higher priorities "overlapping" it. This anomaly indicates a probable error in the policy, which should be reviewed.

Network information flows and policy rules are specified by the following tuples:

$InformationFlow = < host1, host2, user1, user2, interface1, interface2, type >,$

$FilteringRule = < host1, host2, user1, user2, interface1, interface2, type, action >,$

where $host1$, $host2$ – sending and receiving hosts, respectively; $user1$, $user2$ – user sending and receiving user; $interface1$, $interface2$ – types of hardware Interfaces of the sender and recipient; $type$ – type of the information flow.

Type of information flow refers to a kind of data that the flow encapsulates. Information flow types by both the kind of transmitted information (e.g., user data, critical data, checksums, encryption keys, security certificate, etc.) and the format which the information is presented in (e.g., unencrypted and encrypted messages, compressed message).

The essence of model checking, applying to anomaly detection consists in iterating states the system can move into, depending on the emerging information flows and responses from the component making decisions on policy based permission or rejection of such requests. When iterating the sequence of actions depends on conditions formulated in a language of linear temporal logic and express correct states of the system [6, 20]. State of the system is determined by a set of variables and state change is caused by concurrent processes running in the system. A process to be executed in the next time is chosen randomly. The system considers all the possible sequences of steps for specific processes and signals potentially incorrect state. After that, the user is given a track, i.e. a sequence of steps leading to an incorrect state of the system with respect to given conditions. Basic input of verification of network information flows includes, first, descriptions of policy rules and, second, the structure of the network in the system description language and detectable types of anomalies.

At the first stage of verification input data is converted into an internal format of the verification system. Then, at a second stage, a general model of the system is built to verify prohibiting and permitting rules for information flows. The model is presented in the form of a finite state machine and initialized by the input data in internal format. In the model the anomalies are expressed by formal statements. According to model checking paradigm these formal statements represent properties of correctness, which violation brings the analyzed system in an incorrect state. At the third stage the general model is verified by a model checker tool. In the verification process all incorrect state of the system are revealed. At the final verification stage the obtained are subjected to interpretation. If any anomaly instances are detected, it is created a description containing situation and the information flow leading to the appearance of the anomaly and its type [20].

For the case of a shading anomaly the verification includes: (1) generating a set of testing flows (the flows are formed on the basis of the so called "boundary" values of the policy rules, i.e. the flows are constructed through any possible combinations of parameters taken from the rule statements); (2) sequential application of the policy to each information flow; thus each time the rule holds it is marked as *held*; (3) search on the set of rules to identify rules did not hold even once.

Therefore, verification allows getting a set of results, each of them being a pair $<A, (B_1,...B_n)>$, where A represents an anomalous rule, $B_1,...B_n$ are higher priority rules shadowing it. $B_1,...B_n$ are isolated by an extra pass of the policy by running those testing flows that meet the conditions of rule A.

6   Software Implementation and Discussion

A software prototype developed is used within the proposed technique of design and verification of systems with embedded devices. The prototype includes a design-time means for making decisions on choosing optimal configurations and for verification of network information flows.

The architecture of the tool for making decisions on choosing optimal configurations on the basis of UML class diagrams is presented in Fig. 3. At the architecture there are its grouped elements in charge of the protected device and its properties; security components; classifications of properties of the device and its individual security components; optimality criteria as well as configuration function of and check of configuration admissibility. This tool includes the following main features: (1) configuration function, that forms an optimal configuration according to the given constraints and a list of security components (function *configure*); (2) check function for verification of configuration admissibility (function *verify*).

As practice shows, often in the development of combined protection systems with embedded devices the choice of security components is realized by developers intuitively without any experimental evaluations on an already produced device with integrated protection and without taking into account any design-time system models and heuristics. Experiments on modeling strategy for choosing pseudo optimal sets of security components on the base of greedy algorithms have been realized. The strategy represents a procedure for a sequentially organized choice and refinement of security components of the sought configuration iteratively for each security requirement. In fact, this procedure works successively, for each functional protection property choosing a security component from the available ones that consumes the least amount of hardware resources according to their order determined by the heuristic. The averaged experimental data allow us to deduce that the proposed configuration process results in more effective solutions of combined protection. At that the combined protection effectiveness is meant as achievement of minimal resource consumption of a set of security components providing the given security features. More detailed description of the configuration tool, its performance evaluation as well as fragments of the GUI are given in [8].

The proposed verification of network information flows has been implemented for the analysis of security level of the system of automated control of energy consumption by end customers (system *MD*) with the following limitations. Due to technical simplifications, a limitation of the implementation is setting parameters of the policy both by defining concrete values or rules (specific hosts, interfaces, users) and by using special identifiers *any*, defining all possible values for a parameter. Generally it is assumed setting undefined sets of parameters of rules (in particular as the use of structures such as *"all the values, excepting x1, x2, x3"*). The policy rules for the *MD* case study were established based on available system specifications.

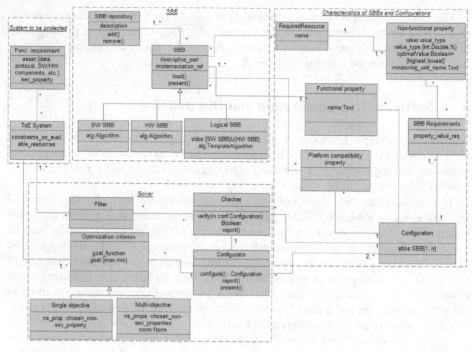

Fig. 3. A tool for configuring security components

We performed experiments, introducing shadowing anomaly instances into the policy. These anomalies simulate potential errors in the process of the policy development. During the technique all the instances were revealed. After verification completed the original policy was subjected to corrections, the verification repeated and new policy admitted as free of shadowing anomalies.

A piece of the requirements got from *MD* case study specification presented below.

> *"The privacy non-relevant data is generated by and temporarily stored on the trusted meter. It is displayed on the trusted meters local display.*
> ny user shall be able to read the privacy non-relevant data by using the local interface of the Trusted Meter, and only by using the local interface."

Fig. 4 shows a fragment of a security policy, two policy rules in PROMELA language specifying the given requirement and presenting a shadowing anomaly (rule 0 is presented in lines 82-92, whereas rule 1 is in lines 94-104). In accordance with the location the rule 0 has a higher priority than the rule 1. This anomaly is the result of an incorrect indication of the values of interfaces of the source device (interface1).

Fig. 5 shows a window with a trace from the use of SPIN. In particular, it is shown that the rule 1 is indicated as abnormal.

The experiments on modeling a large number of involved objects, roles, data types and permitting/prohibiting rules confirmed the effectiveness of the proposed verification for the design of the automated control system of energy consumption (*MD*). Since the typical conflicts and anomalies are detected mostly heuristically, it is difficult to deduce about any universal ways to resolve them. Elimination of a

```
82      rule0.user1 = any_user;
83      rule0.user2 = any_user;
84      rule0.interface1 = any_interface;
85      rule0.interface2 = any_interface;
86      rule0.host1 = TM;
87      rule0.host2 = any_host;
88      rule0.type = Privacy_non_relevant_data;
89      rule0.action = allow;
90      rule0.isHeld = false;
91      rule0.id = 0;
92      storage.policyRules!rule0;
93
94      rule1.user1 = any_user;
95      rule1.user2 = any_user;
96      rule1.interface1 = local_interface;
97      rule1.interface2 = any_interface;
98      rule1.host1 = TM;
99      rule1.host2 = any_host;
100     rule1.type = Privacy_non_relevant_data;
101     rule1.action = deny;
102     rule1.isHeld = false;
103     rule1.id = 1;
104     storage.policyRules!rule1;
```

Fig. 4. Example of rules containing a shadowing anomaly

Fig. 5. The technique output

conflict/anomaly is determined, first of all, by its context including specific security requirements and assumptions, information security risks, modes of the device, involved security components, used interfaces, etc. To verify network control information flows of a security policy it is not sufficient to use pairwise comparisons of the policy rules only. In fact an analysis of the policy rules holdings in dynamic (i.e. model checking) is needed. In general, compared with the classical network architecture, the specificity of information systems with embedded devices in the task of verification of network information flow contains presence of a branched network topology based on heterogeneous embedded devices with different types of communications and types of hardware/software interface being entry and exit points for information flows, and variability of the structure of such systems throughout its work. An advantage of the proposed verification of information flows is to ensure the system security, assuming the same behavior of the model and the real system. Disadvantages include a large amount of computational resources required to analyze complex models; possible false positives, i.e. warnings on anomalies missing the real system; and incompleteness, as instead of the real system its model is verified.

7   Conclusion

The paper focused at the technique for design and verification of information systems with embedded devices. It is oriented at development and comprehensive analysis of the combined security mechanisms to protect embedded devices on the basis of resource consumption metrics, potential conflicts and anomalies between protection components and information flows. The technique is based on domain-specific analysis of several case studies and characterized by specific expert information on hardware resources of embedded devices, typical conflicts and anomalies. The technique peculiarities include the use of specialized heuristic knowledge in the field of embedded security as completed design and verification patterns, applying methods of model checking, discrete optimization and decision-making theory.

As future research we are planning to identify and use additional expert knowledge by analysis of specifications new case studies, research papers, technical and analytical reports in the field. It is expected to expand the list of typical conflicts and anomalies and do the further work on SPIN based verification component. Knowledge identified in the research is planned to be organized in an ontological form, using a modeling environment Protégé. The peculiarity of this representation is unification of expert information for its subsequent use by device developers both in decision-making design directly and as input for automated development tools.

Acknowledgements. This research is being supported by grants of the Russian Foundation of Basic Research (projects 13-01-00843, 13-07-13159, 14-07-00697, 14-07-00417), the Program of fundamental research of the Department for Nanotechnologies and Informational Technologies of the Russian Academy of Sciences (2.2), by Government of the Russian Federation, Grant 074-U01, the State contract #14.604.21.0033, the project ENGENSEC of the TEMPUS program and the FP7 SecFutur project.

References

1. Abraham, D.G., Dolan, G.M., Double, G.P., Stevens, J.V.: Transaction security system. IBM Systems Journal 30(2), 206–228 (1991)
2. Agaskar, A., He, T., Tong, L.: Distributed Detection of Multi-hop Information Flows with Fusion Capacity Constraints. IEEE Transactions on Signal Processing 58(6), 3373–3383 (2010)
3. Arbaugh, W.A., van Doorn, L.: Embedded security: challenges and concerns. Computer Journal 34(10), 40–41 (2001)
4. Braghin, C., Sharygina, N., Barone-Adesi, K.: A model checking-based approach for security policy verification of mobile systems. Formal Aspects of Computing Journal, 627–648 (2011)
5. Burleson, W., Clark, S.S., Ransford, B., Fu, K.: Design challenges for secure implantable medical devices. In: 49th ACM/EDAC/IEEE Design Automation Conference (DAC), pp. 12–17 (2012)
6. Chechulin, A., Kotenko, I., Desnitsky, V.: An approach for network information flow analysis for systems of embedded components. In: Kotenko, I., Skormin, V. (eds.) MMM-ACNS 2012. LNCS, vol. 7531, pp. 146–155. Springer, Heidelberg (2012)
7. Cederquist, J.G., Torabi Dashti, M.: An intruder model for verifying liveness in security protocols. In: Proceedings of FMSE 2006, pp. 23–32 (2006)
8. Desnitsky, V., Kotenko, I., Chechulin, A.: Configuration-based approach to embedded device security. In: Kotenko, I., Skormin, V. (eds.) MMM-ACNS 2012. LNCS, vol. 7531, pp. 270–285. Springer, Heidelberg (2012)

9. Dick, N., McCallum, N.: High-speed security Embedded security. Communications Engineer Journal 2(2), 37–39 (2004)
10. Eisenring, M., Thiele, L., Zitzler, E.: Conflicting criteria in embedded system design. IEEE Design & Test of Computers Journal 17(2), 51–59 (2000)
11. Feigenbaum, J., Freedman, M.J., Tomas, S., Shostack, A.: Privacy Engineering for Digital Rights Management Systems. In: Proceedings of the ACM Workshop on Security and Privacy in Digital Rights Management, pp. 76–105 (2001)
12. Gogniat, G., Wolf, T., Burleson, W.: Reconfigurable Security Primitive for Embedded Systems. In: Proceedings of International Symposium on In System-on-Chip, pp. 23–28 (2005)
13. Grand, J.: Practical Secure Hardware Design for Embedded Systems. In: Proceedings of the 2004 Embedded Systems Conference, San Francisco, California, April 1 (2004)
14. Hedin, D., Sabelfeld, A.: A Perspective on Information-Flow. In: summer school Control Tools for Analysis and Verification of Software Safety and Security, Marktoberdorf, Germany (2011)
15. Juengst, W.E., Heinrich, M.: Using Resource Balancing to Configure Modular Systems. IEEE Computer Society Intelligent Systems and their Applications 13(4), 50–58 (1998)
16. Knezevic, M., Rozic, V., Verbauwhede, I.: Design Methods for Embedded Security. Telfor Journal 1(2) (2009)
17. Kocher, P., Lee, R., Mcgraw, G., Ravi, S.: Security as a new dimension in embedded system design. In: Proceedings of the 41st Design Automation Conference (DAC 2004), pp. 753–760 (2004)
18. Kommerling, O., Kuhn, M.G.: Design principles for tamper-resistant smartcard processors. In: Proceedings of the USENIX Workshop on Smartcard Technology, pp. 9–20 (1999)
19. Koopman, P.: Embedded System Security. IEEE Computer (7) (2004)
20. Kotenko, I., Polubelova, O.: Verification of Security Policy Filtering Rules by Model Checking. In: Proceedings of IEEE Fourth International Workshop on Intelligent Data Acquisition and Advanced Computing Systems: Technology and Applications(IDAACS 2011), pp. 706–710 (2011)
21. Object Management Group, The UML Profile for MARTE: Modeling and Analysis of Real-Time and Embedded Systems, Version 1.1 (2011)
22. Moyers, B.R., Dunning, J.P., Marchany, R.C., Tron, J.G.: Effects of Wi-Fi and Bluetooth Battery Exhaustion Attacks on Mobile Devices. In: Proceedings of the 43rd Hawaii International Conference on System Sciences (HICSS 2010), pp. 1–9. IEEE Computer Society (2010)
23. Pieters, W., Coles-Kemp, L.: Reducing normative conflicts in information security. In: Proceedings of the 2011 Workshop on New Security Paradigms Workshop, pp. 11–24 (2011)
24. Pistoia, M., Chandra, S., Fink, S., Yahav, E.: A Survey of Static Analysis Methods for Identifying Security Vulnerabilities In Software Systems. IBM Systems Journal (2007)
25. Rae, A.J., Wildman, L.P.: A Taxonomy of Attacks on Secure Devices. In: Australian Information Warfare and IT Security, Australia, November 20-21, pp. 251–264 (2003)
26. Rae, A., Fidge, C.: Identifying Critical Components during Information Security Evaluations. Journal of Research and Practice in Information Technology, 391–402 (2005)
27. Ravi, S., Raghunathan, A., Kocher, P., Hattangady, S.: Security in Embedded Systems: Design Challenges. ACM Transactions on Embedded Computing Systems 3(3), 461–491 (2004)

28. Ruiz, J.F., Harjani, R., Maña, A., Desnitsky, V., Kotenko, I., Chechulin, A.: A Methodology for the Analysis and Modeling of Security Threats and Attacks for Systems of Embedded Components. In: Proceedings of the 20th Euromicro International Conference on Parallel, Distributed and Network-Based Computing (PDP 2012), Munich, Germany, February 15-17 (2012)

29. Ruiz, J.F., Rein, A., Arjona, M., Mana, A., Monsifrot, A., Morvan, M.: Security Engineering and Modelling of Set-Top Boxes. In: 2012 ASE/IEEE International Conference on Proceedings of BioMedical Computing (BioMedCom), pp. 113–122 (2012)

30. Sabin, D., Weigel, R.: Product configuration frameworks-a survey. Intelligent Systems and their Applications IEEE Computer Society 13(4), 42–49 (1998)

31. SecFutur. Design of Secure and energy-efficient embedded systems for Future internet applications, FP7 Project Web site, http://www.secfutur.eu

32. Sprintson, A., El Rouayheb, S., Georghiades, C.: A New Construction Method for Networks from Matroids. In: Proceedings of the 2009 Symposium on Information Theory (ISIT 2009) (2009)

33. Wang, Z., Johnson, R., Murmuria, R., Stavrou, A.: Exposing Security Risks for Commercial Mobile Devices. In: Kotenko, I., Skormin, V. (eds.) MMM-ACNS 2012. LNCS, vol. 7531, pp. 3–21. Springer, Heidelberg (2012)

34. Wei, G., Qin, Y.: An Approach of Product Configuration Based on Decision Tree and Minimum Conflicts Repair Algorithm. In: Proceedings of the International Conference on Information Management, Innovation Management and Industrial Engineering (ICII 2009), vol. 1, pp. 126–129 (2009)

35. Yu, B., Skovgaard, H.J.: A Configuration Tool to Increase Product Competitiveness. IEEE Intelligent Systems 13(4), 34–41 (1998)

PrivacyFrost2: A Efficient Data Anonymization Tool Based on Scoring Functions

Shinsaku Kiyomoto and Yutaka Miyake

KDDI R & D Laboratories Inc.
2-1-15 Ohara, Fujimino-shi, Saitama, 356-8502, Japan
kiyomoto@kddilabs.jp

Abstract. In this paper, we propose an anonymization scheme for generating a k-anonymous and l-diverse (or t-close) table, which uses three scoring functions, and we show the evaluation results for two different data sets. Our scheme is based on both top-down and bottom-up approaches for full-domain and partial-domain generalization, and the three different scoring functions automatically incorporate the requirements into the generated table. The generated table meets users' requirements and can be employed in services provided by users without any modification or evaluation.

1 Introduction

Anonymization methods have been considered as a possible solution for protecting private information[8]. One class of models, called *global-recoding*, maps the values of attributes to other values [29] in order to generate an anonymized dataset. This paper uses a specific global-recoding model, *"full-domain generalization"*, and an additional process for local optimization. Generally, some anonymous tables are generated from an original table and users select a table from these based on certain requirements for the services that they provide to the public. A challenging issue in the anonymization of tables is to realize an algorithm that generalizes a table according to the requirements of a data user. If the algorithm incorporates the requirements into a generated table and outputs the most suitable table, then evaluation and selection of candidates for anonymous tables are not required when using an anonymous table.

In this paper, we propose an anonymization mechanism that reflects the user's requirements. The mechanism is an extension of *PrivacyFrost* [12,11], and hold the same properties that are summarized as follows:

- The mechanism generates an anonymous table that satisfies k-anonymity[22], l-diversity-family (l-diversity[18] and recursive (c, l)-diversity[18]).
- The mechanism is constructed based on a combination of top-down and bottom-up methods for full-domain generalization, and produces the anonymous table that has the best score in the execution.
- After full-domain generalization, the mechanism executes the top-down algorithm on each segment to optimize the anonymous table.

S. Teufel et al. (Eds.): CD-ARES 2014, LNCS 8708, pp. 211–225, 2014.
© IFIP International Federation for Information Processing 2014

- A user inputs not only a set of generalization boundary constraints, but also priorities for quasi-identifiers as the user's requirements for the anonymous table.

We improve the tool to generate more valuable data. Extensions presented in this paper are:

- A privacy notion, t-closeness [19], is supported for anonymization, and we compare the transaction time with that of k-anonymity and l-diversity-family cases.
- Three different scoring functions can be selected for anonymization. The three scoring functions outputs anonymous tables that have characteristic properties for the selected scoring function; thus, it can be selected according to a requirement for each anonymous table.
- A pre-sampling process removes *isolated* records in order to output a more useful table. To optimize output data, we can use a pre-sampling process before execution of the algorithm.

It realizes fast generation of an anonymous table to reflect a user's requirements and reduce the number of candidates for an anonymous table. The mechanism evaluates the score of a table for each iteration of generalization and selects the best scoring table for the next iteration. After some iterations, the mechanism provides a k-anonymous and l-diverse (or t-close) table that is suited to the user's requirements.

The rest of the paper is organized as follows: Related work is presented in Section 2. Section 3 presents assumed requirements from data users. Our mechanism is presented in Sections 4, 5, and 6. We show evaluation results in Section 7 and conclude this paper in Section 8.

2   Related Work

Samarati and Sweeney [23,22,26] proposed a primary definition of privacy that is applicable to generalization methods. A data set is said to have k-*anonymity* if each record is indistinguishable from at least $k-1$ other records with respect to certain identifying attributes called *quasi-identifiers* [9]. In other words, at least k records must exist in the data set for each combination of the identifying attributes. Clearly any generalization algorithm that converts a database into one with k-anonymity involves a loss of information in that database.

Minimizing this information loss thus presents a challenging problem in the design of generalization algorithms. The optimization problem is referred to as the k-anonymity problem. Meyerson reported that optimal generalization in this regard is an NP-hard problem[20]. Aggarwal *et al.* proved that finding an optimal table including more than three attributes is NP-hard [2]. Nonetheless, k-anonymity has been widely studied because of its conceptual simplicity [4,18,19,30,28,25]. Machanavajjhala *et al.* proposed another important definition of privacy for a public database [18]. The definition, called l-diversity, assumes a strong adversary having certain background knowledge that allows the adversary to identify object persons in the public database.

Samarati proposed a simple binary search algorithm for finding a k-anonymous table[22]. A drawback of Samarati's algorithm is that for arbitrary definitions of minimality, it is not always guaranteed that this binary search algorithm can find the minimal k-anonymity table. Sun $et.$ $al.$ presented a hash-based algorithm that improves the search algorithm[24]. Aggarwal et $al.$ proposed the $O(k)$-approximation algorithm [3] that is used for executing the k-anonymity problem. A greedy approximation algorithm [14] proposed by LeFevre et $al.$ searches for the optimal multi-dimensional anonymization. A genetic algorithm framework [10] was proposed because of its flexible formulation and its ability to find more efficient anonymizations. Utility-based anonymization [33,32] makes k-anonymous tables using a heuristic local recoding anonymization. Moreover, the k-anonymization problem is viewed as a clustering problem. Clustering-based approaches [7,27,16,34] search a cluster that has k-records. In full-domain generalization, there are two heuristic approaches for generalization algorithms: the top-down approach and the bottom-up approach. Bayardo and Aggrawal proposed a generalization algorithm using the top-down approach [6]. The algorithm finds a generalization that is optimal according to a given fixed cost metric for a systematic search strategy, given generalization hierarchies for a single attribute. Incognito [13] is a bottom-up-based algorithm that produces all possible k-anonymous tables from an original table.

There are several research papers about k-anonymization based on a data owner's requirements for anonymized public data. Loukides et $al.$ considered a k-anonymization approach [17] according to both the data owner's policies and data user's requirements. Aggarwal and Yu discussed a condensation based approach [1] for different privacy requirements. LeFevre et $al.$ provides an anonymization algorithm [15] that produces an anonymous view appropriate for specific data mining tasks. Xiao and Tao proposed the concept of *personalized anonymity* and presented a generalization method [31] that performs the minimum generalization for the requirements of data owners. Miller et $al.$ presented an anonymization mechanism [21] that provides k-anonymous tables under generalization boundaries of quasi-identifiers. The configuration of the boundaries can be considered to be user requirements. We proposed an anonymization mechanism[12,11] to reflect user requirements precisely. However, the mechanism only provides a basic scoring function for the anonymization and a remaining issue is to design appropriate scoring functions for achieving several requirements on anonymous tables. This paper presents an extension of that mechanism that includes pre-sampling and some scoring functions.

3   Requirements

A database table T in which the attributes of each user are denoted in one record is in the public domain and an attacker obtains the table and tries to extract the record of an individual. Suppose that a database table T has m records and

n attributes $\{A_1, \ldots, A_n\}$. Each record $a^i = (a_1^i, \ldots, a_n^i)$ can thus be considered to be an n-tuple of attribute values, where a_j^i is the value of attribute A_j in record a^i. The database table T itself can thus be regarded as the set of records $T = \{\mathbf{a^i} : 1 \le i \le m\}$. In our system, a user can input the following conditions for the anonymization.

- *Priority.* The user defines a positive integer value v_{a^i} for each attribute a^i. The value depends on the priority of the attribute. That is, $v_{a^i} = m v_{a^j}$, where the priority of the attribute a^i is m-times higher than a^j. For example, the user can define $(v_{a^1}, v_{a^2}, v_{a^3}, v_{a^4}) = (10, 5, 1, 1)$. The user gives high priority to an attribute when the user desires more detailed information about the attribute.
- *Minimum Level.* The user can define a minimum level for each attribute. Each attribute has a hierarchical tree structure. The minimum level $w_{a^i}^M$ defined by the user means that a k-anonymized dataset generated by the system includes at least $w_{a^i}^M$-level information for the attribute. The system does not generalize the attribute below the minimum level.

The above two requirements reflect the granularity of information in a generated anonymous table. The mechanism tries to keep attribute values located at the lower node as much as possible in the generalization hierarchy while satisfying the predefined anonymity condition, when the user marks the attribute as high priority. Furthermore, the user controls the limits of generalization using a configuration of minimum levels for attributes.

4   Components

In this section, we explain the basic components of our anonymization method.

4.1   Generalization

Full-domain generalization for obtaining an anonymous table consists of replacing attribute values with a generalized version of those values, and it is based on generalization hierarchies[8]. A quasi-identifier is an attribute that can be joined with external information to re-identify individual records with sufficiently high probability [9]. Generally, a target table $T^x = (T^q | T^s)$ consists of two types of information: a subtable of quasi-identifiers T^q and a subtable of sensitive attributes T^s. Since the sensitive attributes represent the essential information with regard to database queries, a generalization method is used to modify (anonymize) T^q in order to prevent the identification of the owners of the sensitive attributes, while retaining the full information in T^s. Thus, the generalization algorithm focuses on the subtable of quasi-identifier T^q and modifies it to satisfy a predefined anonymity condition. We assume that quasi-identifier attributes are known information for the generalization algorithm.

The full-domain generalization modifies all values of the attribute in the table T. Therefore, the anonymized table is not optimized for regional groups that have the same quasi-identifier T^q and that have lost information due to the global generalization of attributes. The partial-domain generalization replaces the values of an attribute in a small group that has the same quasi-identifier T_q. The partial-domain generalization executes [on] each group independently and modifies T_q subject to the requirement that each group satisfies the predefined anonymity condition. Thus, values of the attribute are generalized as values with different levels for each group.

4.2 Top-Down and Bottom-Up

There are two methods for generating anonymous tables in generalization schemes: the top-down approach and the bottom-up approach. The top-down approach starts at the root table where all attributes have a root value (a maximally generalized value), and finds an anonymous table to change attribute values to lower values (more detailed values) of the generalization hierarchy. In contrast, the initial table in the bottom-up approach is an original table and attribute values are replaced using upper attribute values until an anonymous table is found. Our scheme uses a top-down approach as the basic algorithm to reduce the number of score calculations. Furthermore, we consider a pre-computation in the top-down approach in order to skip some computations by starting at the root table. The details of our scheme are described in a later section.

4.3 Functions

The mechanism generates an anonymous table T^G and calculates its score s based on input data: a table $T = T^q$ that consists of m records and n quasi-identifiers a^i (i=1, ...,n), the parameters for k, a generalization hierarchy for the attributes H_{a^i}, the lowest levels $w_{a^i}^L$ of H_{a^i} and the user's requirements v_{a^i} and $w_{a^i}^M$. The parameters for k are the requirement for privacy (which means k-anonymity) and a system parameter that is defined according to the target table. The score s provides a rating of the degree to which the user's requirements are satisfied. The following subfunctions are used in the algorithm:

- Sort$(T, v_{a^1}, ..., v_{a^n})$. This function sorts attributes a^i $(i = 1, ..., n)$ in Table T by the user-defined priority values v_{a^i}. The function generates $T = (a^1, ..., a^n)$ in an order such that v_{a^1} is the smallest and v_{a^n} is the largest.
- Check$_{k,l,c,t}(T)$. This function calculates the minimum number of group members, where $T = (T_q | T_s)$ and all records in T_q are categorized into groups with the same attribute values. That is, this function calculates x of x-anonymity for T_q. The function calculates l and c of (c, l)-diversity for T_s, or calculates t for t-closeness for T_s. The function outputs OK where T satisfies k-anonymity, (c, l)-diversity, and otherwise outputs NG. The function skips calculations for l-diversity where l is defined as 1, and it only executes l-diversity calculations for (c, l)-diversity where c is defined as 0. The function skips calculations for t-closeness where $t = -1$. First, the function generates the hash value of each record in the table T_q and counts the number

of hash values that are the same. If all hash values are greater than x, the function outputs x. This process is a simple and efficient way for checking k-anonymity and is similar to the process adopted in the previous study. This function is implemented as a modifiable module; we can add other checking logics for anonymity definitions.

- Generalization(a^i, H_{a^i}, w_{a^i}). This function modifies the attribute a^i based on its generalization hierarchy H_{a^i}. The attribute values change to the upper node values of level $w_{a^i}-1$, where the level of the attribute value is w_{a^i}.
- De-Generalization(a^i, H_{a^i}, w_{a^i}). This function modifies the attribute a^i based on its generalization hierarchy H_{a^i}. The attribute values change to the lower node values of level $w_{a^i}+1$, where the level of the attribute value is w_{a^i}.
- Score(T). This function calculates the score of a table T. Our system calculates the score S_t of the anonymized datasets using equations described in Section 6.

5   Algorithm

In the generated table, information that is important for the user is maintained at a level that is as detailed as possible, while other information remains at the level of generalized information. The algorithm consists of two main parts: pre-computation and top-down generation.

5.1   Pre-sampling

To optimize output data, we can use a pre-sampling process before execution of the algorithm. The pre-sampling process finds *isolated* records having attribute sets that very few records have, and removes the *isolated* records to output more useful tables. If the *isolated* records are included in a table, other records tend to be much generalized than expected, so deletion of the records helps to keep the maximum amount of information in the table. The pre-sampling process is an optional process that the user can choose to use, or not. Let $\mathbf{u} = u_{a^1}, ..., u_{a^n}$ be a threshold level of generalization for each attribute a^i, and k' be a threshold value of anonymization. When the user inputs a table T, and threshold values $\mathbf{u}$ and k', the pre-sampling process is executed as follows:

The algorithm uses the updated table T for generating the anonymous table T^G. The whole mechanism is described in Figure 1.

1. Each attribute a_i is generalized up to the level u_{a^i} and the process outputs a temporary generalized table T^P.
2. Using table T^P, the process makes groups whose records have the same attribute sets, and counts the number of records in each group. The process picks up records that belong to a group having records less than k'.
3. The selected records are removed from the original table T. The process outputs the updated table T. Note that the generalized table T^P is just discarded.

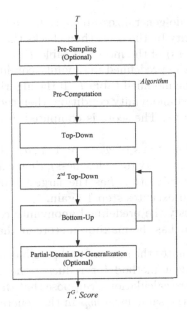

Fig. 1. Mechanism Overview

5.2 Pre-computation

The mechanism uses pre-computation to reduce the total computational cost of anonymization. The pre-computation consists of two steps; step 1 considers single attribute anonymity and generalizes each attribute to satisfy $(k+p)$-anonymity, and step 2 considers the whole table to satisfy k-anonymity. The parameter p is a system parameter, and it should be optimized according to the results of previous trials. The pre-computation is based on the subset property theorem [13]. This theorem means that each single attribute has to satisfy k-anonymity for a k-anonymous table. The mechanism uses the top-down approach and starts with a k-anonymous table as the initial table; thus the algorithm executes the following pre-computation.

1. The algorithm generalizes each attribute of a table $T(=T^q)$ to satisfy $(k+p)$-anonymity, and creates a modified table T.
2. The algorithm checks whether the whole table T satisfies k-anonymity and (c,l)-diversity (or t-closeness). If the table T does not satisfy k-anonymity and (c,l)-diversity (or t-closeness), then the algorithm generalizes each attribute once (one level) and returns to step 2. Note that each attribute is not generalized up to the minimum level defined by the user. If the algorithm finds no table that satisfies k-anonymity and (c,l)-diversity (or t-closeness), then the algorithm outputs *failed*. Otherwise, the algorithm makes an initial anonymous table T^I and inputs it to T^G.

5.3 Top-Down Generalization

The basic steps of top-down generalization are as follows:

1. First, the algorithm de-generalizes an attribute a^n in Table T^G, which is defined as a top priority by the user, then checks the k-anonymity and (c, l)-diversity (or t-closeness) of the modified table T.

2. If the table satisfies the predefined anonymity condition, the algorithm calculates the score of the modified table T. If the algorithm finds no table that satisfies the predefined anonymity condition, then the algorithm outputs the table T^G and its score s. The score is computed using the scoring function Score(T).

3. For all possible modifications of a^i ($i = 1, ..., n$), the algorithm checks k-anonymity and (c, l)-diversity (or t-closeness), then calculates the scores. The algorithm selects the table that has the largest score among the possibly anonymous tables and executes step 1 again.

4. If no more tables satisfy the predefined anonymity condition, the algorithm outputs the table that has the maximum score at that point.

The basic algorithm calculates the scores of all possible anonymous tables. Now, we consider a more efficient method for reducing the computational costs of anonymity checks and score calculations. Suppose that the algorithm obtains the number $b_{w_{a^i}}$ of nodes at the same level w_{a^i} in the generalization hierarchy H_{a^i}. The number indicates the upper bound of e_{a^i} in each level. Thus, we estimate the upper bound of increase in the score to calculate $\delta_s = (b_{w_{a^i}+1} - e_{a^i})v_{a^i}$, where the current generalization level of a^i is w_{a^i}. If $s > s' + \delta_s$, the algorithm can skip de-generalization of a^i. Figure 1 shows the basic algorithm that outputs T^G and s using input parameters. The algorithm first executes pre-computation and generates an initial table T^I; then the algorithm searches the table T^G that has the highest score. The top-down approach is used for the search performed by the basic algorithm.

5.4   Optimization Steps

We present optimization steps to find a better table that has a higher score than the table found using the basic algorithm. The optimization consists of three steps: the second top-down, bottom-up, and partial-domain de-generalization. The extension part is executed after the execution of the basic algorithm. The algorithm repeats two sub-functions until no table has a score higher than the current best score; then the algorithm executes the partial-domain generalization process, if required. An overview of the search process is shown in Figure 2. The figure is a generalization graph of the table T and the top is a root table in which all attributes are level 0. The extended algorithm tries to find a table using both top-down and bottom-up approaches. The algorithm searches for the high-score table on the boundary of anonymous tables and tables that do not satisfy the predefined anonymity condition. The extended algorithm is executed after the basic algorithm as follows:

1. After the basic algorithm, the algorithm generalizes possible a^is in the table T^G and calculates the scores of the tables. Then, the algorithm selects the top score table T^T. Note that table T^T does not satisfy Check$_{k,l,c}(T) = OK$.

2. Next, the algorithm executes a bottom-up generalization to search for tables that satisfy the predefined anonymity condition, then from these tables the algorithm chooses the table with the best score.
3. The algorithm compares the score of the chosen table with the current score s of table T^G, and if the score is higher than s, the algorithm replaces T^G with table T and s by its score. The algorithm executes the above steps using the new T^G. Otherwise, the algorithm stops and outputs the current generalized table T^G. The steps of top-down and bottom-up are repeated until no table has a score higher than the current best score.
4. After finding the best score table, the algorithm executes the top-down approach for each partial-domain using a function named "Partial-Domain De-Generalization (T)". The function selects one group that has the same quasi-identifiers and modifies one attribute using the top-down approach to satisfy the predefined anonymity condition. The algorithm executes the function until the table T^T does not satisfy $\text{Check}_{k,l,c}(T) = OK$. Note that the partial-domain generalization process consists of only the top-down approach, and the score of the output table is larger than that of the best scoring table produced by full-domain generalization. This step is optional; the user decides whether the partial-domain generalization process is executed for the table.

Details of the algorithm are shown in the Appendix.

6   Scoring Functions

In this section, we explain scoring functions that are used in the anonymization algorithm.

6.1   Basic Scoring Function

The basic function is described as follows:

$$S_t = \sum_{\forall a^i} v_{a^i} \cdot e_{a^i}$$

where e_{a^i} is the number of value types of an attribute a^i in the table. The score is high where the user-defined priority value for the attribute is high and the attribute has many types of values. The function produces a single value; thus, different priority values may produce the same value. The function is implemented as a replaceable module; thus, we can adjust the function or add another scoring function according to data types. Note that the table with the best score is not optimal among k-anonymous tables, but is suitable for the user's requirements.

6.2 η-Based Scoring Function

The η-based scoring function focuses on the variation of attribute values for all attributes (calculated as the sum of e_{a^i}) more than in the case that we use the

Table by Logarithm-Based Scoring Function

Quasi-Identifiers			
Birth	Gender	Zip	Nationality
198*	*	012**	UK
198*	*	012**	Italy
198*	*	012**	UK
198*	*	012**	Italy
1984	Male	0123*	USA
1984	Male	0123*	USA

Table by η-Based Scoring Function

Quasi-Identifiers			
Birth	Gender	Zip	Nationality
1984	Male	0124*	Europe
1984	Male	0124*	Europe
1985	Female	0123*	Europe
1985	Female	0123*	Europe
1984	Male	0123*	USA
1984	Male	0123*	USA

Fig. 2. Generated Anonymous Tables

basic scoring function. Thus, the table tends to be uniformly generalized. The η-based scoring function is described as follows:

$$S_t = \sum_{\forall a^i} v_{a^i} \cdot \eta(e_{a^i})$$

The function $\eta(x)$ is defined as:

$$\eta(x) = \begin{cases} 2 & x > d \\ 1 & \frac{d}{2} < x \le d \\ 0 & x \le \frac{d}{2} \end{cases}$$

Where d is a constant parameter. We can extend the function $\eta(x)$ to add conditions for x.

6.3 Logarithm-Based Scoring Function

The logarithm-based scoring function focuses on the priorities (defined as v_{a^i}) more than on the basic scoring function. In particular, the precision of the top-priority attribute is of prime importance in the generalization. The logarithm-based scoring function is described as follows:

$$S_t = \max_{\forall a^i} v_{a^i} \cdot \frac{log(e_{a^i})}{log(e_{a_i}^b)}$$

where $e_{a_i}^b$ is the value of e_{a_i} before anonymization. Figure 2 shows two tables generated by the η-based scoring function and the logarithm-based scoring function, respectively. The left table is generated using the logarithm-based scoring function with a priority that the attribute "Nationality" is the most valuable attribute in the table.

7 Performance Evaluation

We implemented a prototype system on a PC (Core i7 870 2.93 GHz, 4 GB Memory, Windows 7, 32 bit) and evaluated the transaction times for pre-sampling and anonymization. In this section, we show the results of the experiments.

Table 1. Transaction Time of Pre-Sampling

Data	No. of Records	k'	Transaction Time
Adult	32,561	1	1289 ms
Adult	32,561	2	1299 ms
Adult	32,561	5	1307 ms
Adult	32,561	10	1286 ms
Census-income	199,523	1	4401 ms
Census-income	199,523	2	4324 ms
Census-income	199,523	5	4431 ms
Census-income	199,523	10	4464 ms

Table 2. Transaction Time of Anonymization (Adult Data Sets)

Data	No. of Records	k	l	t	Scoring Function	Transaction Time
Adult	32,561	2	2	-	Basic	619 ms
Adult	32,561	2	2	-	Log-Based	592 ms
Adult	32,561	2	2	-	η-Based	680 ms
Adult	32,561	2	-	0.1	Basic	736 ms
Adult	32,561	2	-	0.1	Log-Based	720 ms
Adult	32,561	2	-	0.1	η-Based	675 ms
Adult	32,561	2	-	0.9	Basic	823 ms
Adult	32,561	2	-	0.9	Log-Based	778 ms
Adult	32,561	2	-	0.9	η-Based	723 ms
Adult	32,561	10	10	-	Basic	663 ms
Adult	32,561	10	10	-	Log-Based	631 ms
Adult	32,561	10	10	-	η-Based	669 ms
Adult	32,561	10	-	0.1	Basic	726 ms
Adult	32,561	10	-	0.1	Log-Based	722 ms
Adult	32,561	10	-	0.1	η-Based	696 ms
Adult	32,561	10	-	0.9	Basic	803 ms
Adult	32,561	10	-	0.9	Log-Based	777 ms
Adult	32,561	10	-	0.9	η-Based	833 ms

We evaluated the prototype system using two data sets [5], *Adults Data Sets*, which has 32,561 records of 14 attributes, and *Census-Income Data Sets*, which has 199,523 records of 42 attributes, under several different sets of parameters k, l and c. These data sets had been used for performance evaluation in previous research. The transaction time for pre-sampling is shown in Table 1. The All threshold level of generalization for each attribute a^i was configured as 2 in the experiments. The All transaction time for *Adults Data Sets* was about 1.2 seconds and that for *Census-Income Data Sets* was about 4.4 seconds. The transaction times for anonymization for *Adults Data Sets* and *Census-Income Data Sets* are shown in Table 2 and Table 3, respectively. In all experimenst, we measured transaction time including the partial-domain de-generalization steps.

Table 3. Transaction Time of Anonymization (Census-Income Data Sets)

Data	No. of Records	k	l	t	Scoring Function	Transaction Time
Census-Income	199,523	2	2	-	Basic	18585 ms
Census-Income	199,523	2	2	-	Log-Based	18381 ms
Census-Income	199,523	2	2	-	η-Based	16773 ms
Census-Income	199,523	2	-	0.1	Basic	19839 ms
Census-Income	199,523	2	-	0.1	Log-Based	19832 ms
Census-Income	199,523	2	-	0.1	η-Based	18525 ms
Census-Income	199,523	2	-	0.9	Basic	21889 ms
Census-Income	199,523	2	-	0.9	Log-Based	21363 ms
Census-Income	199,523	2	-	0.9	η-Based	19955 ms
Census-Income	199,523	10	10	-	Basic	22287 ms
Census-Income	199,523	10	10	-	Log-Based	21454 ms
Census-Income	199,523	10	10	-	η-Based	16319 ms
Census-Income	199,523	10	-	0.1	Basic	19788 ms
Census-Income	199,523	10	-	0.1	Log-Based	19871 ms
Census-Income	199,523	10	-	0.1	η-Based	18417 ms
Census-Income	199,523	10	-	0.9	Basic	25477 ms
Census-Income	199,523	10	-	0.9	Log-Based	24552 ms
Census-Income	199,523	10	-	0.9	η-Based	19040 ms

The transaction time when using t-closeness was almost same as that when using l-diversity. There were no significant differences between the three scoring functions.

Thus, our prototype system is expected to generate anonymous tables in a feasible transaction time. In particular, where the table has fewer than 30,000 records and each consists of a reasonable number of attributes, the prototype system will generate an anonymous table for it in real-time.

8   Conclusion

In this paper, we proposed an anonymization scheme for generating a table with k-anonymity. The scheme calculates the scores of intermediate tables based on user-defined priorities for attributes, and from these it selects the table with the highest score. Three scoring functions were designed and they can be selected according to the specific requirements of each case. The generated table meets user's requirements and is employed in the services provided by users without any modification or evaluation. Our mechanism is applicable to full-domain and partial-domain generalization in some types of anonymity definitions to replace the check function. We will evaluate the prototype system using a number of tables for several usersf requirements, and consider an optimization method for parameters in our future work.

References

1. Aggarwal, C.C., Yu, P.S.: On variable constraints in privacy preserving data mining. In: Proc. of the 5th SIAM International Conference on Data Mining, pp. 115–125 (2005)
2. Aggarwal, G., Feder, T., Kenthapadi, K., Motwani, R., Panigrahy, R., Thomas, D., Zhu, A.: Anonymizing tables. In: Eiter, T., Libkin, L. (eds.) ICDT 2005. LNCS, vol. 3363, pp. 246–258. Springer, Heidelberg (2005)
3. Aggarwal, G., Feder, T., Kenthapadi, K., Motwani, R., Panigrahy, R., Thomas, D., Zhu, A.: Approximation algorithms for k-anonymity. Journal of Privacy Technology (2005)
4. Al-Fedaghi, S.S.: Balanced k-anonymity. In: Proc. of WASET, vol. 6, pp. 179–182 (2005)
5. Asuncion, A., Newman, D.J.: UCI machine learning repository (2007)
6. Bayardo, R.J., Agrawal, R.: Data privacy through optimal k-anonymity. In: Proc. of ICDE 2005, pp. 217–228 (2005)
7. Byun, J.-W., Kamra, A., Bertino, E., Li, N.: Efficient k-anonymity using clustering technique. In: Proc. of the International Conference on Database Systems for Advanced Applications, pp. 188–200 (2007)
8. Ciriani, V., De Capitani di Vimercati, S., Foresti, S., Samarati, P.: k-anonymous data mining: A survey. In: Privacy-Preserving Data Mining: Models and Algorithms. Springer (2008)
9. Dalenius, T.: Finding a needle in a haystack —or identifying anonymous census record. Journal of Official Statistics 2(3), 329–336 (1986)
10. Iyengar, V.S.: Transforming data to satisfy privacy constraints. In: Proc. of ACM SIGKDD 2002, pp. 279–288. ACM (2002)
11. Kiyomoto, S., Miyake, Y., Tanaka, T.: Privacy Frost: A user-oriented data anonymization tool. In: 2011 Sixth International Conference on Availability, Reliability and Security (ARES), pp. 442–447 (2011)
12. Kiyomoto, S., Tanaka, T.: A user-oriented anonymization mechanism for public data. In: Garcia-Alfaro, J., Navarro-Arribas, G., Cavalli, A., Leneutre, J. (eds.) DPM 2010 and SETOP 2010. LNCS, vol. 6514, pp. 22–35. Springer, Heidelberg (2011)
13. LeFevre, K., DeWitt, D.J., Ramakrishnan, R.: Incognito: Efficient full-domain k-anonymity. In: Proc. of SIGMOD 2005, pp. 49–60 (2005)
14. LeFevre, K., DeWitt, D.J., Ramakrishnan, R.: Mondrian multidimensional k-anonymity. In: Proc. of the 22nd International Conference on Data Engineering (ICDE 2006), pp. 25–35. IEEE (2006)
15. LeFevre, K., DeWitt, D.J., Ramakrishnan, R.: Workload-aware anonymization. In: Proc. ACM SIGKDD 2006, pp. 277–286. ACM (2006)
16. Lin, J.-L., Wei, M.-C.: An efficient clustering method for k-anonymization. In: Proc. of the 2008 International Workshop on Privacy and Anonymity in Information Society (PAIS 2008), pp. 46–50. ACM (2008)
17. Loukides, G., Tziatzios, A., Shao, J.: Towards preference-constrained k-anonymisation. In: Chen, L., Liu, C., Liu, Q., Deng, K. (eds.) DASFAA 2009. LNCS, vol. 5667, pp. 231–245. Springer, Heidelberg (2009)
18. Machanavajjhala, A., Gehrke, J., Kifer, D.: l-diversity: Privacy beyond k-anonymity. In: Proc. of ICDE 2006, pp. 24–35 (2006)
19. Machanavajjhala, A., Gehrke, J., Kifer, D.: t-closeness: Privacy beyond k-anonymity and l-diversity. In: Proc. of ICDE 2007, pp. 106–115 (2007)

20. Meyerson, A., Williams, R.: On the complexity of optimal k-anonymity. In: Proc. of PODS 2004, pp. 223–228 (2004)
21. Miller, J., Campan, A., Truta, T.M.: Constrained k-anonymity: Privacy with generalization boundaries. In: Proc. of the Practical Preserving Data Mining Workshop, P3DM 2008 (2008)
22. Samarati, P.: Protecting respondents' identities in microdata release. IEEE Trans. on Knowledge and Data Engineering 13(6), 1010–1027 (2001)
23. Samarati, P., Sweeney, L.: Generalizing data to provide anonymity when disclosing information. In: Proc. of the 17th ACM SIGACT-SIGMOD-SIGART Symposium on Principles of Database Systems (PODS 1998), p. 188 (1998)
24. Sun, X., Li, M., Wang, H., Plank, A.: An efficient hash-based algorithm for minimal k-anonymity. In: ACSC 2008: Proceedings of the Thirty-first Australasian Conference on Computer Science, pp. 101–107 (2008)
25. Sun, X., Wang, H., Li, J., Truta, T.M., Li, P.: (p^+, α)-sensitive k-anonymity: a new enhanced privacy protection model. In: Proc. of CIT 2008, pp. 59–64 (2008)
26. Sweeney, L.: Achieving k-anonymity privacy protection using generalization and suppression. J. Uncertainty, Fuzziness, and Knowledge-Base Systems 10(5), 571–588 (2002)
27. Truta, T.M., Campan, A.: K-anonymization incremental maintenance and optimization techniques. In: Proceedings of the 2007 ACM symposium on Applied computing (SAC 2007), pp. 380–387. ACM (2007)
28. Truta, T.M., Vinay, B.: Privacy protection: p-sensitive k-anonymity property. In: Proc. of ICDE 2006, pp. 94–103 (2006)
29. Willenborg, L., de Waal, T.: Elements of Statistical Disclosure Control. LNS, vol. 155. Springer (2001)
30. Wong, R.C.-W., Li, J., Fu, A.W.-C., Wang, K.: (α, k)-anonymity: an enhanced k-anonymity model for privacy preserving data publishing. In: Proc. of ACM SIGKDD 2006, pp. 754–759 (2006)
31. Xiao, X., Tao, Y.: Personalized privacy preservation. In: Proc. of SIGMOD 2006, pp. 229–240. ACM (2006)
32. Xu, J., Wang, W., Pei, J., Wang, X., Shi, B., Fu, A.W.-C.: Utility-based anonymization for privacy preservation with less information loss. SIGKDD Explor. Newsl. 8(2), 21–30 (2006)
33. Xu, J., Wang, W., Pei, J., Wang, X., Shi, B., Fu, A.W.-C.: Utility-based anonymization using local recoding. In: Proc. of ACM SIGKDD 2006, pp. 785–790. ACM (2006)
34. Zhu, H., Ye, X.: Achieving k-anonymity via a density-based clustering method. In: Dong, G., Lin, X., Wang, W., Yang, Y., Yu, J.X. (eds.) APWeb/WAIM 2007. LNCS, vol. 4505, pp. 745–752. Springer, Heidelberg (2007)

A   Details of the Algorithm

Figure 3 shows details of the anonymization algorithm.

Input: a table T, k, l, c, t, p, H_{a^i}, $w_{a^i}^L$, v_{a^i}, $w_{a^i}^M$
$(i=1, ..., n)$, *Score Function*
Output: T^G, s
// *Pre-Sampling before Algorithm (Optional)*
//
// *Precomputation:*
Sort $(T, v_{a^1}, ..., v_{a^n})$
for $i = 1$ **to** n **do**
  $w_{a^i} \leftarrow w_{a^i}^L$
  while Check$(a^i) < k + p$ **do**
    $a^i \leftarrow$ Generalization(a^i, H_{a^i}, w_{a^i})
    $w_{a^i} \leftarrow w_{a^i} - 1$
  end while
end for
while Check$_{k,l,c}(T) = NG$ and all $w_{a^i} > w_{a^i}^M$ **do**
  for $i = 1$ **to** n **do**
    if $w_{a^i} \geq w_{a^i}^M$ **then**
      $a^i \leftarrow$ Generalization(a^i, H_{a^i})
      $w_{a^i} \leftarrow w_{a^i} - 1$
    end if
  end for
end while
$T^I \leftarrow T$
$T^G \leftarrow T^I$
$s, s' \leftarrow$ Score(T)
if Check$_{k,l,c}(T) = NG$ **then**
  return *failed*
end
else
  Top-Down Generalization
  // *Top-Down Generalization:*
  while *state* $\neq$ *stop* **do**
    $T' \leftarrow T^G$
    $s' \leftarrow s$
    state $\leftarrow$ *false*
    for $i = n$ **to** 1 **do**
      $T \leftarrow T'$
      $a^i \leftarrow$ De-Generalization(a^i, H_{a^i}, w_{a^i})
      if Check$_{k,l,c}(T) = OK$ and Score$(T) > s$ **then**
        temp $\leftarrow a^i, w_{a^i} + 1$
        $T^G \leftarrow T$
        $s \leftarrow$ Score(T)
        state $\leftarrow$ *true*
      end if
    end for
    if *state* = *false* **then**
      state $\leftarrow$ *stop*
    end if
    $a^1, ..., a^n, v_{a^1}, ..., v_{a^n} \leftarrow$ *temp*
  end while
  return T^G, s **repeat**
  // *2nd Top-Down:*
  $T' \leftarrow T^G$
  $s' \leftarrow s$
  state $\leftarrow$ *false*
  for $i = n$ **to** 1 **do**

$T \leftarrow T'$
$a^i \leftarrow$ De-Generalization(a^i, H_{a^i}, w_{a^i})
if Score$(T) > s'$ **then**
  temp $\leftarrow a^i, w_{a^i} + 1$
  $T^T \leftarrow T$
  $s^T \leftarrow$ Score(T)
  state $\leftarrow$ *true*
end if
end for
if *state* = *false* **then**
  state $\leftarrow$ *stop*
  return T^G, s
else
  // *Bottom-Up:*
  while Check$_{k,l,c}(T) = NG$ **do**
  $T' \leftarrow T^T$
  state $\leftarrow$ *false*
  $a^1, ..., a^n, v_{a^1}, ..., v_{a^n} \leftarrow$ *temp*
  for $i = 1$ **to** n **do**
    $T \leftarrow T'$
    if $w_{a^i} > w_{a^i}^M$ **then**
      $a^i \leftarrow$ Generalization(a^i, H_{a^i}, w_{a^i})
    end if
    if Check$_{k,l,c}(T) = OK$ and Score$(T) > s$ **then**
      temp $\leftarrow a^i, w_{a^i} - 1$
      $T^G \leftarrow T$
      $s \leftarrow$ Score(T)
      state $\leftarrow$ *true*
    end if
  end for
  if *state* = *true* **then**
    $a^1, ..., a^n, v_{a^1}, ..., v_{a^n} \leftarrow$ *temp*
  else
    for $i = 1$ **to** n **do**
      $T \leftarrow T'$
      if $w_{a^i} > w_{a^i}^M$ **then**
        $a^i \leftarrow$ Generalization(a^i, H_{a^i}, w_{a^i})
      end if
      if Score$(T) > s'$ **then**
        $T^T \leftarrow T$
        temp $\leftarrow a^i, w_{a^i} - 1$
        $s' \leftarrow$ Score(T)
        state $\leftarrow$ *true*
      end if
    end for
    if *state* = *false* **then**
      state $\leftarrow$ *stop*
    end if
  end while
  until *state* = *stop*
  // *Partial-Domain Generalization:*
  while Check$_{k,l,c}(T^P) = NG$ **do**
    $T^G \leftarrow T^P$
    $T^P =$ Pertial-Domain De-Generalization(T^G)
  end while
  return T^G, s

Fig. 3. Algorithm

Detection of Malicious Web Pages
Using System Calls Sequences

Gerardo Canfora[1], Eric Medvet[2], and Francesco Mercaldo[1],
and Corrado Aaron Visaggio[1]

[1] Dept. of Engineering, University of Sannio, Benevento, Italy
[2] Dept. of Engineering and Architecture, University of Trieste, Italy

Abstract. Web sites are often used for diffusing malware; an increasingly number of attacks are performed by delivering malicious code in web pages: drive-by download, malvertisement, rogueware, phishing are just the most common examples. In this scenario, JavaScript plays an important role, as it allows to insert code into the web page that will be executed on the client machine, letting the attacker to perform a plethora of actions which are necessary to successfully accomplish an attack. Existing techniques for detecting malicious JavaScript suffer from some limitations like: the capability of recognizing only known attacks, being tailored only to specific attacks, or being ineffective when appropriate evasion techniques are implemented by attackers. In this paper we propose to use system calls to detect malicious JavaScript. The main advantage is that capturing the system calls allows a description of the attack at a very high level of abstraction. On the one hand, this limits the evasion techniques which could succeed, and, on the other hand, produces a very high detection accuracy (96%), as experimentation demonstrated.

1 Introduction

In recent years, the web applications became an important vector of malware, as many reports state [1, 2]. A number of attacks are performed leveraging malicious web sites: drive-by-download, which consists of downloading and installing or running malware on the machine of the victim; csrf, which deviates the victim's navigation on a malicious web site; phishing, web sites which reproduce existing benign sites for obtaining credentials or other sensitive information from the victim; malvertisement, which is advertisement containing malware; malware serving, which collects traffic with different techniques and hosts malware; and rogueware, which is a fake antivirus which realizes illegal tasks, like stealing information or spying victim's machine.

Existing techniques may be very efficient in identifying specific and well-known attacks [3], but they often fail in detecting web threats which are new or scarcely diffused [4]. Since the attackers know that the approaches for detecting attacks are usually successful only against some kinds of attacks, different combinations of attacks are mixed together in order to evade detection [3].

Furthermore, the turbulent evolution of web technology entails a parallel evolution of web threats, which makes ineffective all those detecting techniques

S. Teufel et al. (Eds.): CD-ARES 2014, LNCS 8708, pp. 226–238, 2014.

which are strictly based on the technology of the web pages, because they observe the behavior of only certain components or characteristics, neglecting others which may be exploited by attackers. The introduction of HTML5, for instance, is bearing new functions like inline multimedia and local storage, which could be leveraged for designing new attacks [5], whose dynamics are not expected by current detectors.

A system for circumventing these hurdles is to analyze the web threats at a finer grain, which is the one of the operating system. The conjecture which we aim to demonstrate with this paper is that observing the behavior of a web application as the sequence of system calls invoked by the system when the browser connects to the web application makes the capability of detection independent of the specific web threat. This should result in a more effective detection system, which is able to exhibit a higher accuracy, i.e., reduce the number of false negatives and false positives. To observe the behavior of a web application at the level of system calls means decomposing at the smallest units of computation, or rather obtaining a very high level of abstraction of the code features.

The conjecture relies on the idea that a web application designed for performing an attack instead of performing some specific (and benign) business logic should show characteristics, in terms of sequence of system calls, which are common to many attacks, independently from the type of attack and its implementation. For instance, a malicious web application is often hosted on web server with poorer performances (often due to the fact that a malicious web application must frequently change hosting server because these servers are blacklisted) than a benign web application (which needs high speed server for business reasons). Moreover, benign web applications have a more complex structure than malicious web application, whose only purpose is to perform attacks and not to provide business services, several functions to user, or many pieces of information. This could cause, for instance, a fewer number of open system calls invoked by the malicious web application, than by the benign ones.

We wish to investigate whether malicious web applications and benign web applications differ in terms of the system calls they invoke. Thus, we pose two research questions:

– RQ1: is there a significant difference in the occurrences of system calls invoked by malicious and by trusted web applications?
– RQ2: are there sequences of system calls which are more frequent in malicious web applications than in trusted web applications?

RQ1 aims at verifying whether malicious web applications have system calls with different occurrences of benign web applications. A similar finding was observed for malware, where some op-codes had a larger or smaller number of occurrences than in non-malware code [6]. RQ2 consists of exploring the possibility that specific sequences of system calls could characterize malicious web applications, i.e., are more (or less) frequent in malicious web applications than in benign ones. As data analysis demonstrates, both RQ1 and RQ2 have a positive answer.

The paper proceeds as follows: Section 2 analyses the related literature, Section 3 and 4 discuss experimentation and results obtained, respectively for RQ1 and RQ2, and, finally, Section 5 draws the conclusions.

2   Related Work

A wealth of techniques exist to detect, prevent or characterize malicious activities carried on using web pages.

Blacklists collect malicious URLs, Ip addresses, and domain names obtained by manual reporting, honeyclients, and custom analysis service [3]. Blacklisting requires trust by the users and a huge management effort for continuously updating the list and verifying the dependability of the information.

Heuristic-based techniques [7, 8] leverage signatures of known malicious codes: if a known attack pattern is found within a web application, it is flagged as malicious. However, signatures can be successfully evaded by malicious code—obfuscation being the most commonly used technique. Moreover, this mechanism is not effective with unknown attacks.

Static Analysis techniques [9–12, 8, 13, 14] extract features from URL string, host identity, HTML, JavaScript code, and reputation metadata of the page. These values are entered in machine learning based classifiers which decide whether the web application is malicious or not. Obfuscated JavaScript, exploiting vulnerabilities in browser plug-ins and crafted URLs are common practices to evade this form of detection.

Dynamic analysis [15–18, 13] observes the execution of the web application. Proxy-level analysis [19] captures suspicious behaviors, such as unusual process spawning, and repeated redirects. Sandboxing techniques [7, 20] produce a log of actions and find for known patterns of attacks or unsual sequence of actions. Honeyclients [21] mimic a human visit in the website, but by using a dedicated sandbox. Execution traces and features are collected and analyzed to discover attacks. Low-interaction honeyclients [22] compare the execution traces with a set of signatures, which makes this approach ineffective with zero-day attacks. High-interaction honeyclients [23–25] look for integrity changes of the system states, which means monitoring registry entries, file systems, processes, network connections, and physical resources (memory, CPU). Honeyclients are powerful, but at a high computational cost, as they need to load and execute the web application. Honeyclients are useless for time-based attacks, and, moreover, malicious server can blacklist honeyclients IP address, or they can be discovered by using Turing Test with CAPTCHAs [3].

Different methods have been proposed for detecting and analyzing malicious Java script code. Zozzle [26] extracts features of context from AST, such as specific variable names or code structure. Cujo [20] obtains q-grams from the execution of JavaScript and classifies them with machine learning algorithms. Code similarity is largely used to understand whether a program is malicious or not, by comparing the candidate JavaScript with a set of known malicious JavaScripts. Revolver [27] computes the similarity by confronting the AST structure of two JavaScript pairs.

Clone detection techniques have been proposed in some papers [28, 29], but they assume that the programs under analysis do not show an adversarial behavior. Such an assumption does not hold when analyzing malicious programs. Attackers usually change the code corresponding to the payload taken form other existing malware for evading clone detection. Another strong limitation is the large number of source code the candidate code sample must be compared with. Bayer et al. [30] intend to solve this problem by leveraging locality sensitive hashing, while Jong et al. [31] make use of feature hashing for reducing the feature space.

At the best knowledge of the authors the method we propose is new in the realm of malicious JavaScript detectors, and its main advantages are: the success is independent from the type of attack, and it is designed to be robust against evasion techniques, as discussed later in the paper.

3 RQ1: System Call Occurrences

3.1 Data Collection

We performed an experimental analysis aimed at investigating the point addressed by RQ1—i.e., whether a significant difference exists in the occurrences of system calls invoked by malicious and by trusted web applications. To this end, we composed a set including malicious and trusted web pages and recorded the system call traces which are generated while visiting them.

We chose at random more than 3000 URLs from the Malware Domain List[1] archive: this archive contains about 80 000 URLs of malicious web pages implementing different attacks patterns. We chose the first 3000 URLs included in the Alexa Global Top Sites[2] ranking for making up the set of trusted websites.

We then systematically visited each of these URLs and recorded the system calls traces. In order to collect system calls traces, we used Strace[3], which is a tool for Unix platform diagnostic and debugging. Strace hooks a running process and intercepts the system calls done by the process and register them within a log. Strace can be configured in two different modes: "verbose", which collects all the system calls of the target process with all the metadata, and "summary", which collects aggregated data, such as the number of calls for each system call, the total time required for the system call, the number of errors, the percentage of user time. We used Strace in "verbose" mode. We automated the collection procedure by means of a Java program which we built for performing the following steps—being u the URL for which the system call trace has to be collected:

1. launch Strace, configured to hook the Firefox process;
2. launch Firefox with u as the only URL to visit;
3. wait 60 s;
4. kill Firefox and Strace;
5. truncate the system call trace to the calls performed during the first 20 s.

---

[1] http://www.malwaredomainlist.com
[2] http://www.alexa.com/topsites
[3] http://sourceforge.net/projects/strace/

We executed the collection procedure for all the URLs in a row, running the Java program on a machine hosted in our campus, provided with good and stable connectivity to the Internet.

We ensured that no errors were generated while visiting URLs. We excluded all those traces for which one of the following abnormal situation occurred: HTTP response codes 302 and 404, "unable to resolve host address" error and "connection time out" error. We stopped the collection after visiting exactly 3000 malicious and 3000 trusted pages.

3.2   Analysis

We denote with N the length of a system call trace and by N_c the number of occurrences of the system call c within a trace.

We observed 106 different system calls. The average number $\overline{N}$ of system calls we collected for each URL was 114 000 and 76 710, respectively for trusted and malicious pages. We think that the difference is justified mainly by the different connectivity and processing power of servers serving trusted and malicious pages. In particular, malicious pages are often served by improvised web server— possibly compromised machines which were not meant to act as servers—and hence with bad connectivity and low processing power. Despite the number of system calls in the 20 s trace might appear a good indicator of a page being malicious, it cannot be actually used alone as a discriminant, since it strongly depends on the setting of the client: client connectivity and processing power were tightly controlled in our data collection settings, but are likely to be more variable in a real scenario.

Concerning the number of occurrences of system calls, Table 1 shows the absolute occurrences $\overline{N_c}$ and relative occurrences $\frac{N_c}{N}$ of the 10 most occurring (considering all traces) system calls, for trusted and malicious pages: for example, the `futex` call occurs on the average 12 895 times in each trusted trace, which corresponds to 11.36% of calls per trace. As expected, the absolute number of occurrences is in general greater for trusted pages. In relative terms, figures are similar for trusted and malicious pages, with some exceptions. The call `gettimeofday` is by far the most occurring across malicious pages: on the average, more than $\frac{1}{3}$ of system calls are `gettimeofday`; this system call could be invoked for time-based attacks and logic bombs. On the other hand, for trusted pages, the most occurring call is `clock_gettime`. This is likely to happen because, for a time-based attack, a temporal grain at level of a day is enough as temporal line after which the attack must be launched. The call `clock_gettime` can be used by many common functions in current trusted websites: for instance in forums and social networks, the local clock time is commonly used to tag the published posts. Moreover the local clock time is used for web page dynamic updates (for instance this is typical in news websites), or for JavaScript timers bound to UI activieties, and so on. The call `open` seems to occur more frequently while visiting malicious web pages than trusted ones: 4.20% vs. 2.88%. This could

Table 1. Most occurrent system calls in our dataset

System call c	Trusted N_c	$\frac{N_c}{N}$ (%)	Malicious N_c	$\frac{N_c}{N}$ (%)
1 clock_gettime	35 444	29.97	17 869	21.81
2 gettimeofday	30 675	27.53	25 622	34.54
3 futex	12 895	11.36	9757	12.55
4 recv	9325	8.25	5105	6.63
5 poll	6919	6.13	4073	5.24
6 open	3108	2.88	3052	4.20
7 read	2336	2.07	1917	2.51
8 writev	2183	1.97	1231	1.64
9 write	1752	1.53	1206	1.57
10 stat64	1348	1.22	1149	1.54

be due to the fact that many kinds of attacks performed through web pages, as previously observed, consist of gathering private information from the victim's machine, obtaining the machine control, changing machine settings (e.g., DNS poisoning, registry modifications, password cracking, cookies, browser settings, and chronology retrieving), causing a denial of service, and so on.

Figure 1 shows the comparison between relative occurrences of the 10 most occurring system calls for trusted and malicious pages, by means of a boxplot. It can be seen that no one of the considered calls can be taken as a discriminant between trusted and malicious pages, because values for all the considered pages overlap for the two categories. For example, despite being the mean value for the open call significantly lower for trusted pages (see Table 1), several trusted pages (at most 25%) exceed the mean value of the open relative occurrence within malicious pages. This happens because nowadays many web applications must implement very complex business goals (e-health, e-government, e-banking, e-commerce) which require a complex architecture, rich of files (images, animations, CSS sheets, JavaScripts), and complex functions, which need to have access to cookies, Internet files (chronology), local folders (for updating files), web services. In this case the number of files which need to be opened can be remarkably higher than the ones opened by many web-based attacks.

Finally, we analyzed the 10 system calls for which the absolute difference $\Delta \frac{N_c}{N}$ between the average relative occurrences in trusted and malicious page was the greatest. The rationale was to find those system calls which were the best candidate to be a good discriminant between trusted and malicious pages, regardless of being the calls rare or frequent. Table 2 lists the 10 system calls, along with the value of the difference in relative occurrences. It can be seen that 9 on 10 of the calls chosen with this procedure were also included in the set of the 10 most occurring calls (i.e., those of Table 1 and Figure 1): the only exception was the _llseek call which took the place of the write call.

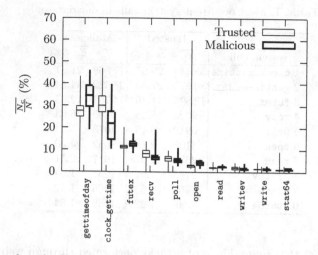

Fig. 1. Boxplot of relative occurrences of the 10 most occurring system calls in our dataset. The top and bottom edges of each box represent third and first quartile, respectively; the line inside the box represents the mean value; the vertical lines above and below each box span to max and min values, respectively.

Table 2. System calls with greatest difference in relative occurrences in our dataset

System call	$\Delta \frac{N_c}{N}$ (%)
1 clock_gettime	8.16
2 gettimeofday	7.01
3 recv	1.62
4 open	1.32
5 futex	1.19
6 poll	0.89
7 read	0.44
8 stat64	0.35
9 writev	0.33
10 _llseek	0.31

3.3   Classification

We tried to exploit the difference in relative occurrences of system calls to build a classifier able to discriminate between trusted and malicious pages. To this end, we defined a method consisting of a training phase and a classification phase.

In the training phase, we proceed as follows. Let T be a set of labeled traces (t, l), where $l \in \{trusted, malicious\}$ is the label and t is the trace, i.e., a sequence of system calls. We build, for each trace t, a feature vector $\mathbf{f} \in [0, 1]^{106}$ composed of all the system call relative occurrences, sorted alphabetically on the calls themselves. Then, we train a Support Vector Machine (SVM) on the feature vectors using the labels in T. We use a third-degree polynomial kernel with cost parameter set to 1.

In the classification phase, we simply obtain the feature vector **f** from the trace under analysis and then applied the learned SVM.

We assessed the effectiveness of the proposed classification method on the dataset D collected as described in Section 3.1, with the following procedure:

1. built a training set $T \subset D$ by picking 2400 trusted traces and 2400 malicious traces;
2. built a testing set $T' = D \setminus T$;
3. run the training phase on T;
4. applied the learned classifier on each element of T'.

We performed a 5-fold cross validation, i.e., we repeated the four steps 5 times varying the composition of T (and hence of T').

We measured the performance in terms of accuracy, False Negative Rate (FNR) and False Positive Rate (FPR), i.e., respectively, the percentage of T' pages which were correctly classified, the percentage of malicious pages in T' which were wrongly classified as trusted and the percentage of trusted pages in T' which were wrongly classified as malicious.

We obtained a classification accuracy of 97.18%, averaged across the 5 repetitions, with a standard deviation $\sigma = 0.44\%$; FPR and FNR were respectively equal to 3.5% and 2.13%. Although such results are good, it is fair to note that a detector based on the number of invocations of a (set of) system calls could be evaded easily: if the number of malicious system calls is expected to be smaller than trusted ones, the attackers should write junk code which does not alter the payload effect but increases the number of those system calls. On the contrary, if the number of malicious system call is expected to be greater than trusted ones, as the value which we are considering is calculated in percentage, it is sufficient to increase the total number of all the system calls, with junk code, as well.

4 RQ2: System Calls Sequences

4.1 Classification

In order to answer RQ2, we considered a classification method for discriminating between trusted and malicious pages which bases on (short) system calls sequences, rather than occurrences. Similarly to the former case, we considered two phases: training and classification.

In the training phase, which operates on a set of labeled traces T, we proceed as follows. We first compute, for each trace, a feature vector **f** of n-gram occurrences (with $n = 3$). Each feature corresponds to ratio between the number of times a given subsequence of 3 system calls occurs in t and the number of 3-grams in t (which is $|t| - 2$). For example, if $t = \{$execve, brk, access, mmap2, access, open, stat64, open, stat64, open$\}$, then $f_{(\text{execve,brk,access})} = \frac{1}{8}$, $f_{(\text{brk,access,mmap2})} = \frac{1}{8}, \ldots, f_{(\text{open,stat64,open})} = \frac{2}{8}$, and so on.

The number $|C|^3$ of possible features is large, being C the set of system calls—recall that in our experimentation $|C| = 106$. For the sake of tractability, we consider only those features for which the corresponding 3-gram occurs at least once in T: this way, we reduce the number of features in our experimentation to $\approx 43\,000$.

Then, we perform a two-steps feature selection procedure. We first select the 5% of features with the greatest absolute difference between the average value computed only on trusted sequences and the average value computed only on malicious sequences. Second, among the remaining features, we select the k features with the highest mutual information with the label l.

Finally, we train a Support Vector Machine (SVM) on the selected features using the labels in T. We use a third-degree polynomial kernel with cost parameter set to 1.

In the classification phase, we simply extract the selected features from the trace under analysis and then apply the learned SVM. Note that the actual extraction of the features in this phase—including the collection of the trace itself—can be computationally cheaper, since only those k subsequences of system calls have to be counted.

4.2   Experimental Evaluation

We assessed the effectiveness of the proposed method on the same dataset and with the same procedure described in Section 3.3.

Table 3 shows the results of the experimental evaluation in terms of average value of accuracy, FNR and FPR across the 5 repetitions. It can be seen that our method is able to discriminate between trusted and malicious pages with an accuracy of 95.83% ($k = 25$): FNR and FPR are balanced, i.e., the method does not tend to misclassify one class of pages more than the other.

Moreover, results show that the best accuracy can be obtained with $k = 25$, but the method itself appears to be quite robust with respect to the parameter k. Considering that an actual implementation of our approach will benefit from low k values—since less data had to be recorded—the fact that the best accuracy can be obtained with $k = 25$ is a plus.

Results of Table 3 suggest that(i) the chosen features (3-gram occurrencies) are indeed informative for malicious pages detection, (ii) a large number of them do not provide any additional information—or the SVM classifier is not able to exploit it—and (iii) the proposed feature selection procedure allows to select the small fraction of features which allow an accurate classification.

For completeness of analysis, in Table 4 we show the 10 3-grams chosen with the feature selection procedure described in Section 4.1 in one repetition of our experimental evaluation—we verified that the list composition was stable across repetitions. It can be seen that the table includes system calls which were not captured by the criterion on call relative occurrences (see Table 1), nor by the criterion on difference in relative occurrences (see Table 2). This is the case of, e.g., `fstat64` and `set_robust_list`. This happens because some system calls fall in several sequences, like `write` , and `close`, so they are more

Table 3. Results in terms of accuracy, FNR and FPR

k	Accuracy (%)	FNR (%)	FPR (%)
10	94.52	5.27	5.70
25	95.83	4.23	4.10
50	95.33	4.70	4.63
100	94.55	5.50	5.40
250	94.63	5.47	5.27

Table 4. 3-grams of system calls chosen by the feature selection procedure in one repetition of our experimental evaluation

	3-gram of system calls
1	clock_gettime, getdents, recv
2	write, send, getdents
3	gettimeofday, ioctl, mkdir
4	write, sendto, futex
5	close, write, connect
6	shutdown, recv, close
7	close, fstat64, set_robust_list
8	clock_gettime, setsockopt, recvmsg
9	open, getrusage, clock_gettime
10	mkdir, getsockname, setsockopt

frequent than others which occur only in one or two sequences, like getdents and shutdown. This suggests that considering the occurrences of sequences of system calls allows to take into account behaviors—defined by short sequences—which characterize benign or malicious activities. In other words, the concept of system calls sequence encloses the concept of a program behavior at a very low-level grain and, at the same time, at a high level of abstraction with respect to the type of attacks and its implementation in the web application. Somehow, the sequences of system calls can be seen as fingerprints or signatures of malicious payload (at a very high level of abstraction). Conversely, occurrences of system calls are not as much clearly representative of an attack as the system calls sequences. In fact, occurrence counting is a too rough feature, as in the counting can be included system calls that are not used in the payload.

Summing up,(i) features considered by RQ2 produce results not significantly worse than those considered by RQ1 (the accuracy is about 96% and 97%, respectively), but (ii) the former appear to be less prone to be circumvented by trivial evasion techniques. As previously explained, the occurrence of a system call can be altered by adding some junk code, which is a relatively straightforward technique. On the contrary, to camouflage a system calls sequence is much harder, because the system calls sequence is a direct image at operating system of the malicious behavior. To define an altered system calls sequence, without affecting the intended payload, could be feasible, but very hard to realize. In fact, being the actual maliciuos code in JavaScript, insertion of junk JavaScript code will likely not impact on short system call sequences. In other words, since the system calls sequence to be invoked depends on the effect which the code should produce, the insertion of junk code may add further system calls, but it cannot remove the sequence of system calls which represents the malicious behavior.

5   Conclusions and Future Work

With this paper we evaluate two methods for detecting malicious web pages based on the system calls which are invoked when the browser connects to the web application under analysis.

The first method consists of counting the occurrences of specific system calls, while the second method consists of retrieving specific sequences of system calls which are more frequent in malicious web applications than in trusted ones. Both the method produced a high classification accuracy, the first method exhibiting an accuracy slightly higher than the second one (97% vs. 96%). However, a detection method which only exploits the occurrences of specific system calls can be evaded easily, by adding junk code which alters the counting. On the contrary, altering a sequence of system calls is much harder, as it depends directly on the specific effect the attacker intends to realize. Adding junk code, in this case, may alter the number of system calls, but not a specific sequence, which may represent a malicious behavior.

As future work, we are planning to enlarge the experimentation by testing the proposed technique on a data with noise, i.e., with data collected by real clients during navigation—an in vivo experimentation. Additionally, we wish to investigate about methods for inferring a pattern for those specific sequences of system calls which correspond to malicious activities. In fact, the proposed method is capable to identify system calls sequences common to malicious web applications, but it is not able to map which ones correspond to which malicious effect.

References

1. 2013 threats predictions (2013), http://www.mcafee.com/us/resources/reports/rp-threat-predictions-2013.pdf
2. Pandalabs quarterly report: January - March 2013 (2013), https://www.switch.ch/export/sites/default/about/news/2013/files/PandaLabs-Quaterly-Report.pdf
3. Eshete, B.: Effective analysis, characterization, and detection of malicious web pages. In: Proceedings of the 22nd International Conference on World Wide Web Companion, pp. 355–360. International World Wide Web Conferences Steering Committee (2013)
4. Trend Micro: Web threats (2012), http://apac.trendmicro.com/apac/threats/enterprise/web-threats
5. Weiss, A.: Top 5 security threats in html5 (2011), http://www.esecurityplanet.com/trends/article.php/3916381/Top-5-Security-Threats-in-HTML5.htm

6. Canfora, G., Iannaccone, A.N., Visaggio, C.A.: Static analysis for the detection of metamorphic computer viruses using repeated-instructions counting heuristics. Journal of Computer Virology and Hacking Techniques, 11–27 (2013)
7. Dewald, A., Holz, T., Freiling, F.C.: Adsandbox: Sandboxing javascript to fight malicious websites. In: Proceedings of the 2010 ACM Symposium on Applied Computing, pp. 1859–1864. ACM (2010)
8. Seifert, C., Welch, I., Komisarczuk, P.: Identification of malicious web pages with static heuristics. In: Australasian Telecommunication Networks and Applications Conference, ATNAC 2008, pp. 91–96. IEEE (2008)
9. Canali, D., Cova, M., Vigna, G., Kruegel, C.: Prophiler: a fast filter for the large-scale detection of malicious web pages. In: Proceedings of the 20th International Conference on World Wide Web, pp. 197–206. ACM (2011)
10. Choi, H., Zhu, B.B., Lee, H.: Detecting malicious web links and identifying their attack types. In: Proceedings of the 2nd USENIX Conference on Web Application Development, p. 11. USENIX Association (2011)
11. Ma, J., Saul, L.K., Savage, S., Voelker, G.M.: Beyond blacklists: learning to detect malicious web sites from suspicious urls. In: Proceedings of the 15th ACM SIGKDD International Conference on Knowledge Discovery and Data Mining, pp. 1245–1254. ACM (2009)
12. Ma, J., Saul, L.K., Savage, S., Voelker, G.M.: Identifying suspicious urls: an application of large-scale online learning. In: Proceedings of the 26th Annual International Conference on Machine Learning, pp. 681–688. ACM (2009)
13. Thomas, K., Grier, C., Ma, J., Paxson, V., Song, D.: Design and evaluation of a real-time url spam filtering service. In: 2011 IEEE Symposium on Security and Privacy (SP), pp. 447–462. IEEE (2011)
14. Sorio, E., Bartoli, A., Medvet, E.: Detection of hidden fraudulent urls within trusted sites using lexical features. In: 2013 Eighth International Conference on Availability, Reliability and Security (ARES), pp. 242–247. IEEE (2013)
15. Kim, B.-I., Im, C.-T., Jung, H.-C.: Suspicious malicious web site detection with strength analysis of a javascript obfuscation. International Journal of Advanced Science & Technology 26 (2011)
16. Ikinci, A., Holz, T., Freiling, F.: Monkey-spider: Detecting malicious websites with low-interaction honeyclients, sicherheit (2008)
17. Kolbitsch, C., Livshits, B., Zorn, B., Seifert, C.: Rozzle: De-cloaking internet malware. In: 2012 IEEE Symposium on Security and Privacy (SP), pp. 443–457. IEEE (2012)
18. Cova, M., Kruegel, C., Vigna, G.: Detection and analysis of drive-by-download attacks and malicious javascript code. In: Proceedings of the 19th International Conference on World Wide Web, pp. 281–290. ACM (2010)
19. Moshchuk, A., Bragin, T., Deville, D., Gribble, S.D., Levy, H.M.: Spyproxy: Execution-based detection of malicious web content. In: Proceedings of 16th USENIX Security Symposium on USENIX Security Symposium, vol. 3, pp. 1–16. USENIX Association (2007)
20. Rieck, K., Krueger, T., Dewald, A.: Cujo: efficient detection and prevention of drive-by-download attacks. In: Proceedings of the 26th Annual Computer Security Applications Conference, pp. 31–39 (2010)
21. Qassrawi, M.T., Zhang, H.: Detecting malicious web servers with honeyclients. Journal of Networks 6(1) (2011)
22. The honeynet project (2011), https://projects.honeynet.org/honeyc
23. Mitre honeyclient project (2011), http://search.cpan.org/~mitrehc

24. Capture-hpc client honeypot / honeyclient (2011), https://projects.honeynet.org/capture-hpc
25. Wang, Y.-M., Beck, D., Jiang, X., Roussev, R., Verbowski, C., Chen, S., King, S.: Automated web patrol with strider honeymonkeys. In: Proceedings of the 2006 Network and Distributed System Security Symposium, pp. 35–49 (2006)
26. Curtsinger, C., Livshits, B., Zorn, B., Seifert, C.: Zozzle: Low-overhead mostly static javascript malware detection. In: Proceedings of the Usenix Security Symposium (2011)
27. Kapravelos, A., Shoshitaishvili, Y., Cova, M., Kruegel, C., Vigna, G.: Revolver: An automated approach to the detection of evasive web-based malware. In: USENIX Security Symposium (2013)
28. Pate, J.R., Tairas, R., Kraft, N.A.: Clone evolution: a systematic review. Journal of Software: Evolution and Process 25(3), 261–283 (2013)
29. Roy, C.K., Cordy, J.R.: A survey on software clone detection research. School of Computing TR 2007-541, Queen's University (2007)
30. Bayer, U., Comparetti, P.M., Hlauschek, C., Kruegel, C., Kirda, E.: Scalable, behavior-based malware clustering. In: NDSS, vol. 9, pp. 8–11. Citeseer (2009)
31. Jang, J., Brumley, D., Venkataraman, S.: Bitshred: feature hashing malware for scalable triage and semantic analysis. In: Proceedings of the 18th ACM Conference on Computer and Communications Security, pp. 309–320. ACM (2011)

Risk Reduction Overview

A Visualization Method for Risk Management

Hellen Nanda Janine Havinga[1] and Olivier Diederik Theobald Sessink[2]

[1] Rijkswaterstaat, Central Information Services, Delft, The Netherlands
hellen.havinga@rws.nl
[2] Ministry of Defense, The Hague, The Netherlands
odt.sessink@mindef.nl

Abstract. The Risk Reduction Overview (RRO) method presents a comprehensible overview of the coherence of risks, measures and residual risks. The method is designed to support communication between different stakeholders in complex risk management. Seven reasons are addressed why risk management in IT security has many uncertainties and fast changing factors, four for IT security in general and three for large organizations specifically. The RRO visualization has been proven valuable to discuss, optimize, evaluate, and audit a design or a change in a complex environment. The method has been used, evaluated, and improved over the last six years in large government and military organizations. Seven areas in design and decision making are identified in which a RRO is found to be beneficial. Despite the widely accepted need for risk management we believe this is the first practical method that delivers a comprehensive overview that improves communication between different stakeholders.

Keywords: Design, Security, Residual risk, Risk management, Security measure, Visualization.

1 Introduction

Risk management in IT security is complex. Large numbers of security measures and many stakeholders make risk management in large organizations even more complex. Risk management involves the balance between the residual risks for the business and the costs of the measures that are taken to reduce the initial risks. In this article we define risk as the product of the chance that a threat causes damage to the business and the damage of that threat to the business. A 5% chance for $100 total damage, for example, will justify the costs for a $5 measure. The costs include not only the cost of the implementation of the measure itself, but also the costs of any loss of functionality.

There have been various approaches to quantify and model the security costs and benefits [6, 7, 11], [13]. However, in large organizations both the chance and the damage are mostly unknown. Furthermore, the estimates of the effect of measures on chance and impact also have a high degree of uncertainty. Those approaches are therefore not practical for real-world risk management in situations with large numbers of

S. Teufel et al. (Eds.): CD-ARES 2014, LNCS 8708, pp. 239–249, 2014.
© IFIP International Federation for Information Processing 2014

security measures. There also have been several approaches to present risk management visually [16, 17]. However, none of these methods present an intuitive overview of the coherence of all risks and measures required for risk management.

1.1 Challenges of Real World IT Risk Management

There are four main reasons why chance and damage are uncertain in IT security and thus why risk management is complex. First, the known vulnerabilities in IT systems change with a high rate. Every computer runs millions of lines of code, and thus the existence of bugs is almost a certainty [12]. At a certain moment, for example, it may seem impossible to gain unauthorized access to a system, a week later there may be a zero-day exploit and an experienced hacker may gain access, one week later an exploit is released on the internet and access is possible for every "script kiddy", and again one week later the vulnerability is patched and unauthorized access seems impossible again. Second, the IT environment itself changes continuously, which changes both the chance and the potential damage to the business. For example the introduction of new software or a new network connection to an external system. New technology developments such as cloud computing and ubiquitous computing that introduce completely new security challenges extend this challenge even more. Third, the chance that a threat causes damage is influenced by unknown external factors. It is for example difficult to quantify how much effort an external entity is willing to take to gain access to your information, or to quantify the number of backdoors in the software you use, or to quantify the bypass rate of your security measures [2]. Last, the cost of the damage is hard to estimate. The damage incurred when IT systems are unavailable, interrupting business processes or critical infrastructure, or when sensitive information is disclosed, affecting competitiveness or causing reputation damage, is not easy to express in monetary terms [3], [5], especially in the public sector where information if often sensitive for political, sovereignty, or privacy reasons [1]. Furthermore, the total cost of ownership of measures is difficult to express in monetary terms. Especially since most measures cause a decrease in productivity as a side effect.

1.2 Challenges of IT Risk Management in Large Organizations

Large organizations add three additional challenges to the complexity of IT risk management. First, where in a small organization a single administrator might be solely responsible for the overall security, in large organizations there are many different roles involved, such as business owner, information security officer, authorizing official, functional application manager, solution architect, and system administrator. This separation of roles causes few people to have the required overview and knowledge to link security measures to chance and impact on the business required for a good cost/benefit analysis. Second, large organizations have large numbers of information systems which are interconnected in many ways: sharing hardware, network infrastructure, storage, and data. Defining a strict boundary for a single information system is therefore almost impossible. A security breach on any level might affect many information systems. NIST 800-37 [9] recommends segmentation of systems with guards in between, but this is not considered feasible for most networks except when dealing with very high classification levels. The chance that a security breach occurs is difficult to estimate because there are thousands of IT components and thousands of unique security measures that affect the chance. The damage is difficult to quantify because a security breach might affect many information systems. Last, the cost/benefit analysis becomes rapidly more complex due to the large number of business processes with different security requirements in large organizations. A new security measure may, for example, reduce the risk for one business unit, but may decrease productivity for another business unit.

1.3   Risk Management Methods and Standards Used in Large Organizations

To overcome the challenges of complexity, large organizations use generic risk management methods and security baseline standards for the generic infrastructure, such as NIST 800-37 [8], CRAMM, and ISO/IEC 27005 [10], to guarantee a minimum security level for all systems. In order to be sustainable over time these methods and standards use generic threats and describe only generic measures that allow for different implementations; only some common cases are described. The generic measures are not clearly linked to threats to the business [4]. When the threats change over time, the implementation might need to be re-assessed and updated. Furthermore, whether or not a specific implementation complies with the standard has to be justified by the IT security architect.

Every implementation thus needs an argumentation why it meets the requirements of the generic measures and how it tailors or supplements baseline security controls. The IT security architect needs to provide insight into three aspects to justify his decisions. First, the different successive complementary and independent technical and procedural measures. Second, the risks which are reduced by each security measure. Last, the residual risks that have to be accepted.

So although these standards help larger organizations to improve the overall security, they do not eliminate the need for communication between those that design the measures and those that have to accept the residual risks.

2   Objectives

The challenges in IT risk management as described have led to the objectives for the RRO method. First, present the relation between risks, measures and residual risks in an intuitive way. Second, present the security design in a way that gives people with different skills and roles the opportunity to either discuss, evaluate or audit if a design meets the required security level. Third, present the security design in a way that people can evaluate the residual risks that a design imposes on the business. Last, the presentation should be applicable independent whether or not the design is already implemented or in design phase. Summarizing, the presentation should help the business to improve risk management: to improve communication and clarify the link between threats, security measures, and residual risk and make IT security designs more comprehensible and auditable.

3   The Risk Reduction Overview

The Risk Reduction Overview (RRO) consists of two parts: a flowchart representation and an appendix. The flowchart provides an intuitive overview of the coherence of all risks, measures, and residual risks. The position and relation of measures in the flowchart show if a measure is successive to another measure (which provides defense in depth), complementary to another measure (the measure reduces a different aspect of the risk), or independent from other measures (the measure acts on a different risk). The appendix provides the details on each risk, measure, and residual risk.

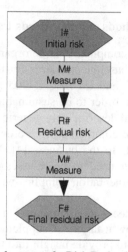

Fig. 1. Basic elements of a Risk Reduction Overview

The flowchart is based on two basic elements: risks and measures. There are three types of risks: the initial risks, the residual risks, and the final residual risks (Fig. 1). All paths in the RRO flowchart follow the same format: initial risks are identified and measures are applied to reduce these risks, which lead to residual risks. The flowchart starts with all the initial risks that are identified for the particular design. All initial risks are followed by one or more measures, which are followed by residual risks and more measures, and finally end with a final residual risk. Arrows depict the flow. The flow is not necessarily linear; multiple measures from different flows may lead to the same residual risk, and multiple residual risks may follow a single measure. Arrows are drawn from risk to the resulting residual risk. When the measure itself introduces a new risk, an arrow can be drawn from that measure to a new risk.

All risks and measures in the flowchart have a unique identifier: Initial risks have the identifier I# (in which # is a unique number), residual risks have the identifier R#, measures have the identifier M#, and final residual risks have the identifier F#. In the flowchart the identifier is followed by a short description of the risk or measure. The appendix of the RRO contains the detailed description for each risk and measure in the flowchart.

3.1   Example

To illustrate the risk reduction flow we use a simplified example: email communication between a network with confidential data and the internet is enabled, and six security measures are proposed to reduce the risks (Fig. 2). This particular example describes a very common application for a risk reduction overview: a change on a secure environment is proposed, and the risk reduction overview is used to show the proposed measures and the residual risks of that change. Figure 2 does not describe a real-life design. Real risk reduction overviews [14] often have over ten initial risks and over twenty measures (Fig. 3).

3.2   Drawing Method

Before making a RRO, an initial set of risks and measures must have been identified already. The initial risks are the risks if one would take no security measures at all. The initial risks can be derived from the threats to the business combined with all

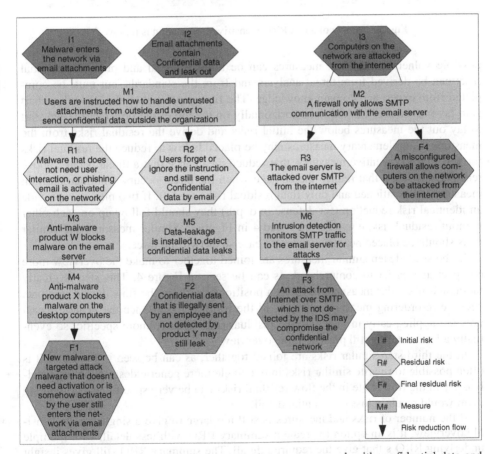

Fig. 2. Example RRO of email communication between a network with confidential data and the internet

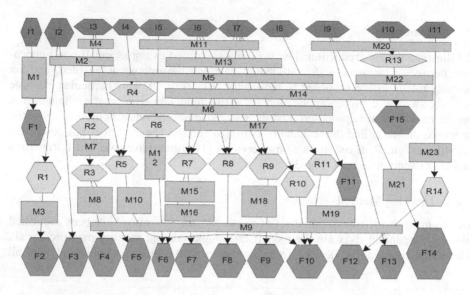

Fig. 3. Example of a real RRO (sensitive information is removed)

possible vulnerabilities. The measures can be both technical and procedural. Initial risks can be derived from threat analysis and from the standards, but must be completed from expert and domain knowledge. The first step to set up the RRO flowchart is to lay out the set of initial risks horizontally on the top of the flow chart. Then start to lay out the measures below the initial risks and derive the residual risks from the measures. Complementary measures may be placed below to reduce the residual risks further. Place preventive measures, that reduce the chance that a threat occurs, above reactive measures, that reduce the damage when the threat occurs. Continue until all measures are positioned and only final residual risks are left. If two measures provide an identical risk reduction (for defense in depth) they should follow up on each other without residual risk, e.g. measure 3 and 4 in Figure 2. Similar measures and similar risks should be placed near each other, to ease steps two and three.

In the second step similar measures are joined together to make the overview more compact and easier to comprehend, as can be seen in Figure 4. This step is greatly facilitated if similar measures have been positioned early in the flow during step one, because re-ordering measures changes all the residual risks. Once the generic measures are applied early in the flow, the residual risks become more specific, so eventually all the detail is still present in the overview.

In the third step similar risks are joined together, as can be seen in Figure 4. It is often possible to rewrite similar risks into a single more generic description, especially early in the flow. Late in the flow residual risks can be very specific and combining them would result in loss of essential detail.

If the number of risks and measures is still too large to give a single comprehensible overview, it is an option to create a summary RRO with less detail, with multiple underlying RRO's that give the required detail. The summary RRO still gives insight in the detailed final residual risks, but summarizes the upstream risks and measures in

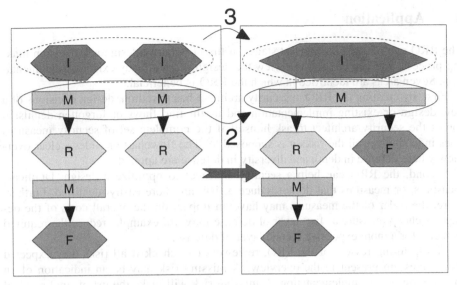

Fig. 4. Before (left) and after (right) step 2 and step 3

the risk reduction flow. For example: different measures like fire alarm, fire extin-guisher, fire blankets and non smoking areas can be summarized as fire fighting measures. Reviewers can still find the details of fire fighting in the underlying de-tailed fire fighting RRO, while business owners might only be interested in the sum-mary RRO, that present them the final residual risk of all fire fighting measures. Evaluation of the method has led to the finding that single RRO's with over 30 meas-ures are generally considered not comprehensible anymore

To support quick reading risks and measures should be described in a uniform sen-tence structure. Start the description of the risks with the vulnerable element. For example: Email attachments may contain malware. Start the description of the meas-ures with the subject that causes the desired effect. For example: Anti virus software scans emails for malware.

The last step is to number and describe each risk and measure of the optimized flowchart in the appendix. The appendix has four sections. The first section describes all initial risks. The second section describes all measures. The level of detail should provide enough information for a reviewer to judge if this measure will indeed reduce the risk to the residual risk. The third section describes all residual risks. The fourth and last section describes all final residual risks. In order to give weight to each of the risks, the description in the appendix should give an indication of the chance that a risk might occur and the damage it may cause to the business. The description should provide a chief security officer or a business owner enough information in a clear and comprehensive way to assess if the final residual risk is acceptable. An indication of the cost of measures and the cost of possible damage could be added to help the deci-sion maker.

Positioning the risks and measures manually can be time consuming, but this process could be automated.

4   Application

The RRO can be used in different stages of the IT security design and decision making process, and can be used to review the design of an already existing implementation. Seven areas are identified in which the RRO is beneficial.

First, by creating the RRO, a security architect has to rethink design decisions of a new design or existing implementation and might find flaws or forgotten details. It forces the security architect to ask himself if the complete set of security measures does indeed cover all the risks it is supposed to. The flowchart provides a clear overview where defense in depth and diversity in defense are applied.

Second, the RRO can help a security architect to optimize a design. Duplicate measures, or measures that do not reduce a risk, are more easily identified. Furthermore, the order of the measures may have an impact on the overall costs of the design. A cheap measure as first layer of defense may, for example, reduce the required capacity for a more expensive second layer of defense.

Third, during review of the RRO, reviewers can check if all risks they expected themselves are present in the overview. A missing risk may be an indication of an insecure design or implementation. A missing risk will make the list of final residual risks incomplete.

Fourth, reviewers of the RRO can check if the suggested risk reduction of a measure is realistic. They are able to see if the assumptions about the effectiveness of technical and procedural measures are correct and if the residual risks are well quantified. Too high residual risk may be an indication of an underestimation of the effectiveness of a measure. Very low residual risks may be an indication of an overestimation. In both cases the corresponding final residual risks will be incorrect too.

Fifth, the chief security officer or business owner of the particular IT system gets an overview of the initial risks, the measures and most importantly the final residual risks. Too high residual risk may be an indication of an insecure design or implementation, very low residual risks may be an indication of too many or too expensive security measures. If the final residual risks in the RRO are not acceptable for the business, there is a clear gap between the business needs and the security implementation.

Sixth, risks can change over time. When the security infrastructure is in use, new vulnerabilities of systems or measures can occur or the chance that vulnerabilities will be exploited can increase or decrease. The RRO gives for example a computer emergency response team the opportunity to immediately see what effect these changes have on the residual risk. The chief security officer or business owner either accepts the new residual risk or requires new measures to be taken to get the residual risks to an acceptable level.

Last, an existing RRO can be used as a source of inspiration for the design of a new similar environment or to review a new design.

5   Conclusions, Limitations, and Lessons Learned

The RRO method has been used and evaluated in two large organizations over thelast six years. The method has been applied to various complex problems in the fields of information security and cyber defense at the Joint IT Command of the

Dutch Ministry of Defense, and for cyber defense of critical infrastructure at the Dutch Rijkswaterstaat. In the Joint IT Command the RRO is now a mandatory document for changes that affect residual risk. At Rijkswaterstaat the RRO is now a mandatory document when exceptions from baseline security requirements are requested for critical infrastructure objects and mission critical systems. In both organizations the RRO is used to clarify, discuss and evaluate the security design of innovative products and services, for which no baseline requirements exist. New baseline requirements are extracted from these RRO's.

The RRO method has been found to be beneficial in all seven application areas described in this article. The RRO is found to deliver a comprehensible overview of the coherence of risks, measures and residual risks. Even first time readers with no previous experience with a RRO have little trouble to identify why measures are taken and which residual risks are left. More experienced readers point out that they need less time to review measures and residual risk with a RRO. Especially if there is a large number of measures or risks involved, the RRO gives far more overview than a traditional technical design document does. The concept of risk reduction is understood by people with different skills and roles, and the use of a RRO does improve their understanding of the coherence of the measures and the residual risks. Business owners of information systems point out that the RRO enables them to discuss measures with IT specialists, something they found very difficult in the past.

The RRO method is, however, not a silver bullet for IT risk management. First, having a RRO does not guarantee that the measures are actually correct and that the real residual risks match the described residual risks. Risks change over time; a new vulnerability that was previously unheard of may introduce a completely new risk, and new threats may require new measures. The competence of the security architect is still one of the most important factors. Second, a RRO covering the security of a large and complex environment will result in a large and complex visualization. The RRO will not make a complex problem simple. Last, the creation of a RRO requires more time than a traditional technical design document that just lists the measures. We do believe, however, that the cost benefit ratio favors the RRO, which is strengthened by the fact that both organizations that have evaluated the RRO have decided to make it a mandatory document in the decision making process.

The most important observation while the method was evaluated was that adjusting the level of detail and the layout of the flowchart manually requires a significant amount of time. This discouraged some authors to improve a RRO after reviewers had sent their comments, especially since there was no obligation to deliver a RRO at the time. A tool to automate this process should therefore be developed and will be published in the future on the RRO website [15].

6   Application Outside IT Security

The RRO is believed to be applicable in any area in which risk management is an issue, such as public safety, fraud prevention, food safety, physical security, military operation planning and medical hygiene. There are three separate situations in which a RRO is beneficial for generic risk management. First, if there is a need for communication about risks, measures and residual risks. Second, if there are stakeholders in the design or decisions making process that do not have the adequate knowledge to derive the residual risk from the different measures taken. For example if stakeholders are not known with the technology of complementary measures from different knowledge domains. Last, if the number of risks or measures in a certain risk assessment is high and a better overview is required to discuss or evaluate the overall situation. If multiple situations are present, the case for a RRO is even stronger.

Acknowledgements. The RRO method was initially developed at the Knowledge and Innovation branch of the Joint IT command of the Dutch Ministry of Defense, and has been further improved together with the CISO office of Rijkswaterstaat in the Netherlands.

References

1. Acquisti, A., Friedman, A., Telang, R. Is there a cost to privacy breaches? An event study. In: Fifth Workshop on the Economics of Information Security. Cambridge (2006)
2. Arora, A., Hall, D., Pinto, C., Ramsey, D., Telang, R.: An ounce of prevention vs. a pound of cure: How can we measure the value of IT security solutions? Lawrence Berkeley National Laboratory, University of California (2004)
3. Berinato, S.: Finally, a real return on security spending. CIO Magazine, 43–52 (2002)
4. Bornman, G., Labuschagne, L.: A comparative framework for evaluating information security risk management methods. In: Proceedings of the Information Security South Africa Conference, ISSA (2004)
5. Garg, A., Curtis, J., Halper, H.: Quantifying the financial impact of IT security breaches. Information Management and Computer Security 11(2), 74–83 (2003)
6. Gordon, L., Loeb, M.: The economics of information security investment. ACM Transaction on Information and System Security 5(4), 438–457 (2002)
7. Hoo, K.J.S.: How much is enough? A risk management approach to computer security. Doctoral Thesis, Stanford University (2000)
8. NIST Special Publication 800-37 Revision 1,
   `http://csrc.nist.gov/publications/nistpubs/`
   `800-37-rev1/sp800-37-rev1-final.pdf`
9. Joint Task Force Transformation Initiative: Guide for Applying the Risk Management Framework to Federal Information Systems: A Security Life Cycle Approach. NIST Special Publication 800-37, Revision 1. Computer Security Division, Information Technology Laboratory, National Institute of Standards and Technology (2010)
10. Joint Technical Committee ISO/IEC JTC 1/SC 27: ISO/IEC 27005:2011 Information technology — Security techniques — Information security risk management. International Organization for Standardization, Geneva (2011)
11. Longstaff, T., Chittister, C., Pethia, R., Haimes, Y.: Are we forgetting the risk of information technology? Computer 33(12), 43–51 (2000)
12. Martin, R.A.: Managing Vulnerabilities in Networked Systems. Computer 34(11), 32–38 (2001)

13. Neubauer, T., Klemen, M., Biffl, S.: Business process-based valuation of IT-security. In: Sullivan, K. (ed.) Proceedings of the 7th International Workshop on Economics-Driven Software Engineering Research, ICSE, pp. 1–5. ACM, New York (2005)
14. Risk Reduction Overview example, http://rro.sourceforge.net/examples.html
15. Risk Reduction Overview website, http://rro.sourceforge.net/
16. Roy, A., Kim, D.S., Trivedi, K.S.: Attack countermeasure trees (ACT): Towards unifying the constructs of attack and defense trees. In: Security and Communication Networks, pp. 929–943 (2012)
17. Schneier, B.: Attack Trees. Dr. Dobb's Journal of Software Tools 24(12), 21–29 (1999)

Towards Analysis of Sophisticated Attacks, with Conditional Probability, Genetic Algorithm and a Crime Function

Wolfgang Boehmer

Technische Universität Darmstadt, Morneweg Str. 30,
CASED building, D-64293 Darmstadt, Germany
wboehmer@cdc.informatik.tu-darmstadt.de

Abstract. In this short article, a proposal to simulate a sophisticated attack on a technical infrastructure is discussed. Attacks on (critical) infrastructures can be modeled with attack trees, but regular (normal) attack trees have some limitation in the case of a sophisticated attack like an advanced persistent (sophisticated) attack. Furthermore, attacks can also be simulated to understand the type of attack, and in order to subsequently develop targeted countermeasures. In this case, a normal, and also a sophisticated attack, is typically carried out in three phases. In the first phase (I) extensive information is gathered about the target object. In the second phase (II), the existing information is verified with a target object scan. In the third phase (III), the actual attack takes place. A normal attack tree is not able to explain this kind of attack behavior. So, we advanced a normal attack tree, which uses conditional probability according to Bayes to go through a certain path - step by step - from the leaf to the root. The learning ability, which typically precedes an attack (phase II), is simulated using a genetic algorithm. To determine the attack, we used threat trees and threat actors. Threat actors are weighted by a function that is called criminal energy. In a first step, it proposes three types of threat actors. The vulnerabilities have been identified as examples for a laboratory network.

Keywords: Conditional probability, genetic algorithm, Bayes theorem, attack trees, threat actor, crime function, risk scenario technology.

1 Introduction

The challenge of Homeland security has significantly changed during the last decade. One of the new challenges is so called advanced persistent threats (APT). APT's have a unique characteristic and current defense strategies have failed against this type of threat. The current main shortcomings of most common security technology are Network/-Host-based Intrusion Detection Systems and antivirus products. Antivirus products are excluded in this analysis. Intrusion detection Systems (IDS) are based on two typical items:

- *Signature-based* is still the most common technique and focuses on the identification of known patterns.

S. Teufel et al. (Eds.): CD-ARES 2014, LNCS 8708, pp. 250–256, 2014.
© IFIP International Federation for Information Processing 2014

- *Anomaly-based*, which consists of monitoring system activity to determine whether an observed activity is normal or anomalous, according to a heuristic or statistical analysis.

Finally, a major challenge for current IDS is the limited window of time for which the connection state can be maintained, as all modern IDSs are focused on real-time detection. Only a few products, like ArcSight from Hewlett Packard, go beyond this limitation. Also the knowledge about sophisticated threats is very rare before a sophisticated attack is faced, but we can point out some typically properties, as Gartner and ISACA has published to name few as a representation. An APT can be characterized as a so called *mission impossible*.

1. APTs make frequent use of zero-day exploits or modify/obfuscate known ones and, thus, are able to evade the majority of signature-based end points and network intrusion detection solutions. Also, in general APTs are spread over a wide period of time and, as a result, are often outside the limited detection/correlation window of these systems.
2. APT attackers focus on a specific target and are willing to spend significant time and explore all possible attack paths until they manage to subvert its defense.
3. APTs are able to jump over an air-gap, like in the case of Stuxnet.
4. Based on the analysis of major APT attacks it is evident that some perpetrators are supported by nation-states that have significant enabling capabilities (intelligence collection, manufacturing, covert physical access) for this type of attacks.
5. APTs are highly selective. Only a small and carefully selected number of victims are targeted, usually in nontechnical departments of an organization, as they are less likely to identify and report an attack.

In this contribution we will deal with sophisticated attacks on a technical infrastructure. We will advance the typical attack tree development methodology with the conditional probability to go step by step from the leaf to root of target. The typical binary logic used on an attack tree is not sufficient for that analysis. Also the search phase of an attack is not represented on a normal attack tree. For this search phase we propose a genetic algorithm (GA) to find a solution to this complex search problem. A genetic algorithm is based on the process of evolution by natural selection, which has been observed in nature. With both of these advanced techniques we combine a threat actor with one possible path of an attack.

The rest of the article is organized as follows. In the next section 2 the related work is discussed and the limitation of a normal attack tree. Afterwards, in section 3, the new type of attack tree, and the strengthes and the weaknesses of this new type of attack tree are discussed. The article concludes with a brief summary, continuing considerations and proposals for further studies.

2 Related Work

The idea of attack trees goes back to the article by Weis in 1991 [1]. In this article he describes *threat logical trees*. Generally, attacks are modeled with graphical, mathematical, decision trees. A few years later, the idea of threat trees was taken up by B.

Schneier, among others, and developed [2]. This work by B. Schneier led to extensive additions and improvements to this technology, such as those published by A.P. Moore et al. [3]. Several tools have been developed and published; representative of the work is [5,6]; the authors provide an overview of the techniques and tools. The contribution of S. Mauw and M. Oostdijk [10] in 2005 formalizes the concepts informally introduced by Schneier [2]. This formalization clarifies which manipulations of attack trees are allowed under which conditions. The commonality of attack trees and game theory has been elaborated on in 2010 by Kordy et al. [11]. Thus, a similar approach for the threat scenarios and threat agent are performed using the game theory.

But all the variations of an attack tree are unable to explain a sophisticated attack, as we explained for APTs in the section 1 (Introduction).

3   A New Type of Attack Tree

We follow the formal definition from [4] of attack graph for a given data structure used to represent all possible attacks.

Definition 3.01. *An attack graph in general, or AG, is a tuple $G = (S, \tau, S_o, S_s)$, where S is a set of states, $\tau \subseteq S \times S$ is a transition relation, $S_0 \subseteq S$ is a set of initial states, and $S_s \subseteq S$ is a set of success states.*

Based on this definition some automated attack graph generators were developed, to name few [8], [5]. But all of these automated attack graphs are unable to explain the infection path e.g. from the Stuxnet Attack. The infection with Stuxnet Virus was of the internal network via a USB stick. The internal network itself was not connected to the internet. Furthermore we want to use an attack graph to prove the possibility of reaching the target (root) up from a leaf. This possibility is often named as the safety condition. In the following definition we follow [9] page 106.

Definition 3.02. *A probabilistic attack graph (scenario) graph or PAG is a tuple $G = (S_n, S_p, s_e, \tau, \pi, S_0, S_a, S_f, S, D)$ where S_n is a set of nondeterministic states, S_p is a set of probabilistic states, $s_e \in S_n$ is a nondeterministic escape state ($s_e \notin S_a$ and $s_e \notin S_f$), $S = S_n \cup S_p$ is the set of all states, $\tau \subseteq S \times A \times S$ is a transition relation, $\pi : S_p \to S \to \mathcal{R}$ are transition probabilities, $S_0 \subseteq$ is a set of initial states, $S_a \subseteq S$ is a set of acceptance states, $S_f \subseteq S$ is a set of finial states, and $D : S \to 2^A (A = 2^{AP})$ is a labeling of states with sets of alphabet letters.*

A probabilistic scenario graph (PSG) distinguishes between nondeterministic states (set S_n) and probabilistic states (set S_p). The sets of nondeterministic and probabilistic states are disjointed ($S_n \cap S_p = \emptyset$). The function π specifies probabilities of transitions from probabilistic states, so that for all transitions (s_1, s_2) such that $s_1 \in S_p$, we have Prob $(s_1 \to s_2) = \pi(s_1)(s_2) > 0$. Thus, $\pi(s)$ can be viewed as a probability distribution on next states. Intuitively, when the system is in a nondeterministic state s_n, we have no information about the relative probabilities of the possible next transitions. When the system is in a probabilistic state s_p, it will choose the next state according to probability distribution (s_p) [9, 12] page 106.

In this work, we expand the idea of T. R. Ingoldsby [6] with conditional probability $\pi(s)$. Threat trees generally have a root or target. Different branches (nodes) can lead to this target, which are to be regarded as parts of goals and each start of a leaf.

Each leaf is initiated by an attacker with different motives. The leaves and branches are weighted and equipped with an actor [14]. The weighting corresponds to the criminal energy (Criminal power, Cp), and contains three functions. The assessment of these three functions reflects the exogenous knowledge which is required in the Bayesian statistics.

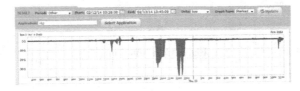

Fig. 1. Attack tree of a telecommunication provider on NTP protocol

The function of the criminal energy (Cp), which in turn is composed of three additive functions, represents the expert knowledge for the Bayesian risk analysis. The criminal energy is represented by the cost function (cost of attack *cf.* Fig. 2), the technical feasibility function (technical function, *cf.* 3) and the noticeability function, *cf.* Fig. 4. The three functions are mentioned by T. R. Ingoldsby [6] and have to be adjusted to the relevant inspection. The following Figures 2 - 4 describe the exogenous knowledge that focuses on the objective of a system.

Fig. 2 states that a threat agent (actor) for an attack is willing to spend money on tools. This willingness varies between 0 - 1 (axis of ordinates) and decreases with increasing costs (axis of abscissae). This can be explained simply because, on the internet, there are a number of free tools that are all well-suited to threaten a system.

Figure 3 indicates how the tools are used and the technical possibilities that exist. It is a statement about the complexity of the tools and the willingness to make use of this complexity. The curve indicates that the greater the technical possibilities and the complexity of the tools, the more the willingness drops. I.e. simple tools are preferred with simple operation. Figure 4 shows the noticeability function expressing how an actor wants to disguise his attack, so that he could not be discovered. From of these three functions, the threat of an attack is determined more precisely. This is called the criminal energy. These functions must be adapted to each situation and reflect the exogenous knowledge again, which is necessary for the conditional probability.

As an example, we can estimate the technical ability rating of 5 (out of 10), and expose the miscreant at a 0.3 noticeability.

Using the utility functions shown, we discover that

$$f_{cost}(25) = 0.9 \tag{3.1}$$

$$f_{tech\,ability}(05) = 0.9 \tag{3.2}$$

$$f_{noticeabiity}(0.3) = 0.85 \tag{3.3}$$

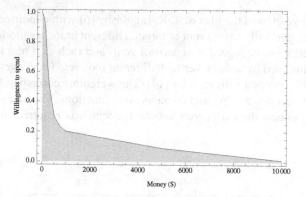

Fig. 2. Cost function

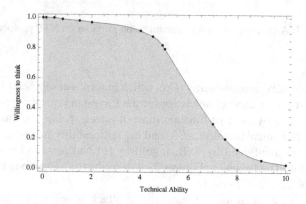

Fig. 3. Technical function

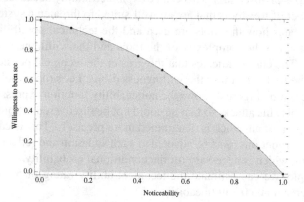

Fig. 4. Noticeability function

and therefore the criminal energy with

$$CE = f_{cost} \cdot f_{tech\,ability} \cdot f_{noticeabiity} \tag{3.4}$$

$$CE = 0.6885 = 0.9 \cdot 0.9 \cdot 0.85 \tag{3.5}$$

With this function of the criminal energy, we could estimate the threat profile in conjunction with a specific threat agent (actor). The three functions of Figures 2 - 4 do not explain anything about the motivation and benefit of the threat agent, but the threat agent's motivation is correlated with attack benefits. These must also be taken into account in order to understand how desirable an attack appears to an adversary. The discussion of the motivation and benefits of a threat agent is not really covered in this article. The criminal function produces the population of the genetic algorithm.

The basic process for a genetic algorithm [13] is:

- Initialization - Create an initial population. This population is usually randomly generated and can be any desired size, from only a few individuals to thousands.
- Evaluation - Each member of the population is then evaluated and we calculate a 'fitness' for that individual. The fitness value is calculated by how well it fits with our desired requirements. These requirements could be simple, 'faster algorithms are better', or more complex, 'stronger materials are better but they shouldn't be too heavy'.
- Selection - We want to be constantly improving our populations overall fitness. Selection helps us do this by discarding the bad designs and only keeping the best individuals in the population. There are a few different selection methods, but the basic idea is the same: make it more likely that fitter individuals will be selected for our next generation.
- Crossover - During crossover we create new individuals by combining aspects of our selected individuals. We can think of this as mimicking how sex works in nature. The hope is that by combining certain traits from two or more individuals we will create an even 'fitter' offspring which will inherit the best traits from each of its parents.
- Mutation - We need to add a little bit randomness into our populations' genetics otherwise every combination of solutions we can create would be in our initial population. Mutation typically works by making very small changes at random to an individuals genome.
- Repeat all steps - Now we have our next generation we can start again from step two until we reach a termination condition.

But, typically the largest benefit of the threat agent is associated with achieving the tree's root node, or with side benefits occurring at the various intermediate nodes. Different threat scenarios run through different paths among leaf nodes and root node. The threat agent's benefits may differ considerably depending on the threat scenario used. We will discuss different threat scenarios and different paths between leaf nodes and root in the next section.

4 Conclusion and Further Investigation

A comparison with real world attacks, like Stuxnet, shows that typical modeled attack graphs and their models in the literature are not able to create a real attack graph. In this paper we proposed a new methodology to use a genetic algorithm and the Bayes theorem to create an attack graph that could explain a real attack graph. The next step is to include not only a network into the model, but also the environment must be taken into account.

References

[1] Weis, J.D.: A system security engineering process. In: Proceedings of the 14th National. Computer Security Conference (1991)
[2] Schneier, B.: Attack trees. Dr. Dobb' s Journal 24(12), 21–29 (1999)
[3] Moore, A.P., Ellison, R.J., Linger, R.C.: Attack modeling for information security and survivability, Technical Note CMU/SEI-2001- TN-001, Carnegie Mellon University (2001)
[4] Sheyner, O., Haines, J., Jha, S., Lippmann, R., Wing, J.: Automated generation and analysis of attack graphs. In: Proceedings of the 2002 IEEE Symposium on Security and Privacy, pp. 273–284 (2002)
[5] Sheyner, O.: Tools for Generating and Analyzing Attack Graphs. In: de Boer, F.S., Bonsangue, M.M., Graf, S., de Roever, W.-P. (eds.) FMCO 2003. LNCS, vol. 3188, pp. 344–371. Springer, Heidelberg (2004)
[6] Ingoldsby, T.R.: Fundamentals of Capabilities-based Attack Tree Analysis. Amenaza Technologies Limited, 406 – 917 85th St SW, m/s 125
[7] Jha, S., Sheyner, O., Wing, J.: Two formal analyses of attack graphs. In: 15th IEEE Proceedings of the Computer Security Foundations Workshop, pp. 49–63 (2002)
[8] Sheyner, O., Haines, J., Jha, S., Lippmann, R., Wing, J.: Automated generation and analysis of attack graphs. In: Proceedings of the 2002 IEEE Symposium on Security and Privacy, pp. 273–284 (2002)
[9] Sheyner, O.M.: Scenario graphs and attack graphs. PhD thesis, University of Wisconsin (2004)
[10] Mauw, S., Oostdijk, M.: Foundations of Attack Trees. In: Won, D.H., Kim, S. (eds.) ICISC 2005. LNCS, vol. 3935, pp. 186–198. Springer, Heidelberg (2006)
[11] Kordy, B., Mauw, S., Melissen, M., Schweitzer, P.: Attack–defense trees and two-player binary zero-sum extensive form games are equivalent. In: Alpcan, T., Buttyán, L., Baras, J.S. (eds.) GameSec 2010. LNCS, vol. 6442, pp. 245–256. Springer, Heidelberg (2010)
[12] Wang, L., Islam, T., Long, T., Singhal, A., Jajodia, S.: An attack graph-based probabilistic security metric. In: Atluri, V. (ed.) DAS 2008. LNCS, vol. 5094, pp. 283–296. Springer, Heidelberg (2008)
[13] Whitley, D.: A genetic algorithm tutorial. Statistics and Computing 4(2), 65–85 (1994)
[14] Poolsappasit, N.: Towards an Efficient Vulnerability Analysis Methodology for better Security Risk Management. PhD thesis, Colorado State University (July 2010)

A High-Speed Network Content Filtering System

Guohong Zhao[1], Shuhui Chen[1], Baokang Zhao[1], Ilsun You[2],
Jinshu Su[1], and Wanrong Yu[1]

[1] School of Computer Science, National University of Defense Technology,
Changsha, Hunan, China
{ghzhao,csh,bkzhao,sjs,wlyu}@nudt.edu.cn
[2] School of Information Science, Korean Bible University, Seoul, South Korea
{ilsunu@gmail.com}

Abstract. Current software based Content Filtering Systems are too computing intensive in large scale packets payload detection and cannot meet the performance requirements of modern networks. Thus, hardware architectures are desired to speed up the detection process. In this paper, hardware based Conjoint Network Content Filtering System (CNCFS) is proposed to solve the problem. In CNCFS, a TCAM based algorithm named Linking Shared Multi-Match (LSMM) is implemented, which can speed up large scale Multi-Pattern Multi-Matching greatly. Also, this system can also be used in high speed mobile networks which need to deal with the security of fast handover of mobile users. The results of performance evaluation show that our solution can provide 5 Gbps wire speed processing capability.

Keywords: Network Security, Hardware Accelerating, Content Filtering, Pattern Match.

1 Introduction

Today, large number of malicious attack, illegal intrusions, worms and other harmful information are spreading over the Internet. CFS (Content Filtering System) and IDS based on software are used to isolate and monitor these harmful information. However, software based CFS and IDS are essentially computing intensive and can't keep up with the traffic rates requested by most of telecom backbone which employed OC48 or OC192 high-speed links. Moreover, they can't afford to support the high performance requirements for secure and fast handover in mobile internet networks including Mobile IPv6 (MIPv6) or PMIPv6 [14-15], Thus, new content filtering based on hardware architectures is a promising way to fill up the gap between network traffic rates and NIDS analysis rates.

Content Filtering is a pattern matching process focus on the payload of network packet. There are many security applications which require content pattern matching, such as network intrusion detection and prevention, content filtering, and load balancing. Measurements on Snort IDS show that 80% of total processing time is spent on

S. Teufel et al. (Eds.): CD-ARES 2014, LNCS 8708, pp. 257–269, 2014.

string matching [4]. Thus, using high-speed algorithms or customized hardware to accelerate the speed of content matching becomes a critical problem.

Currently, network content filtering systems mainly deal with packet reassembly, application recovery, content pattern matching, alarm and event log. Among all, content pattern matching consumes most of the computing resources. The process of pattern matching is as follows: given $P = \{p_0, p_1 \cdots p_k\}$ as a set of patterns, which are the character strings from fixed alphabet $\sum$; given $T = t_1, t_2, \cdots t_N$ as a very large text, whose characters are also from $\sum$, then, the purpose of pattern matching is to find out every p_i in T, where $p_i = t_{k0} t_{k0+1} \cdots t_{k1} (0 \le k0, k1 \le N)$.

Some characteristics of the network content filtering system are listed here:

- The matching speed should be above Gbps.
- The payload of every packet should be matched and there are thousands or more rules, whose length are various.
- Frequently updating of the rules is unnecessary. Adding or deleting single rule can be completed within several seconds.

Since content pattern matching is computing intensive, lots of researches concentrate on how to accelerate the pattern matching. In 1975, Aho [1] proposed the AC Algorithm, which maps the multi-pattern matching process to the state transfer on the state machine. Based on it, many optimized algorithms have been proposed, such as C.J. Coit's AC_BM [3] algorithms and M. Fish's Boyer-Moore-Horspool [4] algorithm. Software based improving algorithms were proposed in [8-9]. In recent years, content filtering turns to use customized hardware to accelerate the pattern matching. TCAM (Ternary Content Addressable Memory) is a component providing tri-state cells of fixed length. Every item (of the TCAM?) contains a bit string and each bit in the string can be 0, 1, or x (do not care). According to the content being searched, TCAM compares this string against all cells of it parallelly, and reports the matched entry. TCAM have the characteristics of deterministic searching time and deterministic capacity, which make it quite suitable for packet classifying applications. Currently TCAM supports more than 100M times searching in parallel over 288 Bit, or even wider ranges. We can store more than 128K matched patterns in one TCAM.

Fang Yu [6] proposed a method which could store long-pattern segments into TCAM and approach Gigabit matching speed. However, this system needs to maintain a Match Table (MT) and its RAM requirement is too much for a network device. Based on the DIRPE method, Karthik Lakshminarayanan [7] proposed a fence code, which was used to solve the multi-matching problem of fixed area (e.g. five-meta item), and there are different characteristics between content rules and fixed field rules .

The architecture and method proposed in this paper are applicable to IDS or Content Filtering Systems. In this architecture, the software compiles rules and downloads them to the hardware, while the hardware completes the packet stream recovery and pattern match. This paper mainly discusses the following contents:

- A Conjoint Network Content Filtering System (CNCFS) is proposed and implemented.
- Based on CNCFS, a long-pattern hardware matching method using TCAM is proposed and actualized.

- By using little resources, a TCAM multi-matching scheme is implemented which can provide more than 5 Gbps wire speed processing ability.

2   Proposed Approach

In CNCFS model, hardware component (Line Card) does packet reception, packet stream recovery, pattern match and event alarm; software component (Control Card) does rule compiling, loads compiled rule image to hardware, interfaces to Administrator and so on, as illustrated in Figure 1. After packets enter the system from the interfaces, they are recovered to streams before being sent to Matching Engine for pattern matching. During the matching, some event results are sent to software for log records, alarming or composite rule processing on higher levels.

Packet reassembly and flow recovery are very critical in the system. In some special applications, e.g. BBS (telnet), every packet only transmits a byte, while the combination of many bytes in different packets may form illegal information. During packet transmission through the network links, large IP packets may be fragmented due to the various MTUs of different links. To escape detection, illegal information promulgators often divide the large data into many small packets and transmit them into the network. Thus, the fingerprints are spread into several packets, which make the detecting of those illegal information very difficult for the Matching Engine. The stream recovery module takes the responsibility of preprocessing packets, combining the data from the same flow to form one message. The stream recovery module reassembles the inactive flows in every $\triangle t$ period, or buffer those data in a certain memory space (Memcap) and reassemble them later. Here, the Memcap and $\triangle t$ should be selected carefully.

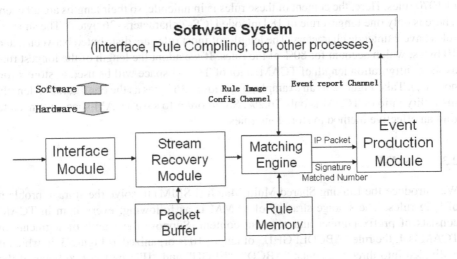

Fig. 1. CNCFS Architecture

The following of this paper mainly expatiates on the matching methods of multi-pattern multi-matching using TCAM.

2.1   TCAM

TCAM is widely used on IP head rules matching, e.g. the longest prefix matching in routing search. Due to its intrinsic ability of parallel searching, it is also used in other high-speed pattern matching cases.

In the field of hardware packets classification, TCAM is one of the most popular methods. Besides 0 and 1, TCAM can store "do not care (x)" state and compare the input keywords with its items in parallel. Given the number of different rules is M, the memory space TCAM requires is only O(M). For a packet of length N, W bytes of the packet are matched in TCAM each time, where W is the width of the TCAM, then shift one byte and check the TCAM again. The search speed TCAM can attain is O(N). Besides its advantages, TCAM also has the shortcomings of low density and high power consumption, so it should be used efficiently.

TCAM is based on first-match, which just exports the lowest index among all matches of the input string if there are two or more matches. However, content filtering system and IDS are based on multi-match, which means that a packet may match multiple keywords. If TCAM is used for multi-matching of content patterns, we should first solve the long rules (rules that exceed the width of TCAM) and the rules storage sequence problems.

2.2   Rule Length

Content Security System often needs to add or delete some rules, but the proportion of various lengths in the rule set is relatively stable. Figure 2 shows the length distribution of 1070 rules. Here, the content of these rules is in unicode, so their lengths are all even. There is only one longest rule of 18 Unicode UCS-2 characters (36 bytes). The shortest rules have 2 unicode characters. The lengths of most rules are distributed between 6 and 10 bytes, which account for 80% of the rules. If we adopt the length of the longest rule as the configuration length of TCAM, a lot of TCAM space will be used to store x (do not care). Take Figure 2 as an example, if we adopt 36 bytes as the configuration length, the utility ratio of TCAM is only 26.2%. So, in order to save TCAM space, we need to find an effective method to store long rules.

2.3   LSMM

We introduce the Linking Shared Multi-Match (LSMM) to solve the storage problem of long rules. The storage strategy of LSMM is as following: every item in TCAM consists of prefix number and segment content. Suppose the length of segments in TCAM is 4, the rule "ABCDEFGHIJ" of length 10 is organized as Figure 3, in which it is divided into three segments: "ABCD", "EFGH" and "IJ", the last two bytes of the last segment are filled by "**" (denoting 16 "do not care" bits). In Figure 3, the leftmost column is the index of TCAM, identified by the addresses. Column 2 stores the address pointer of the preceding segment. Column 3 stores the segment patterns. Column 2 and 3 are stored in TCAM. Column 4 contains matching results which are stored in SRAM.

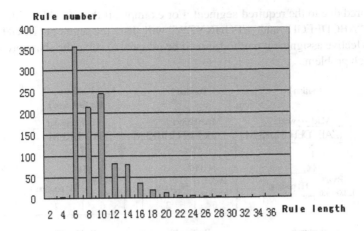

Fig. 2. Rule Length Distribution

Index	B6...B	B3...B	Matched
0	1	IJ**	R$_i$
1	2	EFGH	
2	-1	ABCD	

Fig. 3. Rule Storage Example

If there are n items stored in TCAM, then it is necessary to increase $\log_2 n$ bits for every item to store the addresses of preceding segments (the preceding field). Each time before matching, we add the preceding field in the front of the matched content, then send it to TCAM to do the next comparison. When there is a hit in the preceding segment, we record it in memory. We call the data structure a partial hit list, which records both the position and the index of the hit packets.

Suppose the payload of an input packet is "ZABCDEFGHIJKLMN" and we want to perform content matching using the rules in Figure 3. First, we should add the preceding field "-1" (it is the preceding field value of the first segment). Second, use "-1ZABCDEFGHIJKLMN" to match. If there is no hit, shift one byte so that the string to be matched becomes "-1ABCDEFGHIJKLMN". If there is a hit on the second segment, the partial hit list records this hit. The desired next-hit position of the packet is recorded on the first field, and the current TCAM position of this hit is recorded on the second field. Then, we continue to shift and match "-1BCDEFGHIJKLMN". When reaching the position of the sixth byte, we use "-1EFGHIJKLMN" to match firstly. There is not hit, so we take out address 2 from PHL to constitute "2EFGHIJKLMN", then there is a hit. According to the process, the last match is 0 segment and the matching rule is Ri (Figure 3 and Figure 4).

If the length all the rules are shorter than or equal the TCAM width, they are stored in TCAM according to their lengths in descending order to implement multi-match. If the length of some rules is greater than the TCAM width, then these rules cannot be simply stored due to the required segment. For example, if the TCAM width is 4, then two rules "ABCDEFGH" and "EFGHXYZW" will share the segment "EFGH". In this case, an effective assignment method should be adopted to solve the share problem and multi-match problem.

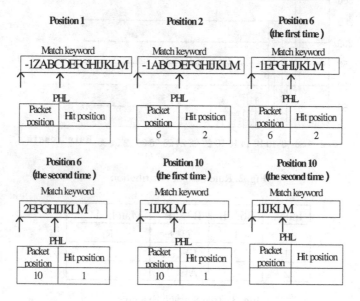

Fig. 4. Long pattern match process example

2.4   Well-Ordered TCAM Rule Assignment

The aim of the Well-ordered TCAM Rule Assignment is that, after the rule assignment of a rule set which consists of various rule lengths is stored in TCAM, there shoud be no match missing for any packet and any rule set.

First, if the rules are within the TCAM width, for two rules R_i and R_j, the matching list are M_i and M_j, the storage position of TCAM are P_i and P_j, and TCAM width for storing content is W, the number of items in TCAM is H. Here are four cases:

(1) If $R_i \cap R_j = \varphi$, the sequence of R_i and R_j is not important for their position.

(2) If $R_i \subseteq R_j$, then $P_j < P_i$, and $M_j \supseteq M_i$.

(3) If $R_j \subset R_i$, then $P_i < P_j$, and $M_i \supseteq M_j$.

(4) If $R_i \cap R_j \neq \varphi$ and never meets the 2nd and 3rd conditions, then the sequence of R_i and R_j is not important for their position.

Definition 1: for the general rule $R = \langle Seg_1, Seg_2, \cdots Seg_n \rangle$, R is an ordered set, $|Seg_i| = W, 1 \leq i \leq n-1$; $|Seg_n| \leq W$, $|R| = \sum_{i=1}^{n} |Seg_i|$, S(R) = n.

Definition 2: for the connection operation "+", $R_i = \langle Seg_{i,1}, Seg_{i,2}, \cdots Seg_{i,n} \rangle$,
$R_j = \langle Seg_{j,1}, Seg_{j,2}, \cdots Seg_{j,m} \rangle$, $R_i + R_j = \langle Seg_{i,1}, \cdots, Seg_{i,n}, Seg_{j,1}, \cdots Seg_{j,m} \rangle$.

Definition 3: given two rules $R_k, R_j \in \Sigma^*$, if there is a max length R_i, that $R_i + R_k = R_j$, then we call R_i is the prefix of R_j, recorded as $R_i \prec R_j$.

Definition 4: given two rules $R_k, R_j \in \Sigma^*$, if there is a max length R_i, that $R_i + R_k = R_j$, $|R_i| = MW$, then we call R_i is the ordered prefix of R_j, recorded as $R_i \prec_o R_j$.

Definition 5: If there are R_i, R_j and max-length R_s, and $R_s \prec_o R_j$, $R_s \prec_o R_i$, then R_i and R_j share prefix R_s. We call R_i and R_j sharing max ordered prefix R_s, recorded as MOP$(R_i, R_j) = R_s$.

There are several relationships between two different rules R_i and R_j:

(1) $R_i \prec_o R_j$, R_j contains R_i and S(R_i)=MW.

(2) $R_j \prec_o R_i$, R_i contains R_j and S(R_j)=MW.

(3) MOP$(R_i, R_j) = R_s$, R_i and R_j share the max-prefix R_s.

(4) R_i and R_j do not contain each other or do not share the max ordered prefix.

When there are rules which contain others, a string matching the "parent rule" should match the "child rule". In order to ensure the TCAM be well-ordered, the "child rule" must be stored after its "parent rule". If there is a max ordered prefix shared between different rules, then we just store the max-prefix R_s once.

2.5   Algorithm

The algorithm converts the rule set ($RuleSet = \{R_1, R_2, \cdots R_k\}$) to a well-ordered TCAM extended rule set E, and loads the rule into TCAM. Insert (R_i, E) is a process which inserts R_i into E, scans all the rules of E, evaluates the relation between R_i and every rule in E, and then makes some disposition. The algorithm is described as follows:

```
CompileRule{
    E = φ ;
    for all the rule  Ri  in RuleSet
        E=Insert( Ri , E);
    Convert PrePoint to Address of Segment and write E into TCAM;
}
Insert( Ri , E){
    int   MinPosition = 0;
    int   MaxPosition =H-1;
    int BeginStore=1;
    for all the  Rj  in E{
        if  Ri ≺o Rj :
            M j,s(Rj) = M j,s(Rj) ∪ Ri ;
            return;
```

```
    if  R_j ≺_o R_i :
      M_{i,S(R_j)} = M_{i,S(R_j)} ∪ R_j ;
      Delete( R_j );
      if  MOP( R_i , R_j )= R_s , R_s ≠ R_i , R_s ≠ R_j
      BeginStore=|R_s|/W +1
      continue;
  }
  for all the  R_j  in E{
    if( R_j ⊂ R_i )    MaxPosition = Position of  Seg_{j,S(R_j)} + 1;
    if( R_i ⊂ R_j )    MinPosition = Position of  Seg_{j,1} - 1;
  }
  if BeginStore<=n
    Insert  Seg_{i,n} … Seg_{i,BeginStore} in any place from MinPosition to MaxPosition;
}
```

Now we explain the algorithm through an example. Supposing we have five rules, which are R_1 = "ABCDEFGHIJKLM", R_2 = "ABCDEFGH", R_3 = "ABCDWXYZ", R_4 = "AB", and R_5 = "EFGH". If the TCAM width is 4, then the storage of these rules is demonstrated in Figure 5.

0	4	WXYZ	R_3
1	2	M***	R_1
2	3	IJKL	
3	4	EFGH	R_2 , R_5
4	-1	ABCD	R_4
5	-1	AB**	R_4
6	-1	EFGH	R_5

Fig. 5. Example of rule assignment

Following is a list of the packet matching algorithm:

```
Match(Packet){
  for CurPositsition from 1 to packetlength{
    for all item in PHL{
      if item.PackPosition=CurPosition
      PHLPop();
      MatchingCont=item.PackPosition+*Packet[CurPosition];
      if(index=MatchTCAM() is valid){
        output(SRAM[index]);
        if(not TCAM[index].LastSeg) PHLPush(CurPostion, index);
      }
```

```
        }
   MatchingCont="-1"+*Packet[CurPosition];
   index=MatchTCAM();
   if(index is valid){
      output(SRAM[index]);
      if(not TCAM[index].LastSeg) Pop(CurPostion, index);
   }
}
```

An example using the algorithm is given in Section 2.3.

3   Analysis and Implementation

3.1   Implementation

The deployment of our system is plotted in Figure1. The control board uses Intel Pentium M 1.6G CPU with 512M memory. The OS is RedHat Linux 9.0. The TCAM of the line card uses Cypress CYN70256. There are two OC48 ports on the line card. One Compact PCI bus is used to connect line card and control board as Control Channel and Event Transfer Channel. We use two Matching Engines to process in parallel.

Packets enter the system through AMCC S4803, and then are sent to the Stream Recovery Module for packet assembling. The stream recovery process adopts the idea of [10]. After that, packets go to the Matching Engine for content matching. If there are some hits, then software will deal with higher-level matching using more complicated rules, such as probability, accumulation, and group, etc.

Section 3.2 indicates that, given a rule set, there is a minimum limit for the capacity of the TCAM. Because there is a determinate configuration limit on the length of TCAM, we should compromise between the configurable TCAM width and the performance requirement [11].

When the length of a content rule is longer than 1 byte, it is necessary to match TCAM many times. Multiple matching is implemented though shifting bytes as following. If the packet length is M bytes, we should shift M-1 times in all. Before each shift, there is a match process for the items of TCAM. We can use S-Double technology to accelerate the shifting step. We shift one byte rightward for each segment of all rules, and then restore it. In order to speed up the matching, every segment is stored twice in the TCAM. After each TCAM matching, we can shift the content rightward two bytes before starting new matching. Thus, by trading space for time, we accelerate the speed of TCAM matching [12-13].

When we use the S-Double technology, our system can automatically decide whether to adopt S-Double or not, according to the number of rules. If the storage space used by the rules decreases to half of the TCAM space, the system adopts this technology. On the contrary, if the space increases to half of the TCAM space, S-Double will be shut down and the duplicated stored rules will be deleted. In order to avoid fluctuation during the process of adding or deleting rules, after many simulations, we select 2 proper threshold-values: waterline_nosd and waterline_sd. When the number of the whole segment falls to waterline_sd, we adopt the S-Double technology; when it grows up to waterline_nosd, we cancel it. This technology can effectively avoid fluctuation during the process of adding or deleting rules and achieve the optimal speed according to different states of the system.

Furthermore, the S-Double technology could be used repetitively. We can store rules 3 times of the original rules number and shift 3 bytes after each match, or store rules 4 times of the original rules number and shift 4 bytes every match, etc.

3.2   Memory Space Analysis

In a rule set of n rules, the length of every rule is L_i, $0 \leq i \leq N-1$, the segment number of the rules is SegNum, SegNum= $\sum_{i=0}^{N-1} (L_i + W - 1)/W$, the TCAM bits required to be extended for every segment are $W_{ext} = \lceil Log_2 (SegNum) \rceil$, and the total TCAM space is $(W_{cont} + W_{ext}) * SegNum$. As mentioned in section 2.2, the parameter W is configurable and smaller W means higher utility ratio of the system. The smaller W is, the larger the segment number will be, the more bits SegNum should be extend. The larger W is, the smaller the segment number will be and fewer bits SegNum should be extend.

Regarding to the rule lengths in Figure 2, we compute corresponding TCAM space size needed. We get the relationship between different segment length and different TCAM space sizes, as shown in Figure 6. Using LSMM, for all those rule lengths, averagely 6% accessional TCAM space is added to solve the long rule problem.

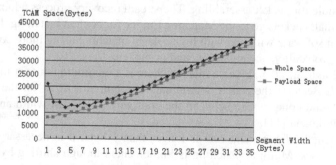

Fig. 6. Relationship between Segment Length and TCAM space size

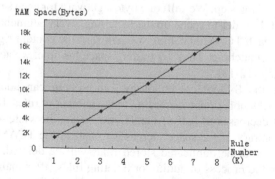

Fig. 7. Relationship between rule number and RAM Space of LSMM

The RAM space size of LSMM can be depicted by the following expression: $\lceil Log_2(N) \rceil * SegNum \sum ((|R_i|+1)/W)$. When the distribution of rule length is steady, the size of the RAM space is almost linear with the rule number. Generally speaking, TCAM width is 36, 72, 144 and 288 bits [2], etc. The frequency of TCAM is low if its width is too small or too large. In our system, we consider the typical case (72 bits width, 8 bytes segment width). Figure 7 shows the changing of the space size along with different rule numbers.

3.3   Performance Analysis

After accessing TCAM, if there is a hit, then accessing SRAM is necessary and the access process can be streamlined. The system performance is limited by the access time of TCAM or SRAM. Because at some positions of some packets, if the PHL is not empty and the desired next-hit position of some items equal the current position, we need to access TCAM many times. Since the packet streamlining is limited, so FIFO is needed to smooth the burst.

Considering random packet contents, for any w bytes in the packet, there are 2^{8w} possible values, so the chance of matching one particular pattern is $1/2^{8w}$. There are $\sum_i S(R_i)$ segments (TCAM items) to be matched. So counting in the address pointer of the preceding segment, the hit probability of one pattern is $\sum S(R_i)/2^{8w+\lceil \log 2 \sum S(R_i) \rceil}$, which decreases dramatically when w increases. For instance, supposing we have 1000 rules (each rule is 64bytes) and the segment width is 8 bytes (which is the typical width with best TCAM performance), the hit rate should be 5.29e-20. The average PHL size is too difficult to compute, theoretically speaking it should be less than $w * \sum S(R_i)/2^{8w+\lceil \log 2 \sum S(R_i) \rceil}$. Since the hit of last segments of all rules do not increase the PHL size, so the average PHL size should be less than 5.29e-20.

The size of the FIFO packet queue is determined by the maximum PHL, while not the average PHL. Through capturing packets on an OC48 interface for 60 seconds (the real-time throughput was about 1.8Gbps, all packets whose sizes were less than 62 bytes were ignored, because they did not match our rules. The total memory space of the packets in the 60 seconds time was about 14.4G Bytes. Using the rules mentioned in section 2.2, registers in Matching Engine showed that 9 rules were matched. The max size of PHL was 3, because the rules we used contained segment inclusive relationships as described in section 2.4. If we modify the rules, the max PHL would be even less.

Table 1 lists the work process during the matching process using LSMM.

LSMM does not induce obvious additional time cost and FPGA logics is comparable to the pure TCAM matching. The addition of preceding field before matching is parallel to the TCAM searching process. If PHL is too long, system may be bottlenecked. In our case, the operating frequency of TCAM is 100MHz and the width of TCAM is 72 bits. For Cypress CYN70256 [2], two time cycles are needed to complete one match. In the real network testing, without using the S-Double technology, CNCFS can obtain throughput about 800Mbps (we had two matching engines work simultaneously, each one achieves 400Mbps throughput), However, after using S-Double 8 times, the throughput of CNCFS can be improved to 6.4 Gbps.

Table 1. Match Process

		LSMM
Before match-ing		Clear out-of-date items of Partial Hitting List, add the preceding field of matched content
Matching process		Send the keywords to be matched into TCAM, two processes is the same.
After matching	Hit	Get hit index and write Partial Hit List Shift bytes
	No Hit	Shift bytes.

We also test our system using the SPRIENT AX4000, with the following setting of traffic flows to simulate real network traffic:

64 bytes   50% of whole traffic

128 bytes   5% of whole traffic

256 bytes   5% of whole traffic

512 bytes   10% of whole traffic

1024 bytes   10% of whole traffic

1600 bytes   10% of whole traffic

2 OC48 ports of the AX4000 were connected to our system. The throughput ratio is set as 100%, which means the whole traffic is about 5Gbps. In this test, our system detects all packets correctly without any loss. In fact, because the packets headers do not enter the matching engine, the actual payload traffic was less than 5Gbps.

Each time the LSMM updates a rule (delete or add), it needs to reorganize the entries of TCAM. We utilize a batching process to load more than 1070 rules. This process takes about 2 seconds for the loading of rules and less than 1.5 seconds for the writing of TCAM, which is acceptable for real applications.

4   Conclusions

In this paper, a novel content filtering architecture (CNCFS) using LSMM in TCAM is proposed to meet the requirements of the high performance processing for the rapid increasing network bandwidth. Our NCFS implementation combines the software and hardware to complete the process of content filtering. The performance evaluation shows that our system can improve the network throughput up to 5Gbps.

This paper mainly addresses the following three issues:

- A new network content filtering system framework is proposed and implemented.
- The content rule matching is implemented using TCAM, which solves the problem of long rules storage.
- Without changing the structure of TCAM, a new solution is proposed to solve the multi-matching problem by using fewer storage resources, which can improve the matching speed up to 5 Gbps.

Acknowledgment. The work described in this paper is partially supported by the project of National Science Foundation of China under grant No. 61202488, 61272482; the National High Technology Research and Development Program of China (863 Program) No. 2012AA01A506, 2013AA013505. This research was also in part supported by Basic Science Research Program through the National Research Foundation of Korea(NRF) funded by the Ministry of Science, ICT & Future Planning(2014R1A1A1005915).

References

1. Aho, A.V., Corasick, M.J.: Efficient string matching: An aid to bibliographic search. Communications of ACM 18(6), 333–334 (1975)
2. Cypress Semiconductor Corp. Content addressable memory, http://www.cypress.com/
3. Coit, C.J., Staniford, S., McAlerney, J.: Towards Faster String Matching for Intrusion Detection or Exceeding the Speed of Snort. In: DARPA Information Survivability Conference and Exposition (DISCEX II 2001) (2001)
4. Fish, M., Varghese, G.: Fast Content-Based Packet Handling for Intrusion Detection. UCSD technical report CS2001-0670 (2001)
5. Antonatos, S., Anagnostakis, K.G., Markatos, E.P.: Generating realistic workloads for network intrusion detection systems. In: Proc. of the 2004 ACM Workshop on Software and Performance (2004)
6. Yu, F., Katz, R.H., Lakshman, T.V.: Gigabit Rate Packet Pattern-Matching Using TCAM. In: Proc. of the 12th IEEE International Conference on Network Protocols, ICNP 2004 (2004)
7. Lakshminarayanan, K., Rangarajan, A., Venkatachary, S.: Algorithms for Advanced Packet Classification with Ternary CAMs. In: SIGCOMM 2005, August 21-26 (2005)
8. Peng, G., Deyun, Z., Qindong, S., Yahui, Z., Wuchun, L.: Multi-Pattern Approximate Matching Algorithm of Network Information Audit System. Journal of Software 15(7), 1074–1080 (2004)
9. Hua, S., Yiqi, D.: A New Fast String Matching Algorithm for Content Filtering and Detection. Computer research and Development 41(6), 940–945 (2004)
10. Zhou, M.-Z., Gong, J., Ding, W.: Study of network flow timeout strategy. Journal on Communications 26(4), 88–93 (2005)
11. Caviglione, L., Merlo, A., Migliardi, M.: Green-Aware Security: Towards a new Research Field. The International Journal of Information Assurance and Security (JIAS) 7(2), 338–346 (2012)
12. Migliardi, M., Merlo, A.: Energy Consumption Simulation of Different Distributed Intrusion Detection Approaches. In: Proc. of the 27th IEEE International Conference on Advanced Information Networking and Applications (AINA 2013), Barcelona, Spain (March 2013)
13. Migliardi, M., Merlo, A.: Improving Energy Efficiency in Distributed Intrusion Detection Systems. Journal of High Speed Networks 19(3), 251–264 (2013)
14. Kim, B., Yang, J., You, I.: A survey of NETLMM in all-IP-based wireless networks. In: Proc. of ACM Mobility 2008, Lan, Taiwan (September 2008)
15. You, I., Lee, J.-H., Sakurai, K.: DSSH: Digital signature based secure handover for network-based mobility management. Computer Systems: Science & Engineering 27(3) (2012)

Feature Grouping for Intrusion Detection System Based on Hierarchical Clustering

Jingping Song[1,2], Zhiliang Zhu[1], and Chris Price[2]

[1] Software College of Northeastern University, Shenyang, Liaoning, China, 110819
{songjp,zhuzl}@swc.neu.edu.cn
[2] Department of Computer Science, Aberystwyth University, United Kingdom, SY23 3DB
{jis17,cjp}@aber.ac.uk

Abstract. Intrusion detection is very important to solve an increasing number of security threats. With new types of attack appearing continually, traditional approaches for detecting hazardous contents are facing a severe challenge. In this work, a new feature grouping method is proposed to select features for intrusion detection. The method is based on agglomerative hierarchical clustering method and is tested against KDD CUP 99 dataset. Agglomerative hierarchical clustering method is used to construct a hierarchical tree and it is combined with mutual information theory. Groups are created from the hierarchical tree by a given number. The largest mutual information between each feature and a class label within a certain group is then selected. The performance evaluation results show that better classification performance can be attained from such selected features.

Keywords: Intrusion detection, Mutual information, Feature grouping, Hierarchical clustering.

1 Introduction

Network intrusion detection system is a tool for network operators to detect hazardous traffic and alert their existence in the networks [1]. Most intrusion detection systems adopt signature based methods to detect intrusion attacks [2]. A signature is a rule set that contains information regarding target patterns from exciting hazardous packet actions against the target patterns. A network intrusion detection system can obtain valuable information from ongoing or local traffic as well. An intrusion detection system is not a standalone system, but works with other systems as a firewall [3]. There are two types of intrusion detection methods, misuse detection and anomaly detection. Misuse detection specifically detects known attacks by using pattern matching approaches, which is the common drawback of this kind of detection method. On the other hand, anomaly detection builds profiles of normal behaviors by detecting attacks first, and then identifies potential attacks when their behaviors are obviously deviated from normal profiles [4].

Anomaly intrusion detection is a classification task, and it consists of building a predictive model which can identify attack instances [5]. Intrusion detection can be

S. Teufel et al. (Eds.): CD-ARES 2014, LNCS 8708, pp. 270–280, 2014.

considered as a two class problem or a multiple class problem. A two class problem regards all attack types as anomaly patterns and the other class is a normal pattern [6]. A multiple class problem deals with the classification based on different attacks. Since there are too many features or attributes which may contain false correlation, classification of anomaly intrusion detection systems is complex work [7]. Moreover, many features may be irrelevant or redundant. For this reason, feature selection methods can be used to get rid of the irrelevant and redundant features without decreasing performance.

Feature selection based on mutual information was initially reported in [8] and subsequently modified in [9] and [10]. The present paper has implemented a feature selection method by grouping features based on the use of mutual information combined with a hierarchical clustering method. The selected features are then employed in the C4.5 classification method for intrusion detection [11]. The performance of the proposed approach is evaluated with respect to different numbers of features and compared with other work in applied feature selection for intrusion detection systems in [9]. [12] and [13] as well. [14] proposed an algorithm to use SVM and simulated annealing to find the best selected features to improve the accuracy of anomaly intrusion detection. [15] reported mutual information-based feature selection method results in detecting intrusions with higher accuracy.

2   Related Works

2.1   Hierarchical Clustering

Hierarchical clustering is a clustering method to build a hierarchy of clusters. There are two types of strategies for hierarchical clustering, agglomerative and divisive [16]. Agglomerative is a bottom-up approach where initially every data item constitutes its own cluster, and pairs of clusters are merged as one moves up the hierarchy. Divisive is a top-down approach and all data is part of the initial cluster and splits are performed recursively as one moves down the hierarchy [17].

In order to decide which clusters should be combined or split, a measure of dissimilarity between sets of observations is required [18]. In most methods of hierarchical clustering, this is achieved by use of an appropriate metric and a linkage criterion [19]. In this paper, an agglomerative hierarchical clustering algorithm is used based on linkage rule.

2.2   Mutual Information

Entropy is an important measurement for information in information theory. It is capable of quantifying the uncertainty of random variables and scaling the amount of information shared by them effectively.

Let X be a random variables with discrete values, its entropy is defined as

$$H(X) = - \sum_{x \in X} p(x) \log p(x) \qquad (1)$$

where $H(\cdot)$ is entropy, and $p(x)=\Pr(X=x)$ is the probability density function of X. Note that entropy depends on the probability distribution of the random variable.

Conditional entropy refers to the uncertainty reduction of one variable when the other is known. Assume that variable Y is given, the conditional entropy $H(X|Y)$ of X with respect to Y is

$$H(X|Y) = -\sum_{y \in Y}\sum_{x \in X} p(x,y)\log p(x|y) \qquad (2)$$

where $p(x,y)$ is the joint probability density function and $p(x|y)$ is the posterior probabilities of X given Y. Similarly, the joint entropy $H(X,Y)$ of X and Y is

$$H(X,Y) = H(X) + H(Y|X) = H(Y) + H(X|Y) = -\sum_{y \in Y}\sum_{x \in X} p(x,y)\log p(x,y) \qquad (3)$$

To quantify how much information is shared by two variables X and Y, a concept termed mutual information $I(X;Y)$ is defined as

$$I(X;Y) = H(X) - H(X|Y) = H(Y) - H(Y|X) = -\sum_{x \in X}\sum_{y \in Y} p(x,y)\log\frac{p(x,y)}{p(x)p(y)} \qquad (4)$$

$I(X;Y)$ will be very high when X and Y are closely related with each other. Otherwise, $I(X;Y)=0$ denotes that these two variables are totally unrelated. In this paper, the mutual information between two variables is calculated.

2.3   C4.5 Algorithm

C4.5 is an algorithm used to generate a decision tree developed by Ross Quinlan and it is an extension of Quinlan's earlier ID3 algorithm. The decision trees generated by C4.5 can be used for classification, and for this reason, C4.5 is often referred to as a statistical classifier.

In this paper, C4.5 will be used to do the classification in section 4. From the classification results we can compare our method with other feature selection methods. C4.5 uses the concept of information gain to make a tree of classificatory decisions with respect to a previously chosen target classification. The information gain can be described as the effective decrease in entropy resulting from making a choice as to which attribute to use and at what level. Compared to other classification algorithms, it is an effective method to deal with a dataset like KDD99 which has new class labels in the test dataset. The reason is C4.5 is a supervised learning method and based on information gain.

3   Implemented Work

In this section, our algorithm based on agglomerative hierarchical clustering is described in detail. The basic idea is grouping the features by agglomerative hierarchical clustering method, and then selecting features from the groups. As we used a clustering method to construct groups, cluster and group have the same meaning in the following formulation.

3.1   Selecting Strategy of Feature Grouping

Feature Grouping is highly beneficial in learning with high dimensional data. It reduces the variance in the estimation and improves the stability of feature selection [20]. Furthermore, it could help in data understanding and interpretation as well. The purpose of feature grouping is creating groups for candidate selecting features and selecting one feature or more features from certain groups to represent the group.

Clustering methods could be used to create groups since they select data in one cluster by specific metrics. Different clustering methods and metrics could compose different cluster constructions. Number of clusters affects how many features will be selected. For example, there are different strategies if we expect to select 8 features from a dataset. We could create 8 groups by a clustering method and select 1 feature in each group. And we could construct 4 groups and select 2 features per group as well. Moreover, we could select different numbers of features in different groups. Where hierarchical clustering method is used to create groups in this work, we chose the selecting 1 feature from each group strategy. This strategy is simple and easy to implement. And another reason is there might be only one feature in one group by using agglomerative hierarchical clustering method.

3.2   Implemented Algorithm

In this section, we will show the algorithm put forward by this paper. The detailed algorithm is shown as follows.

Input: A training dataset $T=D(F,C)$, number of clusters n.
Output: Selected features S.
(1) Initialize parameters: $F \leftarrow$ 'initial set of all features', $C \leftarrow$ 'class labels', $S=\emptyset$.
(2) Calculate the mutual information of every pair of features f_i and f_j in F, denote as $I(f_i; f_j)$.
(3) Create hierarchical cluster tree by using agglomerative hierarchical clustering method base on $I(f_i; f_j)$.
(4) Construct clusters from a hierarchical cluster tree by given n.
(5) For each cluster, calculate mutual information between each feature and class label in C, and then find the maximum value M_c.
(6) Select feature f_s which has the M_c in each group, and put f_s into S, $S \leftarrow$ 'f_s'.

First of all, the algorithm set initialization parameters and F is a set of all the features in the training dataset. And C denotes class labels and C represents class labels. Then, the algorithm calculates the mutual information of every pair of features in F and composes a matrix based on them. After that, it creates a hierarchical cluster tree based on the matrix by using an agglomerative hierarchical clustering method. Moreover, it constructs clusters from a hierarchical cluster tree by given n. And n clusters mean n groups containing candidate features. Furthermore, in each cluster, it calculates mutual information between each feature and class label in C, and then finds the maximum value M_c. Finally, it selects feature f_s which has the M_c in each group, and put f_s into S.

4   Experimental Results

4.1   KDD99 Dataset

KDD99 is the most widely used data set for the evaluation of anomaly detection methods. This data set is built based on 7 weeks of TCP connections in network traffic, and there are about 5 million connection records in the training dataset and around 2 million connection records. Each connection is labeled by either normal or attack. The attack type is divided into four categories of 39 types of attacks [21]. Only 22 types of attacks are in the training dataset and the other 17 unknown types are in the test dataset. It is important to note that the test data is not from the same probability distribution as the training data, and it includes specific attack types not in the training data which makes the task more realistic. The KDD dataset consists of three components, which are detailed in Table 1.

The "10% KDD" dataset is employed for the purpose of training. The KDD training dataset consists of approximately 4,900,000 single connection vectors each of which contains 41 features, with exactly one specific attack type or normal type. This dataset contains 22 attack types and is a more concise version of the "whole KDD" dataset. It contains more connections of attacks than normal connections and the attack types are not represented equally. Denial of service attacks account for the majority of the dataset [22].

Table 1. Basic characteristics of the KDD 99 intrusion detection datasets

Dataset	Normal	DoS	U2R	R2L	Probe
"10%KDD"	97278	391458	52	1126	4107
"Corrected KDD"	60593	229853	70	16347	4166
"Whole KDD"	972780	3883370	52	1126	41102

On the other hand, the "Corrected KDD" dataset (test dataset) provides a dataset with different statistical distributions than either "10% KDD" or "Whole KDD" and contains 14 additional attacks. The list of class labels and their corresponding categories for "10% KDD" are detailed in [23].

4.2   Measures of Performance Evaluation

The implemented method in this paper is conducted by six measures: True Positive Rate (TPR), False Positive Rate (FPR), Precision, Recall, F-Measure. The six measures could be calculated by True Positive (TP), False Positive (FP), True Negative (TN), False Negative (FN), as follows.

True positive rate (TPR): TP/(TP+FN), also known as detection rate (DR) or sensitivity or recall. False positive rate (FPR): FP/(TN+FP) also known as the false alarm rate. Precision (P): TP/(TP+FP) is defined as the proportion of the true positives against all the positive results. Total Accuracy (TA): (TP+TN)/(TP+TN+FP+FN) is the proportion of true results (both true positives and true negatives) in the population.

Recall (R): TP/(TP+FN) is defined as percentage of positive labeled instances that were predicted as positive. F-measure: 2PR/(P+R) is the harmonic mean of precision and recall.

We use the training dataset to construct the decision tree model and then reevaluate on the test dataset and get TP, FP, TN, FN. After that, we calculate precision, total accuracy and F-measure for the test dataset.

4.3   Experiment Evaluation

The experiments were conducted by using KDD 99 dataset and performed on a Windows machine having configuration and Intel (R) Core (TM) i5-2400 CPU@ 3.10GHz, 3.10 GHz, 4GB of RAM, the operating system is Microsoft Windows 7 Professional. We have used an open source machine learning framework Weka 3.5.0. This tool is used to do classification for performance comparison of our method with other feature selection methods. We used C4.5 as the classification algorithm for all the feature selection methods.

Table 2 shows comparison results by different feature selection methods using 13 selected features. The first algorithm C4.5 used 41 features to do the classification. DMIFS is dynamic mutual information feature selection method proposed by Huawen Liu [9]. FGMI is feature grouping based on mutual information method implemented previously by the authors of this paper. This method is construct groups base on mutual information among features. AHC is agglomerative hierarchical clustering algorithm implemented by this paper. We can see from the comparison that AHC algorithm produces better performance on F-measure and achieves good performance on other measures.

Table 2. Comparison results by different algorithms using 13 selected features

Algorithm	TP Rate	FP Rate	Precision	Recall	F-Measure	Class
C4.5 (41)	**0.994**	0.09	0.728	**0.994**	0.841	Normal
	0.91	**0.006**	**0.999**	0.91	0.952	Anomaly
DMIFS	0.993	0.086	0.736	0.993	0.846	Normal
	0.914	0.007	0.998	0.914	0.954	Anomaly
FGMI	**0.994**	0.085	0.739	0.994	0.848	Normal
	0.915	**0.006**	0.998	0.915	0.955	Anomaly
AHC	0.993	**0.077**	**0.757**	0.993	**0.859**	Normal
	0.923	0.007	0.998	**0.923**	**0.959**	Anomaly

Table 3 describes comparison results by different feature selection methods using 10 selected features. C4.5, DMIFS, FGMI and AHC have the meaning as table 2. MMIFS is modified mutual information feature selection method raised by Jingping in 2014 [24]. And we can see from the comparison that AHC could get better performance nearly in all measures.

Table 3. Comparison results by different algorithms using 10 selected features

Algorithm	TP Rate	FP Rate	Precision	Recall	F-Measure	Class
C4.5 (41)	**0.994**	0.09	0.728	**0.994**	0.841	Normal
	0.91	**0.006**	**0.999**	0.91	0.952	Anomaly
DMIFS	0.993	0.086	0.736	0.993	0.846	normal
	0.914	0.007	0.998	0.914	0.954	anomaly
MMIFS	0.99	0.084	0.741	0.99	0.848	normal
	0.916	0.01	0.997	0.916	0.955	anomaly
FGMI	0.994	0.082	0.746	0.994	0.852	Normal
	0.918	0.006	0.998	0.918	0.957	Anomaly
AHC	**0.994**	**0.08**	**0.751**	**0.994**	**0.856**	Normal
	0.92	**0.006**	0.998	**0.92**	0.958	Anomaly

The purpose of comparison in table 2 and table 3 is compare AHC and other algorithms by the same number of selected features. Figure 1 illustrates the precision comparison of AHC by different number of features.

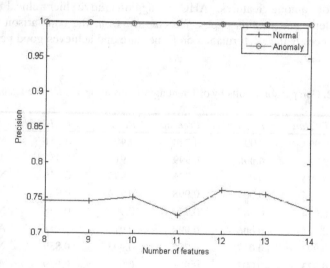

Fig. 1. Precision comparison of AHC by different number of selected features

Figure2 and figure 3 show the F-measure and total accuracy comparison of AHC by different number of features respectively.

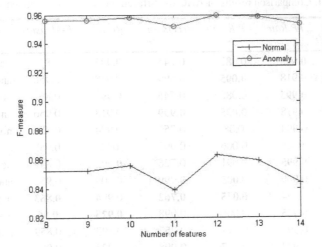

Fig. 2. F-measure comparison of AHC by different number of selected features

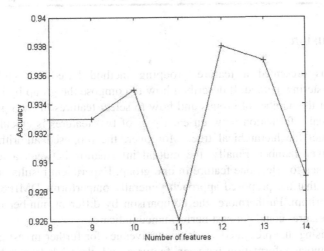

Fig. 3. Total accuracy comparison of AHC by different number of selected features

From the comparison of figure 1 to figure 3, we could see better performance could be achieved when selecting 12 features by AHC. And table 4 shows detailed comparison of AHC by different number of selected features.

We can see from table 4 that AHC algorithm could get best performance by selecting 12 features. And for F-measure, both normal and anomaly could achieve highest value when using 12 selected features.

Table 4. Comparison results of AHC by different number of selected features

NO. of Features	TP Rate	FP Rate	Precision	Recall	F-Measure	Class
8	**0.995**	0.082	0.745	**0.995**	0.852	normal
	0.918	**0.005**	**0.999**	0.918	0.956	anomaly
9	**0.995**	0.082	0.745	**0.995**	0.852	normal
	0.918	**0.005**	**0.999**	0.918	0.956	anomaly
10	0.994	0.08	0.751	0.994	0.856	normal
	0.92	0.006	0.998	0.92	0.958	anomaly
11	**0.995**	0.091	0.726	**0.995**	0.839	normal
	0.909	**0.005**	**0.999**	0.909	0.952	anomaly
12	0.994	**0.075**	**0.762**	0.994	**0.863**	normal
	0.925	0.006	0.998	**0.925**	**0.96**	anomaly
13	0.993	0.077	0.757	0.993	0.859	normal
	0.923	0.007	0.998	0.923	0.959	anomaly
14	0.994	0.087	0.734	0.994	0.844	normal
	0.913	0.006	0.998	0.913	0.954	anomaly

5   Conclusion

This paper has presented a feature grouping method based on agglomerative hierarchical clustering method. It described how to compose the group by hierarchical tree, how to get the number of groups and how to select features in each group. First of all, the mutual information between each pair of two features is calculated to be used to construct the hierarchical tree. Moreover, the proposed algorithm creates groups by a given number. Finally, the mutual information between a feature and class labels is used to select one feature in one group. Experiment results on KDD 99 dataset indicate that the proposed approach generally outperforms DMIFS, MMIFS, and FGMI algorithm. Furthermore, the comparison by different number of features shows that 12 features could get best performance indicator.

Whilst promising, the presented work opens avenues for further investigation. For instance, the mutual information between features and class labels can be used to design new algorithm. And other clustering or classification algorithms can be applied to compose groups. Moreover, more than one feature could be selected in a certain group. In future work, the proposed algorithm will be tested on other datasets and look for more effective measures or methods than mutual information theory.

References

1. Kim, H.J., Kim, H.-S., Kang, S.: A memory-dfficient bit-split parallel string matching using pattern dividing for intrusion detection systems. IEEE Transactions on Parallel and Distributed Systems 22(11), 1904–1911 (2011)

2. García-Teodoroa, P., Díaz-Verdejoa, J., Maciá-Fernández, G., Vázquez, E.: Anomaly-based network intrusion detection: Techniques, systems and challenges. Computers & Security 28, 18–28 (2009)
3. Horng, S.-J., Su, M.-Y., Chen, Y.-H., Kao, T.-W., Chen, R.-J., Lai, J.-L., Perkasa, C.D.: A novel intrusion detection system based on hierarchical clustering and support vector machines. Expert Systems with Applications 38, 306–313 (2011)
4. Bolón-Canedo, V., Sánchez-Maroño, N., Alonso-Betanzos, A.: Feature selection and classification in multiple class datasets: An application to KDD Cup 99 dataset. Expert Systems with Applications 38, 5947–5957 (2011)
5. Sobh, T.S.: Anomaly Detection Based on Hybrid Artificial Immune Principles. Information Management & Computer Security 21(14), 1–25 (2013)
6. Mehdi, M., Zair, S., Anou, A., Bensebti, M.: A Bayesian Networks in Intrusion Detection Systems. Journal of Computer Science 3(5), 259–265 (2007)
7. Shan, S., Karthik, V.: An approach for automatic selection of relevance features in intrusion detection systems. In: Proc. of the 2011 International Conference on Security and Management, pp. 215–219 (2011)
8. Battiti, R.: Using mutual information for selecting features in supervised neural net learning. IEEE Transactions on Neural Networks, 537–550 (1994)
9. Liu, H., Suna, J., Liu, L., Zhang, H.: Feature selection with dynamic mutual information. Pattern Recognition 42, 1330–1339 (2009)
10. Vinh, L.T., Lee, S., Park, Y.-T., d'Auriol, B.J.: A novel feature selection method based on normalized mutual information. International Journal of Artificial Intelligence, Neural Networks, and Complex Problem-Solving Technologies 37(1), 100–120 (2012)
11. Muniyandia, A.P., Rajeswarib, R., Rajaramc, R.: Network Anomaly Detection by Cascading K-Means Clustering and C4.5 Decision Tree algorithm. In: International Conference on Communication Technology and System Design, pp. 174–182 (2012)
12. Chebrolu, S., Abraham, A., Thomas, J.P.: Feature deduction and ensemble design of intrusion detection systems. Journal of Computers & Security 24(4), 295–307 (2005)
13. Mukkamala, S., Sung, A.H.: Feature ranking and selection for intrusion detection systems using support vector machines. In: International Conference on Information and Knowledge Engineering (ICIKE), pp. 503–509 (2002)
14. Lin, S.-W., Ying, K.-C., Lee, C.-Y., Lee, Z.-J.: An intelligent algorithm with feature selection and decision rules applied to anomaly intrusion detection. Applied Soft Computing 12, 3285–3290 (2012)
15. Amiri, F., Yousefi, M.R., Lucas, C., Shakery, A., Yazdani, N.: Mutual information-based feature selection for intrusion detection systems. Journal of Network and Computer Applications 34, 1184–1199 (2011)
16. Oh, S.-J., Kim, J.-Y.: A hierarchical clustering algorithm for categorical sequence data. Information Processing Letters 91, 135–140 (2004)
17. Cilibrasi, R.L., Vitanyi, P.M.B.: A fast quartet tree heuristic for hierarchical clustering. Pattern Recognition 44, 662–677 (2011)
18. Kojadinovic, I.: Agglomerative hierarchical clustering of continuous variables based on mutual information. Computational Statistics & Data Analysis 46, 269–294 (2004)
19. Özdamar, L., Demir, O.: A hierarchical clustering and routing procedure for large scale disaster relief logistics planning. Transportation Research Part E 48, 591–602 (2012)
20. Liu, X., Lang, B., Xu, Y., Cheng, B.: Feature grouping and local soft match for mobile visual search. Pattern Recognition Letters 33, 239–246 (2012)

21. Kayacik, H.G., Zincir-Heywood, A.N., Heywood, M.I.: Selecting features for intrusion detection: A feature relevance analysis on KDD 99 intrusion detection datasets. In: Proceedings of the Third annual Conference on Privacy, Security and Trust (2005)
22. Cho, J., Lee, C., Cho, S., Song, J.H., Lim, J., Moonam, J.: A statistical model for network data analysis: KDD CUP 99' data evaluation and its comparing with MIT Lincoln Laboratory network data. Simulation Modelling Practice and Theory 18, 431–435 (2010)
23. Tavallaee, M., Bagheri, E., Lu, W., Ghorbani, A.A.: A Detailed Analysis of the KDD CUP 99 Data Set. In: Proceedings of the Second IEEE Symposium on Computational Intelligence for Security and Defence Applications (2009)
24. Song, J., Zhu, Z., Scully, P., Price, C.: Modified Mutual Information-based Feature Selection for Intrusion Detection Systems in Decision Tree Learning. Journal of computers 9(7), 1542–1546 (2014)

Towards a Key Consuming Detection in QKD-VoIP Systems

Guohong Zhao, Wanrong Yu, Baokang Zhao, and Chunqing Wu

School of Computer Science, National University of Defense Technology,
Changsha, Hunan, China
{ghzhao,wlyu,bkzhao,wuchunqing}@nudt.edu.cn

Abstract. Quantum Key Distribution (QKD) technology, based on laws of quantum physics, can generate unconditional security keys between two communication parties. QKD is nearly a commercial technology and can make it available to the public. In existing QKD networks and commercial QKD systems, classical network is an essential part of the implementation of QKD protocols. With security keys and encryption scheme (one-time pad), we can protect the security of various network applications. But the public classical channel in QKD network may suffers potential key consuming attacks. In this paper, we focus on how to detect the potential attacks during the security applications in the QKD network. Especially, we propose a Dynamic Key Consuming Detection scheme (DKode) in QKD-VoIP systems which encrypting VoIP streams with security keys from QKD systems.

Keywords: Quantum key distribution, VoIP, detection, security.

1 Introduction

Quantum Key Distribution (QKD) technology, based on laws of quantum physics, rather than the computational complexity of mathematical problems, can generate unconditional security keys between two communication parties [1]. QKD is nearly a commercial technology and can make it available to the public. The world's first QKD network was established by BBN company in 2004 [2]. In 2005, IDQuantique and MagiQ companies have launched second generation products of commercial QKD systems [3, 4]. The European project SECOQC demonstrated the world's first commercial QKD network for about 30 days in 2008 [5].The QKD network with security audio application was established by USTC in 2009 [6]. Nowadays, researchers have focused on improving the performance of QKD systems and integrating QKD technologies into practical security communication systems.

In existing QKD networks and commercial QKD systems, classical network is an essential part of the implementation of QKD protocols. QKD post-processing and security applications are both based on classical communication [7-8]. In the future, for large-scale QKD network, it will be integrated with the existing internet. The public classical channel in QKD network has potential security risks. With security keys and security encryption schemes such as one-time pad, Eve can gain nothing about

S. Teufel et al. (Eds.): CD-ARES 2014, LNCS 8708, pp. 281–285, 2014.

transmitted information. But eve can distinguish the communicating parties by eavesdropping and analyzing network flow data. By dropping or modifying encrypted data, eve may attend to reduce the performance of QKD network. As worst-case scenario, security keys of QKD network will be consumed totally and security messages can't be exchanged between two communication parties.

In this paper, we focus on how to detect the potential attacks during the security applications in the QKD network. Especially, we propose a Dynamic Key Consuming Detection scheme (DKode) in QKD-VoIP systems which encrypting VoIP streams with security keys from QKD systems.

2   Security VoIP Application in QKD Network

2.1   The Framework of QKD-VoIP Systems

QKD network can be logically divided into two layers: quantum layer and classical layer, as it shown in Fig. 1. Quantum signals are transmitted in quantum layer. In classical layer, the communication parties (Alice and Bob) collect quantum information, and conduct post-processing procedures to generate unconditional security keys through security authenticated classical channel.

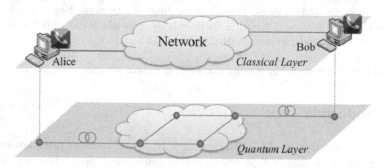

Fig. 1. The QKD network framework

VoIP is unquestionably the most popular real-time service in IP networks today. After Alice and Bob established a VoIP session, their audio stream will be encapsulated into RTP (Real-Time Transport Protocol) packets [9-10]. The framework of QKD-VoIP systems is shown in Fig. 2. During audio stream exchanging between Alice and Bob, QKD-VoIP systems gain the security keys from QKD engines, encrypt/decrypt RTP packets with these keys by one-time pad (OTP) method. Though eavesdropping and analyzing network flow data, eve can gain nothing about transmitted VoIP stream.

2.2   Vulnerability Analysis of QKD-VoIP Systems

Combining security keys generated by QKD network and OTP security encryption method, QKD-VoIP system can provide unconditional security network applications.

Actually, the key generation rate of QKD network is limited. The state of art reported rate is about Mbps [11]. Thus, QKD network can supply only a few network applications. By dropping or modifying encrypted data, eve may attend to reduce the performance of QKD network. As worst-case scenario, security keys of QKD network will be consumed totally and security messages can't be exchanged between two communication parties. Thus, we must detect out the potential key consuming attacks rapidly.

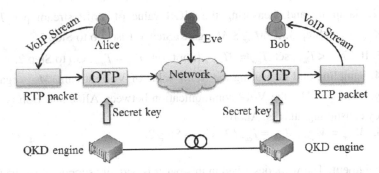

Fig. 2. The Framework of QKD-VoIP Systems

3 Dynamic Key Consuming Detection Scheme in QKD-VoIP Systems

In QKD-VoIP systems, eve can gain nothing by eavesdropping data packets. But eve can modify the transmitted data to consume the security keys generated by QKD systems. When the amount of security keys is not enough to encrypt the VoIP stream, Alice and Bob can't to exchange security messages any more. In this paper, we propose a Dynamic Key Consuming Detection scheme (DKode) in QKD-VoIP systems.

3.1 Detection Principles

In order to provide a numerical indication of perceived quality of received audio stream after transmission and compression, we introduce the Mean Opinion Score (MOS) model defined by ITU-T [12]. The MOS value is expressed from 1 to 5, as it shown in Tab. 1. Values dropping below 3.5 are termed unacceptable by many network users. In order to prevent the audio communication between Alice and Bob, the attacking actions must drop the MOS value of transmitted VoIP stream below 3.5 or even lower [13]. We can use PESQ algorithm which based on MOS model to estimate the stream quality quickly to detect out the potential attacks [14].

Table 1. The MOS Values

MOS	5	4	3	2	1
Quality	Perfect	Fair	Annoying	Very annoying	Impossible to communicate

3.2   The Proposed DKode Scheme

By adjusting the detecting timer dynamically, our proposed Dkode scheme can esti-mate the link state effectively to find the potential key consuming attacks. Dkode includes the following five steps.

Step 1. Initialization. Set up the detecting timer of Dkode $T_{cur} = T_{init}$, the threshold of MOS value $M_t = M_{init}$. Measure the MOS value of initial voice quality M_{ptr}.

Step 2. Sampling and measuring the MOS value of VoIP stream per T_{cur}. If $M_{cur} \geq M_{ptr}$, go to Step 3. If $M_{cur} \leq M_t$, go to Step 4. Else, go to Step 5.

Step 3. If $2T_{cur} < T_{init}$, set $T_{cur} = 2T_{cur}$. If not, set $T_{cur} = T_{init}$. Go to Step 2.

Step 4. Sampling and measuring the MOS value of VoIP stream M_{cur} again im-mediately. If $M_{cur} \leq M_t$, the VoIP communication between Alice and Bob is suffer-ing the key consuming attacks. Abort.

Step 5. $M_{cur} = M_{ptr}$, $T_{cur} = T_{cur} / 2$. Go to Step 2.

Acknowledgment. The work described in this paper is partially supported by the project of National Science Foundation of China under grant No. 61202488, 61272482; the National High Technology Research and Development Program of China (863 Program) No. 2011AA01A103, 2012AA01A506, 2013AA013505.

References

1. Liu, B., Zhao, B.K., Wei, Z.L., Wu, C.Q., Su, J.S., Yu, W.R., Wang, F., Sun, S.H.: Qphone: A Quantum Security VoIP Phone. ACM SIGCOMM Comp. Commun. Rev. 43, 477–478 (2013)
2. Elliott, C., Colvin, A., Pearson, D., Pikalo, O., Schlafer, J., Yeh, H.: Current status of the DARPA quantum network. In: Quantum Information and Computation III, March 29-30, pp. 138–149 (2005)
3. IDQuantique (2014), http://www.idquantique.com/network-encryption/products/network-encryption-overview.html
4. MagiQ (2014), http://www.magiqtech.com/Products.html
5. Peev, M., Poppe, A., Maurhart, O., Lorunser, T., Langer, T., Pacher, C.: The SECOQC quantum key distribution network in Vienna. In: 35th European Conference on Optical Communication, ECOC 2009 (2009)
6. Chen, T.-Y., Liang, H., Liu, Y., Cai, W.-Q., Ju, L., Liu, W.-Y., Wang, J., Yin, H., Chen, K., Chen, Z.-B., Peng, C.-Z., Pan, J.-W.: Field test of a practical secure communication network with decoy-state quantum cryptography. Optics Express 17, 6540–6549 (2009)
7. Liu, B., Liu, B., Zhao, B., Zou, D., Wu, C., Yu, W., You, I.: A real-time privacy amplifica-tion scheme in quantum key distribution. In: Mustofa, K., Neuhold, E.J., Tjoa, A.M., Weippl, E., You, I. (eds.) ICT-EurAsia 2013. LNCS, vol. 7804, pp. 453–458. Springer, Heidelberg (2013)
8. Liu, B., Zhao, B., Liu, B., Wu, C.: A Security Real-time Privacy Amplification Scheme in QKD System. Journal of Universal Computer Science 19, 2420–2436 (2013)

9. Xu, E., Liu, B., Xu, L., Wei, Z., Zhao, B., Su, J.: Adaptive VoIP steganography for information hiding within Network Audio Streams. In: 2011 International Conference on Network-Based Information Systems, NBiS 2011 (September 7, 2011)

10. Wei, Z., Zhao, B., Liu, B., Su, J., Xu, L., Xu, E.: A novel steganography approach for voice over IP. J. Ambient Intell Human Comput., 1–10 (2013)

11. Tanaka, A., Fujiwara, M., Yoshino, K.-I., Takahashi, S., Nambu, Y., Tomita, A., Miki, S., Yamashita, T., Wang, Z., Sasaki, M., Tajima, A.: High-speed quantum key distribution system for 1-mbps real-time key generation. IEEE Journal of Quantum Electronics 48, 542–550 (2012)

12. Wu, Z., Yang, W.: G.711-Based adaptive speech information hiding approach. In: Huang, D.-S., Li, K., Irwin, G.W. (eds.) ICIC 2006. LNCS, vol. 4113, pp. 1139–1144. Springer, Heidelberg (2006)

13. Mean Opinion Score (MOS) - A Measure Of Voice Quality (2014), http://voip.about.com/od/voipbasics/a/MOS.htm

14. Rix, A.W., Beerends, J.G., Hollier, M.P., Hekstra, A.P.: Perceptual evaluation of speech quality (PESQ)-a new method for speech quality assessment of telephone networks and codecs. In: Acoustics, Speech, and Signal Processing, vol. 742, pp. 749–752 (2001)

A Structure P2P Based Web Services Registry with Access and Control

He Qian[1,2], Zhao Baokang[1], Long Yunjian[2], Su Jinshu[1], and Ilsun You[3]

[1] College of Computer, National University of Defense Technology, Changsha 410073, China
[2] Key Laboratory of Cognitive Radio and Information Processing, Ministry of Education,
Guilin University of Electronic Technology, Guilin 541004, China
[3] Korean Bible University, South Korea

Abstract. In the cloud computing, there are massive functions and resources are encapsulated into Web services. The traditional web service registry systems normally using the central architecture can't meet the requirements of cloud computing. A web service registry system based on structured P2P system with secure access and control is implemented. Multiple Universal Description, Discovery and Integration (UDDI) nodes are organized by the P2P based schedule and communication mechanism. The registration and discovery of Web services is redesigned to the new system that provides services like one single UDDI server. The experiment results show that the capacity can be extended dynamically and support large scalable access.

Keywords: Web Service Registry, UDDI, P2P, Pastry, Access and Control.

1 Introduction

The cloud computing is separated into three layers: Infrastructure as a Service (IaasS), Platform as a Service (PaaS) and Software as a Service (SaaS). Service is a main form provided by the cloud, especially in SaaS. The Service Oriented Architecture (SOA) is a new type of mode for software development, deployment and integration, which is behind object-oriented and components based development [1][2]. Flexible design and development program provided for software development is the main way of the cloud computing to provide access to the outside. SOA consists of three roles, including service provider, service registry center and service requestor. The service registry center is the basis for the realization of service composition among the entire SOA. UDDI (Universal Description, Discovery and Integration) is a descriptive specification for information related Web service, and it also includes the standardized specifications of Web services information registry center at the same time [3].

The centralized architecture and complies with the private service registry library of the UDDI specification is normally used in traditional service registration systems [3][4]. In the cloud computation, there are massive functions and resources are encapsulated into Web services. Because of the shortcomings like performance bottlenecks, single-point-of-failure and no easily scalability, which centralized architecture systems have, the traditional service registration systems are almost unable to adapt to

S. Teufel et al. (Eds.): CD-ARES 2014, LNCS 8708, pp. 286–297, 2014.

large-scale service registration and inquiries [5-10]. Architecture for semantic sensor matchmaker was proposed by the authors to make the discovery and integration of web services more efficient. A kind of Web service discovery method called I-Wander which improves efficiency is designed for the unstructured P2P network in literature [9]. However, the service query mechanism of unstructured P2P network is completed by flooding, which has certain blindness and encroaches on a lot of network bandwidth. For the low routing efficiency, poor scalability, load imbalance and other issues which unstructured P2P network have, a service discovery method based on the structured P2P network is proposed, taking advantage of a structured P2P system to use information routing between nodes instead of flooding mechanism. With the development of P2P technology, the P2P networks can provide appropriate exchanging mechanism between the private service registration libraries, avoiding problems like solitary-island service, and it becomes a research tendency to utilize the P2P network's advantages to solve problems like performance bottlenecks of centralized architecture and single-points-of-failure [11]. The introduction of distributed architecture is proposed, using a distributed architecture to reduce the burden of registration centers, improving system efficiency. In response, a service discovery method based on the structured P2P network is proposed, taking advantage of a structured P2P system to use information routing between nodes instead of flooding mechanism. JUDDI is an very famous open source project which realizes UDDI functions [4].

This paper make a scalable architecture to extend JUDDI system, to solve some problems as performance bottlenecks, single-points-of-failure for the cloud computing. Pastry [12], which is a structured P2P protocol, is introduced to organize and coordinate multiple JUDDI. The structure P2P based Web services registration is called PUDDI in the next, and the discovery is redesigned to PUDDI that works like a single JUDDI and can provide a scalable services organization functions for big data analysis. The scalability and performance of PUDDI system is proved and analyzed through the experiments using SoapUI [13] and LoadRunner [14].

The rest of this paper is organized as follows. The framework is proposed in Section 2. The system scheduling and communication algorithm based on Pastry is given in Section 3. The registration and discovery of web service on PUDDI is presented in Section 4. The performance is evaluated in Section 5. Finally, we conclude the paper in Section 6.

2   Framework of P2P Based Service Registration System

The Pastry protocol is introduced to organize multiple UDDI to realize a scalable Web services registration. According to the characteristics of P2P protocols, on the design of system scalability, the number of nodes can be arbitrarily expanded, the system has good scalability and strong expansibility, in other words, the system performance does not decrease with the expansion of nodes and it has a good stability; on the performance of load balancing of the network, each node on the Pastry network only keeps resources managed by itself, network services is distributed substantially and uniformly to each node, and this is conducive to the network load balancing, increasing system throughput, supporting more concurrent users to access; on the reliability of the system, the service request is automatically transferred to the adjacent nodes by Pastry network to avoid a single-point-of-failure when there is a large number of service requests focus on a particular node or a sudden failure of a node. Based on the above advantages, Pastry agreement is introduced to take advantage of the Pastry network to improve the dynamic expandability, load balancing and other properties of the system. The network architecture of Pastry-based Web services registration system is diagrammed in Figure 1. Service requestor can send queries to any UDDI node on PUDDI, the root node is the first node to establish Pastry, based on the Pastry protocol, the routing and communication can be implemented between nodes.

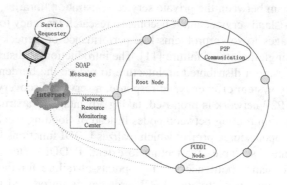

Fig. 1. The network architecture of PUDDI system

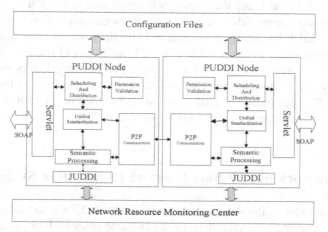

Fig. 2. The function structure of PUDDI

The functional modules of PUDDI system consists of six modules, including configuration, scheduling and distribution, peer to peer communications, access and control, JUDDI and network resource monitoring, the models are shown in Figure 2. To start Pastry, firstly, PastryIdFactory is called to hash the public key to get node ID, if there is no public key, the IP address will be hashed instead. The P2P based scheduling module is mainly used to intercept service request messages, controlling operational processes. The P2P communication module includes sending module and reception module. JUDDI module mainly provides service registration query of nodes. The Access control module realized the Web service authentication, which is the premise of Web service access control and the security call, permission validation module promises the PUDDI system access control and the security call, on the other hand, this module gives safety certification to the users' identity and operation, if the user has not been given relevant rights, the operation will be terminated and an error message returns. If the authentication passed, related operations can be continued.

3   System Scheduling and Communication Algorithm Based on Pastry

System scheduling algorithm and system communication algorithm are the essential algorithm to implement the combination of JUDDIV3 and Pastry. Scheduling algorithm is responsible for distributing tasks, controlling processes and coordinating multiple service requests of UDDI node. System communication algorithm is the key point to implement the exchange of service information between UDDI nodes and it is also the link between the UDDI nodes.

3.1   System Scheduling Algorithms

System scheduling algorithm and system communication algorithm are the essential algorithm to implement the combination of JUDDIV3 and Pastry. Scheduling algorithm is responsible for distributing tasks, controlling processes and coordinating multiple service requests of UDDI node. System communication algorithm is the key point to implement the exchange of service information between UDDI nodes and it is also the link between the UDDI nodes.When the service request messages is sent over the P2P network, the local JUDDI interface is called directly and do corresponding operations of service registry queries. If it is the reply message sent over P2P networks, the message will be returned to the client. If it is the SOAP messages initiated directly by the client, executing purview certification, if the authentication fails, an error message returned to the client. If authenticated, the service will be returned directly if the service in the query buffer, otherwise taking out the information in the message which is named tmodelName, generating a message keyword K by the SHA-1 algorithm, the K is compared with the node ID of UDDI. After that, waiting for the message reply, the reply message will be returned to the client if it is received, if the wait times out, then a times out message is returned, if the wait does not time out, then continue to wait.

   The Pseudo-code of the specific process of the system scheduling algorithm is described as following, in order to a convenient introduction; the following notation is given as the algorithm 1.

Algorithm 1: Pastry based system scheduling.
K : The keyword of the service request message.
NodeId : The ID number of the home node.
1) if isPastrySentMessage then
2)   Invoking JUDDI API ;
3) if isPastryBackMessage then
4)   if timeout then {Putting into register ; }
5)   else {Return to client ; }
else
{
6) if isPassed {
7)   if storedInRegister then
8)   Return storedMessage ;
else
{
9)   StandardWord← getStandardWord(Message.*tModelName*)
10)   K ← SHA-1(Standard*Word*) ;
11) if mostSimilar then
12)   Invoking JUDDI API ;
else
{
13)   Create PastrySentMessage ;
14)   Invoking Pastry API ;
15)   Wait ;
16)   if receivedPastryBackMessage then
17)   Return to client ;
18)   else if timeout then
19)   Return timeoutMessage ;
20)   else Goto (12) ;
}}}
else //the authentication does not pass ;
20)   Return error ;
}

3.2   System Communication Algorithm

The specific process of system communication algorithm is: firstly, the service messages which need to be sent stored into the message buffer, the keyword K of the message is compared and matched to the node ID of UDDI by the Selection manager, (the service messages) will be forwarded to the UDDI node which exists in the UDDI node set which close to the home node, and the condition is, compared to home node, this UDDI node is more closer to the keyword K. If the sending is successful and ACK is received, the next service message will be sent, otherwise there is a retransmit. If the node cannot be found, then the length m of the common prefix which both the ID number of the home node and the keyword of the message have is calculated. If the node ID of UDDI exists in m rows and n columns (i is the value of number m in K) in the routing table, forwarding the service message to the UDDI node, if the node does not exist, the message is forwarded to the node which the length of common prefix is m, and compared to the home node, this node is closer to K.

The Pseudo-code of the specific process of the system communication algorithm is described as following, in order to a convenient introduction, the following notation is given as algorithm 2.

Algorithm 2: Pastry based communication.

K : Keyword of the Pastry message

$NodeId$: The ID number of home node.

R_l^i : The UDDI node exists in l $(0 \leq l < 128/b)$ __rows and i__

$(0 \leq i < 2^b)$ __columns in the routing table.__

L_i : The i-th $(-|L|/2 \leq i \leq |L|/2)$ UDDI node in the UDDI set, L

, which is close to the home node.

K_l : The numerical value in the l-position of the keyword K

of the service request message.

1) Put Message into buffer ;

2) SelectorManager.Match(K) ;

3) if $L_{-|L|/2} \leq K \leq L_{|L|/2}$ then

{

Forward $UDDI_L$, ($UDDI_L \in L \cap \min(|L_i - K|)$) ;

5) if ACK==true then Goto (1) ;

6) else Goto (2) ;

}

else //__forwarding by using of routing table__ ;

{

7) l =prefix($K, nodeId$) ;

8) if $R_l^{K_i} \neq NULL$ then

{

9)   Forward $UDDI_R$, ($UDDI_R$== $R_l^{K_i}$) ;

10)   if ACK==true then Goto (1) ;

11)   else Goto (2) ;

}else //this UDDI node does not exist {

12) Forward $UDDI_R$, ($UDDI_R \in R \cap \min(|R_l^i - K| < |nodeId - K|)$) ;

13)   if ACK==true then Goto (1) ;

14)   else Goto (2) ;

}

}

For example, a message whose key is D617FA is sent to the node whose ID is 74BA2F, according to the system communication algorithms, the forwarding process of the message is shown in Figure 3. After each forwarding message between the nodes, the message is more close to the target node, and finally it will be forwarded to the node which ID is the closest to the K value, and the ID is D615AB.

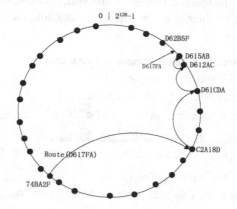

Fig. 3.   Routing process of the system message

4   The Registration and Discovery of Web Service Based on PUDDI

The service provider is responsible for the concrete implementation of the service, and it is also responsible for publishing the service to the registration center. The service requester can find service description in the registration center and obtain binding information, utilizing the binding information to bind to the service provider, and then call the service provided.

The concrete processes that service providers register service to the PUDDI is shown in Fig.4, and described as following.

Step 1: the service providers read the URL(Uniform Resource Locator) of the services' WSDL(Web Services Description Language) file and parse the WSDL file, generating the necessary information when there is service registration (For example, binding information).

Step 2: The related messages of SOAP are generated and the messages will be sent to a known node on the P2P networks through the http requests

Step 3: After the messages of SOAP are received by the node, these messages are transferred from the schedule and distribution module to the access and control module, and operate. According to the results returned by the schedule and distribution module, the purview certification module gives it's judgment, if the purview certification is not passed, an error message is returned, if the purview certification is passed, the next process continues.

Step 4: Analyzing the service-related information, a hash value is obtained through SHA-1 algorithm; According to the hash value, the node judges whether the messages are managed by itself, if so, then jump to the step f, if not, the message of SOAP will be packaged through Pastry protocol and transferred to the P2P communication module, and then the messages will be forwarded to the node which manage the hash value.

Step 5: According to the routing mechanisms of Pastry, the messages will be finally forwarded to the node who manages the services, by P2P communication module. Then the messages will be forwarded to and handled by the schedule and distribution module

Step 6: Calling the registered API of JUDDI, the analyzed information of the WSDL file of service and some related information will be registered to the JUDDI of this node.

Step 7: Returning the registered information of the result to the client.

The process of service registration is shown in Fig.5. The procedure that the service requester query to the PUDDI of the founding service is similar to the procedure of registration and the difference is that the initiated message of request is not the same and no more description here.

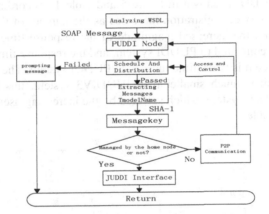

Fig. 4.   Process of service registration

5   Experiments and Analysis

The experiment is tested in the network environment of 100M Ethernet, including 3 physical hosts and 3 virtual machines. The physical hosts are Lenovo foolproof server of R510 (Intel 4-core, 2.80GHz processor, 1G RAM), the 3 virtual machines (single CPU, 1G RAM) are deployed on the Sugon server of W5801-G10 (two Intel 12-core, 2.30GHz processor, 64G memory).The operating systems are centos 6.2 and the software environment includes the Java platform of jdk1.6, database of mysq15.5 and web container of Apache Tomcat6.

The SoapUI is used to test the system function of PUDDI. For the query of Web service, the service requestor firstly queries the WSDL address of the service, and then generates a client based on the WSDL, after that, you can call the service or even combine new service. All the function works like a single JUDDI. The performance of a software system is measured by some common indicators: response time, throughput, the number of concurrent users. The response time is the time which spent on the service which the software system provide for the user, and the response time includes the response time of server, the response time of internet and response time of client. The response time can intuitively reflect the processing capacity of the system, so, according to the response time, we can measure the performance of the JUDDUV3 system and the PUDDI system. Next, The LoadRunner is used to test the service registration performance and the discovery performance of the JUDDI system and the PUDDI system which deploys 6 nodes.

5.1   Web Services Registration

In the experiment, for the original system of JUDDIV3 and the PUDDI of 6 nodes, loadRunner is used to simulate the service registration of multiple users. 5 users is added in every 10 seconds until the concurrent users reaches to 100, and the test has to work for a continuous time. The average response time of the service registration of JUDDIV3 and PUDDI is shown in figure 5 and table 1. According to the chart, the response time of service registration increases as the number of the concurrent users increases, however, the increased magnitude of the response time of JUDDIV3 system is far greater compared to PUDDI system, and the response time of registration of the JUDDIV3 system is twice time more than PUDDI system. The standard deviation of PUDDI system is much smaller than JUDDIV3 system, this illustrates that the impact of the PUDDI system, which suffered by the increasing users, is small, and the system is more stable.

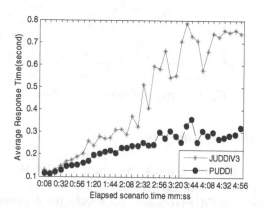

Fig. 5. The contrastive chart of average response time

Table 1. The contrastive table of the response time of registration (second)

Test objects	Average value	Minimum value	Maximal value	Median value	standard deviation
JUDDIV3	0.451	0.12	0.787	0.405	0.23
PUDDI	0.234	0.113	0.36	0.243	0.064

5.2   Web Services Discovery

In this experiment, the service of JUDDIV3 system and PUDDI system is the same, under the circumstance that 2000 different services have been registered, 100 concurrent users are simulated and the query services of each user are random. 5 concurrent users are started in every 10 seconds until the number of the users reaches to 100, and the test has to work for a continuous time. The average response time of the service registration of JUDDIV3 and PUDDI is shown in figure 6 and table 2. According to the result of the experiment, the response time of service discovery increases as the number of the concurrent users increase, however, the time of service discovery of the JUDDIV3 system is twice more than PUDDI system. The standard deviation of PUDDI system is much smaller than JUDDIV3 system, this illustrates that the impact of the PUDDI system, which suffered by the increasing users, is small, and the system is more stable.

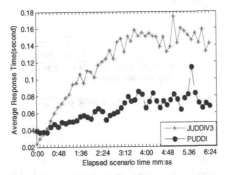

Fig. 6. The contrastive figure of response time of queries

Table 2. The contrastive table of response time of queries (second)

Test objects	Average value	Minimum value	Maximum value	Median value	Standard deviation
JUDDIV3	0.12	0.024	0.174	0.134	0.039
PUDDI	0.064	0.037	0.114	0.066	0.015

The clicks of PUDDI system and JUDDIV3 system while querying the service is shown in Figure 7. In figure 7, X-axis represents the running time; Y-axis represents the clicks per second. The clicks reflect the number of SAOP requests which initiated by the clients, and this reflects the processing ability of the system from the upper side, the more strong the processing ability of the system, the more requests sent from the client will be received. According to the Figure 7, the clicks of PUDDI system is far larger than JUDDIV3 system, and the processing ability of PUDDI system is stronger. The contrastive result of the experimental data is shown in Table 3.

Table 3. The contrastive table of clicks of the systems

Test objects	Average value	Minimum value	Maximum value	Median value	Standard deviation
JUDDIV3	192.251	61.25	246.125	204.125	39.182
PUDDI	286.551	14.375	394.75	305.5	88.68

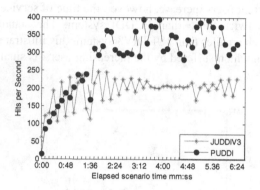

Fig. 7. The contrastive figure of clicks

6   Conclusion

An extendible distributed service registration system is needed for the management of the massive web services. A service registration system based on the structured P2P is designed in this paper. The implemented Pastry based Web service registration system can support magnanimous web services registration if there are enough computers provided and it can adapt to the large-scale registration and access dynamically. PUDDI works like a Web service cloud that provides a scalable services organization capacity for the cloud computation and the big data analysis.

Acknowledgment. This work was partly supported by the National Natural Science Foundation of China (61201250,61163057, 61163058), the Important National Science & Technology Specific Projects (2012ZX03006001) and Guangxi Natural Science Foundation of China (2012GXNSFBA053174).

References

1. Al2Masri, E., Mahmoud, Q.H.: Investigating Web services on the World Wide Web. In: Proc. of the 17th Int Conf. on World Wide Web, pp. 795–780. ACM (2008)
2. Papazoglou, M.P., Traverso, P., Dustdar, S., Leymann, F.: Service-Oriented Computing: A research roadmap. International Journal of Cooperative Information Systems 17, 223–255 (2008)

3. Liu, J.X., Liu, J., Chao, L.: Design and implementation of an extended UDDI registration center for web service graph. In: ICWS 2007: Proceedings of IEEE International Conference on Web Services, pp. 1174–1175. IEEE Press, Salt Lake City (2007)
4. Apache Software Foundation.JUDDI.[EB/OL].[2014-01-17], http://juddi.apache.org/
5. Tamilarasi, K., Ramarkrishnan, M.: Design of an intelligent search engine-based UDDI for web service discovery. In: ICRTIT 2012: Proceedings of International Conference on Recent Trends In Information Technology, pp. 520–525. IEEE Press, Chennai (2012)
6. Yao, Y., Cao, J.X., Liu, B., et al.: Scalable mechanism for semantic web service registry and discovery. Journal of Southeast University (Natural Science Edition) 40(002), 264–269 (2010)
7. Guo, M.Q., Huang, Y., Luo, X.G., et al.: Design and implementation of a distributed web service directory in SOA-oriented urban spatial information sharing platform. In: PACIIA 2009: Proceedings of Asia-Pacific Conference on Computational Intelligence and Industrial Applications, vol. 1, pp. 127–130. IEEE Press, Wuhan (2009)
8. Goodwin, J.C., Russomanno, D.J., Qualls, J.: Survey of Semantic Extensions to UDDI: Implications for Sensor Services, SWWS, pp. 16–22 (2007)
9. Zhang, C.Y., Cao, Y., Liu, D., et al.: I-Wander: A Web Service Discovery Method for Unstructured P2P Network. Transactions of Beijing Institute of Technology 26(6), 521–525 (2008)
10. Sioutas, S., Sakkopoulos, E., Makris, C., et al.: Dynamic Web Service discovery architecture based on a novel peer based overlay network. Journal of Systems and Software 82(5), 809–824 (2009)
11. Steinmetz, R., Wehrle, K.: Peer-Peer-Networking Computing. Informatik Spektrum 27(1), 51–54 (2004)
12. Rowstron, A., Druschel, P.: Pastry: Scalable, decentralized object location, and routing for large-scale peer-to-peer systems. In: Guerraoui, R. (ed.) Middleware 2001. LNCS, vol. 2218, p. 329. Springer, Heidelberg (2001)
13. Luo, Z.M., Zhu, Y., Cheng, M.: Web service testing tool soapui and its analysis. Computer Applications and Software 27(005), 155–157 (2010)
14. Mercury Interactive, LoadRunner[EB/OL], http://www.mercury.com/us/products/loadrunner/ (2007)

Amplification DDoS Attacks: Emerging Threats and Defense Strategies

Antonio Colella[1,*] and Clara Maria Colombini[2]

[1] Italian Army and Italian Atlantic Committee, Piazza di Firenze 27, Roma, Italy
antonio.colella.it@ieee.org
[2] University of Milan, External Researcher, Milano, Italy
cmcolombini@email.it

Abstract. There are too many servers on the Internet that have already been used, or that are vulnerable and can potentially be used to launch DDoS attacks. Even though awareness increases and organizations begin to lock down those systems, there are plenty of other protocols that can be exploited to be used instead of them. One example is the Simple Network Management Protocol (SNMP), which is a common UDP protocol used for network management. Several types of network devices actually come with SNMP "on" by default. A request sent to an SNMP server returns a response that is larger than the query that came in.

The main aim of this paper is to investigate on the increasing prevalence and destructive power of amplification-based distributed denial of service (DDoS) attacks in order to present a solution based on a profiling methodology. The paper encompass three aspects: amplification DDoS attacks and main port used, the profiling methodology as a mean of identifying the threat and shape it. Finally, a proposal solution is given by considering both strategic and technical aspects.

Keywords: DDoS Attack, Amplification of DDoS Attacks, DNS, Digital Profiling.

1 Introduction

A Denial of Service (DoS) attack has the main goal of preventing legitimate usage of a specific resource available on the Internet such as a web portal or any kind of network-based service. A Distributed Denial of Service (DDoS) attack is a coordinated attack against the availability of services belonging to a given target system or network. It is launched indirectly through many compromised computing systems (see Figure 1). The services under attack are those of the "primary victim", while the compromised systems used to launch the attack are often called the intermediate attack vectors or "secondary victims". The use of secondary victims in a DDoS attack provides the attacker with the ability to

---

* Corresponding author: Antonio Colella, Italian Army and Italian Atlantic Committee advisor, Piazza di Firenze 27, I-00186, Rome, Italy. E-mail: antonio.colella.it@ieee.org

S. Teufel et al. (Eds.): CD-ARES 2014, LNCS 8708, pp. 298–310, 2014.

wage a much larger and more disruptive attack while remaining anonymous since
the secondary victims actually perform the attack making it more difficult or
almost impossible for network forensics experts to track down the real attacker
(see Figure 2).

In the first quarter of year 2014, Verisign DDoS Protection Services saw an 83
percent jump in average attack size over Q4 2013, which was primarily attributed
to NTP-based attacks. While DNS amplification was the most common vector
in 2013 and continues to be seen, the NTP attack type is the largest attack
vector seen in 2014. Verisign said that they mitigated multiple amplification
attacks – commonly ranging from 50 to 75 Gbps – for their customers. Directly
related to the popularity of amplification attacks was the sharp decline in more
complex application-layer attacks. With the presence of so many vulnerable NTP
servers and reflection vectors readily available on the Internet, attackers were
able to cause maximum disruption with minimum effort, by ditching smarter
application-layer attacks in favor of volume-based amplification attacks (for a
more detailed study please refer to the "Verisign's Q1 2014 DDoS Trends Report"
in [1]).

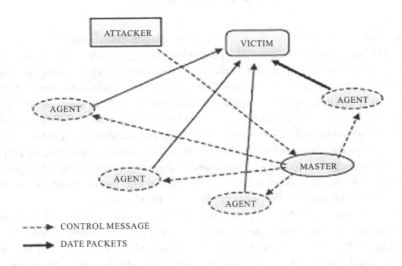

Fig. 1. DDoS Attack components

2   Amplification DDoS Attacks

Amplification DDoS attacks are based on a third-party reflection paradigm in
which the real *source* of the attacks originates a significant number of service
requests, implying the transmission of a certain quantity of small-sized solicita-
tion packets, towards several completely unaware third-party entities, providing
some kind of service on the Internet, and assuming the role of *reflectors*. The
attacker properly forges the source IP address of all the requests (IP spoofing)

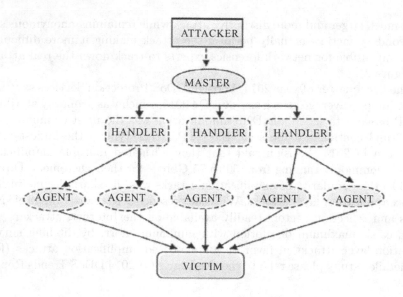

Fig. 2. DDoS Architecture

so that they seem to come from the victim rather than from the real attack source. Furthermore, the requests are crafted to: (i) solicit a large number of individual responses (amplification through flow or reflection multiplication attacks) or (ii) obtaining response messages whose size is much larger that te one of the corresponding request (amplification through payload magnification). Reflection and Magnification can be considered as two separate attributes that can coexist in the same attack, resulting in combined amplification strategies (see Figure 4). Clearly, an attack does not get magnified unless the sizes of response messages are bigger than the request ones and analogously a flow multiplication implies that the number of attack flows received by the victim must be an integer multiple of the number of flows originally sent by the source.

In all the cases, the traffic volume generated by the third-party reflector servers in response to the individual queries received, results to be several order of magnitude higher than the one originated by the attacker alone, so that the above amplification/boosting effects greatly enhance the attack power, by overwhelming the victim's own resources both in terms of available bandwidth and (often) computing power. More formally, the bandwidth waste (in bits/s) associated to an amplification DDoS attack can be expressed as follows:

$$B = 8a \cdot S \cdot N \cdot r \tag{1}$$

where S is the request packet size, a the magnification factor characterizing the response size, N the number of simultaneous reflecting entities (flow multiplier) and r is the attack flow transmission rate (in pakets/s).

One of the first attacks deploying amplification techniques over the internet is known as Smurf [2][3], exploiting in a coordinated way the ICMP replay and the

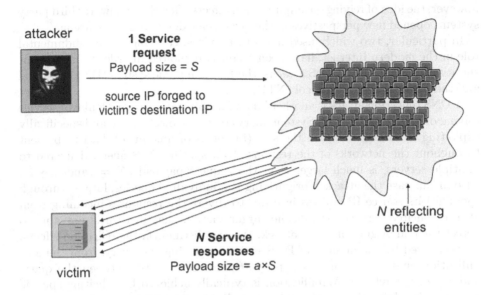

Fig. 3. Amplification DDoS attacks dynamics

direct broadcast propagation mechanisms, together with address spoofing practices, in order to completely saturate the connectivity of the target victims with huge volumes of ICMP reply messages. The great strength of this kind of attack is that it did not required the availability of a large number of compromised hosts to be successful, but only a single source machine, originating the attack flow (made of individual ICMP requests) by spoofing its own address with the one of the victim, as well as one or more third party local area networks exposing a large number of hosts on the Internet and allowing directed broadcast propagation at the gateway level. Clearly, by directly transforming the network-level broadcast packets into link-layer ones, these network provided the amplification effect by forcing each of their host to reflect the ICMP reply messages towards the attack target (whose address has been spoofed as the source of the ICMP requests). In such a way, the greater the number hosts available on the network, the higher the number of flows reflected toward the victim, with obvious consequences on its connectivity. Thus the power of the attack is proportional to the size of the intermediate "reflecting" networks, by operating according to a pure flow multiplication model ($a \approx 1$ and $N \gg 1$).

A very close variant of the Smurf attack, known as Fraggle [4], used UDP ECHO packets and the "Chargen" service, instead of ICMP, to implement the request/response mechanism characterizing the attack flow, but was substantially identical in all the attack dynamics based on direct broadcast propagation.

While devastating in their denial of service effects, both these attacks have been rapidly defeated by inhibiting direct broadcast propagation at the gateway level, however, the idea of relying on amplification effects offered by unaware third party systems opened new perspectives in the large-scale denial of service arena.

In particular, two widely used network services, carrying out a fundamental role in the modern Internet, have been recently exploited in order to implement successful amplification DDoS attacks: the Domain name system (DNS) protocol and the Network Time Protocol (NTP).

A DNS reflection attack is another kind of amplification-based denial of service relying on the Domain Name System query/response mechanism, and specifically exploiting situations in which the size (in terms of amount of data to be sent throughout the network) of the response to a specific DNS query, delivered to multiple servers, is much larger than the request payload ($N = 1$ and $a \gg 1$). Also in this case the attacker, originating the individual queries, forges (through spoofing) its source IP address in order to divert the responses incoming from all the solicited servers towards the target victim, that in turn is not able to detect the real originator of the attack. We can distinguish the reflection effects, characterized by the number of DNS servers receiving the query, from the amplification ones, whose success is proportional to the ratio between the query and response payloads. Amplification is typically achieved by soliciting specific responses involving the use of previously individuated TXT records. For example, specific queries sent to an authoritative DNS server can result in responses with a 10-20x amplification factor (e.g., a 40-byte size DNS query can result in a 400-byte response or greater). Attackers are able to take advantage of a huge number of "open" DNS servers available in the Internet that respond to any request sent to them. This is a quite easy technique that has proven successful in launching very large-scale attacks (i.e., several hundred Gbps in size).

Also the NTP-based attacks rely on the UDP protocol, by taking advantage of some mechanisms commonly used to synchronize the electronic clocks of computers connected to the Internet. The attack dynamics are very similar to those characterizing DNS reflection, based on soliciting the generation of very large response messages. One particularly damaging variant of the NTP attack uses the MONLIST command, supported in older NTP implementation, that returns the last 600 clients that an NTP server has talked to, and hence resulting in responses with an amplification factor of 10-200x with just a single NTP server. Accordingly, large scale attacks that simultaneously solicit thousands of NTP servers can produce incredible damages while requiring a very limited amount of resources on the attacker's side. For example, on February 10, 2014 about 1300 NTP servers on different networks were involved in an unprecedented cyber attack, where each server generated at peak hours approximately 90 Mb/s of traffic towards particular targets located on the Internet.

A taxonomy on the most common amplification DDoS attacks is reported in Figure 3.

3 Profiling a DDoS Attack

One of the biggest problems of cyberdefense in general is represented by anonymity and the resulting non-imputability that cyberspace can offer to the

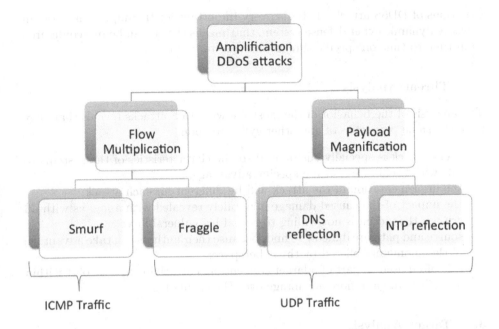

Fig. 4. Amplification DDoS attacks taxonomy

authors of a cyber attack, as it becomes difficult, if not impossible, to identify them [5]. Chief among these is the challenge of *situational awareness* [6,7,8] which is defined as "the continuous extraction of environmental information, the integration of this information with previous knowledge to form a coherent mental picture, and the use of that picture in directing further perception and anticipating future event" [9].

It is therefore essential to gain this view, which allows to acquire those information, more detailed and updated, useful to reach the solution. This is achieved by the method of analysis developed by Colombini and Colella in [10], where authors give a new point of view to common ICT protections, in order to recognize and prevent a DDoS attack.

3.1   The Method

The method consists of four steps:

1. threat analysis;
2. target analysis;
3. motivation analysis;
4. attack results analysis.

The study of these aspects allows to obtain a full profile of the attack, which provides new information useful for a real-time view of the presence of possible situations of DDoS attacks. It is also very important for the implementation an effective dynamic cyber defense system, that means that it can be pre-configured from time to time on specific threats that are to be fought [11].

3.2 Threat Analysis

The analysis of the behavior of the most known DDoS attacks reveals that they have the same properties of any other cyber-weapon:

- every attack is specially customized to the characteristics of the systems to hit, with the aim to reach a specific advantage;
- the implementation of the attack will be different for each attack;
- the impact of the caused damage is publicly revealed with a lag: as with all crimes, the victim is not willing to reveal his vulnerability;
- source and path are difficult to find, because their authors can take advantage of the anonymity offered by the cyberspace;
- it is often used as part of a larger conventional attack in support of it within a conflict, to gain more advantage over the enemy [12].

3.3 Target Analysis

The design of a DDoS attack takes place purely in a strategic way, in which decisions are made to define and guide the course of the attack. In the first place, the choice of the targets, that is, the type of the enemy's critical structure to hit, closely linked to the motivations of the attack, ranging from the threat to use as a deterrent to retaliation or to counterattack as a result of a suffered attack, until the attainment of some strategic advantage: economic, political, military, social [13].

It can thus describe the target with the answer to four questions:

- WHERE - physical location of the target: nation, region, town, building, up to determine whether it is a government institution, an industrial or military installation;
- WHAT - target functions: for example, a military or industrial specific process control equipment, a database that contains sensitive data, the project of a new instrumentation, etc.;
- WHO - owner and users of the target: a person, a company, a government or other groups;
- WHY - motivation of the attack: type of damage and expected results.

In this respect, it determines the type of damage to cause, which can be *digital* (exclusively aimed for delay or interruption of service) or *physical* (such as a consequently material destruction of a control system). It is measured in terms of severity of the indirect effects caused and persistence of the effects.

3.4   Motivation Analysis

The study of known DDoS attacks [14], [15], [16] confirmed that they are most often used as part of a larger conventional attack in support of it, or replacement as invisible as part of a conflict or at least one situation of tension/antagonism in place.

This observation leads to the creation of a monitoring system of political, economic and social, to extrapolate those indicators that show the possibility of an attack on available critical infrastructures, through the analysis of available information from different type of sources:

- *open* (national reports of companies of antivirus production sites, national and international news, analysis sites political, economic, social);
- *semi-open* (sites hacker circles, antagonists, extremists, fundamentalists);
- *closed* (documentation strategic-military).

3.5   Attack Effects Analysis

This step analyses the effects of a possible attack on a specific target, in relation to the information obtained from the previous steps, especially related to the time of the attack, the type of damage, the time duration of the damage on the system and the cost of the damage on the critical infrastructure.

Any impact in the short, medium and long term is evaluated in terms of:

- side effects of damage on systems/people in the environment of the target system;
- impact of the damage out of the environment of the affected system;
- side effects of damage on structures/people outside the affected system;
- social impact of the publicity of the attack;
- immediately and over time effect (military-political-social).

The information obtained by the analysis performed in the previous steps must allow to answer to the seven questions presented in Table 1.

4   The Proposed Solution

Here we propose a multi-dimensional solution, composed by the analysis of the two aspects of the problem: the technical one and the strategic one. From the technical side, analyzing the specific tool that attackers have to use, can prevent attacks first of all configuring client systems and using antivirus protection so that the attacker is unable to recruit his botnet arm, and finally configuring name servers to reduce the attacker's ability to corrupt a zone file with the amplification record. Another important action is to disable open recursion on name servers and accept only recursive DNS from trusted sources. Unfortunately, to prevent the impersonation attack fundamental is the possibility to perform source IP address validation: the botnet hosts cannot generate DNS request

Table 1. The seven questions and related answers useful for the attack analysis

WHO	Possible attackers	Type identification:
		  - external (opposite nations, international terrorism, international organized crime)
		  - internal (domestic terrorism, antagonist groups, organized crime)

WHY	Possible reasons	- Identification of topics of tension / crisis / antagonism in the field:
		        -political
		        -social
		        -economic
		        -military
		- (internal or external)

WHERE	Possible objectives	- Identification of critical infrastructures. - Identification of supersensitive data and their location.
WHAT	Damage type	- Detection of damage type: physical, digital, interruption of service, data theft.
WHEN	Attack time	- Detection of the moment of maximum vulnerability of critical infrastructure in relation to the type of attack.
RESULTS	Damage extent	- Detection of damage in relation to critical infrastructure type and damage type. - Detection of the kind disadvantage that could be caused by specific damage on specific infrastructure.
REACTION	Response actions	- Detection of the moment of maximum vulnerability of critical infrastructure in relation to the type of attack.

messages posing as the targeted name server, which stems the attack at the outset.

A new preventive way is the use of honeypots, that are systems intentionally set up with limited security to be an enticement for an attacker's hostile action. Honeypots serve to deflect attacks from hitting the systems they are protecting as well as serving as a means for gaining information about attackers by storing a record of their activity and learning what types of attacks and software tools the attacker is using. The goal of this type of honeypots is to lure an attacker to install either handler or agent code within the honeypot, thereby allowing the honeypot's [17] owner to track the handler or agent behavior and better understand how to defend against future DDoS installation attacks. Honeypots are also helpful because they can store event logfiles during a DDoS attack.

Data can be analyzed post-attack to look for specific characteristics within the attacking traffic. To help identify the attackers, tracing Internet traffic back to it's source helps to identify the authors. Additionally, when the attacker sends different types of attacking traffic, this method assists in providing the victim system with information that might help develop filters to block the attack. An example of countermeasure in which network profiling can be effective has been reported in the Table 2 .

To work as better, this solution must be based on information obtained by the application of the digital profiling method, explained in Section 3. The result of the study provides information on:

Table 2. Countermeasures

Countermeasures (what)	Actions (in what way)	Aim (why)
detect and neutralize handlers	analyzing the content of source code and detected feature in the malware behavior	comprehension of communication protocol and traffic among handlers, clients, and agents.
detect/prevent secondary victims	heightened awareness of security issues and prevention techniques from all Internet users	to prevent themselves from participating in the attack.
detect/prevent potential attacks	egress filtering	scanning of IP packet headers leaving a network and checking to see if they meet certain criteria.
mitigate/stop attacks	load balancing	network providers can increase bandwidth on critical connections to prevent them from going down in an attack.
mitigate/stop attacks	throttling	the Max-min Fair server-centric router throttle method. This can prevent flood damage to servers.
deflect attacks	honeypots	gaining information about attackers by storing a record of their activity.
post-attack forensics	traffic pattern analysis	these techniques help identify the attackers tracing Internet traffic back to it's source.
post-attack forensics	packet traceback	these techniques help identify the attackers tracing Internet traffic back to it's source.

- critical infrastructure as possible target;
- list of exploitable vulnerabilities;
- time of the attack;
- extent of expected damage;
- origin of attack;
- the identity of the attacker/s.

The obtained information can then be used to implement a series of effective countermeasures, for protection and prevention of a DDoS attack, by improving the physical protection of critical infrastructure, as well as the resolution of digital vulnerability of critical systems and implementation of new security policies for access to critical data [18]. From the point of view of offensive defense, the real-time view of the presence of possible situations of attack allows the implementation of an effective system of cyber defense in a dynamic way, every time capable of pre-self-configure depending on the eventual threats from time to time detected, and to implement countermeasures specifically proportionated to the threat in act [11]. In the analysis of log files, for instance, depending on the purpose it is intended, are used to highlight relationships between data and build a result of behavioral models that describe two types of approach:

- Top down: search for confirmation of facts already known or assumed (e.g., an action resulting from an intrusion has already occurred)

- bottom-up: useful to find information useful to construct hypotheses (e.g., the most likely causes that produce a particular result).

As we have explained in a previous paper [17] the analysis cycle takes place in 6 steps (see Figure 5)

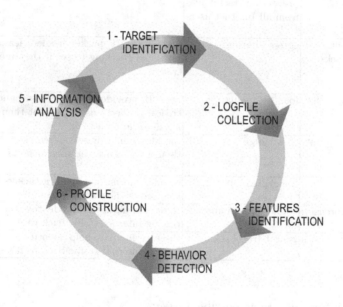

Fig. 5. Network profiling cycle of analysis

Step 1 - Identification of the target.

Step 2 - Collection of data log files.

Step 3 - Identification of characteristic properties (features) from the mass of data collected from log files and collect this information (indicators) contained the features detected.

Step 4 - Detection of possible subjects to which it is possible to attribute behavior Digital.

Step 5 - Analysis of information and construction of the behavior of digital accesses.

Step 6 - Construction of the user profile and usage of digital information obtained, depending on the objective.

5   Conclusions and Future Work

Countering amplification DDoS attacks is an important security issue to be faced with in modern network-empowered organizations. In this work we have presented an alternative defense strategy, obtaining information from profiling techniques that can be used to implement a series of effective protection and prevention countermeasures against such attacks. The intent of the authors for the future is to deeply analyze this approach trying to find a full set of indicators able to foster a complete and effective prevention methodology.

References

1. Verisign Inc.: Verisign Distributed Denial of Service Trends Report, issue 1 ? 1st quarter 2014, www.verisigninc.com/en_US/website-availability/ddos-protection/ddos-report/index.xhtml
2. Kumar, S.: Smurf-based distributed denial of service (ddos) attack amplification in internet. In: IEEE Second International Conference on Internet Monitoring and Protection, ICIMP 2007, p. 25 (2007)
3. CC, C.: Smurf IP Denial-Of-Service Attacks - CERT ADVISORY CA-1998-01 (2000), http://www.cert.org/advisories/CA-1998-01.html
4. Specht, S.M., Lee, R.B.: Distributed Denial of Service: Taxonomies of Attacks, Tools, and Countermeasures. In: ISCA PDCS, pp. 543–550 (2004)
5. Schreier, F.: On Cyberwarfare, DCAF Horizon 2015 Working Paper Series (7) (2012), http://www.dcaf.ch/Publications/On-Cyberwarfare
6. Fenza, G., Furno, D., Loia, V., Veniero, M.: Agent-based Cognitive approach to Airport Security Situation Awareness. In: 2010 International Conference on Complex, Intelligent and Software Intensive Systems, pp. 1057–1062 (2010)
7. Furno, D., Loia, V., Veniero, M., Anisetti, M., Bellandi, V., Ceravolo, P., Damiani, E.: Towards an agent-based architecture for managing uncertainty in situation awareness. In: 2011 IEEE Symposium on Intelligent Agent (IA), pp. 1–6 (April 2011)
8. De Maio, C., Fenza, G., Furno, D., Loia, V.: Swarm-based semantic fuzzy reasoning for situation awareness computing. In: 2012 IEEE International Conference on Fuzzy Systems (FUZZ-IEEE), pp. 1–7 (June 2012)
9. Vidulich, M., Dominguez, C., Vogel, E., McMillan, G.: Situation awareness: papers and annotated bibliography - Armstrong Laboratory, Human System Center, ref. AL/CF-TR-1994-0085 (1994), http://www.dtic.mil/dtic/tr/fulltext/u2/a284752.pdf
10. Colombini, C., Colella, A.: Digital Profiling: A Computer Forensics Approach. In: Tjoa, A.M., Quirchmayr, G., You, I., Xu, L. (eds.) ARES 2011. LNCS, vol. 6908, pp. 330–343. Springer, Heidelberg (2011)
11. Colella, A., Colombini, C.M.: Cyber-space, Cyberware, Cyber-weapons. In: Attanasio, A., Costabile, G. (eds.) IISFA MEMBERBOOK 2012 DIGITAL FORENSICS, Experta Edizioni (2012) (in Italian)
12. Colombini, C.M., Colella, A., Mattiucci, M., Castiglione, A.: Network Profiling: Content Analysis of Users Behavior in Digital Communication Channel. In: Quirchmayr, G., Basl, J., You, I., Xu, L., Weippl, E. (eds.) CD-ARES 2012. LNCS, vol. 7465, pp. 416–429. Springer, Heidelberg (2012)

13. Colombini, C., Colella, A.: Digital scene of crime: technique of profiling users. Journal of Wireless Mobile Networks, Ubiquitous Computing, and Dependable Applications (JoWUA) 3(3), 50–73 (2012)
14. Palmieri, F., Fiore, U.: Network anomaly detection through nonlinear analysis. Computers & Security 29(7), 737–755 (2010)
15. Palmieri, F., Fiore, U., Castiglione, A.: A distributed approach to network anomaly detection based on independent component analysis. Concurrency and Computation: Practice and Experience 26(5), 1113–1129 (2014)
16. Fiore, U., Palmieri, F., Castiglione, A., De Santis, A.: Network anomaly detection with the restricted Boltzmann machine. Neurocomputing 122, 13–23 (2013)
17. Colombini, C.M., Colella, A., Mattiucci, M., Castiglione, A.: Cyber Threats Monitoring: Experimental Analysis of Malware Behavior in Cyberspace. In: Cuzzocrea, A., Kittl, C., Simos, D.E., Weippl, E., Xu, L. (eds.) CD-ARES Workshops 2013. LNCS, vol. 8128, pp. 236–252. Springer, Heidelberg (2013)
18. Colella, A., Colombini, C.M.: La rete e le informazioni, raccolta e uso illecito dei dati. In: Attanasio, A., Costabile, G. (eds.) IISFA MEMBERBOOK 2011 DIGITAL FORENSICS, Experta Edizioni, pp. 201–220 (2012) (in Italian)

Author Index